D0856712

POLITICS, POLICY, AND NATURAL RESOURCES

Politics,
Policy,
AND Natural Resources

EDITED BY *Dennis L Thompson*

THE FREE PRESS, New York

COLLIER-MACMILLAN LIMITED, London

The Free Press
A Division of The Macmillan Company
866 Third Avenue, New York, New York 10022
Collier-Macmillan Canada Ltd., Toronto, Ontario
Library of Congress Catalog Card Number: 76-143506

printing number
1   2   3   4   5   6   7   8   9   10

Contents

POLITICS, POLICY, AND NATURAL RESOURCES

Introduction

The subject of the development and administration of natural resources is both political and technical. Scientists and technicians must understand the political process, and political participants must understand the complex nature of technical problems. Scientists tend to believe that the policy implications of their research should be self-evident to the policy-makers, who in turn complain that the technical knowledge fed to them is inadequate to meet their needs and that very little technical data is self-evident.

What is evident to both the politician and the professional environmental technician is that while each is concerned with natural resources policy, both lack a complete understanding of the political, scientific, and technical problems of conservation. Each could better serve the other's needs and contribute to more responsive decision-making at the various levels if he communicated better. The political process is the procedure by which the various interests are blended into a decision for government action.

One of the difficult tasks in becoming aware of political issues is gaining scope as well as depth. The scientist tends to sacrifice scope for depth, and the politician, who must be concerned with a broad range of problems, sacrifices depth for scope. Yet each is aware that there are other pieces to the picture which he does not have. Legislatures, natural resource professions, and even governmental agencies are sensitive to cultural factors only to a certain degree, but geographic and economic criteria must be dealt with in policy-making decisions and must be at least partially understood by those who are concerned with the environment. And such out-and-out political factors as partisan interests, group interests, and bureaucratic and institutional conflicts also must be considered.

Most natural resource participants admit the need for dialogue but proceed to go their own way (technical, political, or bureaucratic) nevertheless, without complete awareness of the various needs, demands, and expectations of the others. The scientist's reliance on technical competence and scientific accuracy as a sure base for policy decisions is usually misplaced. At the same time, politicians and bureaucrats often make decisions in an unsatisfactory context because all of the available information is not at their disposal or because all interested and informed parties are not participating. Thus, the final decision is limited by an incomplete list of alternative choices, and the decision is not secure because there are often interests for which no account is made.

Because government is so thoroughly entwined in natural resources policy, the environmental technician must be constantly involved in the political process. How well he responds and acquits himself depends largely on how well he understands what is going on in the political system. Similarly, the politician is in regular contact with natural-resource personnel and interests and always must be ready to confront their demands.

In addition to the general reasons which propel issues into the political sphere, there are three which are identified specifically with natural resources: (1) The universal presence of many resources puts them beyond the bounds of parochial or group control; (2) the ownership of many resources by the government makes them of proprietary interest to political institutions; and (3) the extreme importance of some resources to society requires that they be protected and managed by society.

Politics has negative connotations to conservation only when the arena is closed, thus limiting the participants and decisions to a few, while enforcing the consequences upon society as a whole. When the system is open, the scientist must not recoil from politics or leave the solutions to others. He must make his work and information factors in any decision, though he cannot seek final solutions to social problems in his technology alone. Technology does not answer important questions of value and cost, which are negotiated in the political arena.

The political process is fascinating, especially for those who understand it and commit themselves to a participation in it. But there are no easy answers or sure guidelines for political participation. Political scientists are most effective in studying the *what* of politics, in providing information and indicating patterns that help in understanding the *how* of the process. But the actual effective involvement in the political arena is the work of artists who use this information and experience to its fullest advantage. Unfortunately not everyone knows how to wield the brush when he needs to paint a policy decision.

The purpose of this book is to bridge the gap between the politics of policy-making and the technological and substantive matter of natural resources and to show how they are regularly interconnected. It should give the reader an appreciation of the scope of information, interests, institutions and events which must be considered in the political arena. In addition, for the social scientist it will serve as a collection of some of the policy formation studies which have been done on natural resources. For the student or manager of natural resources, the book can be an introduction to the political morass which exists beyond the technological or scientific problems.

Formerly many natural resource technicians and administrators did not conceive of their job as a political one. However, the new hydrologist, forester, ranger, ecologist, or wildlife manager appears to be aware that his task is in part political and expects to be involved in political process. Yet his baptism into politics tends to be by fire, which is a rather rude introduction. Perhaps this book can indicate to him how some of the fires are fought—or at least who can be called upon to fetch water for the rescue.

Part One sets up justifications for the combining of environment with politics. Part Two gives a brief introduction to the policy-making process. Part Three indicates the institutional factors involved in political decisions. In Part Four conservation is presented in terms of the public interests. Part Five considers public perceptions of issues in the resources area. Part Six presents some selections illustrating the kinds of conflicts which arise and demand political solutions; these include air, water, and space pollution. Resource administration and its effect on policy decisions are presented in Part Seven.

Except for the selections used to briefly explain the policy process in Part Two, all of the selections included herein are directly concerned with some natural resource. It is hoped that this will illustrate the ways politics, policy, and natural resources are intertwined.

I wish to acknowledge the encouragment of the students in my course on "Government and Natural Resources" at the University of Arizona who voiced a need for a collection of this sort. Advice and criticism on scope, format, and selections were provided by Dean E. Mann, Vincent L. Marando, N. Jerry Chatterton, and Jay Schultz. My wife, Karen, helped, as wives do, in the preparation of the manuscript. Mrs. Lois Putzier did the typing. Thanks to them all.

Dennis L Thompson

Part One

Natural Resources and Politics

The cry today among pure and applied scientists is for more involvement and relevance on the part of behavioral scientists. Applying science and technology to the issues at hand is a continuing problem, but political science that does not relate to some area of policy-making has little effect on the issues either. Both scientists and politicians recognize the need for each other; yet by finding it difficult to communicate, they thus find it more difficult to cooperate. But the issues of our time demand the best attack we can muster.

Scientists can provide the knowledge of what can be done and "how to do it," and political scientists can provide the "how to get it done." Both must be involved, speaking from their own perspectives, on "what should be done" —a value judgment which is affected by externalities related to our knowledge of other subjects and is shaped by previous policy decisions. Each pure scientist, technician, or behavioral scientist can improve on the choice of alternatives by better understanding the contribution of all the others.

In this introductory section, Stanley A. Cain, a former Undersecretary of the Interior, discusses ecology as a basis for synthesizing the social sciences. Lynton K. Caldwell then presents environment as a focus for public policy, and Hans H. Landsberg summarizes the resource outlook in the United States. Politicians make their contribution with the National Environment Policy Act of 1969 (P.L. 91–190), which was signed into law on January 1, 1970.

Stanley A. Cain

Can Ecology Provide the Basis for Synthesis Among the Social Sciences?*

The inquiry is into the role of the social sciences in research and the formulation of policy to guide action programs affecting the quality of the environment and, presumably, to suggest lines of investigation normally peripheral to the physical sciences *per se*. Furthermore, the suggested title implies that ecology, originally a biological science, is applicable to the social sciences. Finally, there is recognition that ecology is concerned with synthesis more than it is with analysis, and therefore at least the implication that ecology, because it deals with interrelations, may assist in integrating the physical, biological, and social sciences and their programs.

. . . I feel that I should state clearly that my discussion is based, in the first place, on the fact that I am a biologist interested especially in ecology and biogeography, who has become involved in the conservation management of natural resources. By itself, this statement means little, or perhaps too much, for both "ecology" and "conservation" have received various connotations.

Stated simply, ecology is concerned with the interrelations among things, conditions, and processes. Stated from the biological point of view, ecology is the study of the relations between living things and their environment. There is no life in the absence of such relations. All phenomena that characterize the living substance are a consequence of its sensitivity and reaction to conditions of the environment. Stimulus and response, however, are not unique to living substance. Biological uniqueness lies in the phenomena of self-generation of protoplasmic materials and the autochthonous growth and reproduction, which include both hereditary duplication of identical substance as well as variation. Organic growth is never by simple accretion of materials from the environment. It is unlike the growth of mineral crystals, the accumulation of sediments, the condensation of liquids, or the generation of storms. Organic growth, as I have already said, is autochthonous.

*Reprinted by permission from *Social Sciences and the Environment*, ed. Morris Garnsey and James Hibbs (Boulder: University of Colorado Press, 1967), pp. 27–40. © University of Colorado Press, 1967.

These interacting phenomena result in organisms, populations of similar organisms, and communities of mixed organisms. At every level there is organization. Each level is a system, a system that is a consequence of the organizing power of the interrelated actions of stimulus and response.

There follows, then, the conclusion that there is an ecology of organisms, of populations, and of communities that is based on their relations with the environment. Furthermore, this hierarchy can be extended at both ends. Because of geochemical and global thermal phenomena and the existence of the biosphere, there are certain world-encompassing phenomena of an ecological nature such as found in organic evolution, the hydrologic cycle, world temperature relations, cycling of elements, increase of carbon dioxide in the atmosphere from human—largely industrial—activities, and the global distribution of pesticides and radioactive isotopes.

If one focuses attention on man . . . one might add to the global atmosphere, hydrosphere, lithosphere, and biosphere, the noosphere, the latter being the world-encircling aspects of the human intellect and the impact of ideas. Perhaps this is illustrated by the aphorism that nothing travels faster than bad news.

At the other end of the hierarchy there is an internal ecology of the interrelations among organs, tissues, cells, and even of compounds within the organism. This is clear in the interrelations of neural and muscular systems that are affected by the internal as well as the external environment, and by the actions of hormones and enzymes as well as by pharmaceutical ingredients that may be added to the organism.

The approach I am taking would seem to imply that all is ecology. I do not mean it that way. However, whatever the scientific inquiry or the application of scientific knowledge and understanding in engineering or any other action or management program, if it concerns itself primarily with environmental relations, it may truly be called ecology. Much ecology is done by scientists who never think of themselves as ecologists, in fact would disdain calling themselves ecologists. Also, much of the work done by ecologists is not focused on the action system itself.

Ecologists often have to examine things, conditions, and processes in nature in order to have the specific data they need to understand the interrelations that organize the ecological systems they are studying. Because of this, ecologists often do the same kinds of things that are done by micrometeorologists, pedologists, nutrionists, physiologists, etc. They perform in these various ways simply because there are gaps in information that will be filled expeditiously only if they dig out the information themselves. For example, an ecologist interested in the composition and structure of a plant–animal community may need precise micrometeorological data to explain what are essentially morphological features of the community—the numbers and patterns of occurrence in three-dimensional space and in time of perhaps several dozen, even a few hundred species—and this over a space of no more than a few hundred hectares. For such needs, data from standard weather stations are wholly inadequate.

At the same time, the ecologist must use the knowledge and sophisticated instrumentation of the physiologist, adapted to the uncontrolled conditions of nature, if he is to understand the flow of energy and the cycling of mineral nutrients. And when it comes to the animal components of his community, he is confronted also with the whole perplexing field of ethnology and behavioral science.

Still, what makes a scientist an ecologist is his focus of attention on the ecological *action system*. The physical environment *acts* upon the living organisms. The living organisms *react* upon the physical environment, and they *coact* with one another. For example, the physiologist has learned about the relation between temperature rise and the rate of certain chemical reactions that occur in living organisms, and this relationship can be expressed mathematically. In addition, the field ecologist observes certain correlations between temperature and growth rate, but this correlation *per se* proves nothing because of the simultaneous effects of light, moisture, nutritive condition, inherent differences among members of the same species, and general physiological state at the time of observation, including disease, approaching dormancy, etc.

To take another example, there are correlations between temperature and the onset of physiological changes leading to migration and reproduction of birds, but changing day length may also be correlated, as may other conditions of the physical environment. The permutations of the physical environmental actions are certainly very, very many.

On the other hand, all living organisms react upon the environment and change it. This is probably most generally appreciated by nonscientists in the exchange of gases such as oxygen and carbon dioxide and the loss of energy to the environment as the heat of respiration. But here, too, there is a multitude of processes to take into consideration, such as the absorption by plants from soil and water of mineral nutrients, the absorption and accumulation of other minerals such as selenium and uranium, and the discharge into the soil and air of various by-products of the functioning protoplasm, including, according to Dr. Fritz Went, photo-reactive hydrocarbons from the cuticle of certain plants that play a role as condensation nuclei in fog and smog formation.

But more familiar ways in which organisms affect the physical environment include such phenomena as those associated with shading, soil and water stabilization, water losses to the atmosphere, depletion of oxygen in water, accumulation of hydrogen sulphide, creation of humus, building of coral reefs, deposition of marl and peat, increased acidity of substrata, physical and chemical decomposition of rock, the transformation of complex organic compounds to simpler ones, and the release of certain minerals as soluble, usable nitrates, phosphates, sulfates, etc. In this connection we can say once again that the number of permutations is very, very great.

Finally, there are the coactions which, by definition, are the interactions among the living organisms themselves. These include the plant-to-plant coactions, as in the case of bacterial and fungal diseases and certain hemiparasites such as mistletoe growing on oak trees, which we make so much of around Christmas time. There are numerous close animal-to-animal coactions, such as protozoan, worm, and insect parasites. Most subtle and recently studied are such phenomena among animals as territoriality of birds, howling monkeys, and, for that matter, house dogs. And, of course, there are unnumbered plant–animal and animal–plant coactions. Nearly everyone has heard about "insect-eating" plants and knows of insect, bird, and even bat pollination of certain flowering plants.

The most fundamental phenomena of the entire ecological action system, however, are those of the food network, a network that is made up in part of quite familiar food chains such as those that either benefit man or do damage to his interests. Here one places the grass-eating sheep and the lamb-eating coyote, feral dog, and other predators. The seed-eating bird or rodent is of no less interest, whether it is helpful because it eats weed seeds or destructive because it eats cereals that man has so laboriously grown.

We can generalize. Every plant and animal ends up being eaten alive, or by being attacked when dead and their substance and products used by the decomposers and transformers, from earthworms to protozoans, fungi and bacteria.

The food-chain network of relationships is the most fundamental of all coactions because it is through it that the matter and energy, which sustain all life, pass step by step, from the original green plants that are the primary producers of organic material, and which, by that photochemical process, make available energy in chemical form that is usable and necessary for life processes.

Having seen in this brief sketch something of what biological ecology is about, we can now face the question that was posed to me: "Can ecology provide the basis for synthesis among the social sciences?" I am reluctant to say "yes" because the question is posed as "the basis,", instead of just one among other possible means of synthesizing the social sciences. It asks too much of ecology; yet if anything is to be synthesized, it must be on a basis of relationships among what is to be synthesized. And ecology, by its presumptuous definition, is concerned with interrelationships between life and environment. So why not?

But I am reluctant also to say "no" because there are ecological data and concepts that can be useful, as the social scientists discovered long ago: Boulding and other economists; in a sense Malthus himself; Park, Hawley, and other sociologists; and several geographers, cultural anthropologists, psychologists; and even, perhaps, some political scientists and a few lawyers.

I do not believe that any of us would question that there is a field of ecology of man, at least in the sense of the ecology of any other organism. However different man may be from other animals in some regards, he shares with them continuous and intimate relations with the physical environment. He tends to sleep in the dark and to be active when it is light, but has wide adaptability in this relationship. Unprotected, his skin may sunburn. His internal mechanisms for regulation of body heat are supported by his selection of microenvironments that are relatively cool or warm, as the conditions may warrant. His bodily state and muscular activity are affected by high and low vapor-pressure deficit of the air and by the low atmospheric pressure of high altitudes. His mental acuity may be influenced by gases in the air. While the extremes of environmental conditions may induce pathological conditions in individuals, as a species man has developed subpopulations adapted to particular conditions, such as heat or cold stress, high-altitude stress and dryness. Other subpopulations have become adapted to diets high or low in carbohydrates, in fats, or in proteins.

The interests of anthropologists in these aspects of human ecology are paralleled by those of others concerned with nutrition and health. More and more it is being found that environment and health are closely related both in physiological and pathological conditions. The pathology of respiratory diseases, for example, is not only that of parasitic organisms but of their activity in relation to the physiological condition of the organism which, in turn, is related to the environment.

As we explore this area of human ecology, however sketchily, we are immediately aware that man has many means of protecting himself from unfavorable environmental conditions, some of which he shares with other animals. From the common shelters of cave, burrow, and nest, man has gone on to the construction of elaborate houses. In addition, he has further protected himself by clothing of fur, hides, and a variety of textiles. From hunting and food gathering in nature, he long ago went into supplementary animal husbandry and farming. Special needs are met at the water hole and salt lick and by the use of natural pharmaceuticals, the efficacy of which was learned over the course of long, haphazard experimentation.

A further look at human ecology makes inescapable the rudiments of social organization—vested in the family, clan, tribe, and nation. Not only mating pairs, the dominant male and his harem, and blood relatives *in extenso*, but male hunting groups, female farming groups, handicraft specializations, and the leadership roles of the chief and shaman introduce elements of social organization that, with time, have progressed further and further from any counterparts in nature.

Going far beyond the hierarchy of the peck order, we all know of the degrees of individual and group status that are related to physical vigor and aggressiveness to find their bases in the accumulation of physical wealth in land, possession of gold, jewels, livestock, weapons, tools, and means of transport. Coupled with this, of course, are the individual and shared knowledge of ways and means for production, maintenance of social organization and group integrity, the concepts of natural and supernatural phenomena, of law and order, of division of labor and mutual help. All of this, and much more, works together for intragroup cooperation and out-group competition, and leads us to the areas of human concern and endeavor of the modern social sciences— law, religion, politics, administration, economics, sociology, psychology, cultural anthropology, training, and education.

Where, then, one must ask, is the dividing line between ecology as it is pursued in the search for understanding of the phenomena of nature and these social sciences of today's sophistication? The physical environment acts on man as it does on all life. Man reacts, changing the physical environment, as does all life. And man coacts with other men and with other animals and plants, as does all life. There is no escape for man from his environmental interrelations. Yet there is no turning back on a hundred millennia of human social development and its technological accomplishments. Nature *qua* nature is inescapable; yet our whole effort is to ameliorate nature, to overcome it, to adapt it to our needs, while adapting ourselves to it as little as possible.

We seek, as a species, to turn the physical world to our ends, and every passing day sees an increase in the predominance of human intellect in global ecological relationships. The human power that has been developed is an awesome force in the world of a new order of magnitude as man manages his affairs for good or evil.

The slowly changing progress of man through the millennia has given way to accelerating rates of change in nearly every aspect of human life, at least for those of us who live in those parts of the world we call modern, progressive, and developed. The upward sweep of these curves of change is recent in human history. Their significance is marked by the expressions we use, such as the "agricultural revolution," the "industrial revolution," the "medical and public health revolution," the "population explosion," the "age of automation," the "nuclear age," the "space age," and so on. The date of the onset of these changes is decades, or, at most, a few centuries ago. Where the exponential curves of change will lead us, no one yet knows. I will comment briefly on the changing nature of the real world, not for information, but to remind us of what we all know.

Scarcely a person who comments on the current social, economic, and political conditions fails to mention certain significant changes such as the population explosion, the growth of urbanization and industrialization, and the advance of science-based technologies. Others dwell on the increase of expendable income and the rise in level of living, the shortened work time, and the recreation explosion.

According to the interest of the commentator, discussion of such changes is related to the demand placed on natural resources and a need for conservation. Others who are concerned with the more immediate human state emphasize the impact of a changing world on urban renewal, open space and wilderness, social security and the alleviation of poverty, education, health improvement, and crime prevention. Still others seek new political and legal instruments to help meet changing conditions.

Some of the changes, such as the population explosion and rapid urbanization, are essentially worldwide. Only the West has had long experience with industrialization and the growth of science-based technology. A few nations such as U.S.S.R. and Japan have jumped into the modern technological world in a few decades, some others have a spotty modernization, and perhaps half of the world's people have yet to experience little more than hope for the future.

Despite patches of povery and backwardness, the United States has to worry about automation and the shortening work time, the recreation explosion, and a capacity to overproduce. As a consequence, it is sometimes difficult to have a clear view of another world that is faced by more than two billion persons who have limited experience with the abundant fruits of modern technology.

There are, of course, other significant changes that are receiving comment in various quarters. There is a growing interrelatedness of humanity, the increasing reality of a single world being brought about by speed of communication and transport. There is a sense of shared responsibility for human welfare and the quality and rights of existence that are formalized and expressed by means of new international instrumentalities. But at the same time there is a resurgent nationalism that has followed upon the breakup of the old internationalism of colonial empires.

Whether one focuses on signs of unification or fragmentation, we recognize that there is a growing interrelatedness of problems—problems of resources and goods and trade, social problems, economic problems, and political problems.

More subtle than this, perhaps, is the stirring of appreciation of another interrelatedness among the traditionally separate actions of our progress. I refer to the fact that our specialized and single-purpose activities, including those that have led to great advances in science, technology, and engineering, have side effects that are becoming intolerable because they diminish the quality of the environment, as in the case of pollution; distort the scale of common human activities, as in great cities and high-speed travel; and disorient the person with respect to deep-seated personal and cultural needs. At long last, the heedless devotion to material progress, despite its many benefits, is bringing a realization that analysis must be balanced by synthesis, that specialization must be limited by generalization, and that commodities and marketable services cannot be equated with and replace real values that are intangible.

There are two other points that I will mention about the changing nature of the real world. One is that some of the parameters of change I have mentioned are easier to cope with than others. A fact that is harder to accept by some of us is that nations with similar fundamental problems do not have to solve them in the same way. I see no evidence, for example, that it is necessarily easier to meet the problems of a changing world in a representative political system than it is in an authoritarian one. Certainly, the old "machine bosses" could run their cities without the many sources of frustration and opposition that today's mayors face. Neither do I see that a rising level of consumption leads to democracy and peace. There seems to be little inevitability about the details of the complex interrelations among the physical and social facts of life that lead to one and only one solution of a given human problem.

If I judge correctly, a tacit assumption of this conference is that the quality of the physical environment is being deteriorated by human actions; that to check the processes of deterioration and, hopefully, to reverse them, will require new knowledge and policies to guide human actions; and, of course, that the social sciences can be helpful in this regard if, somehow, their understandings can be employed in an integrated manner. Furthermore there is the question whether ecology can somehow weld together the physical, biological, and social sciences to help define and achieve an environment of a quality satisfactory to human well-being and aspirations.

I wish now to come to the conclusion for which my previous remarks have been a preface. It is that we generally have utilized our rapidly growing scientific knowledge in the performance of specific and largely short-term objectives with little or no concern for the side effects of our actions. Stated baldly, this is a serious accusation because it implies that the loss of quality of the physical environment has been a consequence of this narrow vision.

It is a measure of the times, and a very hopeful one, that this conference is directing its attention to the ramifying consequences of our actions, formerly neglected. I will give first a few illustrations from biology:

(1) The development of hybrid corn greatly increased the production per acre with such obvious economic advantages that it spread rapidly to account in a few years for over 90 per cent of U.S. field corn produc-

tion. It was only slowly realized that the rich stock of genetic alleles of hundreds of corn varieties was being lost in the new uniformity. Once lost, these genetic materials would be gone forever and their possible future use foregone in breeding for improved nutritive quality, habitat adaptability, and disease resistance. A sort of living museum of corn varieties may circumvent this loss.

(2) Many efforts to introduce desirable plants and animals failed because little attention was paid to their native habitats and the introductions were not made into areas that were ecologically homologous. And there is the contrary result—the purposeful introduction of plants and animals that have found unoccupied ecological niches and, as a consequence, have developed economically destructive populations. Japanese honeysuckle, escaped from gardens, and kudsu, introduced for soil erosion control, have become stubborn weeds. The mongoose, introduced to control rats in sugar cane fields, has exterminated many species of valuable ground-nesting birds and has become a serious pest. And city and farm people alike now suffer the depredations of starlings and house sparrows.

(3) Many pharmaceuticals have been used for treating human ills without adequate testing of the possible side effects. The embryo-deforming thalidomide is sufficient example.

(4) The great advances in medicine and public health have been applied in reducing the death rate, dropping it from 35 to 40 or more per thousand persons per year to ten or less within about half a century. This is unquestionably good, for human health and longevity are to be desired. But it is not farsighted that the same powers of medical research and social manipulation have not been applied to the birth rate, for every biologist knows that every species has a reproductive potential to expand its numbers to the limits of environmental support at which time starvation, disease, and death balance the account.

(5) Industrial farming with exclusive attention to market crops, monoculture, and mechanization in a few decades resulted in the destruction of millions of acres of agricultural land through erosion because of a lack of soil and water conservation.

If we turn now to industrialization, we find an area of rapid and dramatic changes based largely on the physical sciences and their engineering application. The success of these ventures has produced wealth beyond imagination, each decade surpassing the previous one as the new wonders appeared in chemistry, physics, electronics, and power generation. One cannot gainsay these tools, machines, instruments, devices, and constructions that have increased the productivity of human labor many fold. But one must now, in some cases, at long last, pay attention to the costs as well as to the benefits. A few examples here will be sufficient:

(1) Modern limited-access highways move large volumes of auto

and truck traffic at high speed with comparative safety. They are routed across the landscape with little consideration for anything but engineering feasibility and economy. As a consequence, many rural scenic and natural values have been unnecessarily impaired and urban areas have caused great difficulties in traffic congestion and costs. Only recently has the Federal Bureau of Public Roads charged state highway departments with responsibility of coordination with state and federal forest, park, and wildlife agencies.

(2) Despite the Coordination Act, federal water construction agencies do not have a positive record of compliance with the recommendations of fish and wildlife agencies, especially in regard to dredging and filling permits issued to local governments and private developers. Important improvements in coordination are occurring, but we are still far from giving full consideration to values lost and benefits foregone because of single-purpose actions.

(3) The Federal Power Commission was recently hauled up short by the courts because of issuance of licenses for power installations without having given full consideration to possible losses of scenic beauty and of fish and wildlife.

(4) Thermal pollution of water is a consequence of many industrial uses of cooling water, and this is especially a threat from nuclear reactors. The Atomic Energy Commission apparently has no authority to require mitigation of such side effects.

(5) Innumerable industrial plants are located on water bodies because of transportation efficiency, cheap waste disposal, and a need for processing and cooling water. Except as such mills, plants, and factories have not interfered with navigation, there has been little public concern shown until the recent general interest in water pollution.

(6) Hundreds of chemicals produced by industry and used in households and on farms, including fertilizers, pesticides, detergents, manufacturing waste products, and effluents from food and fiber processing plants, are dumped into the nation's stream and estuaries, and even at sea. Disposal plants are technically incapable of purifying water of many new chemicals, while quantities are dumped directly into water.

(7) Silt pollution from road development, urban construction, and suburban real estate developments has muddied the waters of nearly all our streams.

(8) Domestic wastes are generally handled imperfectly both by septic fields and municipal plants, especially when they are mixed with overflow storm waters and spilled to watercourses without treatment. Moreover, we are finding that storm waters, which in the past may have been relatively "clean," now carry so much unwanted material that they also need treatment before being discharged into our streams.

(9) In a similar way, the gases and solids ejected into the air from

the stacks of public and private enterprises have caused damaging pollution that has been ignored until recently, just as the smoke from homes, trash-burning, and the exhaust of internal combustion engines has generally gone uncorrected.

(10) City, state, and federal parks, established to preserve nature and provide pleasure and nature-related recreation for the people, seem never to be safe from encroachments of all kinds by other public agencies with single-purpose interests, an attitude that has been described as "public vandalism."

This list could be extended to great length, but I wish to turn attention to damages to the social environment that result from a lack of full consideration being given to the consequences of single-minded actions, many of which are undertaken with the best of intentions. Some of the fruits of modern urbanization will provide adequate examples:

(1) The flight from the city to the suburbs has produced an economic and social "dry rot" in the heart of the cities.

(2) The unplanned development of suburban sprawl that is costly of public services, destructive of rural beauty, and without adequate provision of open space in the end is canceling the hopes of many who have moved from the cities.

(3) The deterioration of older parts of cities into slum warrens results in inadequate public services, including police, schools, recreational space, beauty of surroundings, and sanitation. To this can be added the sociological failure of many slum-clearance projects.

(4) Even new urban developments within the great cities usually are not adequately planned in consideration of human scale and ease of movement from home to work, and to recreational and cultural centers. The predominance of the private auto and the weakness of planning agencies which lack authority lead to the betrayal of the best intentions.

(5) The great urban centers generally lack unified authority. On the contrary, a large metropolitan complex may consist of more than a hundred different jurisdictions. This is one of the main causes of loss of quality of the social environment.

Thus in speaking of the effects of change on the biological, physical, and social environments, and especially the rates of change that are consequent to our rapidly expanding technical competences, I know that I have sketched the situations too baldly to be accurate in every instance. But the point is that we have come late to a realization that every action we take has consequences beyond those that are our direct and specific purposes, and, although we are beginning to correct some of the past deficiencies, we are as yet far from stopping the processes of deterioration of our environment and reversing the trend. Every year sees more, not less, pollution of the nation's air, water, and soil. Every year sees more losses of natural landscape by the filling of estuaries, loss of fish and wild-life habitats, and encroachments on park lands and wilderness.

There is need for a much greater investment in research. The proportion that is spent for knowledge to guide our actions and formulate policies is minute in relation to the dollars spent on actions that deteriorate the environment. To redevelop our cities, to cleanse the air and water, to regulate our industrial and other development programs will take vastly increased knowledge as well as money. Part of this knowledge can be supplied by the biological and physical sciences, as in the case of pollution abatement, but the need is also great, possibly even greater, for more knowledge that can be supplied only by the social sciences.

We need new laws to protect the environment. We need to invent new instrumentalities for governing ourselves, to supersede the political and administrative arrangements that antedate modern technology. We need a new economics that can deal with nonmarketable, intangible values. We need more psychological and social understandings that can guide us through the mazes of cultural and racial differences, that can help improve mental health and check delinquency and crime. We need more cultural anthropologists who will tackle the more complex societies of man, even though it is true that isolated human populations need to be studied before they are swamped by contemporary civilization. In short, at every hand there is great need for direct contributions by the social sciences to the processes that are affecting the quality of the environment.

But the question was this: Can ecology provide the basis for synthesis among the social sciences? The answer will be "yes" when each social science discipline takes into consideration, in the formulation of its concepts and conclusions, the fields of knowledge and understanding of the others. If economics takes into consideration the impact of psychology, if psychology takes into consideration the influences of cultural groups, if geography seeks the causes of the patterns it finds on the land, then these and any other social science fields will be dealing with interacting interrelations and their scientists will thereby be practicing human ecologists creating a synthesis of their separate fields.

In all fairness, however, we cannot ask the social sciences to produce a synthesis unless we expect the same from the biological and physical sciences. The only true synthesis would be that which recognizes the real nature of human ecosystems, a recognition of all the significant relationships between man and environment.

If we ever reach the time when internal combustion engines no longer pollute the air, when rivers are not for dumping wastes, when cities have human scale—in fact when all our actions are humane—we will have a physical environment of quality. We will then, as individuals, as economic firms, as participants in political systems and units of government, yes, and as managers and administrators, all be practicing ecologists.

Lynton K. Caldwell

Environment: A New Focus for Public Policy?*

To look at familiar things from an unfamiliar point of view is always a difficult and troublesome experience. The familiarity of the material tends to obscure the novelty of its arrangement. It is a little like looking at a picture consisting of a mass of apparently unrelated dots. If you look intently and from some distance away, the individual dots suddenly resolve themselves into a sharply defined image—perhaps a profile of George Washington. One may wonder why the artist didn't help the viewer by drawing the profile in the first place. But perhaps the profile was created in this curious manner to illustrate an idea rather than to suggest an image. By creating the profile out of a mass of separate dots, the artist is able to show how significant relationships may be discovered among apparently unrelated things. The profile in the picture was there all the time, even though the viewer did not at first perceive it, and then saw it only when distance lent the right perspective.

So it is with the complexities of the human environment and the concept of public policy that this article proposes. Most of us read no special meaning into familiar surroundings. But some, by training or experience, have come to see certain relationships that do not reveal themselves readily to the untrained glance. You see a picture of a traffic jam on a Los Angeles Freeway. This may be all that some see. Others, depending on the specialized character of their interest and perception, may see problems of transportation, public health, or engineering; or perhaps, problems of urban design, metropolitan government, or public finance. But, to one who sees the congested freeway as an aspect of human environment, all of these things and many others come into focus simultaneously, forming a profile of one aspect of our society.

A difficult way to look at things? True—but perhaps it is a more faithful perception of whatever reality we can know than the more

*From *Public Administration Review*, XXIII (Sept., 1963), 132–139. Reprinted by permission of the American Society for Public Administration. (Notes to this selection will be found on pp. 407–408.)

selective version of reality that serves us adequately for the everyday business of life. And just as many apparently insoluble problems have eluded solution until someone discovered the "right" way to view them, so it may be that our failure to cope adequately with certain large and complex problems of our time is a consequence of failure to see the unifying elements in the complexity. In our characteristic concentration on intensive, specialized analysis of our public problems we may omit so many data from our normal field of vision that the integrating profile does not appear.

The purpose of this article is to ask whether "environment" as a generic concept may enable us to see more clearly an integrating profile of our society. Would the perspective gained by looking at the way in which our society shapes its surroundings give us insight into relationships between specific social, economic, or political problems—into interrelations between the parts and the whole? It is not argued that environment is necessarily the only, or even the best, integrating concept. This could not be easily proved or disproved. The proposition that "environment" may be a useful focus for public policy purposes is advanced primarily for reasons of exploration—not advocacy. The merit of the idea can be discovered only by putting it to test.

MEANING OF ENVIRONMENT

To understand this essay, it matters little how environment is defined, provided it is defined comprehensively. A standard dictionary describes environment as "the aggregate of surrounding things, conditions, or influences." This is environment in the generic sense, as distinguished from specific environments. The concept of environment assumes not only "surrounding things" but something that is surrounded—in our preview, man.

Environment thus suggests analogy to the concept "sound." In both concepts, the physical reality of the objective universe is distinguishable from the interaction between that reality and the perceiving object. Practically speaking, sound exists only when there are ears to hear. Environment is not only the complex interrelating reality surrounding us; it includes us. But our environment is not the same as our perception of it. The "real" environment includes much more than we sense in our ordinary day-to-day surroundings. Yet, we are in continuing interaction with this total environment in varying degrees of directness and intensity.

Obviously, the human environment in its complex totality extends far beyond our present comprehension and technology. In its grand phases the environment is inexorably changing beyond our power to influence or even to understand. But we can and do influence our more limited terrestrial environment. We have learned to create artificial environments that increase our health and comfort or extend the range of our activities. But, when we "condition" our surroundings, we find that we must live within the regimen imposed by the artificial environment and the system that maintains it. Man has often altered his immediate natural environment in order to overcome its limitations, only to discover that he must then conform to new conditions imposed by the circumstances or consequences of environmental change. Equipped with space ships and space suits, he can live beyond the earth—but only as a consequence of one of the most exacting administrative and technical operations that human ingenuity has devised. To leave the earth and to return to it again, he must remain within a continuously administered environment. In outer space absolute environmental control is the obvious price of survival.

In all this there is nothing new. Man has been changing environments and adapting his behavior to them ever since he learned to use fire and clothe his body. Environments have been altered on a large scale by deliberate choice as well as by inadvertence. Forests have been felled, grasslands burned, marshes drained, and wild land brought under cultivation. But, in shaping our environments, we have seldom foreseen the full consequences of our action. The more remote and complex results of environmental change could not be perceived without the aid of a scientific knowledge and technology that we are still in the process of creating. With amazing consistency, men have misread the most obvious consequences of their efforts toward environmental control. Their defense cannot rest solely on want of knowledge; historians and geographers as long ago as Herodotus have noted reciprocal influences between men and environments. And in the more recent past, scientific ecology has clarified many cause–effect relationships in environmental change.

One need not accept as proved every argument advanced to support a theory of environmental influence in order to believe that in shaping their environments men shape their own societies.[1] Environments manage men even as men manage environments. Although this lesson has been written large in the landscape as well as in human history, few appear to have read it and fewer still to have read it with understanding.

Since the advent of the republic and the "pork barrel," Americans have been using government to "develop" selected aspects of their environments. But they have seldom seen environment, as such, as an expression of anything in particular. They have seldom thought of it as a general object of public policy. Their readiness to control environment for particular purposes has not been accompanied by recognition of a need for comprehensive environmental policies.

DILEMMA FOR DECISION-MAKERS

In the evolution of American political institutions, thus far, there appears to be no clear doctrine of public responsibility for the human environment as such. It therefore follows that concern for the environment is the business of *almost* no one in our public life. The qualification *almost* is necessary because urban and regional planners are increasingly seeing environment as the end product of their efforts. But, their responsibilities are usually limited to a restricted group of environmental problems and situations—urban renewal, for example. In the professional field of public health, environment is also increasingly a focus of concern. But rarely, aside from urban renewal, is broad environmental planning firmly joined to administrative action. At the higher political levels of government, environment is seldom recognized in other than the vague and generalized sense of "good living conditions" or "safeguarding our national heritage."

Does absence of consensus regarding public responsibility for the environment explain our widespread record of failure to develop stable, self-renewing, and generally desirable communities? Certainly absence of belief that the environment, comprehensively conceived, is, could, or should be a public responsibility, explains the absence of public policies relating to environments as entities different from the sum total of their parts. It would explain the inability of most public officials to think—or thinking, to act—in environmental terms. The political and technological circumstances of American life invite precisely the opposite approach to environmental policy.

In brief, our national tendency is to deal with environmental problems segmentally, as specialists whose frequently conflicting judgments require compromise or arbitration. For example, the history of interagency relations in river basin development illustrates the deeply ingrained exclusiveness of technical thinking on environmental questions and the great difficulty of relating the technical competence of the specialized experts to a comprehensive public policy. Here is an instance of that all-too-common human failing—a seeming inability to mobilize and direct tremendous resources of specialized knowledge and technique into comprehensive, well-conceived, and generally beneficial public action. Where the ultimate task is clear—as to put an astronaut into orbit—the technical task finds guidance toward its proper definition. Where no larger purpose is evident, administrators and technicians conceive policy in their own terms, which, under the circumstances, is perhaps the only thing that they can do.

The public decision-maker—legislative, administrative, or judicial—must deal with environmental questions without the help of a general body of environmental policy to which he may turn for authoritative guidance. And so in the administration of environmental problems he has been compelled to seek some calculus of objectivity that would pass as defensible rationality and simultaneously afford room to maneuver among the fixed or conflicting political forces—the "pressures" of public life. In order to make politically feasible decisions among specialized interests, decisions that could be defended as "in the public interest," a variety of concepts or "principles" have been invoked.[2] Some have been treated almost as if they were formulae for decision-making.

For example, the concept of *highest priority* has been asserted in support of military as against civilian preemption of public lands and waters. This approach assumes a hierarchy of values in the use of lands and waters, but provides no generally accepted authoritative basis for determining priorities among values or their relevance in any given situation. Another concept, that of *multiple use*, has seemed a logical avenue toward determining how varied interests in an environment may be served. But this approach, like the former, runs into a problem of priorities among values and how discrimination among values should be made in any given instance. A third concept, that of weighing environment-affecting decisions on the basis of *costs and benefits*, is limited at the outset to circumstances in which measurement can be expressed in monetary or other tangible terms.

Assuming a set of values to which all subscribed, conflict in environmental development might lead to decisions among interests that would be defensible within the context of the assumed value structure. Unfortunately for him, the public official must usually decide in an atmosphere charged with conflicting values and with no universally accepted guidepost pointing the way toward the "public interest."

Involved in public decision-making regarding natural resources and the environment are two intellectual tendencies or viewpoints that, although not necessarily opposites, are distinctly dissimilar. First of these is the *market* view. It sees the relatively free play of economic forces as the "best" determinant of environmental change. The second viewpoint is *ecological* and sees the natural world, including man and his works, as dependent for well-being and ultimate survival on the maintenance of an equilibrium or balance among the elements of the environment.

Each viewpoint has its mystique—each has practical strength and weakness. The *ecological* viewpoint derives strength from the natural sciences. It is a viewpoint congenial to the scientist-administrator who prefers decisions based on verifiable facts, for example, to those based on political fiat. It tends toward an idealist concept of "good" policy as something that can be "scientifically" determined to be "good" for people, regardless of popular preference or understanding. The *market* or competitive view has the practical advantage of appealing to men of means and action. It does not search for objectively "right" answers, but looks rather for practical solutions among the issues as people see them. The *market* is, of course, not only one of money. It includes the market in which political influence is negotiated and may thrive at political levels in a socialist economy as readily as in an atmosphere of free enterprise. Indeed, there have been rumors of disagreement among Soviet political economists and agricultural experts over whether politics or ecology should have guided Chairman Khrushchev's decision to plow or not to plow the "virgin lands" of Central Asia.

These two viewpoints are based upon strongly contrasting sets of values and assumptions regarding man and nature. They lead to equally contrasting conclusions regarding the role of government in relation to the environment. But, between the extremities of viewpoint there are intermediate stages in which these and other attitudes are mixed. Yet science and politics need not, as often as they do, lead to opposing conclusions regarding environmental policy. A politics better informed by science and a science applied in the service of well-considered values would provide a firmer and broader basis for public environmental decision-making than present circumstances provide.

The administrative dilemma in environmental decisions—and it is also a legislative dilemma—is that public decisions must be taken as if there were a generally accepted, guiding concept of the public interest by which the "rightness" of the decision could be measured. But neither our law, our political tradition, nor the predominant elements of our cultural heritage provide such a guiding concept. And so, on environmental issues affecting lands (urban and rural), waters, forests, wildlife, and air space, conflicting interests clash headlong in what is usually a test of sheer political strength. For want of a common denominator of differing interests, public policy-makers have had to make do with rationalizations of decisions in which *the public interest* has, in fact, become synonymous with effective political power.

EMERGING ENVIRONMENTAL CONCEPTS

No massive research is required to document the inadequacy of our environmental decision-making. The evidence surrounds us. Clearly, a substantial percentage of our public problems, conspicuous at the local level, are the consequences of unfortunate environmental decisions. Local communities throughout the nation struggle with problems of housing, schools, water supply, sewage, transportation, parks, industrial location, and urban renewal—problems made far more difficult than they needed to have been by failure of the community or its decision-makers to think in environmental terms.

Segmental thinking, segmental decision-making—the "practical" approach to practical problems—has again and again produced some very impractical results. Familiar examples are found in cities that conduct vigorous drives for safety on the streets and simultaneously permit built-in safety hazards in street layout, building construction and outdoor advertising. Examples of "practical" nonsense can be found in the application of tax laws which, in effect, penalize the improvement or rehabilitation of run-down property—linking government with landowners as co-defendants in slum-making. And there is the monotonous, colorless, culture-free, mass housing—particularly in urban renewal areas—that may well represent substitution of a new set of environmental problems for the ones presumed to be solved.

American policies affecting the environment have been essentially segmental—largely because most of us, in government and out, taking the environment for granted have dealt with its various elements without regard to their interrelated totality.[3] In our pioneer tradition, we have been too busy cutting trees to think about consequences to the environmental forest. Consequently, American government is continually trying to solve problems and to salvage the wreckage caused by misguided, heedless, or inadvertent environmental change. While significant public environmental needs go unmet, public funds and energies are preempted to remedy the waste and error of technical and economic innovations which proceed without adequate guidance or control, destroying values and creating unforeseen situations harmful and costly to the public welfare.

There are indications, however, that the tempo and magnitude of change are forcing a reshaping of traditional American attitudes toward the environment. Increasing problems and increasing knowledge regarding the distribution of people and their activities in physical space seem certain to stimulate systematic new theories of environmental planning and administration.[4] The transformation of living conditions in mid-20th century is a universal phenomena not peculiar to urban or rural areas, or to developed or underdeveloped countries. The phenomenon is endemic to the times.

The basic problems are seldom new, but their magnitude and urgency have no precedent. Governance of the megalopolis presents a host of problems nowhere adequately solved and, in many cases, not yet adequately defined. Urban planning, for example, cannot now proceed realistically without regard to the larger surrounding region. Meanwhile, the urgency of urban problems has tended to divert attention from no less portentous transformations in the nonurban areas. The mechanization, collectivization, and industrialization of agriculture and other aspects of natural resources management is changing rural life as radically as present-day Tokyo or New York were changed from the traditional cities from which they evolved. Large-scale efforts toward environmental change as in the river valleys of the Columbia, Colorado, or Missouri create obvious and continuing intergovernmental and even international complications.[5] Thus environmental change—its causes, problems, and consequences—emerges as one of the practical and compelling areas for public debate, for policy focus, and for research.

The first effort toward a formulation of comprehensive environmental policy has been through the medium of public planning. But planning, of itself, has seldom succeeded in achieving the vital expression of policy that is evidenced through action. Planning is not self-executory. Plans, to be realized, must reach a point of action—yet this is the conspicuous point of failure in the history of planning.

Even urban renewal, which has been previously noted as a partial exception, has been largely restricted to the remedy of very specific. environmental situations and seldom goes beyond the immediate renewal area to shape the future of the larger surrounding community. At present, town and country planning as understood in Great Britain comes as close as any public effort to uniting planning and action in the control of environmental change. And yet, observation of British experience has suggested that, even where planning policies are clear and generally accepted, conventional administrative practice may tend to contradict objectives.[6] Could it be that objectives have been sought through planning that are realizable only through a new concept of administrative responsibility?[7]

Administration implies action, and action, being the ultimate test of policy, gives administration a practical advantage over planning as a medium for achieving public purposes. The action may, of course, be negative—it may be misguided or it may fail to be instructed by adequate planning. But planning, however excellent, remains ineffectual until it is translated by administration into action. There may be critical or prophetic value in theoretical planning that does not lead to action. But, the practical utility of this type of planning cannot be evaluated. To separate practical planning from administration is like separating cart from horse. In the long run, the objectives sought through urban or regional planning may more likely be realized through the emerging concept of environmental administration.

Environmental administration is a convenient word-symbol representing at least three distinguishable but closely related meanings. *First*, the term represents the policies, methods, and processes by which man shapes his environments; *second*, it provides a name for the study of man's efforts to influence his environments; and *third*, it suggests an attempt to deal with environments comprehensively, as environments, in contrast to focusing upon their component parts. In the first sense, we have always had environmental administration. In the second sense, it is a new multidisciplinary synthesis in the process of being born. In the third sense, we have a concept that could carry with it profound social and political implications.

As with most concepts, environmental administration in any of its meanings can be pushed to the point of absurdity. Dealing with environments comprehensively need not imply endlessly detailed analyses and hopelessly complex syntheses of all environmental factors before policies can be formulated. There is a common-sense balance between the too-often uninformed, expedient, piecemeal methods now generally pursued and a perfectionist effort to take into account absolutely everything relevant to a contemplated environmental change. The concept of environment as a possible focus for public policy is only now emerging. There will no doubt be many theories of environmental administration developed before the best one, if indeed there can be any best one, is discovered.

Among the systematic theories of environmental administration now current is *ekistics*, "the science of human settlements," conceived and most effectively expounded by C. A. Doxiadis. Ekistics is both a general approach to environmental development and a body of specific doctrine. Doxiadis sees ekistics as a science to be developed. "We are," he declares, "only starting to grasp the need for it. . . ." Derived from the Greek word *ekos*, meaning habitat, and from the verb *eko*, meaning to settle down, ekistics has the same conceptual origin as economics and ecology. It is in purpose a practical discipline, drawing upon the substance and methodology of the physical, biological, and social sciences for much of its basic data and directed to the problem: "How to make a settlement so as to fill the two basic requirements laid down by Aristotle: Security and happiness."[8]

The genius of Doxiadis has been to combine a theoretical concept and an operational method with a systematic exposition, and to give the combination an appropriate name. The novelty of ekistics lies in its formulation rather than in its elements. It is no mean accomplishment to discover a name that will crystallize a concept so as to make clear what, for many people, is obscure—to spark imagination and thus persuade to action those whom a conventional analysis of environmental factors would fail to move. Ekistics is therefore more than a theory of planning. It is also a theory of action and its realization assumes an on-going administration of the total environment in accordance with verified ecological understanding.

A FOCUS FOR POLICY?

Examination of the recent literature of human ecology, public health, natural resources management, urbanism, and development planning suggests a growing tendency to see environment as a policy framework within which many specific problems can best be solved.[9] Does this trend presage a greater public concern for environmental policy? It seems highly probable.

The intellectual foundations for an environmental policy focus are being laid. The social and material pressures toward such a focus are already present. The need for a generalizing concept of environmental development that will provide a common denominator among differing values and interests is becoming clearer. And the concept of "good" environment, however one defines it, is certainly no less concrete, tangible, and specific than the concepts of freedom, prosperity, security, and welfare that have on various occasions served to focus public policy.

Environmental thinking has resulted both from an examination of past environmental errors and from a growing awareness of the probable consequences of present environmental decisions. It is doubtful whether circumstances henceforth will allow us as wide a margin for environmental miscalculation as that enjoyed in the past. An accelerating demand on all resources is resulting from our burgeoning technology and from increasing populations, their needs, expectations, and changing ways of life. We have both the occasion and the means to make bigger, more disastrous, and more irremedial environmental mistakes than ever in the past. But, how would policy focus on the environment help us to follow a wiser course, now and in the future?

It can be demonstrated that many of the worst environmental errors are direct or indirect results of segmental public decision-making, of failing to perceive specific environmental situations in comprehensive environmental terms. A policy focus on environment in its fullest practicable sense would make more likely the consideration of all the major elements relevant to an environment-affecting decision. Whatever content is ascribed to the adjective "good," it becomes daily more evident that public administration of the environment will not be "good" if it fails to deal with environmental problems in comprehensive terms.[10] This task would not of necessity be hopelessly involved and time consuming. In contrast to some of our more primitive current methods of environmental decision-making, it would indeed be complex. But methods oversimplified in relation to the problems are not likely to produce satisfactory results.

Consideration of environmental problems in comprehensive terms may lead to fewer errors and hence to better environmental decisions. But, here an important reservation must be added: The approach is not a panacea. A focus on environment may facilitate, but would not lessen, the political task of reconciling a great diversity of interests and values. The scientific base and content of environment-focused decisions would no doubt be increased beyond that employed in our characteristically segmental decisions. But value judgments, particularly with respect to ends, ethics, and accountability in public action, would also gain significance. For through these decisions the futures of communities would be shaped not by accident or inadvertency, but by responsible, deliberate, purposeful design. Scientists may one day tell us what kinds of environment are best for our physical and mental health, but it seems doubtful if scientists alone will be able to determine the environmental conditions that people will seek. There will surely remain an element of personal judgment that cannot be relegated to the computer.

Certainly a major advantage of the comprehensive approach is that it tends to force consideration of the basic value questions involved, as for example: What in a given instance is a "good" environment? What kind of environment should, in a given instance, be sought? What objective data can be found that are valid indicators of the effect of environmental factors upon people? Until we find answers to these questions, better than those we now have, our environmental policies, although capable of great improvement, will still leave much to be desired.

Environment as a focus for public policy has thus grown out of past experience, but its major development extends into the future. In the long run, its advantages will be fully realized only as research broadens and firms our knowledge of environmental influences. In the short run, the environment concept may provide a new and better focus for many public policy decisions. This growth, however, can take place no faster than two other developments occur. *First*, the public must have begun to see the comprehensive environment as a legitimate and necessary field for public action. *Second*, means must be found for more effectively interrelating or integrating the tasks of the public agencies as they bear upon the environment. In both of these developments, research is needed to guide the course of action.[11] It seems unlikely that we will find the legislative, organizational and administrative answers to environmental development and control before we have developed the policy concepts and goals toward which our political efforts can intelligently be directed.[12]

Public policy in the shaping of the environment thus emerges as a vast multidisciplinary field of inquiry in which significant work has been started, but most of it, as yet, restricted to specific environmental factors as, for example, water resources or radioactive radiation. Investigation of specific environmental problems is essential to any larger or more generalized concept of environmental policy. But ultimately, the accumulating special studies must be related to a larger order of generalization, if comprehensive environmental administration is to become a reality. For it does not follow that if the lesser jobs are pursued with diligence, the greater ones will take care of themselves.

Hans H. Landsberg

The U.S. Resource Outlook: Quantity and Quality*

It will soon be sixty years since Gifford Pinchot published *The Fight for Conservation*, as informative and succinct a guide to the Conservation Movement's views and judgments as one can hope to find. With regard to resource adequacy, it presents a generally somber picture, supported by careful projections based on the idea that the volume of economic resources in the United States is defined by their identified physical occurrence. The lesson that only careful husbanding can stretch the supply is the logical sequel. Governor Pinchot summarizes the findings of approaching resource exhaustion as follows:

The five indispensably essential materials in our civilization are wood, water, coal, iron, and agricultural products. . . . We have timber for less than thirty years at the present rate of cutting. We have anthracite coal for but fifty years, and bituminous coal for less than 200. Our supplies of iron ore, mineral oil, and natural gas are being rapidly depleted, and many of the great fields are already exhausted.

Later in the book, Pinchot points to our "limited supply" of coal, a substance that he holds to be "in a sense the vital essence of our civilization:"

If it can be preserved, if the life of the mines can be extended, if by preventing waste there can be more coal left in this country after we of this generation have made every needed use of this source of power, then we shall have deserved well of our descendants.

On that last point there is unfortunately no direct way of judging how well we have, in fact, done. Not only is the evaluation of resources and reserves a very imprecise art at any point in time, but criteria and methods themselves undergo change. Thus, the nation's first estimate

*Reprinted by permission from *Daedalus*, Journal of the American Academy of Arts and Sciences (Boston), XCVI, No. 4 (Fall, 1967), 1034–1057. (Notes to this selection will be found on p. 408.)

of coal resources, published by the U.S. Geological Survey in 1909, one year before Pinchot's book, reckoned that 3,200 billion tons had been in existence "when mining first began." This estimate held for four decades but was trimmed to 2,500 billion tons in 1950, and to 1,900 billion tons in 1953, not because of intervening consumption (not more than 40 billion tons or so, a minute fraction of the amount estimated to exist, has been mined in the entire history of the country), but because of more sophisticated and extensive methods of measurement.

Governor Pinchot would probably judge us kindly on the score of coal consumption, for the American of 1966 used about two-and-a-half tons of coal per year where his forebear of 1910 consumed almost twice as much. The decline was not, however, motivated by thrift or avoidance of waste, as the Conservation Movement understood these terms. Rather, the prime reasons were vastly greater efficiency in burning, especially in steam–electric plants, and the emergence of other energy sources that have almost totally replaced coal in ships, railroads, and homes, and partially replaced it in factories and power plants.

Indeed, in the case of coal, we have come full circle. Today the U.S. Department of the Interior is investing millions of dollars a year in research that is aimed not at conserving coal but at developing new uses. Two of them, liquefaction and gasification, could, if successful, increase future coal consumption spectacularly. But few considerations, we may be sure, prey less on the department's mind than the fact, incontestable as it is, that the country's coal supplies constitute a finite resource and thus are subject to eventual exhaustion.

HOW WE HAVE MADE DO—THE BIG PICTURE

What has wrought this radical change in our view of things is, of course, the cumulative and joint impact of increased knowledge and improved technology—in short, the forces generally lumped under the broad heading "The Scientific Age."[1] Change induces change. Diminishing returns from exhaustion of resources with better characteristics are staved off not by lucky discoveries, as was once the case, but by advances that are both systematic and cumulative. Moreover, we have learned the advantages of "disaggregation"—that is, the separate utilization of the different inherent features of natural resources, as opposed to their joint use in the form in which they occur in nature. To illustrate the technique and realize its advantages from a conservation point of view, one need only think of the way in which the chemical industry, prominently including oil and gas processing, typically breaks down its raw-material stream.

We have thus enhanced our ability to upgrade old resources (for example, cropland through the addition of fertilizer), to discover new ones (oil, gas, nuclear fission, and so forth), to utilize them more efficiently (coal in power generation, low-grade copper ore, wood waste for pulp mills and building board, and the like), and to adjust to relative resource availabilities (aluminum replacing copper, or air-cooling replacing water-cooling). Consequently, the relative importance of the country's resources as inputs into the economic hopper has steadily diminished. A few gross examples will suffice to support this statement.

At the end of the Civil War, 6.5 million people were employed by the resource industries, which represent the sum total of the agriculture, forestry, and extractive industries (lack of suitable data prevents inclusion of water-associated activities). By 1910, this figure had climbed to 12 million, but it has now dropped to 5.5 million—one million less than it was 90 years ago. Resources now claim less than one tenth of all the labor in the country, instead of the half of a century ago, but this tenth produces five times as much as the half did.

Almost the same relationship is revealed when the output of resources industries is compared with the output of all goods and services. A quintupling in the resource field has been accompanied by a 25-fold growth in the economy's total output. Not surprisingly, prices of resource commodities have, in general, not risen above prices for all goods and services.

A QUICK RUNDOWN IN SOME DETAIL

One might, therefore, say so far so good. Things have not worked out badly, at least not for the United States. Fossil fuel reserves have held up well, even though we have drawn on them at rates that were unimaginable not so long ago. Because rising yields allow us to grow what is needed on fewer acres, land in crops has been on the decline. And were it not for booming food exports, partly financed by ourselves, the problem of surplus farm land would loom much larger.

The most recent survey reveals that our forests are adding new growth at a substantially faster rate than that at which the annual cut is removing them. In 1962, when detailed estimates were last made, growth exceeded cut by 60 per cent. To be sure, behind this favorable aggregate comparison lurk problems of quality, species, location, marketing, and so on. For example, we still cut more sawtimber softwood—a highly desirable product—than we grow. Moreover, some of this apparent good fortune derives from improved measurement. This would mean that we were better off in the past than we had thought and that part of the apparent improvement is a mirage, but it would not negate the finding that current growth exceeds cut. The products of new technology—metals, plastics, and other synthetic substances—have reduced the demand for forest products; and in some lines, such as pulp and paper, we have been able to rely extensively on imports to supplement domestic production.

Perhaps nothing reflects so dramatically the changing tide of events as the conditions of timber resources. As Harold J. Barnett and Chandler Morse have pointed out, the Conservation Movement's "sense of impending scarcity derived directly from a concern for the future of America's forests, dating back at least to the 1870s."[2] As early as 1877, Carl Schurz, then Secretary of the Interior under President Hayes, forecast a coming "timber famine," with supplies to last only another 20 years. Today the concern for forests focuses on their role as part of the environment rather than as a source of materials.

In the field of nonfuel minerals, we are intermittently plagued by specific shortages—copper, sulfur, tin, and the like—but a stretch of high prices and concern has never as yet failed to engender successful efforts to locate new deposits, to exploit old ones more efficiently, and to promote substitution of more abundant, natural or man-made, materials, sometimes temporarily, sometimes permanently.

THE ROLE OF TECHNOLOGY

The current condition of ease regarding sufficiency of quantity is rooted largely in advancing technology, with its twin offspring: efficiency and substitutability. This trend has accelerated in the recent past. Only 15 years ago, the authors of "Resources for Freedom" (the name under which President Truman's Materials Policy, or Paley, Commission released its findings in 1952) commented that "in the U.S. the supplies of the evident, the cheap, the accessible are running out."

The commission would probably not phrase it that way today, for there are abundant examples of the nonevident becoming evident, the expensive cheap, and the inaccessible accessible. Broadening scope, increasing variety, and rising volume of man-made products exemplify the nonevident that is becoming evident. So do nuclear power generation and telecommunication by microwave and laser.

Hardness, low-metal content, fine-grained structure, and the non-magnetic nature of part of the deposits made the extensive iron-bearing ores of Minnesota, Michigan, and Wisconsin that are commonly lumped under the generic heading of taconites too costly to mine until after World War II. New processing technology has since made it not merely possible to extract usable material at acceptable costs, but has turned the initial handicap of having to agglomerate the fine particles into pellets into a major advantage, because the pellet feed greatly enhanced the productivity of the industry's furnaces. Similar evidence testifies to the changing circumstances of accessibility. Thus, the deposits of oil in offshore fields, buried under hundreds of feet of water and thousands of feet of ocean bottom, have become accessible. So have many and varied underground ore deposits that have yielded to the search by airborne magnetometer, sensing devices, chemical anomalies, and other new exploration tools.

But while that commission, from the vantage point of 1967, appears to have underestimated the speed of population growth, of economic growth, and of industrially useful new knowledge and technology, its place in history is secure, for its decisive emphasis was not on the "running out of resources," which had been a popular concept in earlier years, but on resource availability at a cost, on the role of costs as a barometer of scarcity, and on future technology as a factor in determining costs and availability. Thus "running out" becomes a relative matter. Copper may "run out" for fabricator A, but not for fabricator B, who, for one reason or another, is able to pay the higher price that reduced availability engenders. At the same time, the higher price is likely to bring closer the threshold at which deposits with poorer characteristics can be commercially exploited. The "running out" process is a dynamic one, subject to changes in direction, and thus is quite different from the straightline, down-trending concept current early in the century.

Barnett and Morse have suggested that a major cause of this development is the flowering of the scientific advances.[3] In such an environment, there are no diminishing returns from improvements, for the improvement is in turn improved upon before its advantages have been dissipated or squeezed to a zero return. We have reached constant cost plateaus, at which increased amounts of resources are available without cost increases.

Others suggest that the curve of technological improvement will soon begin to flatten out and that we may already be moving along the upper leg of the sigmoid development curve. The bigger part of many technical revolutions, says John R. Platt, appears to lie behind us.[4] We have reached "science and technology plateaus." From horse-and-buggy to the current version of the jet plane is a bigger quantum jump than the impending advance to the SST. The invention of the telephone marked a bigger break with past communications methods than will the transition to satellites.

Perhaps this is so, although the odds in speculating on unknown technology are notoriously long. Nevertheless, no amount of speculation on the kind of plateau we may be approaching can relieve us of the need or impair the usefulness of taking a long look ahead for a test of how well, under carefully spelled-out, realistic assumptions, our resource situation is likely to hold up. Such a look involves a wide array of guesses, the worth of which will depend as much on the effort that goes into making them as on the investigator's success in recognizing and overcoming his biases.

A LOOK AHEAD

Resources for the Future* has engaged in making and publishing such informed guesses or projections.[5] I can, therefore, be brief and summarize the picture that emerges for the balance of this century. It is not one to provoke undue concern, at least not on the score of quantity and for this country.

Farm Land

Rising crop yields—based both on further advances in agronomy and on a large-scale catching-up of the bulk of the growers with the best—can confidently be expected to keep land from becoming a limiting factor to food production. A few years ago, contemplation of past history led Resources for the Future to project 1970 corn yields at 70 bushels per acre. Because yields ranged between 53 and 55 bushels per acre in the three years preceding 1961, the year in which we had to make our projections, we thought our prediction a little daring; some scholars who were asked to review what was then a manuscript thought we were very daring. But by 1965 the yield had climbed to 74 bushels and had outrun the projection. The average yield in Iowa had jumped above 80 and in Indiana and Illinois above 90 bushels per acre. Our projected yield of 100 bushels in the year 2000, a faraway guess when made, had begun to move into clearer view. This projection and those for other feed grains stand a good chance of being overtaken before the end of the century. Little can as yet be said about other major crops.[6]

Forests

It is difficult to speak with assurance regarding the long-run adequacy of U.S. forests to supply the domestic market. A few years ago, Resources for the Future had grave doubts that even allowing for a generous drawing on imports, prospective demand could long be satisfied by domestic supply without impairing the size and quality of our forests. These doubts have diminished. Demand continues to lag. Wood prices seem high in comparison with nonwood alternatives, especially when the latter offer advantages in handling and maintenance. Also, there has been a less than buoyant housing market. Moreover, the existing volume of

---

*A privately funded foundation engaged in and sponsoring research on natural resources. – Ed.

trees now appears larger than was believed a few years ago. The most recent figures (1962) compiled by the U.S. Forest Service show a significantly higher timber inventory than does their previous estimate (1953). For the time being, emphasis has shifted from forest products in the aggregate to adequacy and quality of given species.

Outdoor Recreation

Considerable uncertainty attaches to those uses of land that do not lead to production of commodities. This is true especially for outdoor recreation. Even cautious projections of the use trend of parks and other recreation land translate into very large acreage figures.

On what some might consider conservative assumptions regarding both the rate of increase in visits and tolerable. density of recreation acreage, Resources for the Future estimated that by 1980 there might be need for 76 million acres for outdoor recreation; and by the year 2000 this need should call for an additional 58 million acres. For comparison, in 1960 there were only 44 million acres of land in national parks, monuments, recreation areas, state parks, and in national forests used primarily for recreation.

In terms of new policies and of magnitude of outlays required, such figures put a wholly new face on a hitherto secondary aspect of land use. On the other hand, until we know more about such factors as the carrying capacity of outdoor acreage for recreation and the potential of private land for such purposes, we must handle these statistics with some sense of detachment. Unfortunately, it will take some time for research to catch up with the speed at which use of this new resource has been growing.

Other Uses of Land

A common complaint of the sixties is the "asphalting over" of America's land. Houses, offices, factories, highways, airports, parking lots, and the like have such high visibility to so many people that their presence and growth tends to distort perspective. It is the view during the occasional airplane ride that restores it.

In cold figures, the 25 million acres or so occupied by the urban population at this time is less than 1.5 per cent of the country's surface. Highways, railroads, and airports take up perhaps 27 million acres, for a grand total of built-up terrain of, say, 50 million acres, not quite 3 per cent of the face of America. By the end of the century, this might grow by 50 per cent, to 75 million acres, due overwhelmingly to expansion of urban land use.

I do not mean to suggest that problems of land use—especially in urban areas—are meaningfully measured in terms of acres. If they were, the task of finding the additional 25 million acres of land that we may need for urban living between now and the end of the century could be entrusted to a child equipped with nothing more than a map and a ruler. Nor does dealing in aggregates, unqualified by reference to land characteristics, do justice to the issue. Pointing to European population densities that typically run five to ten, and in some cases, fifteen times the U.S. density merely shows that other countries have problems too.

On the other hand, nearly 500 million acres are devoted to commercial raising of trees, and about 700 million acres are primarily grazing land (there is room for arguing over proper land classification here, but these rough figures will do for the purpose). Thus, 75 million acres for urban centers and transportation facilities pose less a problem of "space shortage" due to "asphalting over" than of inventiveness in efficient use of the country's surface.

The Demand for Energy

The demand for energy is likely to be three times as high in the year 2000 as it is now, but the entry of new or newly derived energy resources (from nuclear reactors to oil and gas from coal, shale oil, oil sands, and so forth), combined with more efficient utilization and conversion of conventional energy sources, is likely to ward off rising costs. Indeed, we may well be entering an era of slowly declining energy costs. There is unprecedented activity in developing new coal technology to widen the scope of our largest fossil fuel resource; research and development leading to a breeder reactor, which may begin to bear fruit by the mid-seventies, will multiply many times over the country's uranium resources as a basis for power generation.

Metals

Enough deposits of the major metals, supplemented by imports and rising amounts of scrap, have been identified that emergence of sustained supply problems due to inadequate resources seems unlikely given our demonstrated ability to handle ever lower-grade material. This does not, however, insure against shortfalls in times of national emergency—to be provided for through special measures, such as stockpiles. Nor does it offset temporary and, perhaps, even prolonged difficulties like those that have in recent years plagued copper, which is mined in major quantities in countries that are subject to political upheavals or uncertainties. Supply cannot always keep up with quick rising demand, but it has a habit of catching up, sometimes to a greater extent than is required.

Ability to process low-grade material carries one great advantage: Such material usually exists in very large volume. For example, the previously mentioned taconite ores, most of which are likely to become subject to commercial exploitation during the balance of the century, equal four times the cumulative demand for iron projected through the end of the century. Perhaps a turn to unconventional sources, such as the ocean floor, will help the situation for others, as will substitutions by nonmetallic materials. Thus, despite projected levels of consumption that between now and the year 2000 could cumulate to the equivalent of 60 to 70 times the 1960 consumption for iron, copper, lead, and zinc, 90 to 100 times that for nickel, chromium, and tungsten, and 125 times that for aluminum, it is difficult to envision serious supply problems because of resource limitations.

Water

Judgments about water are often confusing because of fuzzy concepts and poor terminology and complicated because of the attention that must be given to problems of quality. It helps to realize initially that in many of its uses water is either a free or nearly free good and that incentives for economizing are the exception rather than the rule. Thus, projections of future consumption are based more on what people have been led to take for granted as "needed" than on what they would be willing to buy at prices that more nearly reflect cost.

Another aid to understanding is a clear distinction between *withdrawal* of water with subsequent discharge back into the original source and withdrawal followed by consumption, or *depletion*. All uses have elements of both, but the proportions vary greatly. In municipal use, for example, most water—about 90 per cent—is discharged after it has served its function, while irrigation depletes from 60 to 90 per cent, depending upon the circumstances. Since water can be used over and over again, the item to keep one's eye on is, for most purposes, depletion—not withdrawal. Unfortunately, most popular discussion is conducted in terms of water "use," without further definition of the term.

The need for sharpness of definition applies equally to the supply side. The total supply of surface water—precipitation—is a multiple of what becomes accessible in the form of runoff. The latter is, in turn, normally a multiple of withdrawal, and withdrawal typically exceeds depletion. (Instances where the entire flow is diverted without any return to the source are the exceptions.) Moreover, ground water, as distinguished from annual replenishment, constitutes a separate supply. Finally, there is a variety of techniques for adding to available supply. Some, such as storage, predate the era of recorded history, others, such as desalinization, weather modification, and evaporation control, are undergoing active development. They are paralleled on the demand side by techniques for reducing consumption. Substituting air-cooling for water-cooling, less wasteful irrigation techniques, and a more efficient use generally (for example, having a smaller flow or depletion per unit of service required) belong in this category. As our political and administrative approaches to water management, as well as our costing and pricing mechanisms, receive attention and review, channeling water into the highest-yielding alternatives will assume increasing importance.

Differences in natural endowment and climate have combined with a different mix of use categories to produce a sharp cleavage in situation and outlook between the eastern and western United States, using these geographic terms in the loosest of meanings. Because of the large role played by irrigation, the West (excluding the Pacific Northwest) depletes nearly five times the volume of water depleted in the East. Since it only disposes of about 20 per cent of the runoff available to the East (which is, of course, the reason why the West needs irrigation if it wants to have agriculture), the West depletes about 40 per cent of the water it can count on.

Before long, the West may find water supply a serious obstacle to economic growth if flows are not diverted to uses other than irrigation, prices are not brought into line with costs, and techniques for adding new supplies do not soon become commercially feasible for meeting the needs of cities and industries at prices they can afford.

In sharp contrast, and for the opposite reasons, the East depletes less than 2 per cent of its runoff and faces no long-range physical shortage, provided rainfall deficiencies during the past few years do not represent the beginning of a basic long-term change in climatic conditions. Meteorologists are divided on this issue, and conclusive evidence one way or the other will not be forthcoming for some time. Meanwhile, whatever the ultimate trend, the East faces decisions associated with pricing and allocating water and with encouraging economizing by means other than admonitions and exhortations (though in the face of uncertainty the "muddling-through" approach has the merit of preserving options).

Above all, however, the eastern United States is confronted with growing deterioration of water quality. This increasingly narrows the usefulness of many streams and lakes for purposes that demand clean water. It imposes costs on users that draw their supplies from stretches polluted by others. Moreover, it raises in full not only a host of new technical problems but economic, political, and administrative questions about equitable and efficient remedies to the situation. For those who try to appraise the degree of adequacy of the nation's resources, it opens up a new dimension—the quality of resources.

The size and characteristics of domestic resources, in combination with imports, are such as to exclude any significant limitation to U.S. growth because of resources. This picture would no doubt look different if one were to widen the geographic scope and consider the world, or a major portion of it. The number of critical resource areas would increase, and the time horizon for which one would have a reasonable assurance of adequacy would shrink. Specifically, it is unlikely that these conditions will affect the terms on which the United States obtains its imports sufficiently to alter significantly the general perspective outlined above. Except in the case of food, however, only the most general quantitive appraisals have been made of the resources that the developing countries are likely to need for the decades ahead.[7] Analogies of trends and patterns of material use that have prevailed in Western industrialized nations and extrapolations of short trends in the developing countries can both be misleading. Exploration of future development patterns in terms of claims on specific resources is badly needed, however, if we are to gain a realistic picture of what faces this country in its role as a member of the world community.

QUALITY OF RESOURCES: HOW GOOD?

It would be convenient to deal with the quality problem in much the same fashion as with quantitative adequacy. We would, in other words, assess the degree of past acceptability for each of the resources, project the demand into the future, and judge whether the supply will be forthcoming, or whether, where, and when "quality shortages" will develop.

Unfortunately, we can barely begin to measure the state of adequacy at the present. How good or bad the past has been we can deduce, at best, from the presence or absence of comments and protests. Moreover, we are as yet woefully short of methods that can help us pick our way between those who see the population tobogganing toward physical and emotional decay and those who regard the current concern over quality decline as but another phase of modern life with which common sense and technology will in time come to grips.

TECHNOLOGY—TWO SIDES OF THE COIN

Technology, it seems, has played a cruel hoax on us: It has assured enough, but in the process it has led to a degraded quality. Excessive use of the waste assimilative characteristics of water and air by cities, factories, coal mines, oil wells, chemical-bearing agricultural land, and many other concomitants of life in the industrial age has created a complex technological and economic problem: To devise ways and means other than natural stream and air flow for disposing of waste material, and to determine and apportion the costs and benefits that arise in the process. Undesirable by-products have made their mark on both the rural and the urban landscape. The settings are different but the adverse consequences and the problems of measurement, evaluation, and policy are similar.

Deploring technology's side effects—which range from unpleasant to highly dangerous—is not tantamount to decrying technology as such. In one of his recorded songs, Tom Lehrer, Cambridge's gift to social satire, finds it a sobering thought that at his age Mozart had been dead for two years. Similarly I find it a sobering thought that I would have been less likely to accept the invitation to contribute to this symposium at the turn of the century, for a man in his fifties would at that time have outrun his mean chance of survival. Life expectancy at birth in the United States has since moved from less than 50 to 70 years.

One is apt to view the more disagreeable aspects of modern life, including most prominently those due to the impact of technology, with partiality—often unconsciously. We take for granted that we may drink tap water, eat uncooked fruit or vegetables, and consume milk with no thought of falling victim to a lurking bug. We are reminded of our good fortune only when we travel in parts of the world that require preventive or remedial countermeasures, or when the exceptional case in this country hits the front page. But, customarily, we fail to do much balancing of pluses and minuses. We tend to overlook the fact that the chemical industry produces not only controversial pesticides, but also antibiotics and vaccines; that the automobile whose incomplete fuel combustion fouls the city air does, at the same time, enable us to escape its boundaries and to know the world in a way available a generation or two ago only to the daring or the rich. We are quick to lament the fallen sparrow, but slow to celebrate the fall of "Typhoid Mary."

This is not the same as inviting, or welcoming, or even being indifferent to the negative aspects and abuses that can be or are associated with technological advance. To reconstruct what is in terms of what could have been is generally a misleading venture, for people commonly engage in such reconstruction for the purpose of excising the obnoxious features while leaving untouched those they sanction. They forget or ignore that both are usually part of one and the same fabric. To show that we could have had one without the other requires more than saying so.

Nor can it be taken for granted that accurate and timely anticipation of the adverse consequences of a particular action necessarily produces decisions to prevent them. For example, the failure of cigarette-smoking to decline or of repeated disasters to discourage occupancy of flood plains raises doubts about the level of individual response. Failure to have acted long ago on such matters as provision of adequate, common-carrier urban transport or nonpolluting incinerators suggests that we act no more wisely in matters of collective response.

Beyond the need of adequate motivation and appropriate institutions, there is the great difficulty of balancing the gains and the losses. Let us look more closely at the cigarette-smoker, and let us assume that he is well informed about the effects. Presumably the smoker has achieved a balance of gains and losses: The gain from inhalation more than offsets the pain from possible illness and shorter lifetime. Arriving at the balance is likely to involve several elements—among them, the weighing of pleasure *now* against pain *later*, with the distant event, as is customary in such situations, heavily discounted; the reluctance and remoteness of applying to oneself a cause-and-effect relationship that is only statistically demonstrated, a reason for additional discounting; the calculating of odds; allowance for personal habits and characteristics; appeasement through change to presumably less harmful brands. Clearly some such calculus underlies the decision to smoke and how much to smoke.

One might go on to speculate that those smokers who have digested the new knowledge have adjusted to it by setting their daily intake at a level at which they judge reduction would gain them less in future health than they would forego in current pleasure; a level, conversely, at which the improvement in current well-being derived from the extra cigarette, the marginal revenue, is not worth the incremental health hazard, the marginal cost. At that point, the smoker is in equilibrium. This point comes at different levels of smoking for different people, and the motivation—the type of gain extracted—differs widely among smokers. Thus, rationality of decision is not the issue. Rather, what is open to discussion and represents a proper area for education are the value scales on which pleasure from smoking and pain from ill health are traded off.

A serious economic problem arises not when an individual's actions affect adversely only himself (though costs of medical attention will in varying degrees not be defrayed by the individual, and there is, therefore, a public interest), but when those actions affect, primarily and often exclusively, other people. This is the heart of the quality aspect of resources.

QUALITY VERSUS GRADE DIFFERENTIAL

One could argue that to distinguish quality from quantity is merely a semantic nicety; that supply must always be understood as supply corresponding to appropriate specifications; and that if there is not "enough" by whatever the qualitative yardstick, then we have a quantitative shortage, whether it be water, air, iron ore, copper, or softwood sawtimber.

To some extent this is true. For example, within a large excess of aggregate forest growth over aggregate cut, there is too much poor hardwood from small trees and too little good softwood from large ones. Why do we not customarily speak of this as a separate dimension in judging resource adequacy? In part, we do not because there is a market on which poor hardwoods are traded and have, in different uses, found acceptance as satisfactory substitutes for good softwoods. Taconite ores are undoubtedly poorer bearers of iron than the traditional ores, but poor quality did not prevent their acceptance as soon as they could be processed at a cost low enough to make their use lucrative in blast furnaces. Copper mines today go after ores that hold only five pounds of metal per thousand. In the end, there is nothing that distinguishes the copper ingot derived from poor ore from that derived from rich ore; all that matters is that their costs be in a range that finds them a market. These grade differentials are handled satisfactorily by the market that reduces the offerings to quantities of some commonly agreed upon standard or equivalent. Provided we have an appropriate processing technique, six tons of .5 per cent copper ore are neither better nor worse than one ton of 3 per cent copper ore.

But 100 cubic feet of slightly polluted water or air cannot presently substitute for 50 or 10 of clean water or air—at least not for most purposes. Given a choice, one could not be indifferent, as in the case of copper. But above all, the choice is not one the consumer can effectively make, except in the most roundabout way.

Examples of these kinds of quality problems are abundant. There is the discharge of municipal, industrial, and agricultural waste into watercourses, of pollutants into the air; there is disfiguration of the landscape through mining activities, transmission lines, or other symbols of the industrial revolution; there is ugliness along highways, be it beer bottles or billboards, interference with plant life and wildlife through the use of pesticides, disturbance of the atmosphere through vibration caused by fast-flying planes and of the sound waves through indiscriminate use of portable radios.

A new wrinkle in the quantity–quality relationship, best exemplified in the energy field, should be mentioned here. The traditional conservation doctrine maintains that use of natural gas as boiler fuel signifies an "inferior" use of an exhaustible resource. In the past, both the Federal Power Commission and the courts have upheld this viewpoint. As late as 1961, the Supreme Court confirmed the commission's authority to make end use a factor in deciding upon certification for service (in a case involving shipment of gas from Texas to New York for use as boiler fuel). "One apparent method of preventing waste of gas," said the six-man majority, "is to limit the uses to which it may be put, uses for which another, more abundant fuel may serve equally well."

This was before air pollution became a pressing problem and made natural gas the preferred boiler fuel, given its low pollution quotient. The Federal Power Commission has not yet made this feature a basis for granting electric-utility applications for increased gas deliveries. It does not deny that gas is a less polluting fuel; the "inferior use" argument would sit badly with urban communities today. It does, however, contend that steam-electric plants are not the major villains in the situation and that additional gas would be, at best, a temporary palliative—at worst, a block to more radical remedial action. In any event, appraisal of adequacy can obviously be heavily affected by such changes in judgment.

ECONOMIC CHARACTERISTICS OF SIDE EFFECTS

The "side effect" syndrome has a number of characteristics, all of which distinguish it from simple grade differentiations and make it a highly controversial object of economic analysis and public policy.

Certain effects arise apart from and beyond the primary purpose. Not confined to the user, these affect others. Gains are reaped and costs are incurred, but there is no market that relates the two. Most importantly, the costs that arise are borne not by those that cause them but by others that happen to be around but are outside the process—bystanders, so to speak. Not all the costs of the process end up as costs to the producer; a slice is lodged outside. With inventiveness, but at the peril of losing their nontechnical audience, economists refer to these as "external diseconomies" or "externalities"; less elegantly, one might think of them as "someone else's headache."

Unless these headaches are brought home to the originator in such a way that they are included as costs in his profit-and-loss calculations—or "internalized"—private costs will understate total, or social, costs. Consequently, production decisions will lead to misallocation of resources, for the producer will be faced with production costs that are lower than they would be if he had also to foot the bill for the external diseconomies—the unpleasantness, nuisance, or other aggravation caused to his neighbor or environment.

The cause–effect nexus of such phenomena is often difficult to establish. Sometimes this may be due to the low intensity of the degrading substances or activities or to the low degree of quality deterioration that takes place. At other times, damage may be long delayed in appearing, or it may turn up in areas remote from the locus of emission. Finally, effects seldom occur with laboratory-like purity and in isolation, but are intermingled with a variety of other factors. Thus, presumption is more common than proof. And when the causal relationship can be satisfactorily established, it is often difficult to identify the offender, or when he can be identified, to assess his share in the total effect.

Typically, there is a widely dispersed multiplicity of the offended. In marked contrast to traditional "nuisance" cases that are actionable in the courts, this raises questions of both efficiency and equity in remedial action, if not of the feasibility of starting any action at all.

Changes in the environment are not easily, and often not at all, susceptible to meaningful evaluation in dollars and cents. This impedes comparison with costs incurred or avoided by the producer of the side effect in question, which as a rule lends itself to expression in monetary terms.

There is no answer to "what price beauty?" that would furnish a zoning authority a ready method of weighing the claims of, say, a stone quarry, a wildlife refuge, and a resort hotel where they are competing for the same tract of land. Psychic values are not traded in the market, at least not directly and not obviously. One is, therefore, limited to seeking surrogates and proxies that reflect such values. (For example, movements into and out of specific areas may be prompted by changes in environmental conditions and may be reflected in real-estate quotations.) This search has only just begun. Moreover, there are, as yet, few institutional and administrative arrangements that offer a mechanism for bringing together the offended and the offender, even when both can, in principle, be identified.

For the sake of efficient management, it is frequently desirable that measures dealing with questions of environmental quality be considered for large areas at a time. This is almost a necessity where air and water are concerned. Action then tends to become collective and regional, rather than individual and local. The rationale is that the smaller the community considered, the more the costs will be of the "external" kind. As the area widens, they become internal and, therefore, part of the proper economic calculus. If the decision-making unit is my home, then the costs of my dumping trash in my neighbor's backyard are "external" as far as I am concerned. If the unit is my street, then the costs are "internal."

Thus, one way of catching up with side effects is to extend the area within which they cannot be "external." Decisions made on the basis of rather large areas—the community, the river basin—are likely to produce a result closer to the optimum than the sum total of many individual decisions. One consequence of this spatial relationship, incidentally, is that for reasons of both efficiency and equity the role of the federal government as well as that of interstate and regional compacts, commissions, and similar multistate bodies will inescapably grow larger.

While it may sound as though stressing the size of the decision-making unit as an important element in quality management is a highly academic point, it is actually a very practical one. A good topical illustration is the use of pesticides in crop production. One's balancing of the gains and losses incurred from use of pesticides would differ according to whether one focuses on the individual farmer and his immediate surroundings, the county, the state, a region, the country, or an even larger supranational area. It is one thing to weigh damage to the environment against gains in crop protection in a given locality, but quite another to do so in a national or supranational framework. It could be argued that the United States might not now be able to ship one fourth of its wheat crop to India had it not been for the prolonged application of various chemicals to soil and vegetation. Such chemicals not only raise productivity in their own right but permit many other changes in farm practices and organization that jointly form a tight, almost ecological system. Evaluation of gains and losses from use of pesticides, thus, can be seen to depend greatly on the size of the decision-making unit—on where one draws the line.

THE CASE FOR QUANTIFICATION

The above categorizing makes no claim to either comprehensiveness or uniqueness. But it does serve to bring out the principal difficulties that beset improvement of resource quality: Identification of gainers and losers, ascertainment and valuation of gains and losses in the absence of a market, and lack of channels and institutions for arbitration of rival claims. If economists have not yet found many answers, they have begun to bring to this relatively new field of concern the integrating element of a common denominator—cost. Its applicability can be exaggerated, but its neglect surely leaves the field open to pressure and emotion. At the very least, even a rough casting of gains and losses into dollars and cents will convey a sense of magnitude that would otherwise be lacking. There is nothing dehumanizing in the process of monetary quantification.[8] Where efforts must be expanded to achieve a given objective, they are not available for alternative uses, and it is only fair that we establish at least the magnitude of what we must forego, so we can gain some idea of whether the environmental change contemplated is worth the price tag. This approach suggests a number of areas that call for better understanding. To a degree, they are corollaries of the characteristics discussed above.

We must learn more about the physical characteristics of the desirable objectives, of the undesirable side effects, and of the relationship of the one to the other. In such studies, attention should be directed not to the spectacular, which is usually accidental and ephemeral, but to the pedestrian, which is usually basic and lasting. From the study of physical aspects, we must move to the dollar values associated with them. Above all, we must ascertain and analyze cost relationships. We know, for example, that it is extraordinarily expensive to remove the final traces of pollution. In water treatment, costs double and triple as we approach a state of pristine purity. In removing successive amounts of coal dust from power-plant smokestacks, the capacity of precipitators must increase proportionately with the added removal efficiency, measured in terms of the remaining dust. Thus, if removal efficiency is to be raised from 96 to, say, 98 per cent, the increase is not 2, but 50 per cent, and consequently represents a steep rise in equipment size and cost. We must, therefore, ask how we determine the point of equilibrium, beyond which additional purity costs more than is gained in terms of health or aesthetics? Where does one reasonably stop? The more we can learn about cost behavior under different conditions, the easier it will become to establish criteria around which compromises can be built, even in the face of the difficulties that beset ascertainment of corresponding benefits.

Indignation over the manifestations of pollution comes easily; remedies do not. It has been estimated, for example, that it would cost some $20 billion annually to return all watercourses to an unspoiled state. This is about what the country spends each year on primary and secondary education. Will such knowledge affect specific decisions? It might, for decisions will tend to be more in accord with explicit value scales, openly arrived at. And these will frequently differ from what is merely presumed.

We must find ways of measuring society's demands for improving the quality of resources, the environment. The bafflingly unmeasurable must be made measurable. There are small beginnings today and much groping for answers, for it is clear that in the absence of acceptable measurements the debate will continue to produce more heat than light. Moreover, since funds will be appropriated and spent without greater guidance from any demand gauge, responsibility will remain above all with the resource manager, who must construe a demand schedule out of his own scale of preferences, what he believes are other people's preferences, and what he thinks ought to be other people's preferences. He will get some help from the political process, but that process is clumsy, especially when it comes to detail. Customarily, it permits choices only between approval and rejection, between yes and no; rarely between more and less, or among a whole spectrum of alternatives. As a consequence, decisions tend to be reached with little factual knowledge of the values that society as a whole puts on the results of the contemplated action.

Nor does the matter end here. Even though the individual consumer's choice is limited to the range of goods and services that are offered in the market, there *is* choice, both in quantity and in kind. This is not so in most decisions that are arrived at politically. As little as I can have a federal government that is part Democratic and part Republican, can I have a river that is both wild and provides storage for water supply and power. Thus, there is a problem of meeting the wants and needs of minorities whose desires are swamped in political decisions.

Finally, we must recognize that the decision-maker can err. Let us assume, for the sake of argument, that cigarette smoking were considered a form of pollution and its practice made subject to public regulation. In the light of the last few years' experience, there can be little doubt that any restrictions put on smoking would not be in accord with the aggregate of private valuations rationally arrived at—not only, as J. W. Milliman has suggested,[9] because the political process is no freer from imperfection than the market mechanism, but because there is a real conflict between a theoretical cost–benefit calculus, made in all good faith, and one derived from the summation of an individual's preferences. Only by cranking in society's interest in a healthier population as a plus could one hope to redress the balance toward a net gain from restrictive regulation.

All of this demonstrates the need for greatly increased research efforts directed toward methods of ascertaining where in the hierarchy of rival claims people rank quality improvement and similar intangibles. Even without accurate measurements, however, we are not quite lost. Establishing a range of arbitrary quality standards and estimating the costs their imposition would imply is one way out. To initially recommend itself, the cost of an action would have to be at least commensurate with the value of the improvement that is sought or the deterioration that is to be prevented. With the aid of such calculations of alternatives, we can begin to make intelligent choices among policy decisions—intelligent, but not necessarily easy. The cost tag is an indispensable aid: "No intangible has infinite value. All intangibles have cost."[10] Nevertheless, it is not the only nor perhaps always the determining criterion for decision. Still, the magnitude of what one has to forego, which is what cost is all about, is always relevant and usually lurks somewhere in the decision-maker's mind. Instead, it should be explicitly and prominently on the decision-maker's agenda.

Calculation of both gains and losses greatly facilitates dealing with quality changes. Whether it is more efficient to allow degradation to stand, or to reduce or suppress it, the course followed should leave nobody worse off and somebody better off than before. Without cost tags, this is hard to judge.

If the effluent from a paper mill muddies the water for the downstream resident, and the cost of removing the cause exceeds the cost of reducing such disturbance by treatment at the intake, it would clearly be efficient to let the offending effluent continue and to treat the water prior to its further use. In that event, the "winner," the paper mill, could compensate the "loser," the municipality, out of the savings that would accrue from not having to treat the effluent. Thus, both efficiency and equity would be served. The added cost (added, that is, in comparison to the previous condition of pollution without compensation) would most likely be reflected in higher costs of paper, at least initially, which only proves that you do not get something for nothing.

As has been pointed out, most situations of this kind are very complex, involving a multitude of participants, actions, and reactions. But it is easy to see the need for finding ways in which the external cost—in the simplified case above, the nuisance to the city residents—can be gauged and added to the private, or internal, cost, with the result that the polluter's cost will fully reflect the social cost of his activity.

Existing institutions and mechanisms need to be modified or new ones invented to facilitate making the cost of side effects a cost to the originator—that is, "internalizing" them. Imposition of taxes, charges, or other financial burdens on the producer is one way. These might be rigid or flexible so that the punishment could fit the crime. Their rationale lies in the consideration that the use of a congested facility, be this a watercourse, the air, a highway, or a park, should be reduced by putting a price on it.

At times, particularly when it is impractical or too costly to bar free access to the resource, a charge can be levied not on the activity itself but on the agent that causes the adverse effect (a pesticide, a detergent, a fuel), in the expectation that this will promote more sparing use of the offending substance and thus lead to a reduction of the noxious side effects. Also, raising the cost may stimulate the development of new technology, and the charges collected can be tapped for remedying the effects of the activity in question. In other situations, collective, administrative action may be more efficient. Unlike taxes, standard-setting regulations will not, however, produce revenue; also, flexibility will be less easily achieved, and policing and enforcement will present major administrative burdens, if not problems.

Technical considerations may, however, suggest collective action of a different sort—not through regulation—but through doing on a large centralized scale what is harder and more expensive to accomplish through the aggregation of a multitude of individual actions. To illustrate, a dollar's worth of aeration of dirty water performed by a public body according to a carefully laid plan is likely to beat a dollar's worth of waste-discharge treatment undertaken separately by a score of users.

When we can compare meaningfully the costs to society—which are, as we have tried to show, the producer's private costs plus costs to others that are not part of his calculus—with the many-sided benefits that are the counterpart of those costs, we shall have taken a long stride toward evolving a workable policy of preserving the quality of the environment without sacrificing the beneficial effects of advancing technology. Only then will we be able to appraise the present and future adequacy of quality of the resources as we have appraised that of quantity. If this means having the best of two worlds, then the time may be at hand to cease calling economics the dismal science. Until then, the economist will have to insist that the frontiers of cost and benefit measurement be vigorously extended—not necessarily to dictate action but to allow it to be shaped in the presence of the newly gained knowledge.[11]

"National Environmental Policy Act of 1969"

Purpose

Sec. 2—The purposes of this Act are: To declare a national policy which will encourage productive and enjoyable harmony between man and his environment; to promote efforts which will prevent or eliminate damage to the environment and biosphere and stimulate the health and welfare of man; to enrich the understanding of the ecological systems and natural resources important to the Nation; and to establish a Council on Environmental Quality.

TITLE I

Declaration of National Environmental Policy

Sec. 101—(a) The Congress, recognizing the profound impact of man's activity on the interrelations of all components of the natural environment, particularly the profound influences of population growth, high-density urbanization, industrial expansion, resource exploitation, and new and expanding technological advances and recognizing further the critical importance of restoring and maintaining environmental quality to the overall welfare and development of man, declares that it is the continuing policy of the Federal Government, in cooperation with State and local governments, and other concerned public and private organizations, to use all practicable means and measures, including financial and technical assistance, in a manner calculated to foster and promote the general welfare, to create and maintain conditions under which man and nature can exist in productive harmony, and fulfill the social, economic, and other requirements of present and future generations of Americans.

(b) In order to carry out the policy set forth in this Act, it is the continuing responsibility of the Federal Government to use all practicable means, consistent with other essential considerations of national policy, to improve and coordinate Federal plans, functions, programs, and resources to the end that the Nation may—

   (1) fulfill the responsibilities of each generation as trustee of the environment for succeeding generations;

(2) assure for all Americans safe, healthful, productive, and esthetically and culturally pleasing surroundings;

(3) attain the widest range of beneficial uses of the environment without degradation, risk to health or safety, or other undesirable and unintended consequences;

(4) preserve important historic, cultural, and natural aspects of our national heritage, and maintain, wherever possible, an environment which supports diversity and variety of individual choice;

(5) achieve a balance between population and resource use which will permit high standards of living and a wide sharing of life's amenities; and

(6) enhance the quality of renewable resources and approach the maximum attainable recycling of depletable resources.

(c) The Congress recognizes that each person should enjoy a healthful environment and that each person has a responsibility to contribute to the preservation and enhancement of the environment.

Sec. 102—The Congress authorizes and directs that, to the fullest extent possible: (1) the policies, regulations, and public laws of the United States shall be interpreted and administered in accordance with the policies set forth in this Act, and (2) all agencies of the Federal Government shall—

(A) utilize a systematic, interdisciplinary approach which will insure the integrated use of the natural and social sciences and the environmental design arts in planning and in decisionmaking which may have an impact on man's environment;

(B) identify and develop methods and procedures, in consultation with the Council on Environmental Quality established by title II of this Act, which will insure that presently unquantified environmental amenities and values may be given appropriate consideration in decisionmaking along with economic and technical considerations;

(C) include in every recommendation or report on proposals for legislation and other major Federal actions significantly affecting the quality of the human environment, a detailed statement by the responsible official on—

(i) the environmental impact of the proposed action,

(ii) any adverse environmental effects which cannot be avoided should the proposal be implemented,

(iii) alternatives to the proposed action,

(iv) the relationship between local short-term uses of man's environment and the maintenance and enhancement of long-term productivity, and

(v) any irreversible and irretrievable commitments of resources which would be involved in the proposed action should it be implemented.

Prior to making any detailed statement, the responsible Federal official shall consult with and obtain the comments of any Federal agency which has jurisdiction by law or special expertise with respect to any environmental impact involved. Copies of such statement and the comments and views of the appropriate Federal, State, and local agencies, which are authorized to develop and enforce environmental standards, shall be made available to the President, the Council on Environmental Quality and to the public as provided by section 552 of title 5, United States Code, and shall accompany the proposal through the existing agency review processes;

(D) study, develop, and describe appropriate alternatives to recommended courses of action in any proposal which involves unresolved conflicts concerning alternative uses of available resources;

(E) recognize the worldwide and long-range character of environmental problems and, where consistent with the foreign policy of the United States, lend appropriate support to initiatives, resolutions, and programs designed to maximize international cooperation in anticipating and preventing a decline in the quality of mankind's world environment;

(F) make available to States, counties, municipalities, institutions, and individuals, advice and information useful in restoring, maintaining, and enhancing the quality of the environment;

(G) initiate and utilize ecological information in the planning and development of resource-oriented projects; and

(H) assist the Council on Environmental Quality established by title II of this Act.

Sec. 103—All agencies of the Federal Government shall review their present statutory authority, administrative regulations, and current policies and procedures for the purpose of determining whether there are any deficiencies or inconsistencies therein which prohibit full compliance with the purposes and provisions of this Act and shall propose to the President not later than July 1, 1971, such measures as may be necessary to bring their authority and policies into conformity with the intent, purposes, and procedures set forth in this Act.

Sec. 104—Nothing in Section 102 or 103 shall in any way affect the specific statutory obligations of any Federal agency (1) to comply with criteria or standards of environmental quality, (2) to coordinate or consult with any other Federal or State agency, or (3) to act, or refrain from acting contingent upon the recommendations or certification of any other Federal or State agency.

Sec. 105—The policies and goals set forth in this Act are supplementary to those set forth in existing authorizations of Federal agencies.

TITLE II

Council on Environmental Quality

Sec. 201—The President shall transmit to the Congress anually beginning July 1, 1970, an Environmental Quality Report (hereinafter referred to as the "report") which shall set forth (1) the status and condition of the major natural, manmade or altered environmental classes of the Nation, including, but not limited to, the air, the aquatic, including marine, estuarine, and fresh water, and the terrestrial environment, including, but not limited to, the forest, dryland, wetland, range, urban, suburban, and rural environment; (2) current and foreseeable trends in the quality, management and utilization of such environments and the effects of those trends on the social, economic, and other requirements of the Nation; (3) the adequacy of available natural resources for fulfilling human and economic requirements of the Nation in the light of expected population pressures; (4) a review of the programs and activities (including regulatory activities) of the Federal Government, the State and local governments, and nongovernmental entities or individuals, with particular reference to their effect on the environment and on the conservation, development and utilization of natural resources; and (5) a program for remedying the deficiencies of existing programs and activities, together with recommendations for legislation.

Sec. 202—There is created in the Executive Office of the President a Council on Environmental Quality (hereinafter referred to as the "Council"). The Council shall be composed of three members who shall be appointed by the President to serve at his pleasure, by and with the advice and consent of the Senate. The President shall designate one of the members of the Council to serve as Chairman. Each member shall be a person who, as a result of his training, experience, and attainments, is exceptionally well qualified to analyze and interpret environmental trends and information of all kinds: to appraise programs and activities of the Federal Government in the light of the policy set forth in title I of this Act; to be conscious of and responsive to the scientific, economic, social, esthetic, and cultural needs and interests of the Nation; and to formulate and recommend national policies to promote the improvement of the quality of the environment.

Sec. 203—The Council may employ such officers and employees as may be necessary to carry out its functions under this Act. In addition, the Council may employ and fix the compensation of such experts and consultants as may be necessary for the carrying out of its functions under this Act, in accordance with section 3109 of title 5, United States Code (but without regard to the last sentence thereof).

Sec. 204—It shall be the duty and function of the Council—

(1) to assist and advise the President in the preparation of the Environmental Quality Report required by section 201;

(2) to gather timely and authoritative information concerning the conditions and trends in the quality of the environment both current and prospective, to analyze and interpret such information for the purpose of determining whether such conditions and trends are interfering, or are likely to interfere, with the achievement of the policy set forth in title I of this Act, and to compile and submit to the President studies relating to such conditions and trends;

(3) to review and appraise the various programs and activities of the Federal Government in the light of the policy set forth in title I of this Act for the purpose of determining the extent to which such programs and activities are contributing to the achievement of such policy, and to make recommendations to the President with respect thereto;

(4) to develop and recommend to the President national policies to foster and promote the improvement of environmental quality to meet the conservation, social, economic, health, and other requirements and goals of the Nation;

(5) to conduct investigations, studies, surveys, research, and analyses relating to ecological systems and environmental quality;

(6) to document and define changes in the natural environment, including the plant and animal systems, and to accumulate necessary data and other information for a continuing analysis of these changes or trends and an interpretation of their underlying causes;

(7) to report at least once each year to the President on the state and condition of the environment; and

(8) to make and furnish such studies, reports thereon, and recommendations with respect to matters of policy and legislation as the President may request.

Sec. 205—In exercising its powers, functions, and duties under this Act, the Council shall—

(1) consult with the Citizens' Advisory Committee on Environmental Quality established by Executive Order numbered 11472, dated May 29, 1969, and with such representatives of science, industry, agriculture, labor, conservation organizations, State and local governments and other groups, as it deems advisable; and

(2) utilize, to the fullest extent possible, the services, facilities, and information (including statistical information) of public and private agencies and organizations, and individuals, in order that duplication of effort and expense may be avoided, thus assuring that the Council's activities will not unnecessarily overlap or conflict with similar activities authorized by law and performed by established agencies.

Sec. 206—Members of the Council shall serve full time and the Chairman of the Council shall be compensated at the rate provided for Level II of the Executive Schedule Pay Rates (5 U.S.C. 5313). The other members of the Council shall be compensated at the rate provided for Level IV or the Executive Schedule Pay Rates (5 U.S.C. 5315).

Sec. 207—There are authorized to be appropriated to carry out the provisions of this Act not to exceed $300,000 for fiscal year 1970, $700,000 for fiscal year 1971, and $1,000,000 for each fiscal year thereafter.

Part Two

The Policy Process

The policy approach to politics differs from other ways of looking at governmental activity in its focus on issues and its concern with the actual operation of the policy-making system. Thus it offers an understanding of government in greater depth because of its attempts to integrate substantive and procedural knowledge.* In this book we are concerned only with the government of natural resources, so "policy" here tends to describe "the information collected." However, the politics of natural resource policy-making occurs throughout a broad spectrum of government; therefore, what begins as a narrow focus in principle has a broad focus in fact.

Charles O. Jones states that the "policy approach offers more in-depth analysis of specific public problems, how they are acted on in government, and how policy is administered to the problem." The difference of this approach from other ways of studying political science is one of the emphasis. The potential advantage is that the policy approach provides a framework for a more comprehensive analysis than any other method.**

There are some general ways of examining governmental policies, and there is a framework within which one can study issue-oriented decisions. This chapter presents four general pieces of "policy" literature in an attempt to provide a general basis for studying policies. None of these articles has a natural resources orientation, but each provides useful guidelines and insight into the policy process. Raymond A. Bauer's "The Formation of Public Policy" gives a good, but precise, survey of the policy process. Robert H. Salisbury evaluates contemporary conceptions of policy analysis. Arthur Maass critically reviews the economic constraints on policy. Charles E. Lindblom's "The Science of 'Muddling Through'" is a standard, and by now classic, description of how things really *are done*. There is always the hope that muddling can be improved upon.

---

*See Yehezkel Dror, *Public Policymaking Reexamined* (San Francisco: Chandler Publishing Co., 1968), Chaps. 1 and 2.

**See Charles O. Jones, "The Policy-making Approach: An Essay on Teaching American Politics," p. 2 [unpublished paper delivered at the Annual Meeting of the American Political Science Association, September, 5–9, 1967].

Raymond A. Bauer

The Policy Process[*]

The best point of departure for an understanding of the policy process is to consider more fully the assertion made earlier that "decision-making" is an inappropriate concept for characterizing policy formation and the conclusion reached by Zeckhauser and Schaefer that there is no determinate *best* solution to a policy problem. The two propositions are closely linked.

The term decision-making, when used by psychologists, decision theorists and other students of the phenomenon ordinarily implies a specific model of cognitive activity. This model assumes a single decision-making unit with a single set of utility preferences; knowledge of a reasonably full range of action alternatives and of their consequences; this intention of selecting that course of action of maximum utility; and, the opportunity, disposition, and capacity to make the appropriate calculations.[1] In the process of policy formation every one of these assumptions is violated. However, both the connotations of the term *decision-making* and the ordinary discussion of decision-making on policy issues preserve the illusion of these assumptions. The difficulty created by this circumstance is dual. It diverts the attention of the student of the process from what actually occurs and thereby hampers our efforts to understand the process. Furthermore, it furnishes the policy-maker with an inappropriate model of how he ought to behave. It does not help him, and it will confuse him if he takes the phrase seriously.

Some of the ways in which the assumptions of decision-making are violated in the policy process are amenable to practical solutions. Specifically, to the extent that an individual's information and capacity to process information are finite he can operate as rationally as possible by formalizing the state of his imperfect information. Thus, there is a sophisticated modern approach to decision-making that is based on formalizing one's judgments, however subjective they may be and however tenuous the information may be, with the view of reaching the best decision that can be made on the basis of this imperfect knowledge.[2] Nevertheless, even

*Reprinted by permission from Raymond A. Bauer and Kenneth J. Gergen (eds.), *The Study of Policy Formation* (New York: The Free Press, 1968), pp. 11–20. © The Free Press, 1968.
(Notes to this selection will be found on p. 408.)

this approach tells *an individual* what he *ought* to do. Furthermore, it does not and is not designed to help us understand what people *actually* do. Most important is the fact that it does not touch on the impossibility of hitting on a single "best" solution for a group of people. Any optimizing model for decision-making (a model for a best solution) is built around the notion that some preference scheme can be established according to which the solution is optimal. Such a preference schedule, in turn, assumes some single set of values against which possible future outcomes can be matched in order to establish the order of their desirability. (If more than one set of values is involved, it must be translatable into a common set. There is the rub.) The key difficulty in conceiving of an "optimal" public policy is that of conceiving what would constitute the single system of values against which to judge the solution. Any group of individuals of reasonable size will not have identical values. Furthermore, individuals, although having substantially identical values, will be located at different points in the organization and therefore would receive different benefits from the same policy.

If we conceive of the organization as an abstraction, it is possible to say that a given policy is or is not "in the interest of the firm" or "in the national interest." The implication of such an assertion is that at some future time the firm or the nation will in some sense be better off as a result of a given policy (than it would be as a result of some other set of circumstances). However, it is worth noting that concepts such as "the interest of the firm" or "the national interest" are never invoked except when the policy in question is one for which *someone* will, or thinks he will, suffer an immediate and perhaps permanent disadvantage. Often, when the benefits are widely distributed the costs are highly concentrated. This, for example, has been the essence of the controversy over foreign trade policy in recent decades. While there can be general agreement that a liberal trade policy is good for "the economy," the fact is that there will be some small number of firms and people who will pay a cost, and in some instances that cost will be disastrous.

Any notion of judging a policy by its contribution to an overall system, as Zeckhauser and Schaefer demonstrate by their review to the relevant literature, poses the possibility and usually the inevitability of an inequity to some person or unit within the system. Overall contribution of benefit to the system usually produces some perceived inequity in the distribution of benefits. For example, it is well known that the rich in any society have never as a group looked favorably on any redistribution of property. At the opposite extreme, however, one way of looking at the welfare of "this group" would favor a policy that benefited a rich man by $1 million if it cost a group of poorer people any measurably smaller sum.

In principle, it has been argued that such inequities can be handled by side payments to the disadvantaged parties. If the gain to the system as a whole is sufficient, the magnitude of such payments can be such that everybody is better off. A policy that produced such a situation could unequivocally be called a "good" policy. But, in no meaningful sense is it an optimal policy, because different people will have different preferences among the many "good" policies that might be pursued.

In the absence of any method of determining a "best" public policy (even in principle), there are but two alternatives for selection of policies. The first is the delegation to or usurpation of this task by some small group of persons. The other possibility is negotiation among interested parties to arrive at some policy sufficiently satisfactory to enough of them so that they can or will impose it on the others. Examples of the delegation of preference setting are the granting of formal authority in business organizations or the making of the federal budget. However, any such situation, whether authority is delegated or usurped, can be regarded as a form of deferred negotiation.

The federal budget is based on the assumption that it is acceptable to the American people and to the Congress which, in varying ways, represents the American people. It must also be acceptable to the agencies that will implement it. These agencies are not merely rote executors of the Presidential will, nor could they ever be, since they are faced with the day-to-day opportunity and necessity of interpreting that policy. Similarly, the head of a business organization can initiate policies, but these policies must produce results over the reasonably short run that will maintain the morale of his organization. Even a dictator can only, at best, defer negotiation. It is true that he may be able to impose his will for a long time, perhaps even for the duration of his life. But to the extent that his policies do not build him a base of support, he will have to spend organizational resources to maintain his position.

It would appear that the bargaining process is at the heart of the policy process. One of the functions of a formal organization is to build a delay into the bargaining. Formal delegation of authority makes it possible for certain persons to exercise initiative in establishing and implementing policies. Exercise of that authority involves the formulation of policies and their articulation such that a minimum winning coalition of parties will be aligned behind those policies. This idea of the "minimum winning coalition" was first posed by Riker as the basis on which public policies are formed, but the work of Cyert and March suggests that this is also a useful way of looking at how policies are formed in business organizations.

From a research point of view, one disconcerting characteristic of policy problems is that they do not exist as units. The student of policy tends to think of "the problem" such as urban mass transportation as a unitary problem. In fact, there is no unity with respect to the problems people actually have, the way in which they perceive the problem or, as has been pointed out, of their interests and their values. Furthermore, since the policy process has a time dimension, each of these elements changes over time.

Let us consider the question of the lack of unity of "the problem" through an example from urban mass transportation: in a given case, should the city build a subway or an elevated road? A businessman in an adjacent suburb may be concerned with parking space for his executives who would not take mass transportation under any circumstances but might benefit from less congestion on the highways. He may also be concerned with how to get competent secretaries to commute to his plant as well as with the changing local tax rate. Perhaps, but not necessarily, he will see all these separate issues as part of *the problem* of urban mass transportation. It may even be that he will see that his interest is simply that *some* form of transportation be built but with a reasonable impact on the local tax rate.

This businessman has no "problems" in common with his local politician in the core city. The local politician may concentrate most of his attention on the question of whether the transportation goes underground or above the ground. His concerns will be the possible displacement of people, a changing ethnic composition of his constituency, a changing tax *base* if taxable land is usurped, and so on.

We can quickly imagine various other groups which have different versions of "the problem." One might be concerned with preservation of historical sites and "the traditional appearance of our city," and so forth.

Even when their actual and their perceived problems are identical, and they have the same values, the interests of actors may differ. The mayors of two towns may be in wholehearted agreement over the need for a particular type of transit service but differ widely in the preferred methods of financing the service. Their perceptions and values may be identical but their interests conflict because one method of financing will benefit one community more than the other.

This lack of unity of the problem is important to us in two ways. In the first instance the diversity of interests and values precludes, as pointed out, the sort of determinate identification of a single "best" policy that is implied in the conception of decision-making. The second implication of the lack of unity of "the problem" is a problem for the researcher. Because the problem cannot be taken as given, it becomes necessary to establish the pattern of distribution of perceptions of the problem held by the various relevant actors in the system of action. But in saying this, we pose a whole series of questions for research.

Who are the relevant actors? The policy system is an "open system" in that the relevant actors in any policy issue cannot be specified in advance. Attempts both to use the formal system of authority and the reputation of a supposed "power elite" have been tested and found inadequate for identifying the relevant actors in any specific policy problem. Both the system of formal authority and the reputation of some persons as being influential are *relevant* in the sense that persons identified by such routes are more likely to be involved in a policy problem than people selected randomly from the population. However, such persons are never completely involved in every policy problem. Furthermore, for any one problem some of the crucial actors will be persons who have neither formal authority nor a general position of informal influence. Their role is highly specific to the particular issue. . . .

Once such persons (or the institutions they represent) are identified, we find that other traditionally cherished concepts must be reexamined. The notion that people (or organizations) act in their "self-interest" turns out to be an uninformative tautology. As this assertion is usually used in the discussion of policy formation, it clearly implies that an organization or an individual has an obvious, unitary, unequivocal interest in any given issue. It further implies that the organization or individual is aware of what this is and that certainly any intelligent observer ought to be able to infer this interest from the clear logic of the situation.

In point of fact, the "interests" of people and organizations are multiple and complex and policy problems are sufficiently complex that for the vast majority of individuals or organizations it is conceivable—given the objective features of the situation—to imagine them ending up on *any* side of the issue.

We are also faced with the definition of the "self" which has a self-interest. Does a British-owned American distributor of Scotch whisky consider his obligation to be the parent company or to the American subsidiary? Is the "self" interest of a firm that of the chief executive officer, the top executive group, the firm as an abstraction, or does it include the stockholders and the customers? On the governmental level, various bureaus of the executive branch have developed constituencies for whose interests they are expected to work. However, under certain circumstances the executive branch stands more unified. The question of the self whose interest is pursued cannot be settled on an *a priori* basis.

Once the self has been identified, there is still the latitude of definition of interest to which we have referred. "Interests" are articulated by the various participants in the policy process and an integral part of the process of negotiation is the presentation of policy proposals in such a form as to engage the perceived interests of members of a winning coalition.

Of course, there are constraints of reality beyond which a sane man cannot be persuaded his interests lie. But within these limits there is sufficient latitude that self-interests cannot be taken for granted. We need to determine empirically not only how the persons in the policy process define their self-interest, but how the social process of communication brings about the definition and redefinition of self-interest over the course of time.

The definition and redefinition of the issue are central to the process of debate and negotiation that takes place over time. In this view of the policy process, a key skill of leadership is that of formulating policy so that a winning coalition can be mobilized behind it. The skill does not end with the formulation of the policy but extends to spelling out to the potential members of the potential winning coalition the ways in which the policy will serve their interest.

It will probably be agreed that negotiation of the sort we have been describing is a social as well as an intellectual process. Additionally, there is a certain amount of social context implied in what we have said so far. We have already referred to the question of who are the relevant actors. But these actors exist and act in a series of structured relationships. Certainly people, institutions, and groups vary not only in values, interests, and perceptions of the issue, but also in their access to means of communication, ability to formulate and communicate issues, and in access to resources that can be used for persuasion or coercion.

Up to this point we have treated the policy process as a *relatively* closed system that can, for practical purposes, be isolated for analysis. Regrettably this is an exaggeration. The parties involved in any policy issue have other responsibilities and obligations. They also have a past and a future. They live in an institutional context that has relevance beyond any one policy issue. One of the fallacies of treating the policy process simply as "decision-making" is that it assumes that someone is aware of the problem, that he can devote full time and attention to it, and that the issue has a clear-cut beginning and end. This picture does describe to some extent the situation of the staff analyst who, by virtue of the extent to which he is able to free his time and attention to analyze a given issue, can thereby be misled to assume that this is true of the man with action responsibility whom he is advising.

Regardless of the amount and quality of analysis done, the men who must take final responsibility for policy setting are faced with other events that compete for their time, attention, and energy. These other events involve interests and values that must be traded off against the interests and values involved in the policy issue in which the reseacher is interested. Some events, which might actually have low priority in a given actor's scheme of values, may have the capacity to grab and hold his attention and command his resources. For these reasons we have coined the phrase "the envelope of events and issues" to refer to those events and issues that must be considered as the context within which to analyze a given policy problem. This "envelope" will be distinctive of individuals, or at least of classes of individuals.

Because of the formidable (although hopefully feasible) data-gathering demands that this context of events and issues poses, a fairly strong case should be made that this exploration of the broader contest in which actors deal with specific issues is more than interesting, more than important, but (at least in some cases) crucial. The argument and evidence to support the preceding assertions about the importance of context follow.

The simplest aspect of the importance of context of the problem is that busy men do not have the resources to treat many issues as salient and that their strategies for handling salient and nonsalient issues are probably quite different. Furthermore, the researcher, because *he* is interested in the problem, tacitly assumes that other people find it equally important. Because people are polite, they will answer the researcher's questions generally, but not always, in his terms. In the study of the making of foreign trade policy by Bauer, Pool, and Dexter,[3] it became gradually apparent to them that the issue was for most of the businessmen and most of the Congressmen interviewed one of very low priority.

In any ongoing instutition, the ability to get important things done is dependent upon maintaining a reservoir of goodwill. The person who fights every issue as though it were vital exhausts his resources including, most especially, the patience and goodwill of those on whom he has to depend to get things done. Therefore, it should be considered neither surprising nor immoral that, when an issue is of low salience the sensible individual may use it to build goodwill for the future—or pay off past obligations—by going along with some individual for whom the issue is of high salience. Bauer, Pool, and Dexter found many men in Congress treating foreign trade legislation in this way. On the other hand, businessmen for whom this was an issue of low salience were careful not to expend an excessive amount of their finite goodwill on it.

Hence, in order to understand or predict the way in which a given issue will be handled, we must determine the salience which the issue has relative to other things with which the individual has to cope. And this is seldom self-evident.

The salience of an issue *can* be considered in an atemporal sense in that, at a given moment in time, a person has a limitation on the resources, including time, that he can muster. But as we have already hinted, an issue of low salience may be used to settle past debts and build up future goodwill. The time-binding nature of the policy process manifested itself in many ways in the Bauer, Pool, and Dexter study. During one session of Congress the Eisenhower Administration had put considerable demands on the chairman of a relevant committee to secure the passage of another bill. As a result of the amount of goodwill and committee time they had expended on the previous bill, the Administration was reluctant to, and did not, ask the chairman to hold full hearings on the Reciprocal Trade Act. In effect, what had happened before foreign trade legislation came to the committee was decisive in determining how the bill was handled.

On the other hand, since policy-making is by definition setting a course to be followed in the future, it is redundant to say that consideration of future consequences is part of the "envelope" that affects the policy process. However, the policy-maker's view of the future world, if he has wisdom, is different from that implied in concepts like decision-making, problem-solving, or goal-seeking. All these usual concepts imply a discreet sequence of events with a single definite point of termination.[4] Serious policy-making does not involve such decisive resolutions of a problem. A Supreme Court ruling of 1954 did not abolish segregation in public education, nor did the Civil Rights Act of 1965 eliminate discrimination in politics. Each of these events redefined the terms in which an ongoing struggle was conducted. The experienced policy-maker knows that as he resolves one issue he is posing others. He realizes that he is frequently not settling an issue but redefining the rules of the game and if, in any meaningful sense, he has been "victorious" he hedges his victory to give himself room for maneuver in the future.

One of the ways in which he does this is not to force on the losing coalition terms that will make it unduly difficult to work with the losing parties in the future. In 1965, a private study that involved a considerable number of interviews with key figures in Congress, indicated that the relative speed with which civil rights legislation has been passed—or if you prefer, not been passed—has not been a result of lack of sufficient support for such legislation in the Congress. It has been more a result of the reluctance of many Congressmen and Senators to force such measures on their southern colleagues more rapidly than the Southerners could adjust *vis-à-vis* their constituents. A similar explanation would apply to President Johnson's behavior during the crucial week of turmoil in Selma, Alabama. Johnson appeared to be waiting for public pressure to build up to the point that when he made his address to the Congress he could not be viewed by the Southerners as arbitrarily "pushing them around."

It is true that this model of an intellectual process embedded in a social process which, in turn, has to be understood in the context of past, present, and future events and issues, can be masked. For one thing I have not denied that there are situations in which men have enough power for a finite period of time to override the sort of negotiating process to which we referred. Such actions generally build up future trouble. Nor do I deny that negotiation is sometimes deferred This occurs most often in situations in which authority is delegated to handle some range of issues. Thus an office holder is not in constant explicit negotiation with his constituents but returns to them from time to time to seek out their reaction, in the form of votes, to what he has been doing.

Finally, I do not deny that there are situations in which the formation of policy is a highly intellectual, highly deliberate process. It is conceivable that the Kennedy Administration's reaction to the Cuban missile crisis was of that nature. However, the published accounts of the Bay of Pigs episode suggest that the earlier crisis is better understood as a complex social process in which circumstances kept the new President from understanding the nature of the commitment he was making; his recent campaign had made him sensitive to being seen as "soft on Castro"; he envisaged a group of disgruntled, disappointed refugees spreading anti-American sentiment throughout Latin America if he called it off; some advisers were afraid to speak up; others had become so committed to the invasion plan that they glossed over the difficulties; and so on.

What I am suggesting is that we should approach each policy issue as though the process were as complex as has been suggested, and converge on the intellectual or "decision" aspects of the problem rather than hope that the problem can be understood in terms of its solely intellectual component. There are two reasons for *not* working *outward* to the social context. The first is that much of the record and people's verbalization of what has happened and is happening will be highly rationalized, and the researcher may be deceived into believing he has an adequate picture of what is transpiring or has transpired. The other is that much of what occurs will not make sense in the more limited context. This is the reason that much behavior of congressmen and businessmen is labeled "irrational." And this, in turn, is also deceptive, at least in many instances in which the man involved is concerned with more issues than the observer has taken account of.

Our position that the student of any policy problem should proceed with the assumption that the process may be as complex and as social as we have described should not be taken as a statement of our preference of the way in which people *ought* to solve such problems. We do believe that to some extent it is impossible and undesirable that individual policy decisions be approached in isolation or as though they did not impinge on a wider range of issues. And we also believe that, even though it might be desirable, it is not possible to eliminate entirely the essentially irrelevant factors that influence policy formation.

It is difficult to conceive of a way in which the intellectual aspects of policy formation can ever be completely isolated from their social context. Policies will always be made by and for human beings who inhabit human institutions. But, to the extent that we can handle deliberately those variables that have influenced us without our knowledge or with which we have been able to cope only vaguely, we can with a certain amount of justification say that we have been able to bring the policy process closer to the intellectual models of "problem-solving" or "decision-making." We would hope, therefore, that as the individuals faced with specific policy problems understand better the complexity of the events with which they are confronted, they will become less the victims and more the masters of those events.

Robert H. Salisbury

The Analysis of Public Policy*

I. WHAT WE MEAN BY POLICY

It is commonplace to lament the absence of clear understanding concerning the basic terms of political analysis, but it appears that the range of disagreement concerning the notion òf "policy" is not so very great. One may distinguish three major positions on the question, sometimes taken separately and sometimes in combination. The most common usage of the term "policy," surely, is derived from some version of David Easton's definition of the proper object of political analysis: "the authoritative allocation of values for the whole society."[1] Public policy consists in authoritative or sanctioned decisions by governmental actors. It refers to the "substance" of what government does and is to be distinguished from the processes by which decisions are made. Policy here means the outcomes or outputs of governmental processes.[2]

A second view of policy would confine the usage to "broad" or general questions, and use another term for detailed choices made within the framework of "policy." Thus policy consists of a general frame of authoritative rules, and, while the precise boundary between policy and nonpolicy is nearly always debatable in the particular situation, the distinction crops up over and over. Dichotomies like "discretionary versus ministerial acts," "political versus nonpolitical," "controversial versus routine," and, of course, "policy versus administration" suggest the manifold permutations on the theme and remind us of the wide currency of the usage.[3]

A third way of talking about policy is rooted in the assumption that political behavior is goal-oriented or purposive. Policy here means those actions calculated to achieve the goal or purpose. Thus one may speak of "policy orientations," or "the policy of the AFL–CIO." Lasswell and Kaplan define policy as "a projected program of goal values and practices."[4] Closely related would be the Bentleyan conception that political behavior is always to be understood in terms of its interest or purposive

*Reprinted by permission from *Political Science and Public Policy*, ed. Austin Ranney (Chicago: Markham Publishing Co., 1968), 152–174. © Markham Publishing Co., 1968.
(Notes to this selection will be found on pp. 409–413.)

orientation. According to this view, all political activity should be viewed as policy-oriented, and one must logically encompass the policy substance if one is to comprehend the behavior directed toward that set of goals.

These conceptions of policy are combined in Friedrich's definition:

a proposed course of action of a person, group or government within a given environment providing obstacles and opportunities which the policy was proposed to utilize and overcome in an effort to reach a goal or realize an objective or a purpose. . . . It is essential for the policy concept that there be a goal, objective or purpose.[5]

Friedrich and most other writers agree that there is a difference between specific decisions or actions and a program or course of action, and that it is the latter to which the term "policy" refers.[6] Policy is necessarily an abstraction, therefore, to be approached through aggregative or summarizing analytic procedures. It is *patterns* of behavior rather than separate, discrete acts which constitute policy. The concept of policy is thus anti-case study in its implications for research strategy and encourages controlling for idiosyncratic variables.

Unless one wishes to contend that policy refers only to broad decisional rules and that implementation or other subsequent behavior is to be examined in terms of some other focus, it follows from these conceptions that political science can hardly avoid being policy-centered. That is, if authoritative outputs of the political system, actions aimed at affecting those outputs, and the goals or purposes or interests at stake in authoritative decisions are what we mean by policy, we cannot logically escape dealing with it.

The apparent paradox is, of course, that so much political science inquiry has escaped this logical necessity, or at least seemed to do so. I believe the answer lies in two directions at once. One is revealed in the recent literature suggesting that variations in political processes, with which political scientists have undoubtedly been concerned, may have relatively little explanatory value in accounting for variations in policy outputs. We shall examine these findings later, but, insofar as they are valid, it follows that we may have spent so much time investigating process factors of relatively minor importance that it has been easy to ignore the substance of public policy, for which our research has little relevance.

A second part of the explanation, however, is that in fact political scientists have long been concerned, and vitally so, with policy analysis, but only of a particular kind of policy, namely, *constitutional policy*. That is, we have spent much labor analyzing authoritative decisions that prescribe the rules and specify the structural characteristics of the authoritative decisional system, i.e., government. That these questions are policy issues is obvious, and that political scientists have invested heavily in their analysis is even more so. Whether the investment has turned an explanatory profit may be debated, but in consequence of this work I think we are richer in what Froman calls "policy theory"[7] than we may realize.

Later I shall explore the matter of constitutional policy in more detail, but first it may be well to consider two general problems that plague research in this, or any, area: How may we observe and measure policy data, and how may we classify and categorize these data for purposes of building empirical theory?

II. THE FORMS OF DATA FOR POLICY ANALYSIS

A good many of the uncertainties of policy-centered studies, I think, stem from doubts about how to order the data of policy decisions. Often they are not directly amenable to quantification. The terms in which they may be compared, cross-sectionally or longitudinally, are unclear. And therefore, unless one is willing to settle for the insights of a case-study narrative, it has been difficult to see how empirical theory of any breadth could emerge from such a focus. Let us consider these problems.

Several possibilities for the treatment of policy variables are present. The simplest, and one that has been used in the study of such policies as urban renewal adoption, fluoridation, and several issues in the realm of constitutional policy, is a straight dichotomy between adoption and non-adoption. Policies are passed or they are not. There are all the virtues of simplicity in such a treatment, but two considerations make it less than satisfactory, even when the data permit it. For one thing, many if not most policies that may appear as dichotomous variables will do so only if one takes a rather narrow cross section for one's observations. Thus, while at a given point in time one group of communities may have adopted urban renewal and another group may not, at a later point some portion of the latter is likely to have undertaken the policy. If one adds a time dimension to the observations, one then looks at such things as speed and facility of adoption, continuous variables, rather than a simple yes or no.[8] Secondly, the policy may be adopted in one set of subsystems, rejected in another, and never proposed at all in a third. To lump groups two and three in the same category may lead to spurious results. Again it would seem incumbent upon policy analysts to search for ways of representing the policy data in more continuous form.

This recognition has led a large number of students of policy outcomes to concentrate their attention on expenditures. The data are always expressed in quantities that, so long as accounting conventions are stable, can be neatly arrayed for comparative analysis both longitudinally and cross-sectionally. Spending data have given us much the most systematic policy analyses we have, and their characteristics surely provide guideposts for research on other forms of policy data. That is to say, if we are to engage in systematic inquiry that adequately represents the relevant dimensions of policy types and variations, we must devise ways of specifying what is "more" and what is "less," and so we must learn to count.

How are we to count the dimensions of policy which are not originally expressed in quantitative units? We need not shy away from the recognition that the problem is often difficult, but there are certainly technical strategies for attacking it which have as yet been inadequately exploited. Thus one can imagine devising measures that represent the intensity and direction of communications flows respecting policies,[9] measures of intensity of conflict over policies, or measures of complexity of themes or subjects contained in policies. Measurement is never sufficient for analysis, but it is surely necessary.

Equally necessary, and far more dependent on conceptual than on technical imagination, is the development of appropriate typologies for categorizing and thereby ordering for theoretical purposes the nearly infinite array of authoritative decisional behaviors which we refer to as policies and which we are seeking to understand. As we noted earlier, the very notion of policy itself implies some degree of aggregation of specific decisions, either over time or among different decisional units or both. But this realization only helps to name the problem; it does not answer it.

The literature contains a considerable shopping list of typologies specifically designed for categorizing the content of policy outputs.[10] The least ambiguous and most often employed is a straightforward nominalist typology. That is, one accepts as theoretically meaningful the categories employed by the participants in the decisional systems. Many of these categories—for example, agriculture or education—are based on differentials in client groups pressing for or affected by the policies. Some may be based on distinctions in the structure of the decisions; e.g., self-executing versus nonself-executing, constitutional versus substantive, or appropriation versus authorization. Still others are derived from differences in the decisional units involved: federal, state, local; executive, legislative, judicial; subcommittee, committee, floor; etc. And more may come to mind. Regardless of which nominal categories one uses, the theoretical potentialities are restricted to the extent of the uniformities in use of the categories. They are taken as they are found in the real world, and the real world is often uncomfortably slippery and devious.[11]

In order to move theory to higher levels of generality, more abstract typologies must be invented with the capacity to order a more inclusive range of data, and they must be theoretically meaningful without regard to the names the real world assigns to its activities. At the same time, however, there are cogent reasons for continuing to invest in the analysis of policy cast within nominal categories. For one thing, the object of analysis may not always be the building of more general theory. We are not so rich in lower-level descriptive statements that we can afford to stop seeking them, even if we were agreed, as we are not, that we are never to be interested in explaining, let us say, variations in educational policy because we are interested in educational policy. Moreover, even if we were to agree that the sole object of our inquiry should be to build general theory, it is not clear that we always advance the cause by abandoning the nominal categories in favor of more abstract formulations. As an example, Froman's effort to aggregate community policies into categories of areal and segmental appears to me to founder on an inadequate understanding of the substance of the particular or nominal policies he is attempting to aggregate. Thus there is much reason to dispute his classification of employment in educational services as an areal policy— one that affects "all the families within a school system . . . simultaneously."[12] Depending on the *kind* of urban renewal project, it may or may not be segmental, as he classifies it. And clearly, if city manager adoptions are areal in impact, so also are mayor–council retentions. It is not simply captious criticism to suggest that theoretically suggestive typologies may sometimes do such violence to the complexity of the data as to render the theory irrelevant. The prudent strategy will surely be one of critical pluralism, with many scholars exploiting a variety of approaches at different levels of generality while critically and continuously reviewing and refining the work of other participants in the enterprise.

In that portion of the enterprise which operates at a more abstract level there are several typological possibilities, most of which have been only essayed rather than fully utilized, but they provide at the least a useful starting point. I shall not review them all in detail, but I shall attempt to identify their similarities and differences and see what might be done with them.

Policy typologies may be based on data that are composed of perceptions of the actors. Thus whether a particular policy is classified as zero-sum or non-zero-sum may depend on how the relevant actors perceive it, and similarly with the distinction between symbolic and material policies. Lowi, in a different approach, attempts to classify policies as distributive, redistributive, or regulatory in part according to their "impact on the society."[13] Or one might classify according to the internal structure of the decisions, using such criteria as amount, complexity, or self-execution. Froman's areal-versus-segmental distinction appears to involve some combination of internal characteristics of the policies with their impact on the system. In evaluating the utility of the alternatives we must go immediately to the operational problem, and this appreciably narrows the real research alternatives. "Impact on the society" appears to me beyond our present capacity to measure in any way that goes beyond the plausible hunch. If this is so, then the criterion itself is really a special case of the criterion of actor's perceptions, with observers replacing decision-makers as the active parties. We know, at least in principle, how to approach the data of perception, and if we recognize the accessible data as largely of this kind, we may enhance our abilities even more. From this point of view, whether a policy is classified as distributive or redistributive depends on how it is seen by the actors, and I suggest that any hypotheses we might advance relating process variables to policy types would, in fact, assume that policy types were so derived. It would be odd, I think, if actors very often behaved in systematically variable ways without perceiving some parallel variations in the substance of their actions.

This still leaves an option in the form of internal decision structures as the classification criterion. Where observers can agree on variations in decision form—as they obviously can when using nominal categories, and also probably by using distinctions in amount or complexity of policy—this criterion is especially valuable because it shortcuts the necessity of interviewing the actors.[14] But there are many potentially interesting questions that are not yet amenable to such shortcuts and which do take advantage of unambiguous features of the public record. Moreover, as Froman's effort has illustrated, categories invented by the observer may create as many problems as they solve.

From the array of extant possibilities, I propose to employ a typology that is adapted from Lowi's formulation and uses data derived from actor perceptions.[15] The typology differentiates four possible main types: distributive, redistributive, regulatory, and self-regulatory. Distributive policies are those perceived to confer direct benefits upon one or more groups. Typically such policies are determined with little or no conflict over the passage of the legislation, but only over the size and specific distribution of the shares. Redistributive policies likewise confer benefits, but also are perceived to take benefits away from other groups. They therefore involve more intense conflict over passage itself, over the legitimacy of the action as well as the specific content. Regulatory policies impose constraints on subsequent behavior of particular groups and thus indirectly deny or confirm potentially beneficial option in the future. Conflict over regulatory policy is likely to be ambiguous and shifting, since the specific content and direction of benefits and costs are not known; only, so to speak, the "guidelines."[16]

Self-regulatory policies also impose constraints upon a group, but are perceived only to increase, not decrease, the beneficial options to the group. The relevant perceptions in each case are those of the active participants in the policy-making process. This would include all those making explicit demands on the decisional system, as well as those taking an active part in it. In the self-regulatory policy situation, only a small group, such as lawyers or oil companies, makes demands, and typically there is little or no opposition.[17]

A question that immediately arises is how this formulation fits the distinction between zero-sum and non-zero-sum policies. The argument may be advanced that none of the four types necessarily implies zero-sum conditions. Distributive and self-regulatory policies are, one would suppose, invariable non-zero-sum, since there is comparatively little implication of conflict or even of overt self-perceived losers in such situations. Redistributive and regulatory policies, on the other hand, may approach zero-sum conditions. But if side payments are permitted, these conditions are mitigated, and I shall argue that in American politics even redistributive policies are generally decided in distinctly positive-sum games.[18]

A special case of regulatory policy is what I have termed constitutional policy. The making of this equation has some theoretical implications I shall consider later, but political scientists have traditionally been so preoccupied with this set of policy issues that I think it requires special attention. This attention will also give me the opportunity to raise another range of considerations; namely, evaluative criteria, which are more readily discussed apart from the typology and analytic model I shall employ to discuss substantive policy.

III. CONSTITUTIONAL POLICY AND EVALUATIVE CRITERIA

The question of what sets of decisions are to be included within the meaning of constitutional policy is not a simple one. The category is probably both broader and narrower than traditional inquiries might imply. Thus I would think that many issues of political participation, whether structural–legal or behavioral, are properly thought of as aspects of the decisional system and its rules. So, perhaps, with the norms of decision-maker behavior which Matthews calls "legislative folkways." On the other hand, although many constitutional policy questions are decided by judges, not all judicial policy-making deals with constitutional policy. The line is often a hazy one, but I would suppose that a distinction may be maintained, if only in relative emphasis, between decisional rules by which subsequent policy actions are to be determined and decisions that directly confer material or expressive benefits upon one or another contending group. Thus many of the decisions regarding equal protection or the First Amendment or criminal procedure seem to me to confer quite immediate and specific benefits (or costs) upon particular groups, while the issue of apportionment, no matter who decides it, is one primarily specifying rules that help to shape subsequent decisions over substantive concerns.

The analysis of constitutional policy, as of other kinds, may place the policy variable either as dependent or independent. There is a rather substantial body of literature which in a general sort of way attempts to relate constitutional policies to one of two other broad types of data. One portion of this literature explores the connections between constitutional policies and the pattern of demands of politically relevant groups in the polity.[19] Of particular interest, perhaps, has been the long-standing inquiry into the interaction between a pluralistic society and a fragmented constitutional or decisional system.[20] A major issue in these efforts has always been, of course, to determine in which direction the predominant influence runs, i.e., whether constitutional policy is dependent or independent. A variation on this broad theme is represented by the recent literature dealing with the relationship between community characteristics and forms of local government.[21] This literature, I think, is reasonably unambiguous in its assumption that the constitutional policy in question, e.g., the incidence of city-manager government, is best understood as a dependent variable, with region, size, and homogeneity of population looming large as the decisive independent factors.[22] Whether from a Madisonian or Bentleyan or Marxian perspective, I suspect that this is the generally prevailing mood concerning the form of the constitutional policy–demand pattern interaction: that the policies are best viewed primarily as the consequence of group activities or whatever, rather than as their cause.[23]

On the other hand, if one looks at the literature analyzing the relationship between constitutional policies and what one might term system resources or systemic conditions, the analysis tends often to run the other way. There is a considerable body of argumentation and a lesser amount of analysis suggesting that decisional rules and structures of authority have some meaningful, causal effect on such broad features of the system as its consensus or its integration or its capacity for problem-solving.[24]

I shall explore further the analysis of policy taken as a dependent variable at a later point. Here let me concentrate on the impact of policy as an independent variable by considering what seems to me to be the criterion of overriding significance in the literature respecting constitutional policy, namely, the degree of integration or fragmentation of the decisional system. For illustrative purposes, and to see what can be said regarding policy-centered analysis, I shall suggest a number of other criteria by which to order the examination of the dependent variables, either system resources or demand patterns. Much of what is said here is relevant also to the later discussion of substantive policy. There, however, I shall employ only one or two major ordering criteria, and the reader may transfer the argument at his leisure.

There would appear to be at least three criteria for examining the effect of constitutional policy on demand patterns: *group benefits*, *equity*, and *integration.* Thus one may inquire into the differential advantages conferred upon various groups or putative groups by alternative decisional rules. A familiar hypothesis, for example, is that fragmented structures of authority tend to benefit status quo interests.[25] The criterion of equity is closely related in that it too calls for an assessment of relative potentials for access and advantage among contending groups. It differs in the greater likelihood that it will be employed for normative purposes than the more neutral criterion of group benefits. But also the equity criterion impels the analyst to consider longer and broader spans of time and issues in order to assess the evenhandedness with which the decisional system operates. Thus a Beardian may reach rather different conclusions about the U.S. constitution using a group-benefit criterion than a Madisonian, who, using in part an equity criterion, might conclude that many groups would enjoy roughly equivalent access under the constitutional policies adopted at Philadelphia.

The integration of demand patterns has been invoked as a criterion to evaluate constitutional policy in two important areas of concern. One relates to the matter of consensus, especially regarding the rules of the game. It is often argued, for example, that in a heterogeneous society fragmented decisional systems play a part in facilitating such consensus, since, if the system is to work at all, some agreement is essential on the rules of play.[26] The other prominent argument holds that a fragmented decisional system reduces integration on substantive demands by making it more difficult for effective aggregation mechanisms, such as cohesive parties, to develop.[27]

It could certainly be argued that a criterion of *stability* referred to consensus underlying the demand patterns of a political system, but discussions that employ this criterion seem to me generally to treat it as a more abstract characteristic of the system, evidenced by other indicators such as literacy, radios, or riots rather than by explicit politically relevant demands as such.[28] Other criteria concerned with the impact of constitutional policy upon system resources would certainly include *development, efficiency,* and *rationality.* Again, for purposes of illustrating the classic nature of the questions, we may adduce the following hypotheses:

(1) Fragmentation of the decisional system encourages consensus on rules, which enhances system stability.[29]

(2) Fragmentation, with its multiple and competing subsystems, encourages innovation, leading to development.[30]

(3) Given complex and uncertain demand patterns, fragmentation leads to efficient resource allocation.[31]

(4) But, given clear and transitively ordered preferences, fragmentation leads to inefficient resource allocation.[32]

(5) Fragmentation makes individual rationality of choice more difficult.

(6) But, given an aggregate array of complex and intransitively ordered preferences, fragmentation may enhance system rationality.

(7) Fragmentation makes problem cognition more difficult and major systemic change more expensive, and may therefore reduce system stability under conditions of great stress.

It should be apparent that the partially contradictory nature of these hypotheses suggests the paramount need of systematic inquiry into the questions. It should be apparent too that these criteria may be employed both for normative purposes and for purposes of empirical theory. It is also clear, I think, that if one is to be concerned with constitutional policy, one cannot escape involvement, implicit or explicit, in the analysis of system resources and demand patterns as well. The converse, however, is not so evident. That is, it does not necessarily follow that in order to understand the level of wealth and economic development or the pattern of group activity in a society one needs to understand very much about the formal decisional system. Indeed, there is considerable evidence to support the contrary position. Unless, therefore, we are to content ourselves by saying with Dye that constitutional policy may be important primarily for its own sake, that we value the "way we do things" even though it makes no substantive difference to what we do,[33] we must concern ourselves with a larger problem, namely, whether the decisional system can be regarded as a significant independent variable at all. The examination of this question leads us into a broad consideration of substantive policy analysis, and we turn now to that task.

IV. SUBSTANTIVE POLICY: AN ANALYTIC MODEL

The profound implications for political scientists of the pioneering study by Dawson and Robinson have not altogether been realized.[34] What they showed, and what Hofferbert, Dye and others have subsequently confirmed and elaborated, is that the principal variables with which we have traditionally been concerned, e.g., demand patterns reflected in party competition, do not "explain" variations in the authoritative outputs of a polity.[35] With Easton many political scientists have accepted outputs as the ultimate dependent variable to be accounted for. But now it appears that not only party competition and interest-group demand patterns, but such decisional system characteristics as apportionment made little difference to output. What do matter are system resources. Wealth, urbanization, perhaps settlement patterns, and other such factors account for both political system characteristics *and* decisional outputs.[36] No doubt the political system constitutes a kind of "black box" through which system resources are processed in order to result in policy decisions. But the implication of these studies is that, except for its own sake, analysis of the black box will yield little of interest respecting outputs or policies.

This, I submit, is a devastating set of findings and cannot be dismissed as not meaning what it plainly says—that analysis of political systems will not explain policy decisions made by those systems. Moreover, there is another, quite different kind of argument which leads to much the same conclusion. This is the argument of incrementalism: that nearly all the time policy will vary only marginally from what it has been. Accordingly, the best predictor of future expenditure may be past expenditures, which seem to account for some 90 per cent of the variance.[37] And if this is so, there is little room for any other variables except for the odd case of significant or innovative departures from the norm. To be sure, the innovation cases are likely to be the most exciting to study, but in the United States they are pretty largely exceptions. Incrementalism as an empirical theory of organizational behavior surely requires drastic changes in the focus of political science research, and it implies that at least in stable political systems there are at best very narrow parameters within which "political" variables can function.

Both kinds of studies, those stressing system resources and those taking the incremental approach, conceive of policies mainly in terms of expenditures and employ nominal categories for classifying them. Does the contention hold when we conceive of policies along other lines? Much of the argument that follows is to the effect that (1) under an alternative conceptualization of policy outcomes, political system variables again become of critical importance, though the continuing strength of the relationship between system–resource variation and the *amount* of policy output is conceded; and (2) it is absolutely essential, if we are to justify the relevance of examining political system characteristics, to incorporate substantive policy as an explicit part of our analytic model.

The adaptation of Lowi's formulation described earlier presents formidable problems of observation and measurement, but as against other abstract types derived from "policy theory," I doubt they are more severe. In any event, I wish to argue that each of the four policy types defined—distributive, redistributive, regulatory, and self-regulatory—may plausibly be linked theoretically with different interactions between political demand patterns and decisional system patterns. Let us consider the diagram in Figure 6–1.

I have already alluded to most of the terms represented in the figure, and I do not want to define them more than is absolutely necessary. The model resembles other political system models in contemporary vogue, differing chiefly I think in the distinction made—and it is crucial for the argument that follows—between demand patterns and the decisional system. What we have termed constitutional policy is represented by linkage D in the model, and the hypotheses we suggested relating constitutional policy to demand patterns and system resources are represented by linkages D' and D''.

FIGURE 6-1

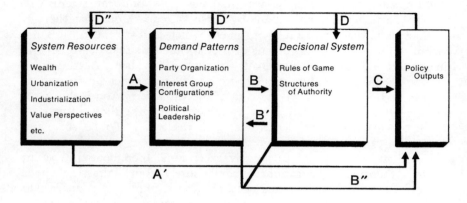

Now the argument of Dawson and Robinson and the others is essentially to the effect that linkage A' is primary for explaining policy output variation. Implicit in that argument is that demand patterns and decisional systems vary mainly as functions of system–resource variation and that, rather than exerting any important independent effect on the *amount* of policy outputs, they function essentially as neutral transmission mechanisms. My argument is that the interactions of demand patterns and the decisional system (linkages B and B') are systematically associated with differentiated *types* of policy, though probably not with amounts. That is, while system resources may account for the amount of money that is spent, the active political system continues to be decisive in determining the kind of policy, including the groups that benefit or suffer, the extent of conflict, the ability to innovate or adapt, and other questions discussed earlier under the heading of evaluative criteria. Let me explain.

Demand patterns refer to the patterns of groups and individuals— interest groups, parties, and other political entrepreneurs—articulating demands and pressing them upon the decisional system. Employing a venerable analytic dimension, we may consider the extent to which demand patterns are integrated or fragmented. The ultimate in an integrated demand pattern might be reached in a secure authoritarian regime where one class or group, homogeneous in its own values, is the only effective actor in the play. The ultimate fragmentation would be an extremely heterogeneous, disaggregated array of interests, each pressing its claim for an authoritative decision on the same issue independently of all the others.

We are not here speaking of the range of values in a community, but of the range of those values expressed in the form of demands for governmental action. Such demands may be cast in the form of a "claim upon other groups," but so far as the perceptions of political actors are concerned, it need not be so. Only in a logical, holistic view must one demand for subsidy necessarily be at the expense of some other group. Moreover, we must assess demand integration separately on each issue and allow for the genuine possibility that it will vary from one issue to the next.[38]

Within the continuum of demand integration–fragmentation many configurations are possible. A strong one-party system whose leaders effectively aggregate and control demand (Byrd's Virginia?) is highly integrated. A weak one-party system is not.[39] An effective "lib–lab" coalition of interest groups may be relatively integrated,[40] but an alliance of disparate farm groups attempting to facilitate mutual cooperation among the groups would be less so.[41] Integration is measured by the range, diversity, and compatibility of substantive demands made as well as by the unity or disunity of activity among groups making them.

Now we lack any very good general theories about the conditions under which various types of demand patterns are likely to emerge. Nevertheless, there are some fragments of theory which speak to the American case, at least, and they will give us a starting point.[42]

The American polity began with a highly heterogeneous pattern of demands, and this heterogeneity has continued until quite recently to dominate much of the policy content of political decisions. But urbanization and industrialization operate to aggregate putative class interests with the result that over time, and especially during the New Deal and after, the demand patterns have been increasingly aggregated, partly in the form of large organized interest groups allied with one another according to shared ideological perspectives, and partly in the form of moderately strong political parties. Further and contrariwise, however, technological innovations have the effect of facilitating specialization of function, and hence of interest, and hence of demand. A technological society is one in which interests proliferate, and one thus finds the paradox of urbanized industrial society with increasing aggregation of demands unjoined with technology-induced proliferation of interests. Yet both tendencies seem to me observable facts about contemporary American politics with significant implications for policy analysis.

Before we encounter further complexity, however, let us consider the probable content of policy demands made under varying conditions of demand pattern. That is, are the demands stemming from integrated groups different in kind from those in a fragmented situation? Consider a homogeneous class in an authoritarian system. Pretty clearly its demands are largely redistributive in the sense that the class seeks to take from one group and give to another. Similarly, the rhetoric of class-struggle ideologies, on both sides, has stressed the redistributive effects of their policy demands once the desired coordination of effort and self-consciousness of interest, i.e., integration of demand, is achieved.

Conversely, fragmented demand patterns are commonly thought of in association with distributive policies. Many diverse groups seeking governmental distribution to themselves of public lands, or pensions, or river and harbor improvements, or income subsidies, or other kinds of assistance—these have been characteristic of much traditional American politics. And even today, despite the undoubted increase in redistributive rhetoric, much policy continues to be viewed as primarily distributive, even as American society continues to manifest substantial pluralism in demand patterns.

Thus far we have said that integrated demand patterns are associated with redistributive policies, fragmented demand patterns are associated with distributive policies. Yet there are other possibilities. For example, when a professional or quasi-professional group presents a policy claim to a legislature, the total relevant demand is typically highly integrated in the sense that members of the group are cohesive and no one else pays any attention to the issue. The result is likely to be a licensing law that delegates the control over entry into the profession to the members of the profession.[43] This is an example of self-regulation policy, and it can be shown, I think, that a considerable portion of the policy demands of economic groups in America has been of this type.[44] The active interests are integrated but they seek self-regulation, not redistribution. Why? Part of the answer, surely, is that groups seeking self-regulation are likely to be small relative to the total polity and do not believe they could win a redistributive game. But this, in turn, is related to the decisional system from which they seek support. An important factor in persuading a group to seek self-regulation rather than redistribution is their perception that other groups who would be adversely affected by redistributive policy could with relative ease enter the decisional arena and frustrate the demand.[45] The first group cannot indefinitely control the decisional system against competing groups, though it can secure a delegation of authority to itself. And the reason for this is that the decisional system itself is fragmented. That is, there are multiple nodes or points of power within the system which opposing groups activated by redistributive policy demands might capture and thereby block the demands. And so the group seeks self-regulation.

In short, the type of policy which is demanded is a function of the degree of integration in both the demand pattern and the decisional system. If the decisional system is fragmented, as American legislatures have characteristically been, an integrated demand pattern will be manifested in a quest for self-regulative policies. If the decisional system is integrated, on the other hand, as in a system dominated by a strong executive, one may expect integrated demand groups to seek more redistributive policies. More on this later.

It remains to describe the fourth policy type in our original formulation, regulative policy. Perhaps the best illustration of regulative policy characteristically is associated with the judiciary. The courts are highly integrated decisional systems, hierarchical in structure, with powerful norms constraining the lower courts to conform to the decisions of higher courts. And in many policy areas, though certainly not all, that pattern of demands upon the judiciary is diverse and fragmented. It may be so regarding many issues of criminal law, for example, or with regard to First Amendment freedoms. The resultant policy output is constraining upon subsequent actions of the interested parties and an unknown array of future parties, specifying that at least some of them will not be permitted to engage in certain kinds of activities. When the pattern of demand upon the courts is also integrated, however, as in the business-dominated era of the courts in the late nineteenth and early twentieth centuries, or in the recent period of civil rights litigation, the policy results are best understood as redistributive.

It was mentioned earlier that constitutional policy is a special case of regulatory policy. Such policy is normally made by integrated decisional systems. By this I mean decisional units with unambiguous authority over subordinates or subjects, unchallenged by competing units. A court, a constitutional convention, or a referendum vote are typical examples. Now if the demand pattern were also integrated, I think it plausible to argue that the conflict would not result in a constitutional decision, but in a redistributive showdown. Historically, it has been precisely because demand was fragmented that the United States and some other systems have been genuinely, not just *pro forma*, concerned with constitutional issues. The fragmentation of demands leads participants to seek agreement on rules of the game.

Our paradigm is summarized in Figure 6–2. Let us now consider

FIGURE   6-2

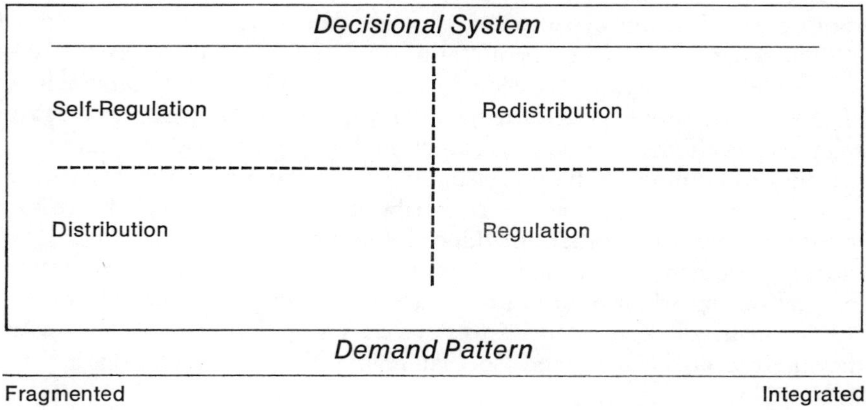

Decisional System	
Self-Regulation	Redistribution
Distribution	Regulation

Demand Pattern

Fragmented   Integrated some of the dynamics of the model. It seems a reasonable reading of American political history that demand patterns have become somewhat more integrated over time, and that, in broad outline at least, so have decisional systems. Thus we do not doubt that executive leadership of the decisional systems has increased, and this is clearly integrative. We would predict, therefore, that American public policy would become increasingly redistributive. To what extent is this prediction borne out by reality?

Had this paper been written in the 1930's, or even perhaps during the heyday of the Fair Deal, one would not have hesitated much over the *general* conclusion that redistribution was more and more the hallmark of public policy. Now it seems a more complex process, and I think there are at least two classes of reasons. One is that redistributive policies are rendered less redistributive in the perceptions of those who contend over them by the introduction of distributive features. That is, if an initially redistributive game is perceived to have a positive sum result, its conflict potentialities are reduced as the extra benefits are distributed. Thus a poverty program taxes the rich to give to the poor, but it is perceived as providing advantages to the nonpoor also in the form of reduced unrest, expanded markets, and greater social equity. Progressive taxation is defended not simply on its redistributive merits, but also because it generates social capital for public-sector investment, which benefits many groups, including the wealthy. In the United States the demand patterns have, despite the rhetoric of the NAM, been subject to renewed *dis*aggregation as distributive possibilities for all sorts of groups continue to appear. In one sense, this is a way of describing the continued vitality of American pluralism. In another, it identifies the sharing of middle-class values, which are preeminently distributive, by all, or nearly all, sectors of the society. In still another sense, the continued salience of distributive aspects of public policy reflects the prosperity of an affluent society in which zero-sum redistribution has not been a necessary means to reallocate either material or symbolic goods. And, recalling the point made earlier, technological specialization has in any case operated to bring about a proliferation of substantive policy demands.

The other group of factors militating against a growth of redistributive policies relate to changes in the decisional system. One major consequence of the redistributive policies associated with the notion of the welfare state has been the creation of larger and more complex bureaucratic agencies to administer the programs. Some of these began as regulative agencies, some as agencies for redistribution of benefits. All, however, to one degree or another introduced fragmenting influences into the executive branch and reduced thereby the effect of increased executive integration regarding policy initiation.[46] Moreover, it has been characteristic of many of these agencies to develop a symbiotic relationship with the interests to be regulated, so that regulation turns into a variety of self-regulation.[47] In other cases, the initial impetus toward redistribution may be mitigated by the incorporation of the groups expecting to be hurt in the actual administration of the program. Thus, as Eckstein tells us for the British case,[48] doctors may denounce Medicare as injuriously redistributive, but they end up running the program.[49]

If demand patterns become disaggregated in the face of continuing integration of the decisional systems, we would expect policies that had begun as redistributive to become increasingly regulative. One might argue that labor–management relations have, in part, followed such a course since 1935. If demand patterns remain integrated and the decisional system becomes fragmented, as it might with administrative decentralization, we would expect self-regulation to supersede redistribution. Probably the most characteristic pattern, however, is for some fragmentation to occur in both the demand and the decisional system. In any case, there is a kind of redefinitional process constantly at work to shift policies out of the redistributive quadrant, often back into the distributive portion of the matrix (see Figure 6–3).

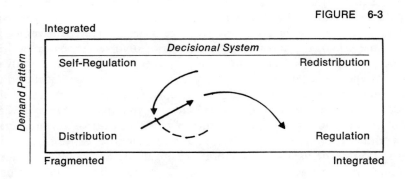

FIGURE 6-3

Another point of importance should be apparent from this analysis. Groups make demands not only about substantive policy, but also about constitutional policy. That is, they advocate more or less integration in the decisional system, and it follows from our analysis that, let us say, business groups might well be expected to prefer a fragmented decisional system in order to secure self-regulation when the given demand pattern there will be a preferred type of decisional system and hence a preferred constitutional policy.[50]

We have spoken thus far of general system interactions and tendencies, but it seems apparent that at a given point in time there will be wide variations in the operative demand patterns and relevant decisional systems for particular substantive policies. That is, tariff policy or farm policy may be more regulative (integrated decisional system, fragmented demand), while education policy or housing policy may be more distributive (fragmented decisional system, fragmented demand) and policy regarding entry into the professions or television broadcasting may be self-regulative (integrated demand, fragmented decisional system). Variability notwithstanding, are there any tendencies that may be generalized concerning the behavior of the variables we have identified as crucial to the type of policy which emerges? We have already noted some tendency toward a kind of oscillation in the two variables, increased integration followed by increased fragmentation, with a resultant tendency for policy outputs of a system to follow a looping pattern back and away from the redistributive quadrant of the matrix.

Is there any general tendency toward an equilibrium point in the matrix, and if so, where will it be located? Lowi argues, following Truman, that in industrial societies the number of tangent relations among groups is increased, and with the increase comes a correlative increase in the necessity of regulation.[51] This is certainly a classical argument and one we should not discard lightly. It is surely plausible to interpret the growth of such regulative (and integrative) mechanisms as the executive budget process as possessing continuing effect not altogether overcome by the reassertion of bureaucratic autonomy.[52] Nor is executive leadership entirely negated by the stubborn presence of legislative recalcitrance. By the same token, the autonomous interests of diverse unions or business trade associations or farm commodity groups or whatever do not always destroy the aggregative effect of peak associations or party coalitions. A general statement might be that secular changes in the location of policy modes in a system tend toward the regulatory quadrant of the matrix and that equilibrium is reached to the extent that formal organizations, government or group, stabilize and structure the expression and/or resolution of demands.[53] In short, organizations are stabilizing factors and may facilitate achievement of a regulatory equilibrium in the system's policy output.

Whether the above hypothesis, or any other that employs the conceptualization of policy types suggested here, is empirically valid depends upon whether the variables adduced can be observed and measured with sufficient reliability to make this more than a literary theory. Bad measures may be worse than none, of course, but it is not an advantage to be unable to make the analysis operational. How might we proceed?

The analysis of American states and cities has proceeded somewhat farther in this matter and may offer some clues. For example, Zeigler has suggested that the judgments of expert informants about the "strength" of the interest group system may yield useful data that can then be related to other characteristics of the polity.[54] In various ways, scholars have long been assessing the "strength" and centralization of control (integration) of the party system. Schlesinger has attempted to specify components of gubernatorial strength[55] which might be adapted to measures of decisional system integration, especially if taken in combination with comparable readings on executive–legislative relations.

Let us suppose that we were to examine the states systematically regarding a range of substantive policies on which all made decisions. If we observed the number and variety of groups making demands concerning each set of policies, we should be able to say that there were many diverse groups expressing demands on each, or one or a few groups on each, or one or a few groups on all. The range of content of the demands might also vary from little to much. We might construct for each state a matrix similar to that in Figure 6–4. The upper left case would

FIGURE 6-4

Number of Issues	Number of Groups					
	1	2	3	4	5	6
1	XXXX	XXX	X	X	XX	XXXX
2	XXX	XX		X	XX	XX
3	X	X	X	XX		X
4	X	XX	X		X	XX
5	XXX	XXX		X	XX	XXX
6	XXXXX	XX	X	X	XX	XXX

bespeak an integrated demand pattern of limited scope which we would expect, *ceteris paribus*, to be associated with self-regulative policy concerns. The lower left case, on the other hand, suggests integrated demand on a broad range of issues leading toward redistributive policy. The upper right case shows fragmented demand of limited scope; the lower right shows fragmented demand of broad scope. Comparisons of demand patterns among states, issues, and groups would be illuminating by itself, and ought to have theory-building consequences too.

The third task, and perhaps the most difficult, is to reclassify policies that in the real world are necessarily nominal in type into the conceptual types we have set forth. To do this we might begin by agreeing that appropriations are mainly distributive policies[56] and that taxation questions are typically redistributive. An issue in these two sets is the extent to which the taxation issues are mitigated by expectations of favorable appropriations or related program benefits. The less conflict generated by taxation issues, the more distributive the policy output. And, hypothetically, the more fragmented the demand pattern, the less heat would be generated over taxation. To take another area, home rule for local governments would be self-regulative policy at the state level.[57] So also would occupational licensing legislation.

If I interpret Gilbert Steiner's fine study correctly, national welfare policies tend to fall somewhere near the distributive–self-regulative line. He observes a relative lack of integration in the decisional system and low salience of demand, but it is not entirely clear whether such demand as exists is fragmented among categorical client groups or more integrated in social work organizations. To the extent that the latter is true, one would expect policy to be self-regulative, with social workers definining the standards and levels of support, while the total moneys available would reflect a distributive pattern resulting from competition with other claimant groups. Steiner uses the term "automated" to describe the process, which would seem to suggest what we have here termed self-regulation.[58] At the local level the extent of spot zoning as against comprehensive zoning might indicate something of the extent of distributive as against regulative policy in a city, and so might a comparison between the number of stop signs and the extent of synchronized traffic lights. The point here is not to categorize every conceivable kind of policy, but to suggest that categorization is possible. The possibility probably requires, however, that there be some comparative data. That is, policy A is more readily classed as distributive when there are policies B, C, and D available with which to compare it. And clearly comparison of political systems is essential if any reliable observations are to be made concerning demand patterns and decisional systems.

I do not intend these efforts at rehabilitating political variables to suggest that they supersede system–resource variables in explanatory power. Rather I mean to suggest that they are relevant to changes in the type of policy outputs in a polity at any given level of amount of those outputs. We are always, no doubt, interested in explaining the political system for its own sake (and ours), but, within the limits that the recent literature alluded to forces us to acknowledge, we may still find work to do which is relevant to the explanation of policy outputs also.

Arthur Maass

Benefit–Cost Analysis:
Its Relevance to Public
Investment Decisions*

The United States government has for some time used benefit–cost analysis in the design and justification of dams and other water resources improvements. Currently the government is trying o adapt the technique to other public investment programs. At the request of the Bureau of the Budget, the Brookings Institution held a major conference on the topic in November, 1963, with papers on applying benefit–cost analysis to urban highways, urban renewal, outdoor recreation, civil aviation, government research and development, and public health.[1] In 1965 the Bureau of the Budget established a special unit to adapt and apply benefit–cost and cost–effectiveness studies to a broad range of government programs. It is appropriate, therefore, to examine and evaluate this important branch of welfare economics.

WHAT IS THE PROBLEM?

The major limitation of benefit–cost analysis, as it has been applied to public investments in the United States, is that it ranks projects and programs in terms only of economic efficiency. (At the national level this means that projects and programs are judged by the amount that they increase the national product.) But the objective of most public programs is not simply, not even principally, economic efficiency. The redistribution of income to classes or to regions is an important objective in government plans—witness the Appalachia program; and there are other objectives, too, the promotion of national self-sufficiency, for example.

In other words, the objective functions of most government programs

*Reprinted by permission from *The Quarterly Journal of Economics*, LXXX (May, 1966), 208–226.
(Notes to this selection will be found on pp. 413–414.)

are complex; yet benefit–cost analysis has been adapted to only a single objective—economic efficiency. Thus, benefit–cost analysis may be largely irrelevant, or relevant to only a small part of the problem of evaluating public projects and programs. We should not settle for the current state of benefit–cost analysis, but rather find ways to make it applicable to the real issues of public investment.

Now in all complex objective functions for government programs, economic efficiency will be one term. A second is frequently income redistribution, as we have noted, to classes (e.g., the poor) or to regions (e.g., depressed areas). These two objectives may be complementary in some ways; a program designed to transfer income from the rest of the nation to Appalachia or from the wealthy to the poor may also increase national product.[2] But a government program that maximizes efficiency will not necessarily, indeed is not likely to, achieve a specified high level of income redistribution. Thus, a planner who is responsible for developing a program or project for both purposes will need to know the relative weights to assign to efficiency and income redistribution.

Assume that the problem is to design an irrigation project on an Indian reservation so as to increase the income of the Indians as a group and to increase food production for the nation as a whole. The relation between income for the Indians (income redistribution) and food production (national economic efficiency) in this case can be stated in any one of three ways as follows:[3]

(1) Maximize net income to the Indians, subject to a constraint that the ratio of efficiency benefits to efficiency costs is at least 1.0 to 1.0, or 0.9 to 1.0, or some other.

(2) Maximize net benefits from food production in national terms— i.e., economic efficiency—subject to a constraint that the Indians net $X thousand per year.

(3) Maximize a weighted sum of net benefits from economic efficiency and income redistribution in which $1 of income to the Indians is valued at $(1 + X) of efficiency. (In this case the X can be called a shadow premium on redistribution benefits.)

With proper values these three statements will be equivalent. Any constraint can be converted into a shadow price and any shadow price, into a constraint.

The efficiency benefits and costs of this two-term objective function can be measured fairly well by the art of benefit–cost analysis in its present state. There are problems, to be sure, resulting from such factors as the collective character of the benefits of many public programs, the need to measure costs in terms of resource displacements rather than market prices where these two measures diverge, the selection of an appropriate discount rate, various so-called external effects; but great progress has been made on these in recent years.[4] Thus, all that is needed to solve the maximization equation is to specify the trade-off ratio between efficiency and income redistribution. If there is a way of finding this ratio, the maximization problem can be solved in any of its three forms, and we can design projects and programs that are responsive to a realistic two-factor objective function.

There is a way to determine the trade-off—through the political process. For the federal government my studies indicate that there is a capacity in the legislative process to make the trade-off decisions that can then govern the design of projects and programs. The President initiates the legislative process; the Congress examines the President's proposals in the light of alternatives and accepts, modifies, or rejects them. Thus, the experts in the executive departments need to develop data that show the effects on the design of programs and projects of different trade-off ratios. This the executive can do. The President needs to select one or a range of these ratios and thereby initiate formally the legislative process. This the President can do. And finally, the Congress, when presented with such data and such a presidential initiative, needs to and can, as we shall see, respond in order.

Ironically but understandably, the field of public investment for which the present benefit–cost technique is most advanced, water resources, is the field for which the political technique for determining trade-offs among efficiency and other objectives is most primitive. The legislative process for water resources consists principally of omnibus bills that authorize individual projects, rather than of legislation that sets standards and criteria. In the housing and urban renewal area, by contrast, standards and criteria based on both income redistribution and economic efficiency, are determined in the legislative process, and benefit–cost analysis is primitive.

The problem is to combine the advanced state of the art of efficiency benefit–cost analysis, as found in water resources planning, with an equally sophisticated technique for relating efficiency benefits and costs to those stemming from other objectives.

HAVE BENEFITS BEEN OVERESTIMATED?

In this context it is interesting to examine the arguments over so-called secondary benefits and how they should be included, if at all, in project analyses. There is no such thing as a secondary benefit. A secondary benefit, as the phrase has been used in the benefit–cost literature, is in fact a benefit in support of an objective other than efficiency.[5] The word benefit (and the word cost, too) has no meaning by itself, but only in association with an objective; there are efficiency benefits, income redistribution benefits, and others. Thus, if the objective function for a public program involves more than economic efficiency—and it will in most cases—there is no legitimate reason for holding that the efficiency benefits are primary and should be included in the benefit–cost analysis whereas benefits in support of other objectives are secondary and should be mentioned, if at all, in separate subsidiary paragraphs of the survey report. Using the current language and current standards, most of the benefits to the Indians in the Indian irrigation project are secondary benefits. How silly!

In this context it is interesting also to examine the conclusion of many nongovernmental studies of government planning for water resources projects, namely, that benefits have been overestimated. Professor Hubert Marshall recently recited the evidences of chronic overestimation in a major address before the Western Resources Conference at Fort Collins.[6] The principal cause of such benefit "overestimation" is, I believe, the unreal restrictions placed on the analysis of projects by the unreal but virtual standard that the relation of efficiency benefits to efficiency costs is the indicator of a project's worth, when in fact the project is conceived and planned for objectives in addition to efficiency. In such an incongruous circumstance one might expect project planners to use a broad definition of efficiency benefits. The critics, either not understanding or unsympathetic to the planners' plight, have judged them by a more rigorous definition of efficiency.[7]

HOW DID WE GET TO WHERE WE ARE?

Why has benefit–cost analysis developed in this way? Certainly not because of any myopia on the part of the Congress, though executive officers are frequently quick to blame Congress for their ills. To be sure, we do not have adequate legislative objectives, standards, or trade-off ratios for the design and evaluation of water resources projects, but this is because the President has failed to initiate the legislative process, not because of a lack of receptivity to such initiatives by Congress. In fact certain committees of Congress, impatient with the President for not proposing legislation to set standards, have tried to initiate the legislative process themselves; but without cooperation from the executive they have failed, understandably. The task of assembling and analyzing data, the necessary first step in the legislative process, is beyond the capacity of the Congress and its staff in complex areas like this one. Insofar as there is a general standard for the design of water projects that has been approved by Congress in legislation, it is a 30-year old statement that "the benefits to whomsoever they may accrue should exceed the costs."[9] This standard, you will note, does not specify efficiency benefits, but "benefits to whomsoever they may accrue."

The executive agencies have painted themselves into the efficiency box. In 1950 the Subcommittee on Benefits and Costs of the Federal Inter-Agency River Basin Committee gave overwhelming emphasis to the efficiency ranking function in its now well-known "Green Book" report.[10] In 1952 the Bureau of the Budget, in a budget circular that neither required nor invited formal review and approval by the Congress, nailed this emphasis into national policy, adopting it as the standard by which the bureau would review agency projects to determine their standing in the President's program.[11] And soon thereafter agency planning manuals were revised, where necessary, to reflect this budget circular. In this way benefits to all became virtually restricted to benefits that increase national product.

The federal bureaucrats, it should be noted, were not acting in a vacuum; they were reflecting the doctrines of the new welfare economics which has focused entirely on economic efficiency. Nonefficiency considerations have been held to be outside the domain of the welfare economist. They have been called by such loaded names as inefficient, value-laden, altruistic, merit wants, uneconomical.[12]

WHAT CHANGES IN WELFARE ECONOMIC THEORY ARE NEEDED?

From a practical point of view the new welfare economics has dealt exclusively with efficiency because for it, and not for other objectives, benefit and cost data are provided automatically by the market, though market prices sometimes have to be doctored. Theoretically, however, the preoccupation of present-day welfare economics, and its branch of benefit–cost analysis, with economic efficiency results from its very basic assumptions, and two of these in my view can and should be abandoned.

First is indifference to the distribution of income generated by a government program or project—the assumption that each dollar of income from the program is of equal social value regardless of who receives it. In benefit–cost analysis that maximizes efficiency, an extra dollar to a Texas oil man is as desirable socially as one to an Arkansas tenant farmer, and an additional dollar of benefits for Appalachia, West Virginia is no more worthwhile than one for Grosse Pointe, Michigan.

Few welfare economists support the social implications of this basic assumption, and they would compensate for them in one of two ways. Some hold that the professional planners should design projects and programs for economic efficiency, for which benefit–cost analysis can provide the necessary ranking function; and that thereafter these project designs can be doctored and modified by a political process to account for any "uneconomic" objectives.[13] But this response is unsatisfactory for reasons already given. Where government programs are intended for complex objectives they should be designed, where this is possible, for such objectives, not designed for one objective which may not be the most important, and subsequently modified in an effort to account for others. Almost inevitably economic efficiency will be overweighted in such a scheme. How relevant is this type of planning for our Indian irrigation project? Furthermore, such a planning process calls on political institutions to perform a task for which they are not well equipped. Where the approval and modification of individual projects, rather than a debate on objectives and standards for designing projects in the first place, is the *principal* activity of the legislative process, decision-making for the nation can disintegrate into project-trading. In the legislature, for example, the voices of the whole house and of committees are muted at the expense of those of individual members, each making decisions for projects in his district and accepting reciprocally the decisions of his colleagues. Nor does the executive under these circumstances play a more general or high-minded role. The public investment decision process can be organized, hopefully, to play to the strengths rather than to the weaknesses of political institutions.

An alternative response of some welfare economists to the inequitable social consequences of the basic assumption of indifference to income distribution is as follows. It is more efficient to redistribute income directly from one group of individuals to another, through government programs of taxation and subsidies, than to do so indirectly through government investment programs that are designed also to increase national product. If the government's objectives are, for example, to increase both national food production and income of the Indians, it should plan to accomplish these by two programs rather than by a single one. Government planners should design the most efficient program for increasing food production, which may mean additional irrigation facilities in the Imperial valley of California where there are no Indians. Then, with taxes collected from the irrigators that represent their willingness to pay for their new benefits, the government should make subsidy payments to the Indians. In this way, so goes the argument, the government can achieve the best of both worlds. Best in this context means efficient, however, and there is no reason why a community need prefer the most efficient method for redistributing income, especially if it requires transferring cash from one group to another. As Marglin points out in his treatment of this subject, the means by which a desired distribution of income is achieved may be of great importance to the community.[14] In our example, the community would probably be willing to give up some efficiency to see the living standard of the Indians improved by their own labors rather than by the dole. In short, the community may quite properly want to realize multiple purposes through public investment projects and programs, and if benefit–cost analysis is to be of great use in planning these activities, then the basic assumption of indifference to their distributive consequences must be abandoned.

It should be noted, however, that where, as in the case of the Indian irrigation project, a government program produces benefits that can be sold or otherwise charged for, a desired redistribution of income can be achieved by both the quantity of benefits produced and the prices charged for them. For any given quantity of irrigation water, the smaller the repayment required from the Indians, the greater the income they will receive. Thus, when the agency men prepare data showing the effects on public programs of alternative trade-offs between economic efficiency and income redistribution, these alternatives should include different repayment possibilities.

The second basic assumption of the new welfare economics and of benefit–cost analysis that needs to be challenged is consumers' sovereignty —reliance solely on market-exhibited preferences of individuals. This assumption, to be sure, provides normative significance for the familiar prescriptions of welfare economics on which the efficiency calculus is based—for example, that price ought to equal marginal costs. Nonetheless, it is not relevant to all public investment decisions, for an individual's market preference is a response in terms of what he believes to be good for his own economic interest, not for the community.

Each individual plays a number of roles in his life—social science literature is filled with studies of role differentiation—and each role can lead him to a unique response to a given choice situation. Thus an individual has the capacity to respond in a given case, to formulate his preferences, in several ways, including these two: (1) what he believes to be good for himself—largely his economic self-interest, and (2) what he believes to be good for the political community. The difference between these two can be defined in terms of breadth of view. To the extent that an individual's response is community, rather than privately, oriented, it places greater emphasis on the individual's estimate of the consequences of his choice for the larger community.

Now, the response that an individual gives in any choice situation will depend in significant part on how the question is asked of him, and this means not simply the way a question is worded, but the total environment in which it is put and discussed. This can be illustrated with a small group experiment. Questions with relevance for the church (e.g., should birth control information be provided to married individuals who desire it?) were asked of Catholic students randomly divided into two groups. One group met in a small room where they were made aware of their common religious membership. The other group met in a large auditorium, along with hundreds of other students of many religions, where no effort was made to establish awareness of common religious beliefs. Although all of the students were instructed to respond with their "own personal opinions," there was a significant difference between the replies of the group that were aware of their common religious membership and the unaware group, the former approximating more closely the orthodox Catholic position against birth control.[15]

An individual's response depends, then, on the institutional environment in which the question is asked. Since the relevant response for public investment analysis is a community, not privately, oriented one, the great challenge for welfare economics is to frame questions in such a way as to elicit from individuals community-oriented answers. The market is an institution designed to elicit privately oriented responses from individuals and to relate these responses to each other. For the federal government the electoral, legislative, and administrative processes together constitute the institution designed to elicit community-oriented responses. The Maass–Cooper model describes these processes within such a context.[16]

Although several welfare economists have recognized explicitly that individuals play several roles and that these roles influence preferences, they go on to say that in making decisions relating to social welfare each individual uses a composite utility function, a total net position representing a balance of all of his roles.[17] This last hypothesis, which is not supported by experimental evidence, is unfortunate. It misses the point that an individual will respond differently depending on how the question is asked of him, and it fails to give proper emphasis to the differentiation of institutions for putting the question—e.g., the market institution to elicit private-oriented responses and political institutions for those which are community oriented.

Ideally we want the community, not market, responses of individuals with respect to both factors in our complex objective function—economic efficiency and income redistribution. Fortunately, however, market-determined prices are a fairly good surrogate for the economic efficiency factor, providing adjustments are made for so-called externalities and the like.[18] This is opportune. Were it not for the propriety of using market-related prices for efficiency benefits and costs, benefit–cost analysis for public projects and programs would be beyond the capacity of available economic techniques and of political institutions as they operate today.

Some day, I am confident, we shall be able to use institutions that elicit community-oriented responses to measure all factors in a complex objective function—efficiency, income redistribution, and others. The very recent search by a few economists, inspired largely by the work of Kenneth Arrow, for a new criterion of social welfare may contribute to this end.[19] The more modest proposal of this article is that we use political institutions to measure the trade-off ratio between a basically market-determined efficiency and the single most important nonefficiency objective of a government program, which is likely to be income redistribution but may be some other.

WHAT IS THE EVIDENCE THAT TRADE-OFFS CAN BE DETERMINED?

It remains to be demonstrated that there is a capacity in the legislative process to select trade-off ratios in a way that will be useful for the design of government programs and projects. As stated earlier, the legislative process involves three steps. First, the officials in the executive departments prepare data showing what would be the effects on programs and projects of alternative trade-offs between economic efficiency and another objective; second, the President, with these data in hand, selects a trade-off ratio and proposes it to Congress as the legislative standard; and third, Congress examines the President's proposal, in the light of the alternatives developed in the departments and of others that may come form outside sources, and accepts, rejects, or modifies it.

The first step should not involve great difficulties, especially in water resources where analysis of the efficiency factor is well advanced, although there will be obvious problems in areas where economic efficiency analysis is primitive. For continuing programs, the data necessary to initiate the legislative process need not relate to projects and programs being designed or to be designed; they can be drawn from projects already in operation and in some cases from hypothetical or prototype projects. Agency men can reexamine completed projects and programs and estimate how differently they would have been built and would have operated with different trade-offs among objectives. At the same time they can reflect in the data that they prepare for new investment programs information generated during previous planning periods, thereby using a sequential planning process.[20]

It is at the final, or Congressional, stage that doubters will raise most questions, and it is, of course, this stage that is most difficult to prove, because in the water resources area, for which the legislative initiative could be taken most clearly, the President has failed to act. To demonstrate Congress's capacity we must, therefore, turn to public investment programs for which standards have been set in legislation, and these are ones for which efficiency benefit–cost analysis is so rudimentary that it is necessary to examine the record very carefully for implicit evidence of a concern for trade-offs between efficiency and other objectives.

Legislation authorizing the National System of Interstate Highways, principally the Act of 1956, furnishes one example.[21] The legislation provides that the system should consist of 41,000 miles of roads which are identified generally as to location, and it sets design criteria for these roads. The criteria depart from those of earlier highway legislation in three important respects, apart from the taxing methods for financing the federal government's share of the costs. First, roads are to be designed for predicted traffic volumes of 1975, and the monetary authorizations are calculated from this standard.[22] Second, the federal–state matching ratio is changed from 50:50 to 90:10. Third, the formula for apportioning funds among the states is changed. The earlier formula for the primary system of roads was one-third on the basis of each of the following ratios: a state's population to the total U.S. population, a state's area to the total U.S. land area, a state's rural delivery and star routes to the total U.S. mileage of such roads. The new formula provides a single ratio: the estimated cost of completing the interstate system within the borders of a state to the total estimated cost of completing the entire system by a fixed date, 1972.[23] This last criterion was agreed to after considerable discussion involving numerous alternatives, but principally two: the one adopted and one that would continue to give considerable weight to a state's area and its population. As Major has shown, these alternatives represent respectively economic efficiency, or more properly a surrogate for efficiency, and income redistribution. Given the requirement of completing a given mileage, by a given date, to a given capacity (1975 traffic volume), an apportionment based on cost of completion would be efficient; and one based on such factors as a state's area would introduce other objectives into the program, namely, redistribution of income (largely federal construction funds) to rural states where traffic volumes and highway construction costs per mile are typically lower. This is especially true because the alternative provided that if a state received more funds than necessary to complete its portion of the interstate system, it could divert a percentage of the excess for use on its other federally aided roads.

A study of the legislative process in which these new program criteria, especially the third one, were adopted has some useful lessons for our inquiry. There was a vigorous and effective executive initiative of the process. The concept of uniform completion of an interstate system in all states at approximately the same time appears to have been recommended first by a nonfederal entity, the American Association of State Highway Officials. Thereafter the Bureau of Public Roads made a detailed factual study of the costs of building an interstate system. The President, in an address before the 1954 Governors' Conference, proposed that the nation develop a new master plan for highways, and he appointed an Advisory Committee on a National Highway Program, chaired by General Lucius Clay, to prepare one. The Clay committee used the Bureau of Public Roads report as its empirical base. It recommended the three design standards that were finally adopted, presenting them in the context of alternatives about which debate in the legislative process could and did revolve.[24] Both the BPR and the Clay reports were sent to the Congress, along with a Presidential recommendation. The discussion in Congress, in committee and on the floor, was informed and extensive. Information was available on the expected consequences in terms of investment of choosing alternative standards, the participants were aware of the nature of the choices they had to make, and their debate was rich in relevant arguments pro and con on the alternatives, especially on apportionment formulae.

What we have called economic efficiency in this case—i.e., the most efficient way of satisfying a fixed requirement—is of course quite different from economic efficiency as an objective in benefit–cost analysis for water resources, where it means to maximize the contribution of a project to national product. The latter concept played no part in setting the standards for the highway program. The art of efficiency benefit–cost analysis is much less well developed for public investments in highways than in water resources developments, and this was even more true ten years ago than it is today. It is not unreasonable to suggest, from the record of the legislative process for the Interstate Highway System, that had data been available on real economic efficiency and on alternative trade-offs between it and income redistribution, these would have been used intelligently in setting standards.

Comparing the legislative processes for the Interstate Highway System and water resources, the former is less concerned with authorizing individual projects that have been designed and more concerned with setting standards for project design. To be sure, the highway act authorized 41,000 miles of roads and fixed their general locations. Design of the roads, including definite locations for them, was left, however, for administrative action insofar as the federal government was concerned.

In federal programs for housing and urban renewal, standards and design criteria have been set in the legislative process, and the recent legislative history of the rent supplement program is an instructive example.[25] In his Housing Message of 1965, President Johnson described a proposed program for rent supplement payments as "the most crucial new instrument in our effort to improve the American city." The federal government was to guarantee to certain private builders the payment of a significant part of the rent for housing units built for occupancy by moderate-income families. These are families with incomes below the level necessary to obtain standard housing at area market prices, but above the level required for admission to publicly owned low-rent housing units. The rent payments were to be the difference between 20 per cent of a family's income (the proportion of income that a moderate income family is expected to allocate to housing) and the fair market rental of the standard housing to be built. The President proposed an authorization of $200 million over four years which was designed to encourage the construction of 500,000 new housing units in this period. The housing supported in this way would constitute some but not all of the rental units in new housing projects.

The Housing Act of 1961 had also included a program designed specifically for moderate-income families, but this program had encountered certain problems that slowed its expected impact. Section 221d(3) of the 1961 Act provided for 100 per cent loans to qualified private builders at below-market interest rates. The low interest rates were to keep rents within the reach of moderate-income families. The law provided, however, that the interest rate was to be the average rate on all outstanding marketable federal obligations. This was $3\frac{1}{8}$ per cent when the program began, but it had risen to approximately $4\frac{1}{8}$ per cent by mid-1965. This meant that rents would be significantly higher and beyond the capacity of most moderate-income families. Another problem with the 1961 program was that the low-interest mortgages constituted a heavy drain on the special assistance funds of the Federal National Mortgage Association (FNMA), the federal housing credit agency that purchased them. Because these mortgages were below market rates, FNMA could not issue against them debentures for sale in private capital markets, and they remained a 100 per cent charge on federal funds. Nonetheless the Administration recommended in 1965 that the 221d(3) program be continued for four years with a mortgage authorization of $1.5 billion, for about 125,000 new housing units. But this program was to be phased out if the rent supplement proposal worked as its backers hoped that it would.

The Administration had three principal objectives in proposing rent supplements. The first was to increase the number of housing starts. This derived from a desire to expand the national housing stock and a concern about the possibly failing health of the housing industry and the industry's impact on the national economy. We can equate this objective roughly with increasing national product, or economic efficiency. The government's housing experts found that there was a large untapped market for new housing among moderate-income families, and that rent supplements for them would stimulate the rapid construction of substantial amounts of new housing.

The second principal objective of the Administration in recommending a rent supplement program was to give direct assistance to a large group of families with incomes above the public housing level but below the level needed to obtain standard housing at market prices. This objective we can equate with income redistribution—to moderate-income families.

As for direct assistance to low-income families, the Administration bill would authorize additional public housing units. Over a four-year period 140,000 new units were to be built and 100,000 units purchased or leased from private owners and rehabilitated. Using the trickle-down theory, the Administration could claim that all other housing programs that increased the national stock of standard housing would ultimately improve the housing of the poor, but certainly the primary and direct impact of the rent supplement program, insofar as its objective was income redistribution, favored moderate-income families.

The Administration's rent supplement program contained, then, as one design criterion a trade-off ratio relating the objectives of efficiency and income redistribution and as a second, a specification of the group to be favored by the redistribution. The second criterion was explicit in the Administration's legislative initiative, though the first was largely implicit.

The Administration's third principal objective for the rent supplement program was "economic integration." Families being aided by the government would live in projects with families who would pay normal market rentals for their housing. In this respect the new program differed from most other federal housing programs for disadvantaged groups, for the latter promoted economic segregation. Only the poor live in public housing; all units in 221d(3) projects are for occupancy by designated groups. To encourage economic integration even where local authorities may oppose it, the Administration proposed that in certain cases projects supported by rent supplements need not conform to locally approved "workable programs" for housing development.

After hearings, and debates, and conferences, Congress modified drastically the Administration's design criteria for a rent supplement program. Briefly, the supplements are to be given for standard housing units that are to be occupied by low-income families. As a result, both the trade-off ratio between efficiency and income redistribution and the impact of the redistribution itself have been changed.

The relative contributions of the program to increasing national product and to redistributing income have been altered because, with a given authorization or appropriation, there will be fewer housing starts if rents of low-, rather than moderate-income families are supplemented. The unit costs of standard housing are the same in either case, but the supplement required to make up the difference between what the family can pay and what is needed to support the new housing varies greatly. The new law authorizes $150 million for rent supplements (rather than the $200 million proposed by the President. According to current (December, 1965) estimates of housing experts, this $150 million would result in 350–375,000 housing starts over four years if it were available for the Administration's program of aiding moderate-income families. As rent supplements for low-income families, the same money will induce only 250–300,000 starts.[26]

As for the criterion that governs the group to be benefited, the relative impacts on low- and moderate-income families of the original and revised programs for rent supplements and closely related activities are shown in Table 7–1.

Table 7-1—Impact on Low- and Moderate-Income Families of Certain Provisions of 1965 Housing Act

Program	ADMINISTRATION PROPOSAL	CONGRESSIONAL ACTION
Low Income		
Public housing	240*	240
Trickle down from all programs that increase national stock of standard housing	ok	ok
Rent supplement program	zero	250–300
Moderate income		
Rent supplements	467–500	zero
221d(3)	125 (*but* problems in achieving this because of high interest rate and drain on FNMA funds)	125 (*and* this likely to be achieved because interest rate fixed at 3% and provision made for tapping private capital)

* All figures are thousands of housing units over four years.

The impact of Congress' revisions on the Administration's third objective of economic integration is not so clear. Insofar as it is poor rather than moderate-income families who are enabled to live in housing developments along with families that are able to pay normal rents, a more dramatic integration can be achieved. On the other hand, it is clear from the legislative history that Congress does not intend that the housing agency exempt any rent supplement projects from the "workable plan" requirement, which means that local controls will continue.

The housing case study, like that of the highway program, shows that there is a capacity in the legislative process to discuss and adopt standards and criteria to control the design of public projects and programs; that the Congress is prepared to focus its efforts on such standards and forego authorization of the projects themselves—public works for housing, urban renewal, and community facilities are not individually authorized by law; and that the legislative process for setting standards can be used to select trade-off ratios where a program has two objectives. On this latter point, the rent supplement case is a bit weak, to be sure. The Administration in its legislative initiative did not make sufficiently explicit the trade-off between economic efficiency and income redistribution that was involved in its proposal for approximately 500,000 new housing starts for the benefit of moderate-income families. Administration witnesses failed to give a clear statement of how the two objectives were related and how the program would differ if alternative trade-off ratios were assumed. One reason for this failure is that efficiency benefit–cost analysis has not been perfected for housing programs as it has for water resources. Nonetheless, the Congress, in reviewing the President's program managed to focus on the relevant design criteria and, after extensive consideration, including some confused debate, revised them in a way that apparently was consistent with its policy preferences. Also, the executive now has a legislated standard that it can use in redesigning the relevant housing programs. How much better the process would have been if the initiative had been better prepared!

THE LESSON

To those in the executive departments of the United States government, the lessons of this article should be clear. If the subject is water resources, initiate a legislative proposal for setting a trade-off value between economic efficiency and the most important nonefficiency objective that is relevant to your agency's program. Once this is approved, you can forget about secondary benefits, probably be relieved from the repetitive and profession-wise insulting charges that you persistently overestimate benefits, and you can design projects that are more in accord with the nation's objectives. If the subject is highways, or housing, or most other public investment programs, perfect the efficiency benefit–cost technique for your agency's program. Once this is done, there should be no difficulty in deriving through the legislative process a trade-off between efficiency and another objective. As a result, the design and selection of projects will be more intelligent and the program should be more convincing to those who judge it.

After the agencies have learned how to work with two-term objective functions, they can try to solve far more complex ones. For the time being, however, purposes other than efficiency and the most important nonefficiency objective will need to be treated descriptively in the familiar "additional paragraphs" of program and project reports.

Charles E. Lindblom

The Science of
"Muddling Through"*

Suppose an administrator is given responsibility for formulating policy with respect to inflation. He might start by trying to list all related values in order of importance, e.g., full employment, reasonable business profit, protection of small savings, prevention of a stock market crash. Then all possible outcomes could be rated as more or less efficient in attaining a maximum of these values. This would of course require a prodigious inquiry into values held by members of society and an equally prodigious set of calculations on how much of each value is equal to how much of each other value. He could then proceed to outline all possible policy alternatives. In a third step, he would undertake systematic comparison of his multitude of alternatives to determine which attains the greatest amount of values.

In comparing policies, he would take advantage of any theory available that generalized about classes of policies. In considering inflation, for example, he would compare all policies in the light of the theory of prices. Since no alternatives are beyond his investigation, he would consider strict central control and the abolition of all prices and markets on the one hand and elimination of all public controls with reliance completely on the free market on the other, both in the light of whatever theoretical generalizations he could find on such hypothetical economies.

Finally, he would try to make the choice that would in fact maximize his values.

An alternative line of attack would be to set as his principal objective, either explicitly or without conscious thought, the relatively simple goal of keeping prices level. This objective might be compromised or complicated by only a few other goals, such as full employment. He would in fact disregard most other social values as beyond his present interest, and he would for the moment not even attempt to rank the few values that he regarded as immediately relevant. Were he pressed, he would

*From the *Public Administration Review*, XIX (Spring, 1959), 79–88. Reprinted by permission of the American Society for Public Administration. (Notes to this selection will be found on p. 415.)

quickly admit that he was ignoring many related values and many possible important consequences of his policies.

As a second step, he would outline those relatively few policy alternatives that occurred to him. He would then compare them. In comparing his limited number of alternatives, most of them familiar from past controversies, he would not ordinarily find a body of theory precise enough to carry him through a comparison of their respective consequences. Instead he would rely heavily on the record of past experience with small policy steps to predict the consequences of similar steps extended into the future.

Moreover, he would find that the policy alternatives combined objectives or values in different ways. For example, one policy might offer price-level stability at the cost of some risk of unemployment; another might offer less price stability but also less risk of unemployment. Hence, the next step in his approach—the final selection—would combine into one the choice among values and the choice among instruments for reaching values. It would not, as in the first method of policy-making, approximate a more mechanical process of choosing the means that best satisfied goals that were previously clarified and ranked. Because practitioners of the second approach expect to achieve their goals only partially, they would expect to repeat endlessly the sequence just described, as conditions and aspirations changed and as accuracy of prediction improved.

BY ROOT OR BY BRANCH

For complex problems, the first of these two approaches is, of course, impossible. Although such an approach can be described, it cannot be practiced except for relatively simple problems and even then only in a somewhat modified form. It assumes intellectual capacities and sources of information that men simply do not possess, and it is even more absurd as an approach to policy when the time and money that can be allocated to a policy problem is limited, as is always the case. Of particular importance to public administrators is the fact that public agencies are in effect usually instructed not to practice the first method. That is to say, their prescribed functions and constraints—the politically or legally possible—restrict their attention to relatively few values and relatively few alternative policies among the countless alternatives that might be imagined. It is the second method that is practiced.

Curiously, however, the literatures of decision-making, policy formulation, planning, and public administration formalize the first approach rather than the second, leaving public administrators who handle complex decisions in the position of practicing what few preach. For emphasis I run some risk of overstatement. True enough, the literature is well aware of limits on man's capacities and of the inevitability that policies will be approached in some such style as the second. But attempts to formalize rational policy formulation—to lay out explicitly the necessary steps in the process—usually describe the first approach and not the second.[1]

The common tendency to describe policy formulation even for complex problems as though it followed the first approach has been strengthened by the attention given to, and successes enjoyed by, operations research, statistical decision theory, and systems analysis. The hallmarks of these procedures, typical of the first approach, are clarity of objective, explicitness of evaluation, a high degree of comprehensiveness of overview, and, wherever possible, quantification of values for mathematical analysis. But these advanced procedures remain largely the appropriate techniques of relatively small-scale problem-solving where the total number of variables to be considered is small and value problems restricted. Charles Hitch, head of the Economics Division of RAND Corporation, one of the leading centers for application of these techniques, has written:

I would make the empirical generalization from my experience at RAND and elsewhere that operations research is the art of sub-optimizing, i.e., of solving some lower-level problems, and that difficulties increase and our special competence diminishes by an order of magnitude with every level of decision making we attempt to ascend. The sort of simple explicit model which operations researchers are so proficient in using can certainly reflect most of the significant factors influencing traffic control on the George Washington Bridge, but the proportion of the relevant reality which we can represent by any such model or models in studying, say, a major foreign-policy decision, appears to be almost trivial.[2]

Accordingly, I propose in this paper to clarify and formalize the second method, much neglected in the literature. This might be described as the method of *successive limited comparisons*. I will contrast it with the first approach, which might be called the rational–comprehensive method.[3] More impressionistically and briefly—and therefore generally used in this article—they could be characterized as the branch method and root method, the former continually building out from the current situation, step-by-step and by small degrees; the latter starting from fundamentals anew each time, building on the past only as experience is embodied in a theory, and always prepared to start completely from the ground up.

Let us put the characteristics of the two methods side by side in simplest terms, as in Table 8–1.

Table 8-1

Rational–Comprehensive (Root):	Successive Limited Comparisons (Branch):
(1a) Clarification of values or objectives distinct from and usually prerequisite to empirical analysis of alternative policies.	(1b) Selection of value goals and empirical analysis of the needed action are not distinct from one another but are closely intertwined.
(2a) Policy formulation is therefore approached through means–end analysis: First the ends are isolated, then the means to achieve them are sought.	(2b) Since means and ends are not distinct, means–end analysis is often inappropriate or limited.
(3a) The test of a "good" policy is that it can be shown to be the most appropriate means to desired ends.	(3b) The test of a "good" policy is typically that various analysts find themselves directly agreeing on a policy (without their agreeing that it is the most appropriate means to an agreed objective).
(4a) Analysis is comprehensive; every important relevant factor is taken into account.	(4b) Analysis is drastically limited: (i) Important possible outcomes are neglected. (ii) Important alternative potential policies are neglected. (iii) Important affected values are neglected.
(5a) Theory is often heavily relied upon.	(5b) A succession of comparisons greatly reduces or eliminates reliance on theory.

Assuming that the root method is familiar and understandable, we proceed directly to clarification of its alternative by contrast. In explaining the second, we shall be describing how most administrators do in fact approach complex questions, for the root method, the "best" way as a blueprint or model, is in fact not workable for complex policy questions, and administrators are forced to use the method of successive limited comparisons.

Intertwining Evaluation and Empirical Analysis (1b)

The quickest way to understand how values are handled in the method of successive limited comparisons is to see how the root method often breaks down in *its* handling of values or objectives. The idea that values should be clarified, and in advance of the examination of alternative policies, is appealing. But what happens when we attempt it for complex social problems? The first difficulty is that on many critical values or objectives, citizens disagree, congressmen disagree, and public administrators disagree. Even where a fairly specific objective is prescribed for the administrator, there remains considerable room for disagreement on subobjectives. Consider, for example, the conflict with respect to locating public housing, described in Meyerson and Banfield's study of the Chicago Housing Authority[4]—disagreement which occurred despite the clear objective of providing a certain number of public housing units in the city. Similarly conflicting are objectives in highway location, traffic control, minimum wage administration, development of tourist facilities in national parks, or insect control.

Administrators cannot escape these conflicts by ascertaining the majority's preference, for preferences have not been registered on most issues; indeed, there often *are* no preferences in the absence of public discussion sufficient to bring an issue to the attention of the electorate. Furthermore, there is a question of whether intensity of feeling should be considered as well as the number of persons preferring each alternative. By the impossibility of doing otherwise, administrators often are reduced to deciding policy without clarifying objectives first.

Even when an administrator resolves to follow his own values as a criterion for decisions, he often will not know how to rank them when they conflict with one another, as they usually do. Suppose, for example, that an administrator must relocate tenants living in tenements scheduled for destruction. One objective is to empty the buildings fairly promptly, another is to find suitable accommodation for persons displaced, another is to avoid friction with residents in other areas in which a large influx would be unwelcome, another is to deal with all concerned through persuasion if possible, and so on.

How does one state even to himself the relative importance of these partially conflicting values? A simple ranking of them is not enough; one needs ideally to know how much of one value is worth sacrificing for some of another value. The answer is that typically the administrator chooses—and must choose—directly among policies in which these values are combined in different ways. He cannot first clarify his values and then choose among policies.

A more subtle third point underlies both the first two. Social objectives do not always have the same relative values. One objective may be highly prized in one circumstance, another in another circumstance. If, for example, an administrator values highly both the dispatch with which his agency can carry through its projects *and* good public relations, it matters little which of the two possibly conflicting values he favors in some abstract or general sense. Policy questions arise in forms which put to administrators such a question as: Given the degree to which we are or are not already achieving the values of dispatch and the values of good public relations, is it worth sacrificing a little speed for a happier clientele, or is it better to risk offending the clientele so that we can get on with our work? The answer to such a question varies with circumstances.

The value problem is, as the example shows, always a problem of adjustments at a margin. But there is no practicable way to state marginal objectives or values except in terms of particular policies. That one value is preferred to another in one decision situation does not mean that it will be preferred in another decision situation in which it can be had only at great sacrifice of another value. Attempts to rank or order values in general and abstract terms so that they do not shift from decision to decision end up by ignoring the relevant marginal preferences. The significance of this third point thus goes very far. Even if all administrators had at hand an agreed set of values, objectives, and constraints, and an agreed ranking of these values, objectives, and constraints, their marginal values in actual choice situations would be impossible to formulate.

Unable consequently to formulate the relevant values first and then choose among policies to achieve them, administrators must choose directly among alternative policies that offer different marginal combinations of values. Somewhat paradoxically, the only practicable way to disclose one's relevant marginal values even to oneself is to describe the policy one chooses to achieve them. Except roughly and vaguely, I know of no way to describe—or even to understand—what my relative evaluations are for, say, freedom and security, speed and accuracy in governmental decisions, or low taxes and better schools than to describe my preferences among specific policy choices that might be made between the alternatives in each of the pairs.

In summary, two aspects of the process by which values are actually handled can be distinguished. The first is clear: Evaluation and empirical analysis are intertwined; that is, one chooses among values and among policies at one and the same time. Put a little more elaborately, one simultaneously chooses a policy to attain certain objectives and chooses the objectives themselves. The second aspect is related but distinct: The administrator focuses his attention on marginal or incremental values. Whether he is aware of it or not, he does not find general formulations of objectives very helpful and in fact makes specific marginal or incremental comparisons. Two policies, X and Y, confront him. Both promise the same degree of attainment of objectives a, b, c, d, and e. But X promises him somewhat more of f than does Y, while Y promises him somewhat more of g than does X. In choosing between them, he is in fact offered the alternative of a marginal or incremental amount of f at the expense of a marginal or incremental amount of g. The only values that are relevant to his choice are these increments by which the two policies differ; and, when he finally chooses between the two marginal values, he does so by making a choice between policies.[5]

As to whether the attempt to clarify objectives in advance of policy selection is more or less rational than the close intertwining of marginal evaluation and empirical analysis, the principal difference established is that for complex problems the first is impossible and irrelevant, and the second is both possible and relevant. The second is possible because the administrator need not try to analyze any values except the values by which alternative policies differ and need not be concerned with them except as they differ marginally. His need for information on values or objectives is drastically reduced as compared with the root method; and his capacity for grasping, comprehending, and relating values to one another is not strained beyond the breaking point.

Relations Between Means and Ends (2b)

Decision-making is ordinarily formalized as a means–end relationship: Means are conceived to be evaluated and chosen in the light of ends finally selected independently of and prior to the choice of means. This is the means–ends relationship of the root method. But it follows from all that has just been said that such a means–ends relationship is possible only to the extent that values are agreed upon, are reconcilable, and are stable at the margin. Typically, therefore, such a means–ends relationship is absent from the branch method, where means and ends are simultaneously chosen.

Yet any departure from the means–ends relationship of the root method will strike some readers as inconceivable. For it will appear to them that only in such a relationship is it possible to determine whether one policy choice is better or worse than another. How can an administrator know whether he has made a wise or foolish decision if he is without prior values or objectives by which to judge his decisions? The answer to this question calls up the third distinctive difference between root and branch methods: how to decide the best policy.

The Test of "Good" Policy (3b)

In the root method, a decision is "correct," "good," or "rational" if it can be shown to attain some specified objective, where the objective can be specified without simply describing the decision itself. Where objectives are defined only through the marginal or incremental approach to values described above, it is still sometimes possible to test whether a policy does in fact attain the desired objectives; but a precise statement of the objectives takes the form of a description of the policy chosen or some alternative to it. To show that a policy is mistaken one cannot offer an abstract argument that important objectives are not achieved; one must instead argue that another policy is more to be preferred.

So far, the departure from customary ways of looking at problem-solving is not troublesome, for many administrators will be quick to agree that the most effective discussion of the correctness of policy does take the form of comparison with other policies that might have been chosen. But what of the situation in which administrators cannot agree on values or objectives, either abstractly or in marginal terms? What then is the test of "good" policy? For the root method, there is no test. Agreement on objectives failing, there is no standard of "correctness." For the method of successive limited comparisons, the test is agreement on policy itself, which remains possible even when agreement on values is not.

It has been suggested that continuing agreement in Congress on the desirability of extending old age insurance stems from liberal desires to strengthen the welfare programs of the federal government and from conservative desires to reduce union demands for private pension plans. If so, this is an excellent demonstration of the ease with which individuals of different ideologies often can agree on concrete policy. Labor mediators report a similar phenomenon: The contestants cannot agree on criteria for settling their disputes but can agree on specific proposals. Similarly, when one administrator's objective turns out to be another's means, they often can agree on policy.

Agreement on policy thus becomes the only practicable test of the policy's correctness. And for one administrator to seek to win the other over to agreement on ends as well would accomplish nothing and create quite unnecessary controversy.

If agreement directly on policy as a test for "best" policy seems a poor substitute for testing the policy against its objectives, it ought to be remembered that objectives themselves have no ultimate validity other than they are agreed upon. Hence agreement is the test of "best" policy in both methods. But where the root method requires agreement on what elements in the decision constitute objectives and on which of these objectives should be sought, the branch method falls back on agreement wherever it can be found.

In an important sense, therefore, it is not irrational for an administrator to defend a policy as good without being able to specify what it is good for.

Noncomprehensive Analysis (4b)

Ideally, rational–comprehensive analysis leaves out nothing important. But it is impossible to take everything important into consideration unless "important" is so narrowly defined that analysis is in fact quite limited. Limits on human intellectual capacities and on available information set definite limits to man's capacity to be comprehensive. In actual fact, therefore, no one can practice the rational–comprehensive method for really complex problems, and every administrator faced with a sufficiently complex problem must find ways drastically to simplify.

An administrator assisting in the formulation of agricultural economic policy cannot in the first place be competent on all possible policies. He cannot even comprehend one policy entirely. In planning a soil bank program, he cannot successfully anticipate the impact of higher or lower farm income on, say, urbanization—the possible consequent loosening of family ties, possible consequent eventual need for revisions in social security and further implications for tax problems arising out of new federal responsibilities for social security and municipal responsibilities for urban services. Nor, to follow another line of repercussions, can he work through the soil bank program's effects on prices for agricultural products in foreign markets and consequent implications for foreign relations, including those arising out of economic rivalry between the United States and the U.S.S.R.

In the method of successive limited comparisons, simplification is systematically achieved in two principal ways. First, it is achieved through limitation of policy comparisons to those policies that differ in relatively small degree from policies presently in effect. Such a limitation immediately reduces the number of alternatives to be investigated and also drastically simplifies the character of the investigation of each. For it is not necessary to undertake fundamental inquiry into an alternative and its consequences; it is necessary only to study those respects in which the proposed alternative and its consequences differ from the status quo. The empirical comparison of marginal differences among alternative policies that differ only marginally is, of course, a counterpart to the incremental or marginal comparison of values discussed above.[6]

Relevance as Well as Realism—It is a matter of common observation that in Western democracies public administrators and policy analysts in general do largely limit their analyses to incremental or marginal differences in policies that are chosen to differ only incrementally. They do not do so, however, solely because they desperately need some way to simplify their problems; they also do so in order to be relevant. Democracies change their policies almost entirely through incremental adjustments. Policy does not move in leaps and bounds.

The incremental character of political change in the United States has often been remarked. The two major political parties agree on fundamentals; they offer alternative policies to the voters only on relatively small points of difference. Both parties favor full employment, but they define it somewhat differently; both favor the development of water power resources, but in slightly different ways; and both favor unemployment compensation, but not the same level of benefits. Similarly, shifts of policy within a party take place largely through a series of relatively small changes, as can be seen in their only gradual acceptance of the idea of governmental responsibility for support of the unemployed, a change in party positions beginning in the early thirties and culminating in a sense in the Employment Act of 1946.

Party behavior is in turn rooted in public attitudes, and political theorists cannot conceive of democracy's surviving in the United States in the absence of fundamental agreement on potentially disruptive issues, with consequent limitation of policy debates to relatively small differences in policy.

Since the policies ignored by the administrator are politically impossible and so irrelevant, the simplification of analysis achieved by concentrating on policies that differ only incrementally is not a capricious kind of simplification. In addition, it can be argued that, given the limits on knowledge within which policy-makers are confined, simplifying by limiting the focus to small variations from present policy makes the most of available knowledge. Because policies being considered are like present and past policies, the administrator can obtain information and claim some insight. Nonincremental policy proposals are therefore typically not only politically irrelevant but also unpredictable in their consequences.

The second method of simplification of analysis is the practice of ignoring important possible consequences of possible policies, as well as the values attached to the neglected consequences. If this appears to disclose a shocking shortcoming of successive limited comparisons, it can be replied that, even if the exclusions are random, policies may nevertheless be more intelligently formulated than through futile attempts to achieve a comprehensiveness beyond human capacity. Actually, however, the exclusions, seeming arbitrary or random from one point of view, need be neither.

Achieving a Degree of Comprehensiveness—Suppose that each value neglected by one policy-making agency were a major concern of at least one other agency. In that case, a helpful division of labor would be achieved, and no agency need find its task beyond its capacities. The shortcomings of such a system would be that one agency might destroy a value either before another agency could be activated to safeguard it or in spite of another agency's efforts. But the possibility that important values may be lost is present in any form of organization, even where agencies attempt to comprehend in planning more than is humanly possible.

The virtue of such a hypothetical division of labor is that every important interest or value has its watchdog. And these watchdogs can protect the interests in their jurisdiction in two quite different ways: first, by redressing damages done by other agencies; and, second, by anticipating and heading off injury before it occurs.

In a society like that of the United States in which individuals are free to combine to pursue almost any possible common interest they might have and in which government agencies are sensitive to the pressures of these groups, the system described is approximated. Almost every interest has its watchdog. Without claiming that every interest has a sufficiently powerful watchdog, it can be argued that our system often can assure a more comprehensive regard for the values of the whole society than any attempt at intellectual comprehensiveness.

In the United States, for example, no part of government attempts a comprehensive overview of policy on income distribution. A policy nevertheless evolves, and one responding to a wide variety of interests.

A process of mutual adjustment among farm groups, labor unions, municipalities and school boards, tax authorities, and government agencies with responsibilities in the fields of housing, health, highways, national parks, fire, and police accomplishes a distribution of income in which particular income problems neglected at one point in the decision processes become central at another point.

Mutual adjustment is more pervasive than the explicit forms it takes in negotiation between groups; it persists through the mutual impacts of groups upon each other even where they are not in communication. For all the imperfections and latent dangers in this ubiquitous process of mutual adjustment, it will often accomplish an adaptation of policies to a wider range of interests than could be done by one group centrally.

Note, too, how the incremental pattern of policy-making fits with the multiple pressure pattern. For when decisions are only incremental—closely related to known policies—it is easier for one group to anticipate the kind of moves another might make and easier too for it to make correction for injury already accomplished.[7]

Even partisanship and narrowness, to use pejorative terms, will sometimes be assets to rational decision-making, for they can doubly insure that what one agency neglects, another will not; they specialize personnel to distinct points of view. The claim is valid that effective rational co-ordination of the federal administration, if possible to achieve at all, would require an agreed set of values[8]—if "rational" is defined as the practice of the root method of decision-making. But a high degree of administrative coordination occurs as each agency adjusts its policies to the concerns of the other agencies in the process of fragmented decision-making I have just described.

For all the apparent shortcomings of the incremental approach to policy alternatives with its arbitrary exclusion coupled with fragmentation, when compared to the root method, the branch method often looks far superior. In the root method, the inevitable exclusion of factors is accidental, unsystematic, and not defensible by any argument so far developed, while in the branch method the exclusions are deliberate, systematic, and defensible. Ideally, of course, the root method does not exclude; in practice it must.

Nor does the branch method necessarily neglect long-run considerations and objectives. It is clear that important values must be omitted in considering policy, and sometimes the only way long-run objectives can be given adequate attention is through the neglect of short-run considerations. But the values omitted can be either long-run or short-run.

Succession of Comparisons (5b)

The final distinctive element in the branch method is that the comparisons, together with the policy choice, proceed in a chronological series. Policy is not made once and for all; it is made and re-made end-lessly. Policy-making is a process of successive approximation to some desired objectives in which what is desired itself continues to change under reconsideration.

Making policy is at best a very rough process. Neither social scientists, nor politicians, nor public administrators yet know enough about the social world to avoid repeated error in predicting the consequences of policy moves. A wise policy-maker consequently expects that his policies will achieve only part of what he hopes and at the same time will produce unanticipated consequences he would have preferred to avoid. If he proceeds through a *succession* of incremental changes, he avoids serious lasting mistakes in several ways.

In the first place, past sequences of policy steps have given him knowledge about the probable consequences of further similar steps. Second, he need not attempt big jumps toward his goals that would require predictions beyond his or anyone else's knowledge, because he never expects his policy to be a final resolution of a problem. His decision is only one step, one that if successful can quickly be followed by another. Third, he is in effect able to test his previous predictions as he moves on to each further step. Lastly, he often can remedy a past error fairly quickly—more quickly than if policy proceeded through more distinct steps widely spaced in time.

Compare this comparative analysis of incremental changes with the aspiration to employ theory in the root method. Man cannot think without classifying, without subsuming one experience under a more general category of experiences. The attempt to push categorization as far as possible and to find general propositions which can be applied to specific situations is what I refer to with the word "theory." Where root analysis often leans heavily on theory in this sense, the branch method does not.

The assumption of root analysts is that theory is the most systematic and economical way to bring relevant knowledge to bear on a specific problem. Granting the assumption, an unhappy fact is that we do not have adequate theory to apply to problems in any policy area, although theory is more adequate in some areas—monetary policy, for example—than in others. Comparative analysis, as in the branch method, is some-times a systematic alternative to theory.

Suppose an administrator must choose among a small group of policies that differ only incrementally from each other and from present policy. He might aspire to "understand" each of the alternatives—for example, to know all the consequences of each aspect of each policy. If so, he would indeed require theory. In fact, however, he would usually decide that, *for policy-making purposes*, he need know, as explained above, only the consequences of each of those aspects of the policies in which they differed from one another. For this much more modest aspiration, he requires no theory (although it might be helpful, if available), for he can proceed to isolate probable differences by examining the differences in consequences associated with past differences in policies, a feasible program because he can take his observations from a long sequence of incremental changes.

For example, without a more comprehensive social theory about juvenile delinquency than scholars have yet produced, one cannot possibly understand the ways in which a variety of public policies—say on education, housing, recreation, employment, race relations, and policing—might encourage or discourage delinquency. And one needs such an understanding if he undertakes the comprehensive overview of the problem prescribed in the models of the root method. If, however, one merely wants to mobilize knowledge sufficient to assist in a choice among a small group of similar policies—alternative policies on juvenile court procedures, for example—he can do so by comparative analysis of the results of similar past policy moves.

THEORISTS AND PRACTITIONERS

This difference explains—in some cases at least—why the administrator often feels that the outside expert or academic problem-solver is sometimes not helpful and why they in turn often urge more theory on him. And it explains why an administrator often feels more confident when "flying by the seat of his pants" than when following the advice of theorists. Theorists often ask the administrator to go the long way round to the solution of his problems, in effect ask him to follow the best canons of the scientific method, when the administrator knows that the best available theory will work less well than more modest incremental comparisons. Theorists do not realize that the administrator is often in fact practicing a systematic method. It would be foolish to push this explanation too far, for sometimes practical decision-makers are pursuing neither a theoretical approach nor successive comparisons, nor any other systematic method.

It may be worth emphasizing that theory is sometimes of extremely limited helpfulness in policy-making for at least two rather different reasons. It is greedy for facts; it can be constructed only through a great collection of observations. And it is typically insufficiently precise for application to a policy process that moves through small changes. In contrast, the comparative method both economizes on the need for facts and directs the analyst's attention to just those facts that are relevant to the fine choices faced by the decision-maker.

With respect to precision of theory, economic theory serves as an example. It predicts that an economy without money or prices would in certain specified ways misallocate resources, but this finding pertains to an alternative far removed from the kind of policies on which administrators need help. On the other hand, it is not precise enough to predict the consequences of policies restricting business mergers, and this is the kind of issue on which the administrators need help. Only in relatively restricted areas does economic theory achieve sufficient precision to go far in resolving policy questions; its helpfulness in policy-making is always so limited that it requires supplementation through comparative analysis.

SUCCESSIVE COMPARISON AS A SYSTEM

Successive limited comparisons is, then, indeed a method or system; it is not a failure of method for which administrators ought to apologize. None the less, its imperfections, which have not been explored in this paper, are many. For example, the method is without a built-in safeguard for all relevant values, and it also may lead the decision-maker to over-look excellent policies for no other reason than that they are not suggested by the chain of successive policy steps leading up to the present. Hence, it ought to be said that under this method, as well as under some of the most sophisticated variants of the root method—operations research, for example—policies will continue to be as foolish as they are wise.

Why then bother to describe the method in all the above detail? Because it is in fact a common method of policy formulation, and is, for complex problems, the principal reliance of administrators as well as of other policy analysts.[9] And because it will be superior to any other decision-making method available for complex problems in many circumstances, certainly superior to a futile attempt at superhuman comprehensiveness. The reaction of the public administrator to the exposition of method doubtless will be less a discovery of a new method than a better acquaintance with an old. But by becoming more conscious of their practice of this method, administrators might practice it with more skill and know when to extend or constrict its use. (That they sometimes practice it effectively and sometimes not may explain the extremes of opinion on "muddling through," which is both praised as a highly sophisticated form of problem-solving and denounced as no method at all. For I suspect that in so far as there is a system in what is known as "muddling through," this method is it.)

One of the noteworthy incidental consequences of clarification of the method is the light it throws on the suspicion an administrator sometimes entertains that a consultant or adviser is not speaking relevantly and responsibly when in fact by all ordinary objective evidence he is. The trouble lies in the fact that most of us approach policy problems within a framework given by our view of a chain of successive policy choices made up to the present. One's thinking about appropriate policies with respect, say, to urban traffic control is greatly influenced by one's knowledge of the incremental steps taken up to the present. An administrator enjoys an intimate knowledge of his past sequences that "outsiders" do not share, and his thinking and that of the "outsider" will consequently be different in ways that may puzzle both. Both may appear to be talking intelligently, yet each may find the other unsatisfactory. The relevance of the policy chain of succession is even more clear when an American tries to discuss, say, antitrust policy with a Swiss, for the chains of policy in the two countries are strikingly different and the two individuals consequently have organized their knowledge in quite different ways.

If this phenomenon is a barrier to communication, an understanding of it promises an enrichment of intellectual interaction in policy formulation. Once the source of difference is understood, it will sometimes be stimulating for an administrator to seek out a policy analyst whose recent experience is with a policy chain different from his own.

This raises again a question only briefly discussed above on the merits of like-mindedness among government administrators. While much of organization theory argues the virtues of common values and agreed organizational objectives, for complex problems in which the root method is inapplicable, agencies will want among their own personnel two types of diversification: administrators whose thinking is organized by reference to policy chains other than those familiar to most members of the organization, and, even more commonly, administrators whose professional or personal values or interests create diversity of view (perhaps coming from different specialties, social classes, geographical areas) so that, even within a single agency, decision-making can be fragmented and parts of the agency can serve as watchdogs for other parts.

Part Three

The Political Institutions

*P*olitical participants are, in the final analysis, persons. But these persons also usually represent various agencies, organizations, government institutions, or even the governments themselves, such as cities, states, or nations. The nature of the relationships between these loyalties has a great impact on policy development and policy outcome. These basic relationships in the United States are established by the Constitution, but this has not forestalled innumerable problems, both intragovernmental and intergovernmental.

The fact that the United States has a federal system of government has many implications for governmental policy and administration. Stationary natural resources, such as land minerals, may have several governments concerned about their use or condition at the same time. Mobile resources, such as wildlife, water, or fish, may have different sets of rules applied to them at different times. And a resource may vary in character: Water can be used for irrigation or for a certain urban need, which brings up the question of its governance and regulation by two different levels of government. In addition, because many natural resources (i.e., water, oil or forests) are claimed as proprietary by different governments, different sets of laws have different levels of applicability and importance.

A contemporary view of federalism sees it as a cooperative system. Years ago Morton Grodzins convinced us that "the American system is best conceived as one government serving one people."* He pointed out that all levels of government participate in providing the various services which people demand.

Though cooperation is recognized as the norm in American federal relations, it is not without its squeak points—nor does it function successfully for all issues. The multitude of natural resources issues abound in case histories of unsolved problems or poorly resolved decisions resulting, to a large degree, from the complexities of federalism. Often the sheer number of governments involved creates serious problems.

*From "The American Federal System" in Robert A. Goldwin (ed.), *A Nation of States,* Chicago: Rand, McNally and Co., 1963, p. 23.

In this part the selections point out the problems which result from multigovernment policy-making and the nature of our institutions. The article by Norton Long is concerned with multigovernmental action and environmental pollution. Morton Grodzins' selection is a federal report indicating the wide variety of governmental and private interests that can focus on one issue. An anonymous author writes of the desirability of reorganizing all of the federal resource agencies into a single department. And also included is the important message of President Nixon on the environment, in which he emphasizes increased governmental awareness and interest in our natural resources.

Norton E. Long

New Tasks for All Levels
of Government*

The subject of environmental quality ranges from the health hazards of water and air pollution to the eyesores of billboards and junk yards. Accordingly, agreement on what constitutes quality varies from subject to subject. Indeed, what constitutes hazard is a matter not only of dispute among laymen but even among the experts. Despite the impressive statistical evidence, even the experts still exhibit significant disagreement about the effects of smoking. The improvement of environmental quality requires, as at least an initial condition, some sufficient concern on the part of important elements of the public with its present and likely future condition. The highly individualistic, every-man-for-himself, ideology has only recently given way to belated recognition of its practical impossibility in an increasingly crowded urban environment.

Present governmental structure reflects a past whose problems could be dealt with in limited areas and with limited resources. The problems of environmental quality, except where approaching the catastrophic, are poorly recognized in the conventional wisdom and are ill-adapted to receive appropriate recognition through the existing structure of government, especially at state and local levels. A glance at the appropriations and staffing for air pollution control at state and local levels outside of California indicates that whatever the objective facts, public recognition and appreciation is a needed precondition for governmental action.

We are today in the process of changing the governmental structure of the United States in such a way that the diversity of environmental values will receive more effective representation in the decision-making structure of government.

The United States has become an overwhelmingly urban and preponderantly metropolitan nation, and will in all probability become overwhelmingly metropolitan. It is certainly clear that the institutions developed in Anglo–American constitutional history were not designed to

*Reprinted by permission from *Environmental Quality in a Growing Economy*, Henry Jarrett, ed. (The Johns Hopkins Press, 1966), 141–155. © 1966, The Johns Hopkins Press, for Resources for the Future.

deal with either the technology or the emergent culture of the modern United States.

Certain kinds of conflicts are built into the effort to maintain or improve the environment. Insofar as we think of the environment as physical, solutions usually are possible. But it is not enough to know the appropriate technical means; the area in which the methods are to be applied must be sufficiently comprehensive to permit a solution. Consequently, at the level of technical competence there is need for different areal solutions. This raises a whole string of questions about the propriety of governments being multipurpose affairs. Furthermore, it is very difficult to satisfy all the lines of preference, let alone optimize on them, because the preferences themselves are in conflict. We do not have any clear-cut common set of values.

Americans are only now in the business of building such values. Today these values have much more potentiality for being given political recognition than they have had previously. The Vietnamese war and possibilities of further escalation apart, our society can afford considerable expenditures to achieve kinds of qualities we desire if we can become sufficiently united in desiring certain kinds of end products of public goods. The problem is one of how to develop a sufficient amount of public support at the right level that has the resource capability, the political power, and the legal jurisdiction to take the kind of actions that the technical people say are required for accomplishing these purposes.

I rather suspect that the answer is largely a matter of leadership—of providing some kinds of new standards for people who up to the present had thought they were doing pretty well. Disagreement among the experts may be one of the major problems that the politicians have to face. A country that has so little concern about the environment of its lungs in the face of the statistics produced by the Surgeon General is likely to be less impressed, I think, with the question of the environment outside its lungs.

If we could move to a Brave New World in which we could simply say, "We trust our experts; they know;" we should not wait for scientific evidence. If we had even scientific fears, that would be enough: We would act immediately, even if the consequences affected life a hundred years ahead. But if we should do all this we would be very gravely changing the quality of the American political life.

That kind of asserted claim for the authority of the experts goes beyond any scientific warrant in terms of public verifiability or of the way in which conclusions can be arrived at. I think concern with this is one of the reasons why many of those who haven't been trained to middle-class acquiescence in expertise voted in a hostile fashion in the fluoridation referenda that Gilbert White mentions in his essay.*

*See his selection, "Formation and Role of Public Attitudes," in this volume, Part Five.

We are moving into a society whose politics are going to be characterized by half-educated members of the middle class who have been able to afford to go to some kind of college. We can expect that as a result there will be a considerable increase in demand for expertise, and in docility before expertise.

Nonetheless, we must not let this carry us to the point where the voting public ceases to be deeply concerned with measures for checking on the experts and verifying their conclusions on what should be controlled and what should not be controlled, instead of just assuming that the doctor knows best, rather than the patient. As citizens we are patients, and while in every case the expert may know a great deal more than the patient about some one subject, every expert is himself a patient outside of his expertise. Our society is made up of the nonexperts in area after area, and these areas will grow as expertise grows. One of the deepest of current problems is that of how to maintain a democratic society in a world of experts in which the democratic society can be reasonably convinced that it is being persuaded rather than manipulated, and in which the institutions that generate, criticize, and control the expertise are adequate. Only then can society repose some kind of faith that the scientific processes that are being carried on are adequate and credible, and the intellectual processes by which people make decisions are not those of achieving consensus through crisis, through fear and through manipulation.

We have as a society been manipulated and we are being manipulated; this is being done by people who, with the best of intentions and in a great hurry, are concerned about the way in which they can save us from our folly.

Our traditional structure of government is to a very considerable extent designed to maximize vetoes, to maximize our capacity for saying "No," for disrupting, for preventing things from happening. This has its uses, but from the point of view of accomplishing things, and doing urgently needed things, it is a very serious liability. Changes are in order, and there are signs that a beginning is being made.

A major federal function is the activation of local publics whose existence makes possible the realistic political enterprise of pressing for needed public goods that have been underevaluated or not valued at all. The density and communication nets of elite populations at the Washington–New York political and media level make it possible to exert style leadership that is usually only feasible under the gun of dire necessity elsewhere. Rachel Carson's *Silent Spring,* like Upton Sinclair's *The Jungle,* could have far greater impact on the elite national media and the relevant Washington elites than it would have in most state capitals. A major policy initiative for Washington is the determination of what is the case, the dissemination in intelligible form of the facts and what they mean, and the development of standards as to minimal goals and further ranges of desirability. As Franklin Roosevelt once said, the Presidency is the best pulpit in the land and the message on environmental quality can nowhere be given more effective attention.

The job is one of giving saliency to neglected but potentially popular political issues and thus making it possible and even necessary for state and local politicians to take up the task of moving the issues at the local level. National politicians, elected and bureaucratic, at any rate some of them, have constituencies—both local and those reached through the media—that make various aspects of environmental quality feasible and attractive public goods for them to promote.

Their constituencies may often conflict, as would be the case with the automotive industry and its governmental allies and those seeking to enforce expensive devices to lessen exhaust fumes. The range of forces lined up pro and con on the issue of pesticides is illustrative of the internal conflict that differing bureaucratic constituencies produce within the federal establishment. But the fact that manufacturers and farmers fail to stifle inconvenient protests underlines the peculiar value of Washington as a center for wide and varied representation of positions that only achieve strength and visibility in a national theater.

There is some evidence that the President is aware of the highly limited range of the indicators that are at present included in his reports to the Congress and the public. The statistics are narrowly economic and even narrow within economics. A State of the Union message that deals with a more inclusive and more broadly relevant body of data representing the human condition is badly needed. The philistinism that has concerned itself more with statistical accuracy than relevance, and that has eschewed the qualitatively significant for the quantitatively measurable, distorts the public definitions of the situations that confront us. We are in important ways the prisoners of the measures that now determine the facts we collect and hence the limited and peculiar range of facts to which we attend.

Indicators of environmental quality need to be built into the national public reporting system at the Presidential level. This would be a major policy and institutional change, for it would place front and center a definition of what the situation is and what it is becoming. The fact that measurements cannot be precisely made is no excuse for not making them, especially if what is possible is vastly better than doing nothing. We need to realize that standards are tools that serve our purposes and are created out of human efforts. They do not emerge fully accredited from nature. To await such a miracle is to avoid the necessary political task of hammering out agreement on purposes and the necessarily imperfect, but improvable, means of their attainment.

As the disposer of the greatest poll of relatively painlessly collected tax surplus in the country, the federal government has the greatest freedom from fiscal constraint in its initiatives. As the jurisdiction that includes all others, the federal government internalizes the costs of the ills of environmental quality and the benefits from their removal. The United States can meaningfully calculate the costs of man days lost through illness or strikes and the gain in national product from the reduction of these limitations on the economy's performance. Similarly, the costs of air pollution and the inefficiencies of waste disposal are at least roughly calculable and the benefits, including increased federal fiscal resources from the reduction of this filth, are subject to determination sufficiently persuasive to suffice for rational policy-making. We have long since realized that repetitive flood hazards are worth dealing with even though federal rather than local funds carry the lion's share of the burden.

A Milton Friedman type of analysis might suggest that the particularized investment of the nation's capital in a particular area amounts to an unsound interference with free market determination of location. There is merit in the concern that federal policy with respect to environmental quality may become another rivers and harbors or urban renewal program in which the logic of political expediency becomes the paramount logic. A contest for limited prizes can be the reality that masquerades under the cloud of general national policy. The political arithmetic of the situation could result in the illusion of a national policy and the reality of an expedient division of the loaves and the fishes. Yet the stimulation of the public appetite may be the first prerequisite to sufficient public support for adequate funding to pursue a truly national policy. Alternatively the winners of the contest for federal prizes may produce demonstrations that will inspire other local governments to emulate them even at their own expense.

Ambiguities as to which of these two policies are intended by federal politicians are rife in many national programs. The Poverty Program with its initial 90 per cent and subsequently diminishing federal share is a good example. No one knows for sure whether the federal phase-out is a gambit to pass the legislation through Congress that will be removed if public demand develops in the way hoped for, or whether it is just bait to get local governments to increase and enter into new programs that they will then have to fund from their own resources.

At one level the ambiguities in policy can be regarded as part of the national process of search by which individual and institutional actors respond to challenges and opportunities in the environment. Just as the mixed bag of contradictory policies thrown up by the New Deal seemed to offend against rational planning so today's mixed bag is likely to look like so much expedient politics as the actors involved in air and water pollution, pesticides, urban transport, blight, and aesthetics maneuver for advantage in terms of their various perspectives. The politically expedient is a mainspring of the technology through which we get things done. The number of tries is related to the likelihood that one of them will work and catch on if our social editing devices destroy the monsters and the drones that are bound to be produced. The Darwinism of social adjustment to change looks crude and untidy, but we lack alternatives.

Given the ambiguity of policy, those with a purpose in mind must press for its clarification. The federal policies in agriculture, rivers and harbors, and urban renewal are so many examples of a manifest policy that merely covers the satisfaction of latent pressure group ends. Whether broad general publics concerned with manifest goals can overcome their distortion by latent pressure group interests is always problematic. The likely payoff is in terms of symbolic recognition of broad goals with material representation of narrower purposes entertained by those capable of mobilizing sustained influence at critical places. Representation of environmental quality goals requires their institutionalization in the committees of Congress, the bureaucracy and the routines of the President.

From the point of view of the federal bureaucracy, the various aspects of environmental quality are so many items of new or expanded business. These items represent opportunities for some, threats for others. Minimally, as additional charges on the budget, they contend for scarce resources with other end items as diverse as the moon race and the war in Vietnam. In addition, they throw the apple of discord into the bureaucracy as departments and bureaus contend for jurisdiction. The departments and their bureaus are deeply set in institutionalized habits of thought and procedure. In addition, their allies, both among pressure groups and the organs of state and local governments, insure differential representation of interests, values and points of view. It was for reasons such as these that the friends of urban transportation legislation fought long and hard to keep their enterprise from the Department of Commerce and its committees on the Hill. The fragmentation of the aspects of environmental quality control among the federal departments presents ultimate problems of program coordination among institutions who not only compete among themselves, but are frequently committed to buttressing the status quo of their local friends. Appraisal of the alternatives for the institutionalization of the various aspects of environmental quality control in Washington requires a shrewd appreciation of the facts of bureaucratic life.

The contenders for a share in the emerging political market for environmental quality control are first and foremost the departments of Housing and Urban Development; Health, Education and Welfare; Commerce; Interior; Agriculture; and Labor; with the rest, such as NASA and the Department of Defense, competitors for funds and objects for coordination rather than principals. However, even here, recognition should be given to DOD's role in sparking the poverty program, and its interest in alternative markets for its suppliers in the event of military cutbacks. In the short run, DOD and NASA are likely to appear in an adversary role in their claims against the budget for Vietnam and space. The hearings before the Reuss committee indicate that the Administration is not likely to support a shift in research and development expenditures toward the solution of environmental problems. Some testimony went to show that further research made little sense until present knowledge had been utilized. Whether the attitude toward R & D expenditures would extend to federal funding to secure greater use of existing knowledge is logically a separate question. However, given Vietnam, a negative response seems likely. Of course Vietnam and a major Asian war overhang not just environmental quality control programs but the Great Society and society itself. Down the road, funds freed from DOD and possibly NASA will be available as well as other funds from growth in federal tax income.

Among the federal competitors for the job of environmental quality control, the Housing and Urban Development Department seems the most likely candidate for the job of administration and coordination. Health, Education, and Welfare, as the federal government's health department and the locus of the Public Health Service, will certainly have a technical research and in all probability some administrative concern with the health aspects of air and water pollution. Commerce's failure to capture urban transportation was a victory for the central cities and a blow to the Bureau of Public Roads and its allies. The conflict between central cities and suburbs is embedded in the constituencies of the two agencies. Suburbs, state governments, and the Bureau of Public Roads have long worked together. The effects of the "one man— one vote" doctrine will increase suburban power in state legislatures and decrease that of central cities.

The importance of the conflict between central cities and suburbs is not limited to probable acute differences over desirable transportation policy. Choice of emphasis on rail and mass transit will have major consequences for air pollution as well as transport. Beyond this, and even more important, the central city forces are likely to support regional approaches to transport planning. The success of mass transit depends on such an approach. As Lyle Fitch and his associates have pointed out, effective transport planning implies land use control. Such control is also highly desirable for any effective waste disposal or air pollution control program. There are joint political costs involved and there may well need to be a critical governmental press for an effective coordinated attack to be possible.

The constituency of the Housing and Urban Development Department is likely to be the 212 metropolitan areas where the bulk of our population already live and will increasingly live. This constituency is also the constituency of the President and it forms a vital element in the constituency of most senators. At present these 212 metropolitan areas are more census statistics than political entities. They are, however, potential communities. They share common problems whose effective solution may require common action of an area-wide nature. Of course there is no certainty that shared problems will produce a cooperation rather than adversary and divisive action. There are powerful reasons limiting cooperation to piecemeal and ad hoc palliatives.

Most federal programs have been directed at urban areas, and one might even say most federal programs have been piecemeal, ad hoc, and by way of exceptional interventions. These actions have been taken through the spending power with some constitutional bad conscience. While marble-cake federalism is currently gaining a measure of acceptance, the normal view was one of fairly clear-cut separation of levels and appropriate competences of government. Federal intervention still raises hackles. The ideology of sovereign states with their local governments was compounded by the general lip service to the politico-economic ideology of *laissez faire*. A truly national government has emerged from a federation of states without a theory to replace the outworn ideology, and this national government is groping towards the creation of a *national* system of local government compounded of the inherited political institutions, the pattern of state and local government. Much of what has been done in the past has served to buttress the institutional status quo by fiscally bailing it out and making it viable. There are now signs of impatience with this result and awareness of the need and possibility to exert creative pressure for the restructuring of our local institutions and the creation of a national system of local government responsive to the range of demands that are nationally salient but require local implementation.

A major force working against restructuring local governments into regional patterns whose resources and territories would be more adequate to achieve control of the quality of the physical environment is the deep-rooted desire to maintain inequalities in the human environment. Our society is committed to the two conflicting norms of equality and achievement. The commitment to equality has meant formal and increasingly substantive equality among citizens. The commitment to achievement has meant inequality among incomes. The latter in the past has been given effect mainly through the market by the device of rationing through price. With the increasing significance of public goods, e.g. schools, the problem has been how to give effect to unequal incomes in their consumption. The equality norm among citizens has presented increasing obstacles to providing a differential range of public goods to differing income holders in the same jurisdiction. While in the past and to a considerable degree today, public goods are not equalized to all citizens in the same jurisdiction, the pressure and the burdens mount. The answer to the problem has been found in the territorial segregation of public goods consumption—in a word, suburbs.

Those who would like control of the physical quality of the environment, air and water pollution, and even transport, are fearful of the further political consequences of creating institutions of the power and comprehensiveness requisite to the job. Metropolitan Toronto was a spectacular success as long as its George Washington Gardener was able to keep to sewerage, water and transport. A metropolitan public works department headed by a Bob Moses with a staff like that of the Port of New York Authority is a viable middle-class ideal. But now that Toronto is moving from concrete to redistribution, the success story is running into difficulties. As things are, housing determines education, education determines jobs and marriage, jobs and marriage determine income, and income determines housing. As a number of political scientists and sociologists have begun to point out, the metropolitan area is an admirable array of governments with differential services to fit the pocketbook of our range of incomes. One buys one's house or rents one's apartment and the government goes with it, like membership in the country club. Most important, a quality school goes with a quality neighborhood, and the differential exposure of one's children to those one feels will do them the most good in work, socializing, and matrimony. This is a highly desired quality of an environment.

It is only to be expected that those for whom the quality of the environment that counts is access to housing, schools, jobs, income, and upward mobility should wish to use governmental change as a means to promote a breakthrough into the charmed circle. Those, on the other hand, who benefit from their position in the charmed circle by differential access to the opportunity structure, are highly reluctant to countenance its change. Suburbs are frequently willing to avail themselves of city water and sewerage, but resist bitterly central city attempts to use these assets as leverage to bring about annexation or a redistribution of public burdens. Suburbs are also fearful of extension of mass transit, because lowered cost of transport might produce a change in their population mix. On the other hand, central city Negroes with increasing political power are less and less willing to risk this increase of power through dilution in a white metropolitan area.

Given the suburban goals, it is readily understandable that piecemeal ad hoc solutions, single purpose districts, authorities, and unifunctional governmental departments make sense. The existing pattern of federal intervention has followed this line. Areal impacts of Washington programs have been coordinated neither nationally nor in the field. The Bureau of Public Roads and the Housing Agency have frequently worked at cross-purposes. They and their allies in the states and local government have shown remarkably little interest in regional planning. Some lip service is now being given to the desirability of meshing programs to produce long-term foreseeable regional results. In the past, and to a large extent still, programs have been used to provide federal aid for favored participants in the battle to preserve and enhance positions in the local status quo. Thus urban renewal has frequently been used by hard-pressed central city mayors to bulldoze out segments of their "tax eating" poor and replace them with the inhabitants of low service, high tax yield, luxury apartments. Even highway programs have been used as a kind of ruthless form of slum clearance.

A further problem for the improvement of environmental quality beyond the conflict over the politics of redistribution stems from the capabilities and motivations of local governments and their inhabitants. In our highly and increasingly mobile society, the marginal commitment of many residents makes long-term investment in major public goods a dubious proposition. As on the old frontier, the modern frontiersman of suburbia finds the solution to his problems in wearing the shine off his FHA- or VA-insured mortgaged tract house and escaping the consequences of the septic tank culture by moving on. Public officials responding to such constituencies are rarely in a position to live for more than from hand to mouth even when they are technically competent to entertain more professional standards of civic housekeeping. Again the resources of suburbia have not even a close fit with governmental needs.

The marginal middle class, the upper working class mortgaged to the hilt for housing and consumer capital goods, has more than enough to handle in meeting the sharply mounting school costs its child-centered culture entails. The cycle of septic tanks, piecemeal low-cost inadequate solutions, and eventual areal solutions with cumulatively mounting costs is typical. Experience in the Seattle metropolitan area and in that of Minneapolis–St. Paul indicates that even highly educated suburbs heavily discount the future. Of course, it is standard to show little concern for the sewerage that pollutes one's neighbors' beaches and water supply. Detroit and the state of Michigan hold Chicago to account before the Supreme Court for diverting waters of Lake Michigan to dilute and divert its sewage while merrily polluting Lake Erie themselves.

Local governments are afflicted with what Edward Banfield termed the moral basis of a backward society immoral familism. In plain English this means every man for himself and the devil take the hindermost. If all could be trusted to cooperate, all might benefit and the game would be transformed from zero sum to multiple payoff. However, when the edifice of trust is hopelessly shaky or nonexistent, Machiavelli is the better guide. Indeed, a regional plan which locates the industrial park in one town and the open space in another, and fails to provide for the pooling of tax yield is an exercise in utopian futility. The existing structure of local government is territorially and fiscally inadequate to undertake in any major way to improve the quality of the environment. The very well-meaning conferences and the useful informal relations among the professionals of local government can do little more than help the status quo to rock along.

Beyond the adequacy of territorial and fiscal resources, local governments are limited by the availability of elite populations, institutions and media to sustain the kinds of concern involved in improving the quality of enviroments in other than response to crisis and on piecemeal and ad hoc bases. The problems to which governments attend are as James G. Coke has shown likely to be phenomena of scale. Coke (in *The Lesser Metropolitan Areas of Illinois,* University of Illinois Institute of Government and Public Affairs, 1962) found that the smaller cities of Illinois were suffering from all the problems of core decay, grey areas, and suburban sprawl that afflicted the large metropolis. However, the problems of these smaller cities failed to achieve articulation by reason of lack of density of relevant elite population of architects, planners and groups likely to form citizens' housing councils and like organizations. Local government fragmentation can have the effect of so dispersing elite populations and limiting media effect in concentrating issues that concern with the improvement of environment quality is politically realistic only at the level of the national government and some central cities.

The realistic promotion of improvement in the quality of environment is most likely to achieve its lead from Washington. The Housing and Urban Development Department promises to become the American equivalent of a ministry of local government. The federal carrot and stick can be used to promote the reality of planning at the metropolitan level and, where technically required by the problem, in jurisdictions that include relevant watersheds or drainage basins.

Improving the quality of the environment in the 212 metropolitan areas where most of the people of the United States live is a realistic objective for the new agency. If, as is projected, it regionalizes to these areas and staffs its regional executives at the assistant secretary level, it has an excellent chance of becoming the chosen arm for presidential field coordination. Should the President use the department in this way, the President would for the first time have an instrument for effectuating the field coordination and the Washington coordination of the impact of the disparate federal programs on our cities.

The tools available range from personnel to funds for planning, housing, public facilities, highways, and research. Federal funds in the past have not been used to promote governmental integration at the local level. Constitutional scruples may still cause some to shy away from a deliberately concerted federal effort to restructure local government so as to make it more effective in promoting improvement in the quality of the environment. Doubtless, there will be considerable circumlocution in the public relations presentation of the objective. Some such device as the "workable program" concept developed in urban renewal (though the latter has tended to be a sham) could be adapted to planning and effectuating regional sewerage and water programs, transportation, air pollution, housing, open space, and such other federally assisted local programs as need regional planning effectively carried into action to amount to anything. Since most of the programs required for improving the quality of the environment would benefit greatly from it if they do not demand land-use control, there is a powerful argument for placing overall planning and responsibility in a single agency. It is possible that the fears of a local politics of redistribution and the ingrained habits of rugged individualism may not prove insuperable.

The restructuring of local government to provide jurisdictions with the territory, the fiscal ability, and the motivation to improve the quality of the environment will move ahead more rapidly if it avoids commitment to any doctrinaire, uniform panacea. In many cases the states may prove the most promising level of government for achieving metropolitan integration. This is likely to be the case in Massachusetts where some 60 per cent of the state's population is included within the Boston metropolitan area. It is certainly the case with Rhode Island. While the "one man—one vote" doctrine is likely to strengthen the suburbs as against the central cities, it is not inevitable that the states will continue unresponsive to the needs of a politics of redistribution, Clearly, for water resource development, quite probably for efficient drainage basin management, and probably for reserving and developing open space, there must be a major role for the states if for no other reason because of their legal powers and the likely need to use interstate compacts in many cases.

Perhaps more important than the likely suburban bias of state legislatures is the orientation and prestige of the old-line agencies and bureaucrats in the states and even in the local governments. These normally worship at the shrines of the gods of things as they are. Much can be done by the federal government to change program emphasis by using the carrot of funds along with provisions for personnel that insure professional competence and appropriate compensation. Much can be done from Washington to induce upgrading of environmental improvement functions at city, county, and state levels through grants with controls. The achievement of some modicum of institutionalized professional elite at state and local levels is a prerequisite to the activation and direction of potential publics and the instruction and programming of the media. Much of the professionalism that exists in many states owes its existence to federal grants with merit—requirement strings.

Representation of the emerging functions of environmental control at appropriate levels in state and local bureaucracies is essential to counterbalancing entrenched representatives of habitual methods of handling highway and other activities with little or no regard for the newly emerging concerns. It is probably wiser to attempt to create allies in the state bureaucracies than to attempt to completely bypass them. Experience with the poverty program indicates that the bypass route may prove ultimately more costly than the longer road of developing compatible counterpart units in the states.

Placing of research funds with state and other universities and private industry at least potentially increases knowledge and lowers the costs of attaining goals. It also broadens the base of those with an informed concern about environmental quality. Activated elites in academic and university circles are especially effective in the dissemination of ideas. Since much of the problem of obtaining improvement depends on the creation of elite and general public opinion favoring such an enterprise, funds directing the interest of strategically placed elites toward the problems are likely to bear fruit all out of proportion to their amount. An informed concern with environmental quality is badly needed in industry because in many cases the most serious and uncontrollable offenders are in the private sector.

Many local and even state governments are reluctant to tackle the problems of industrial pollution for fear of reducing their attractiveness as a location for industry. Indeed, many industries have capitalized their permission to inflict their wastes on others, as many slum properties have capitalized their failure to meet codes. In both cases any sudden crackdown could produce painful and even disastrous increases in costs. Beyond this, if competing locations can offer freedom from desirable standards, many communities will put jobs and tax revenues ahead of pollution abatement. It may well be that only the federal government can provide the sanctions that will free state and local governments from paralyzing fear of economic loss.

There seems little doubt that the costs of controlling waste disposal whether into the air, into water, or so-called nondegradable objects like tin cans will be steeply increasing in the affluent society. If the cost could be internalized to industry, the problem of policing by government could be enormously simplified. The insurance companies and their counterpart units in industry are probably far more effective in achieving plant safety than is state inspection. When pollution control becomes a routinely calculable cost of industry, represented in the corporate decision-making hierarchy rather than a governmental threat to be parried by house counsel and public relations, progress will be expedited. This would suggest federal tax incentives, either in the form of write-off or credit to induce investment or of nuisance taxation to penalize pollution. The receipts of the latter tax could be returned to state or local governments with appropriate legislation and administration.

It is likely that industry's own ranks will be increasingly divided over pollution. At least the growing tourist industry is likely to be more and more concerned with environmental quality. States that used to show a tender regard for the convenience of pulp mills and power companies are waking up to the competing lucrative uses of their streams. There are few more rabid groups than fishermen who, in their frenzy, even assault reservoirs for drinking water. The affluent society is producing a mass leisure public with a capacity for appreciation of environmental quality. To be sure, the affluence of this society produces the rocketing energy consumption and waste production that it is now affluent enough to find objectionable. Doubtless, this could result in a stand-off. Conceivably the cost of waste disposal could approach the cost of energy consumed. One can only hope that the affluent society's waste will not bring about its cumulative impoverishment. Estimates of hot waste disposal from atomic power (whose increase could be fantastic) are so high that little careful thought seems to be now given to it.

As the U.S. Department of Agriculture runs out of farmers, it seems (like other organizations) to search for new customers to keep it going. The same holds true for the land-grant universities and colleges. Recent regional conferences held under the auspices of land-grant institutions have brought together people from the departments of Agriculture and Interior and the Corps of Engineers to consider the problems and possibilities of planning for people in nonmetropolitan areas. Fifty million or more Americans live outside the standard metropolitan areas. These too are a constituency for environmental improvement. Karl Fox at Iowa State has pressed for the significant possibilities of planning in these nonmetropolitan areas. There seems to be a significant responsibility that might be met by the Department of Agriculture and some other departments in acting as the Washington sponsors for this area of local government. Existing relations with state government make likely a favorable climate for cooperation. The concern of many of these areas with tourism gives promise of influence on the state legislatures that will favor some aspects of environmental quality improvement.

The improvement of the quality of the environment is a high priority goal in giving reality to the conception of a Great Society. The articulation of this goal and its gradual development through standards and reporting is a necessity for developing the state of public oninion. The new Department of Housing and Urban Development can be expected to make this issue a major objective of important programs. The opinion leadership of Washington and its fiscal assistance can only go part way. The development of metropolitan or regional governments that can afford, and be motivated to undertake, the improvement of the quality of environment is the major institutional requisite for serious and fundamental action.

Morton Grodzins

The Many American Governments and Outdoor Recreation*

Recreation in the United States is a chaos of activity. It is no less a chaos of private and public responsibilities.

Consider first what people do for recreation. They swim on and under water. They walk, dig for archaeological relics, descend into caves, ascend in gliders and planes. They shoot (with camera or gun) birds and game. They seek the fresh air of mountains and the smoky atmosphere of boxing and wrestling arenas. They bowl and booze, separately or simultaneously. They build in wood, plastic, and metal everything from model aircraft to summer homes. They play musical instruments in jazz combos, chamber music quartets, and business men's symphonies. They play baseball, football, basketball, soccer, volleyball, croquet, tennis, table tennis, badminton, and shuffleboard. They participate in horse shows, dog shows, cat shows, bird shows, and flower shows as well as horse-racing, dogracing, autoracing, turtleracing, and people-racing. They manipulate dolls in puppet shows and toss each other around in judo. Americans trade stamps, coins, seashells, post cards, matchboxes, clocks, rocks, and color slides. They sing together (there are more than 28,000 members in the Society for the Preservation and Encouragement of Barber Shop Quartet Singing in America), and they search for silence in the solitude of wilderness areas. Some 68 million people—more than half of all Americans 12 years of age and older—"drive for pleasure," and each of these spends more than 11 days a year at it. Those who don't drive, and a large fraction of those who do, hike, bicycle, ride horses, canoe, sail, water ski, climb, skate, or ski. Or they stalk prairie chickens, encouraged by a national committee formally organized for preserving that bird. The only recreation activity more popular than driving is picnicking, and picnicking is also enjoyed under the widest range of circumstances. It includes the family roasting hamburgers in the back-

*Reprinted from *Trends in American Living and Outdoor Recreation: A Report of the Outdoor Recreation Resources Review Commission* (Washington: U.S. Government Printing Office, 1962), pp. 62–68.
(Notes to this selection will be found on pp. 415–416.)

yard and more than 10,000 citizens of Polish extraction eating and otherwise celebrating in one of Chicago's parks.

For many, paid hours of work may be more joyful than the unpaid ones which are usually regarded as recreation time. Here one finds those who work at play, whether it be the sort of work that improves homes or demonstrates wealth or muscular power. Others view recreation as absolute rest: just plain loafing. Still a third related view of recreation is the acquisition of new vigor, a literal re-creation of mind and body. This may be sought in many ways, studying the mating habits of reptiles and scaling near-vertical rocks, among others. And a fourth meaning is represented by those who use nonworking hours as a catharsis, letting off steam in weekend wenching, drag-racing, rock-fighting, or beer-busting.

Even this list barely suggests what Americans do for recreation. There must be added a vast range of more-or-less unacknowledged activities and purposes. We know from novels, if not more precisely, that an important aim of "two weeks in the country" for young urban workers is not recreation in any ordinary sense, but marriage. White slacks and blue jackets for men and artfully wired bathing suits for the girls effectively obscure ordinary indications of occupation, income, and physique. So prepared, young people use their two weeks of nonwork in looking for mates. Some resort hotels in the Catskills advertise themselves as propitious sites for this ritual, but few participants would admit even to themselves that they attend for any reason except enjoyment of the lake, trees, dancing, drama, and bigtime basketball, also provided by the management. This is the least well-hidden of many covert recreation activities. The backwoods hunter or fisherman may seek not sport but the joys of not-washing, or all-masculine companionship, or a three-day poker game. The awesome first sight of the Grand Canyon is completely lost upon the foursome who skid their car to an abrupt stop, quickly unload golf paraphernalia, and spend their time at the gorge hitting balls into it. Their only joy is that of smacking a golf ball for a mile, a joy undiminished by the fact that the park service prohibits such practices. The traveler to exotic places may be interested chiefly in the slides or post cards he can bring home to show his neighbors. The motor-launch owner may be terrified of water but enthusiastic over the idea of meeting his social betters at the yacht club.

THE CHAOS OF RESPONSIBILITY

Facilities and services for this infinite variety of recreation activities are provided by an equally inchoate collection of private, semipublic, and public bodies. The industrial society begets industrialized recreation.

Just as the automobile culture produces driving as a favorite "outdoor recreation," so the development and promotion of outboard motors have produced a new impetus to boating, and so the technical development of portable oxygen-supplying equipment has spawned a new and rapidly growing breed of underwater creatures. Television has taken people out of movies; aircraft have made skiing in Aspen (or Kitzbühel) easy.

The recreation industry is big business. Dollar estimates of exactly how big it is vary enormously. Using a restricted definition (excluding such items as liquor, soft drinks, tobacco, sports clothes, and recreation transportation), an authoritative study for 1952 showed recreation costs of $11 billion. Adding only vacation travel would bring this figure (in 1960) to well over $23 billion, almost twice as much as Americans spent that year for clothing, accessories, and jewelry. If such items as liquor consumption are added, the figure easily exceeds $40 billion, roughly double all public costs for primary, secondary, and higher education.[1] The principal suppliers of recreation commodities and services are the vast complex called American business enterprise. The enterprise consists of everything from a multimillion dollar business, manufacturing guns or fishing rods or outboard motors, to a family fishing camp. It meets and stimulates demand by its advertising, its products, and its services. It provides swimmers with ear plugs and hunters with shooting preserves for pheasant and elk, complete with guide and a guarantee of success. Private beaches, woodlands, and swimming places, open to the public for a fee and operated as investment properties, complete with government-operated areas and in some sections of the country serve more people than do public facilities. As in other aspects of commerce, one recreation business begets others. Traveling stimulates picture-taking and vice versa. Motorboats boom water skis, camping equipment goes along with a canoe.

There is great overlap of the private and public in the American culture, including the recreation sector. One facet is reciprocal dependence: the sale of fishing gear (almost $160 million in 1959)[2] is largely dependent upon public waters, not only the oceans, the Great Lakes and the Gulf of Mexico, but also the streams (81,000 miles) and lakes (2.7 million acres) of the Forest Service and the reservoirs built by the Tennessee Valley Authority, the Army Corps of Engineers, and the Bureau of Reclamation. This is not to mention the seeding of streams and other waters by federal and state agencies. (In the spring of 1961, Colorado put 2,515,926 fish into its streams.)[3] Most private recreation camps are adjacent to public parks or water, and many operate on public land, as at TVA reservoirs and in national forests. There would be far fewer horses rented, and a corresponding decrease in the sale of riding boots and clothes, without public bridle paths. The boating industry is similarly dependent upon public waters, docks and launching areas.

A second aspect of the public–private overlap results from enlightened self-interest. Most of the nation's large timber growers allow their lands to be used for some forms of public recreation. At least 60 million acres are involved.[4] Hunting, fishing, hiking, picnicking, among other activities, are invited. Some companies have full-fledged park and recreation programs.

A third manifestation of the overlap is the familiar group pressure on public policy. The boating industry participated in drawing up the Federal Boating Act of 1958 and a complementary draft statute, recommended for passage by the states. The Izaak Walton League, the motorboat industry, wilderness adherents, and fishing buffs (not always without conflict among themselves or without opposition from mining, grazing, and lumbering interests) attempt to mold public policy at innumerable points in the process of administrative–legislative decision-making. The chains of influence are often circular. The U.S. Fish and Wildlife Service, for example, seeks support for its program from state fish and game commissions, which in turn depend on business and sportsmen's groups organized to promote hunting, fishing, and wildlife management. It is difficult in such cases to determine who is influencing whom. Federal and state programs could not exist without the legislative lobbying of private groups; but the success and implementation of those lobbying activities are in turn dependent upon federal administrative officers and their state counterparts. Influence is symbiotic, and the result is a typical confusion of public and private spheres of responsibility.

The confusion becomes extreme when private groups perform what *a priori* appear to be public services. This is a final manifestation of the public–private overlap. Private acquisition of public recreation lands is a good example. The Trustees of Reservations in Massachusetts (an organization that receives no financial support from any government) spend privately donated funds for parks and forests or acquire such lands by gift. As a public agency might, the trustees base their acquisition program on a statewide survey of scenic sites. Land once acquired is either maintained for public use or, the more usual practice, given to the state or a local government for recreation purposes. A number of states have similar organizations, one of the oldest being The Society for the Protection of New Hampshire Forests. California's Save-the-Redwoods League has had an important role in establishing the state park system, not least of all through its purchase by private subscription of prime park land. Even where formal groups for land purchase do not exist, an analogous function is performed in many states by community trusts and private philanthropies. They purchase parkland that may come on the market at a time when governmental funds for this purpose are not available. The land is subsequently resold to public agencies, thus freeing the private funds for another cycle of land purchase and transfer.

Land purchases are only one sample of private organizations doing the public's business. Often a community park will be improved by action of private groups. The Rotary Club will install lighting and picnic benches, and the Lions will provide funds for the community swimming pool. In larger communities, the private contribution to public recreation is more likely to take the form of camps for the underprivileged operated by civic, church, and other welfare-oriented organizations. Thousands of such programs exist. If they didn't, public programs would almost certainly take their place.

The substitution of private for public programs is found in other areas of recreation work. The National Recreation Association, a private organization, carries on an extensive consultation service, aiding local governments and other public bodies to establish and improve recreation programs. The association has also assisted state boards of education in the development of school recreation programs and has supervised the training of state and local recreation workers. Very similar services are offered by a number of state governments as well as by the National Park Service.

The welter of private and semipublic sources of recreation facilities and services is matched by a diverse group of governmental units. As a task force of the Second Hoover Commission noted, the concern of the federal government with recreation resources and activities has been incidental to other functions. Recreation has been a byproduct of the objectives of conserving forest, water, and land resources and of effectively utilizing manpower during wartime. Nevertheless, the federal government now operates an extensive network of recreation programs. No fewer than ten agencies (see Table 10–1) are represented in the Federal Inter-Agency Committee on Recreation. All of these, except the Public Housing Administration, have important responsibilities for providing facilities for outdoor recreation. But the members of the Inter-Agency Committee On Recreation by no means exhaust the list of federal bureaus concerned with recreation. For example, the General Services Administration has a key role in the final transfer of surplus federal properties to states and localities for recreation purposes. In the nation's newest outdoor recreation program, the Urban Renewal Administration (Housing and Home Finance Agency) is charged with carrying out provisions of Title VII of the Housing Act of 1961, which provides grants to assist in the acquisition of open-space land in urban areas. The extensive system of dams constructed by the Tennessee Valley Authority provides the major source of recreation opportunities in what was previously a lake-poor region of the nation. The Soil Conservation Service (U.S. Department of Agriculture) has developed a number of recreation areas as a part of its land utilization projects (in 1954 these areas were transferred to the Forest Service). The SCS has also made important contributions to the

Table 10-1—Agencies Represented in the Federal Inter-Agency Committee on Recreation

National Park Service, U.S. Department of the Interior.
Administration of the national parks, monuments, historical sites and other areas which comprise the national park system and national recreation areas; planning of recreation facilities at Bureau of Reclamation reservoir sites; cooperation with federal and state and local agencies in planning for their park, parkway, and recreation area programs.

Forest Service, U.S. Department of Agriculture.
Recreation on the 186 million acres of national forest system, including national grasslands. Also research in forest recreation.

Fish and Wildlife, U.S. Department of the Interior.
Recreation in national wildlife refuges and federal fish and culture stations. Administers program of grants to state agencies for conservation and fish and game management.

Corps of Engineers, U.S. Department of the Army.
Recreation in navigation and flood control project areas under jurisdiction of the corps. Other aids to recreation through beach erosion control and other related programs.

Bureau of Reclamation, U.S. Department of the Interior.
Recreation at reservoir sites of the Bureau. For most reclamation reservoirs a master and development plan for recreation is prepared by the National Park Service.

Bureau of Land Management, U.S. Department of the Interior.
Recreation in the public lands of United States. Conveys land to state and local governments for recreation purposes.

Federal Extension Service, U.S. Department of Agriculture.
Rural community recreation through state agricultural college and county extension services.

Public Health Service, U.S. Department of Health, Education and Welfare.
Public health, including environmental sanitation and control of stream pollution, in recreation areas.

Office of Education, U.S. Department of Health, Education, and Welfare.
School and community recreation; outdoor education and school camping.

Public Housing Administration, Housing and Home Finance Agency.
Concerned that local housing authorities which own projects in federally assisted low-rent housing program obtain the same community services (including recreation) for their tenants as are available to other residents in the community. Indoor community activities space and outdoor play areas may be provided on the project.

Source: Release (undated) of Federal Inter-Agency Committee on Recreation, supplemented by data from agencies.

preservation of wildlife in agricultural lands and privately owned forests, through its 2,900 soil conservation districts of the country, and to the development of facilities for recreation through its small watersheds program. The Coast and Geodetic Survey provides maps, charts, and tidetables to boaters, among other recreation services. Even the Department of State, through the Under Secretary's Special Assistant for Fisheries and Wildlife, contributes to recreation. These are only samples of a very long list.

The Federal Inter-Agency Committee on Recreation works under a general policy statement that declares "recreation is a human need which is essential at all times to the well being of the people;" and "the national welfare is promoted by providing opportunities for wholesome and adequate recreation." Legislative authorizations are often far less clear-cut, and administrative practices have often subordinated recreation to other purposes.

The Corps of Engineers, for example, constructs reservoirs primarily for flood control, navigation, and power development. No authorization existed at all for the development of recreation activities at reservoirs until 1944. Even under that authorization, recreation became, at best, a secondary or tertiary purpose of the reservoirs. Recreation specialists have often criticized the Corps of Engineers (as well as the Bureau of Reclamation) for their failure to provide sufficient recreation land at reservoir sites.[5] The Bureau of Land Management, the federal government's largest landholder, similarly recognizes recreation as only one of a number of purposes it must fulfill. The bureau's large-scale disposal of the public domain for commercial purposes has been opposed in recent years by many recreation and conservation leaders. Soon after assuming office in 1961, Secretary of the Interior Udall declared a moratorium on BLM land disposals for commercial use, awaiting completion of a classification study and, presumably, the allocation of prime land for recreation.[6]

Substantially all of the national forests and grasslands (186 million acres) are open to the public and used for hunting, fishing, and hiking. Wilderness areas, comprising more than 14 million acres, are operated to preserve their primitive condition, and in these areas all other uses are subordinate. Wilderness areas aside, a relatively tiny fraction of the national forests, are set aside for exclusive recreation use (estimates range from one-tenth of 1 per cent to 2.5 per cent). Over the rest of the national forests, management is based on multiple-use principles. Some types of recreation use are compatible with some types of commercial use on a given area of forest land. But full development of one purpose must, in most cases, result in decreased utilization for the other. The sharpness of the conflict has tended to increase with the upsurge of both recreation and commercial lumbering on forest lands during the postwar years. The difficulty was by no means solved by the 1960 Congressional legislation which established outdoor recreation on the same plane as "range, timber, watershed, and wildlife and fish purposes" in the Forest Service's program. Such legislation simply transfers struggle for actual land-use priority (in the large number of cases where equal intensity of commercial and recreation use is not possible) from the legislative to the administrative arena. Commercial pressures on the Forest Service are immense and well organized. Large gains in the recreation use of the national forests depend upon concerted public efforts in support of that use. Steps in the direction are the Forest Service's "Operation Outdoors," a five-year program of recreation development begun in 1957, and a program for the national forests which lays great stress on recreation.[7]

The Fish and Wildlife Service is primarily concerned with increasing and protecting fish and wildlife resources and enforcing federal game laws. "Incident to these responsibilities," according to an official policy statement, "the Service has recognized the necessity and desirability of providing, when not inconsistent with these primary objectives, the optimum of its facilities and services for recreation use."[8] Again recreation is not the primary legislated function. The several hundred national wildlife refuges make a direct contribution to recreation through the production and protection of wildlife, particularly migratory waterfowl. Facilities in the refuges are also provided for fishing, camping, boating, picnicking, and nature study. Furthermore, in this case the powerful, well-organized citizens' groups devoted to hunting, fishing, and wildlife preservation have produced an overall fish and wildlife program that substantially serves recreation purposes. The task has been easier because of the long-run compatibility between hunting and fishing, on the one hand, and production and management of fish and game, on the other. A powerful lever for sportsmen is the fact that their hunting and fishing licence fees (plus taxes on their equipment) substantially pay for state fish and wildlife programs.

Of all federal agencies related to recreation, the National Park Service is most clearly focused on recreation. But even its mission contains ambiguities. It is charged with the conservation of "scenery and . . . natural and historical objects and wildlife," as well as with providing "for the enjoyment of same in such manner and by such means as will leave them unimpaired for the enjoyment of future generations." Park areas must be preserved if they are to be enjoyed. Yet at any particular moment enjoyment of resources can conflict with their conservation, as when very large numbers of those coming to enjoy may, by their very overuse, threaten the natural scene with destruction. The Park Service in 1956 moved to solve this dilemma by its Mission 66 program, a ten-year effort to meet rising demand for park use by increased facilities and staffs and, in the process, to provide for the protection of natural and historic areas. The Park Service has been actively supported through the years by a large number of citizen groups, including the National Parks Association.

The states and localities present equally complicated patterns of organization for recreation purposes. Each State has at least one park agency (Massachusetts has ten). Agencies charged with park and recreation responsibilities range from rudimentary, parttime custodial commissions to highly professional, large-scale staffs doing specialized tasks, as in California, New York, Pennsylvania, Michigan, and Indiana. Only about 12 states have unified recreation agencies whose responsibilities include both wildlife management (essentially programs for hunting and fishing) and park management for general recreation purposes. The largest number of states have separate administrative organizations for these purposes, each usually with its own governing commission, and almost uniformly the fish and wildlife program is supported by larger budgets, larger and more professional staffs, and better-organized citizen support. Other independent agencies in most states perform peripheral recreation services. The maintenance of state forests is undertaken by a forestry commission in almost every state. Roadside parks are usually the responsibility of the highway department. Historical landmarks are frequently administered by a private historical society. A water resources bureau in some states controls lakes or reservoirs which are the source of water for communities, agriculture, and industry.[9]

Competition and cross-purposes among public bodies sometimes exist as they do among private suppliers of recreation. Roads for tourists are the enemy of wilderness areas. The management of fish and game for sportsmen may conflict with the development of intensive-use park areas. Demands for water purity for household use may limit or prohibit recreation use of lakes and reservoirs. And private business may of course interfere with public pleasure. The lumbering industry has often opposed significant increases in the exclusive recreation use of national forest land (as in the designation of new wilderness areas). In Arizona a state park system was opposed for many years by livestock interest which feared reduction of grazing areas. When a State Parks Board was finally established in 1957, the livestock industry effectively curtailed its scope of action through two provisions in the law: no fewer than two of the seven board members must represent the livestock industry, and no park of more than 100 acres can be established without special legislative action.[10] In its first three years of operation, the state parks board acquired 14 acres of parkland.

On the local plane, virtually every city with 10,000 people or more, and many smaller ones, have park and recreation departments. The largest cities almost uniformly have well-developed recreation programs, and city facilities may include parks, golf courses, tennis courts, amphitheatres, bridle paths, zoos, museums, arboretums, outside-the-city camps, stadiums, scenic drives, and beaches and boat harbors. Special programs are offered for the young, old, indigent, potentially delinquent, and non-English-speaking, as well as for special skill groups in areas ranging from archery and bowling to boatbuilding and flying high-powered model airplanes. The smaller the city, the more likely that private groups (Boy Scouts, YMCA, Rotary) are chiefly responsible for public recreation, and the more certain, too, that facilities will be fewer in number, the bare minimum being a picnic area, a Little League ball park, or a swimming pool.

County recreation programs vary even more widely, from none at all in perhaps one-half the nation's 3,000 counties to elaborate undertakings in a few places such as Kern County, Calif., Westchester County, N.Y., and Douglas County, Ore. Where programs are rudimentary they are likely to be operated by nonprofit groups, financed in some cases through informal community fundraising and in others through community chests or united funds. The trend almost everywhere is toward formal, publicly financed agencies. Twenty-four of Oregon's 36 counties, for example, have some type of recreation program.[11] Many counties have developed recreation facilities jointly with schools or with schools and cities. Counties in highly urbanized areas have been especially active in recreation, and some urban counties have taken the lead in establishing joint programs with cities or adjoining counties. The Huron–Clinton Metropolitan Authority, for example, is a five-county, special tax-levying government, providing a wide range of park and recreation facilities for the Detroit Metropolitan area. The Metropolitan Park District of Boston, the East Bay Regional Park District of California (serving Oakland, Berkeley, and other cities in two counties), and Cleveland's Metropolitan Park District are other examples of cross-county and county–city recreation areas.

Still other public agencies and facilities for recreation abound. Data on municipal and county forests are inexact, but holdings are extensive and growing. The town forest is common in Europe, and the first such forest in the United States was planted in Newington, N.H. in 1710. There are today at least 3,600 community forests in 40 states, most of them in the Northeast (especially New York, Pennsylvania, and New England), in the Great Lakes region, and on the Pacific Coast. Michigan, New York, and Wisconsin have the most community forests. Over the country, the forests range in size from an acre or two to the 83,000 acres owned by Seattle. Ownership is vested variously in towns, townships, cities, counties, schools, hospitals, and churches. Many community forests are used to produce income, but recreation is an important function in most states. An important recreation resource of Chicago, for example, is the land of the Forest Preserve District of Cook County. The district owns more than 45,000 acres, principally strung out in irregular strips along major water courses on the outskirts of Chicago. Facilities include golf courses, swimming pools, and picnic areas, as well as large wildlife areas. A half-million people use the forest preserves on a peak summer day. In Wisconsin, more than 350 county and town forests include over 2.2 million acres, an area greater than the state's combined acreage of national and state recreation land.

THE VIRTUES OF CHAOS

Those with a reformist bent or a directive to recommend policy are likely to look aghast at the chaos of services and facilities that exist for recreation purposes in the United States. There is no neatness in the situation. Responsibilities overlap. Concern and effort are widely shared and appear to be poorly coordinated. It is difficult even to describe who is accountable for what or to understand where one government's responsibility begins and another's ends. If for no other reason than to aid his understanding—to bring some order out of apparent disorder—the observer is tempted to recommend that the system be made more simple and therefore more rational. He who recommends policy is by nature a neatener. The first progress report of the Outdoor Recreation Resources Review Commission comes to this sort of conclusion:

There are a proliferation of policies, a multitude of agencies, ten score activities, and an interest group or clientele for each activity. . . . it is this very overabundance of concern and fragmentation of responsibility, that complicate, and in part even create, "the outdoor recreation problem."[12]

The opposite view in fact recommends itself. "Overabundance of concern" does not in any sense create the outdoor recreation "problem"; that concern rather is the best route to solving the problem, however it may be defined. Nor is "fragmentation of responsibility" a source of difficulty. Rather it is the desirable method by which American governments characteristically carry out almost all of their functional tasks.

Why does lack of neatness recommend itself?

First of all, the overlapping concern of many governments in a single problem in no way prohibits, indeed it invites, the establishment of general goals by the central government. It also invites central authorities, usually through grants of money, to stimulate activity by the smaller governments. These are functions of the American national government in virtually every major domestic public program. The central government has carried out these tasks since the beginning of the Union and even before the Union, as in the allocation of public lands for education in the Northwest Ordinance of 1785. In recreation, as in other programs, the goal-setting and stimulating roles do not mean that the central government's program becomes an exclusive program. Typically, it leaves room for a vast proliferation of ancillary, if not competing, programs in the same area. This is a nation rarely possessing a single goal in a given field. We specialize in goals.

Second, the existence of many governments operating freely in a single program area preserves a desirable openness in the system. There is no single source of initiative, rather there are many. There is no single standard for determining what is desirable, and no single set of officials with the power to define the desirable and undesirable. Power, as well as function, is dispersed.

Third, a system of many power centers is well suited to meet the infinite variety of expressed needs. It responds quickly (sometimes too quickly) to citizen demand. Because there are many points for decision, citizens and citizen groups have multiple opportunities to influence decision-makers. If a group does not get satisfaction at one place, it can try another. And if the second is unresponsive, there may exist a third or a fourth. This openness in the system for making government decisions is particularly appropriate for recreation because it is not a single, but many, things. The very diversity of activities that are labeled "recreation" makes it unwise to vest any single set of public officials with the power to make decisions concerning them all. Even for a single recreation need, exclusive responsibility is both difficult to achieve and unwise if achievable. Many points of public power, with different degrees of accommodation to different sorts of recreation demand, mean, in the end, that no reasonably widespread recreation need will be unfulfilled.

Fourth, many governments operating in recreation, even if they do roughly the same thing, are effective in meeting the growing pressure on recreation resources. Parks, like roads, seem to play the role of food in the old Malthusian calculus: rather than relieving the pressures of population on them, new resources produce new use. There is little chance in the foreseeable future of providing too much recreation land, especially since recreation, as a political issue, does not sustain widespread public attention. One recreation area frequently substitutes for another, and development of new recreation facilities by states and localities directly relieves pressure on areas under federal management, and vice versa. All this argues for more duplication of effort, not less.

Many governments doing one job may appear inefficient and wasteful. Neither charge, except for units of small population, has been effectively demonstrated. The situation does lack neatness and thus is difficult to comprehend fully. In healthy institutions, ambiguities of this sort must be tolerated. In government, as in family life, business, and educational institutions, the absence of complete direction from above disperses initiative and releases energies. It should be preserved. Hierarchy, order, and the delegation of neatly packaged responsibilities are not adequate substitutes. No function of American government—not even so-called local functions such as education or so-called national functions such as foreign affairs—are so packaged. Lack of neatness in the allocation of government functions is a good thing.

THE SHARING OF RECREATION FUNCTIONS

North of San Francisco, near the entrance to Muir Woods, a park of giant redwoods in a wilderness setting, a visitor meets the following sign:

Muir Woods is a geographic
part of a unified public
recreational area reaching over
and beyond Mount Tamalpais.

Muir Woods National Monument
is administered by the National
Park Service of the United States
Department of the Interior.

Adjoining to the North is
Mount Tamalpais State Park.
This, and the Samuel P. Taylor
State Park, are administered by
the California Division of
Beaches and Parks.

Between and connecting
these two state parks are the
lands of the Marin Municipal
Water District.

Trails open to the public
link the entire area. Only fire
precautions and plant and
wildlife protection are required.

These lines reveal what the multiplicity of public recreation bodies easily obscures: the cooperative sharing of the recreation function by governments. This sharing of functions does not prevent different governments from doing the same thing. It does prevent them from working at cross-purposes through ignorance of what each is doing. Frequently, in fact, efforts can be dovetailed, and what appears to be duplication of effort turns out to be an attempt to increase the total resources for recreation. In some areas of activity a rough division of labor among governments has been achieved.

Supplemental Types of Recreation Areas

One small measure of this division of labor is found in the types of park land held by federal, state, and local governments. The National Park Service, for the most part, holds land of outstanding natural beauty or historical interest. Accessibility to nearby population has counted only slightly in the establishment of national parks. At the opposite extreme, city and county parks are use- rather than resource-oriented (the terminology is Marion Clawson's): They are open spaces chosen because they are convenient to the people nearby. If they possess no natural beauty, developers add trees, grass, lakes, and other amenities. State holdings follow an intermediate principle. In the early years of the state park movement, parks were chosen on the same basis as national parks without regard for their proximity to population but rather for their scenic, scientific, or historical significance. In the last 30 years state parks have largely been selected to provide recreation opportunities accessible to large population concentrates. Total state holdings reflect these dual purposes.

Exceptions of all sorts, of course, exist. Some locally operated facilities are a considerable distance from the population which supports them (San Francisco operates a summer camp in the High Sierras, several hundred miles from the city). On the other hand, nearby populations are the heaviest users of some national parks, Yosemite constituting a prime example. Some state parks (California's Point Lobos and Michigan's Porcupine Mountain State Park) possess natural attractions comparable to many sites of the national park system. Many state parks have more out-of-state than in-state visitors.

The distinctions in purpose and acquisition-principle become obliterated when other holdings used, or potentially usable, for recreation are considered. National forests, the residual public domain, revested railroad lands, and reservoirs of the Bureau of Reclamation and the Corps of Engineers were not chosen for recreation purposes at all. TVA reservoirs and most state forests were selected with recreation as only the most minor consideration. Recreation on all these properties is lagniappe: an added use of land secured for other purposes. On some of these properties, however, recreation has now become a major use. And these lands, because of their very size, will provide a major fraction of the future recreation resources in the United States. The disparities in acreage between parks and other public lands make this clear. Though the latter category contains large areas relatively unsuited for recreation purposes, comparisons are nevertheless illuminating. For example, state forests contain almost four times the acreage of state parks, and lands of the Forest Service and Bureau of Land Management (excluding large holdings in Alaska) together constitute an area 24 times the size of all national parks.

Although there are genuine differences in the character of state, local and national park lands, those differences are relatively unimportant when one views the broader field of outdoor recreation. On the one hand, parks, as such, are only a small fraction of the nation's present, and needed, outdoor recreation resources. On the other, as park holdings increase, their national–state–local differences will inevitably tend to become less important. So-called "level" distinctions in type of park land are, therefore, not the principal basis of cooperative sharing among the governments of the federal system. And no differences in park character can be used to justify the fact that all planes of government are in the recreation business. That justification exists, as we have seen, only in the need for recreation space, the impossibility of providing enough such space in the hands of "pure" recreation agencies, and the virtues of preserving multiple points of policy and administration in this continentwide nation.

The Case for a Department of Natural Resources*

The following article is offered to stimulate discussion of a controversial sub-ject. . . . To guarantee that attention will be focused on the issues, and not on personalities, the author prefers to remain anonymous.

Our growing population, our industrial demands for raw materials and our commitments abroad all put pressure on our natural resource base. Our ability to maintain the productive capacity of our soils, forests, water, mineral, and energy sources is in question. Yet United States public policy towards natural resources is developed and ad-ministered by a complex, confusing, and conflicting array of agencies, offices, and departments. Large amounts of money, talent, ideas, and ability are directed towards protecting the national interest in developing and conserving our resources. The concrete results of all this effort have been few. An important obstacle to forward planning is the lack of unifying coordination. A symphony orchestra composed of outstanding musicians each dedicated to producing beautiful music will produce only discordant noise in the absence of a conductor. This analogy applies perfectly to current natural resource policy in the United States.

I. THE PROBLEM

Present divisions and duplications of authority restrict true compre-hensive development. They pit agency against agency in jurisdictional disputes and in contention for executive and legislative approval. Con-sider some random examples. There is a running battle between the Forest Service (Department of Agriculture) and the Park Service (Depart-ment of the Interior) over the role of recreation on public lands. The Forest Service advocates the multiple-use of forests with recreation just

*Reprinted by permission of the *Natural Resources Journal* (School of Law, University of New Mexico), I (1961), 197–206.
(Notes to this selection will be found on p. 416.)

one of many commodities produced. The Park Service argues that such management destroys many of the values of recreation. The result is that much of the administrative energy needed to develop recreational facilities is dissipated in internecine strife. The classic example of the wastes of duplication is in the water resources development field. Four departments are involved: Interior; Defense (Army Corps of Engineers); Health, Education, and Welfare; and Agriculture. Each department uses different methods of computing expected costs and benefits from projects; each department stresses different aspects of water development; each department views the others' activities with a suspicion that borders on the paranoid.

This list of conflicts could be extended indefinitely. The Soil Conservation Service (Agriculture) is promoting the draining of wetlands in the northern midwest while the Fish and Wildlife Service (Interior) is trying to maintain wetlands for waterfowl. The Corps of Engineers is advocating the development of the Potomac River in conflict with the plans of the Park Service for a national park in the area. Undoubtedly the reader can add many more examples to this dreary account of intramural feuds.

The good will and devotion of the agencies concerned is not to be questioned. There are no heroes or villains in this story. The major troubles with present resource policies stem from the administrative organization of federal activities.

The form in which resource conservation and development planning takes place affects the substance of the programs. Irrevocable decisions are made on major natural resource matters within the framework of laws which restrict the developing agency to certain purposes, on the basis of agency traditions, and on the basis of artificially generated political support. Rarely, if ever, are these decisions based on informed judgment about overall national needs and goals. The result is that present public policy towards resources is indefensible if evaluated by economic, political, or social criteria.

The present situation can be summarized in ten propositions. They are:

(1) In nature, the resources of soil, water, forests, wildlife, and minerals are all a closely interrelated whole. Conservation practices designed for their protection, management, and development are similarly related: e.g., water and watershed management, forestry, soil conservation and wildlife, recreational uses of national parks and national forests, mineral development as well as reclamation water developments, flood control and pollution abatement.

As an illustration, consider a national forest. It will usually be the case that, in addition to timber, the forest will provide protection for municipal water supplies. The forest will also be an important factor in any program of water pollution control. There may be extensive campsites, picnic areas, and perhaps wilderness trails. Wildlife management will be practiced. A program of soil conservation will likely be undertaken. This latter program will affect downstream navigation, power production, and flood control. Mineral exploration and production may take place on the forest. All of these uses of the forest are interrelated parts of the forest management. Many of these may take place simultaneously on the same land area. Each of them is related to the programs of some other agency in a different department. Despite administrative divisions, resource management cannot be separated.

(2) Natural resource programs of the federal government are dispersed and scattered among separate departments and agencies, although primarily concentrated in Interior. Consider the list in Table 11–1.

Table 11-1

Interior

Bureau of Land Management	Bureau of Sport Fisheries and Wildlife
National Park Service	Bureau of Commercial Fisheries
Geological Survey	Bonneville Power Administration
Bureau of Mines	Southwestern Power Administration
Bureau of Reclamation	Southeastern Power Administration
Bureau of Indian Affairs	

Agriculture

Forest Service	Agricultural Conservation Program
Soil Conservation Service	Rural Electrification Administration

Defense (Army)
Corps of Engineers (water development and flood control)

Health, Education, and Welfare
Water supply and pollution control

Federal Power Commission
Staff develops positions on pending applications, and also provides statistics and economics surveillance—concerning both gas and electric power.

In addition, a number of independent offices or commissions have, or have had, a role in policy formation and management. Examples are Outdoor Recreation Resources Review Commission, President's Materials Policy Commission, The President's Water Resources Review Commission, and the Tennessee Valley Authority.

(3) The scattering of program responsibility among departments has resulted in a welter of confusion and cross-purposes. This applies both to the development of consistent legislative policy and to program administration. This is especially important at the local level. This situation is spectacularly inefficient and actually dangerous to the public interest in our divided water programs. The present responsibilities of the federal government put great strains on the budget. Yet competition among agencies "to get business" contributes to inefficient water resource development and waste of public funds. Water resource development,

instead of taking place within a framework of consideration of national objectives and resources, takes place as a result of "logrolling" and "pork-barrel" politics. This is tragic when one considers the expanding demands for water-derived products as well as for all other natural resources.

(4) Many conflicts arise because of the special interests of the various agencies. A typical situation in water resource development would find the Corps of Engineers (Defense) concerned with river basin planning and flood control; Soil Conservation Service (Agriculture) concerned with watersheds; Bureau of Sport Fisheries and Wildlife (Interior) concerned with fish habitat and recreation.

Attempts to resolve these conflicts have been made. One popular device has been the establishment of interagency coordinating committees in Washington and on local levels. Nevertheless, lacking any central authority short of the President, the member Bureau and Department representatives on these permissive committees are unable to resolve basic conflicts of interest. Line-operating authority disputes cannot be reconciled by discussion.

This proposition holds even when the coordinating committee is composed of cabinet-level officials. Even here, integration requires presidential directives for each and every issue which arises.

(5) For many years efforts have been made to reorganize federal resource development and conservation responsibilities. Secretary Harold Ickes in 1938 desired to change Interior into a Department of Conservation. In 1949 some of the task forces of the first Hoover Commission suggested a Department of Natural Resources,[1] the establishment of which President Truman tried to obtain up until 1951. In his last Budget Message, President Eisenhower suggested that the Army Corps of Engineers' water functions be transferred to Interior.[2]

President Kennedy's explanation of his decision to offer a Special Message of Natural Resources revealed his concern with the problem of coordination. He said:

This statement is designed to bring together in one message the widely scattered resource policies of the Federal Government. In the past, these policies have overlapped and often conflicted. Funds were wasted on competing efforts. Widely differing standards were applied to measure the Federal contribution to similar projects. Funds and attention devoted to annual appropriations or immediate pressures diverted energies away from long-range planning for national economic growth. Fees and user charges wholly inconsistent with each other, with value received and with public policy have been imposed at some Federal developments.[3]

The President pledged action in his special message to redefine resource responsibilities within the executive office, strengthen the Council of Economic Advisers for this purpose, and establish a Presidential Advisory Committee on Natural Resources under the Council of Economic Advisers.

(6) Present divisions have no logical justification. With respect to the land resource agencies now in the Department of Agriculture, the Forest Service and the Soil Conservation Service, the supposed justification for the former agency is that "trees are crops," and for the latter that farm lands suffer the most from erosion. Neither claim has validity in fact.

Most Forest Service activity is centered on the management of 180 million acres of public lands, the national forests; that which is directed towards private forestry assistance is kept completely separate from all regular farm crop programs and is not even integrated with Soil Conservation plans on the same ownership. At least half of the private forest lands on which assistance is given are held by nonfarm landowners. Even the Forest Service research function is separate from the Agricultural Research Service.

The Soil Conservation Service program is also unrelated to other Agriculture Department efforts. It is concerned with practices for the protection of the basic soil resource, regardless of ownership. It is not integrated with other farm programs concerned primarily with production, marketing, price, and supply regulation. Some of the most serious erosion problems are connected with new highways and suburban developments and have no relationship to farm land.

The Soil Conservation Service program conflicts at many points with programs of the Interior Department, particularly those concerned with fish and wildlife and with reclamation. The conflict over draining of the northern midwest wetlands has already been mentioned. Conciliation of competing soil and water programs is far away.

The division of water agencies among four departments (Agriculture with SCS and Small Watershed Programs; Interior with Reclamation, Saline Water, Geological Survey, etc.; Defense with Army Corps of Engineers; and HEW with pollution control and water supply programs) has reached the proportions of a national crisis. No real justification has ever been offered for a continuation of the present situation except that it is "politically impossible" to remedy. The rapidly developing water problem is forcing the issue to the point where continued inaction will result in embarrassment to the Administration.

(7) Lacking any central responsibility at the cabinet level for resources policy and management, the Bureau of the Budget is forced into the role of coordinator and arbiter between the various agencies. Probably in no other area of federal responsibility does the Budget Bureau exercise so strong an influence and leverage over programming.

The present role of the Budget Bureau exceeds its normal responsibilities. Given the present structure of federal natural resource activities, it has been the only agency which has any interest in, or capability for, developing a truly national resource program. This is particularly important for the development of new programs. New needs require new activities. The evaluation of goals and means to meet these goals require specialized attention and expertise that cannot be provided by fiscal specialists in the Bureau of the Budget.

(8) Natural resource agency appropriations are developed as a group by the Bureau of the Budget and (since 1954) the House and Senate Appropriations Subcommittees, regardless of the fact that functional agencies are scattered among many departments. The legislative committees in the Congress continue to divide responsibilities along older but less consistent lines.

(9) Federal organization of resource activities is in sharp contrast to the organization of those states with the most successful conservation programs. These states, e.g., Michigan, New York, Wisconsin and Minnesota, have single departments which embrace all phases of resource management under central direction.

(10) Federal organization of resource activities is also in sharp contrast to the organization of other major federal programs. Every other sector of federal responsibility, e.g., labor, agriculture, health, foreign affairs, is assigned to a single governmental department, which is publicly understood to have central responsibility. Unified centers of authority give citizens a sense of involvement in public activity and a concern for the results.

II. WHAT IS NEEDED

Some order must be made out of the present chaos of resource policy. A centralized responsibility under a Department of Natural Resources is a necessity. This is not the only possible change in present organization, but other suggested solutions do not hold much promise.

The most popular alternative suggestion is to create coordinating and advisory committees. The Congress recognizes the need for developing policy and programs related to national needs rather than to the traditions and prejudices of competing agencies. A distinguished group of Democratic Senators in both the 86th and 87th Congresses have sponsored legislation to establish a Council of Resource and Conservation Advisers in the Executive Office of the President in order to coordinate resource conservation on the basis of national goals.[4]

This change would go only part of the way towards providing the necessary coordination. The past history of trying to obtain unity through committees and advisory groups illustrates the futility of expecting much from these proposals. At present, only if the President himself operates as his own Secretary of Natural Resources (to the near exclusion of many other important matters) can the problem of divided authority be resolved. Adding more councils and advisory agencies will merely provide more organizations to coordinate—regardless of the value of the specific contributions the new organizations could make. Present problems cannot be solved by grafting still more decision-making or policy-advising units onto the present structure. We need fewer and more responsible centers of authority. Measures such as interagency committees, cabinet-level coordinating committees, and other forms of direction through consensus have resulted, and will continue to result, in divided responsibility and failure to face up to the need to center authority. The basic problem will remain unremedied and more time, effort, and money will be wasted on efforts to coordinate programs rather than being devoted to the development and execution of programs.

At this juncture of American history, it is imperative that our resource management programs be accelerated to provide for the increased productivity needed by an expanding population. A broad resource program involving the application of specialized techniques and investments of billions of dollars can be carried out only by a well-designed and co-ordinated federal organization. It is clear that the present clumsy operation of the government in the natural resources field will not only result in wasteful duplication, but fail to meet the goals set forth. Public disillusion will be inevitable. Nor are the alternatives thus far discussed adequate. A Department of Natural Resources is vital if the federal government is to meet its responsibilities for the conservation and development of natural resources.

Because of the present concentration of resource activities in the Department of the Interior, the easiest way to obtain a Department of Natural Resources would be to transfer other resource agencies to Interior. The major obstacle in the past to such a transfer has been the organized special interest clientele of the agencies involved. These groups fear that their relationships to the government would be affected.

The most adamant group blocking the way to reorganization of federal water functions is the Rivers and Harbors Conference, backed by water development contractors who strongly support certain Congressional relations of the Army Corps of Engineers. This, however, is only one example of a general condition. Many other agencies have special interest clientele groups which do not want their interests disturbed. Few agencies or clientele groups have a direct interest in the improved efficiency which could result from a reorganization.

On the other hand, public citizens' organizations such as the wildlife, park, forestry, and similar groups, the League of Women Voters, organized labor, and the several farm organizations are strong backers of an integrated resource program and would probably support unification through reorganization. Business groups sincerely interested in government efficiency would find resistance difficult. Efforts of these groups could be organized to offset the pressures resisting change. The support of these citizens' organizations will be essential.

The time to take this action is during the first year or so of the President's new term before resistances and pressure group policies harden. The President can evoke great public support for this move if he will go directly to the people for support. The present crisis in foreign affairs provides a further reason for taking civil water programs from the Department of Defense.

It is of central importance that a distinction be made between federal programs for protection, management, and development of basic land, water, and mineral resources, including primary extraction (except agricultural crops) and those which deal with product processing, economics, etc. It is the first phase with which a Department of Natural Resources would be primarily concerned.

On the other hand, resource programs which affect privately owned resources and those which affect publicly owned resources should be combined in one department. For example, direct investment and management, as in the national forests, should be combined with programs designed to aid private owners, such as technical assistance, cost-sharing, etc., for private forest owners. While there are distinct differences between programs for publicly owned resources and those applied to privately owned resources, the techniques and practices followed are so similar in application as to more easily lend themselves to central direction than to split authority. Further, the goals and objectives of the public and private programs are so intertwined that the programs should not be separated administratively.

III. HOW IT SHOULD BE DONE

How should reorganization of the federal natural resource agencies take place? Three possible choices present themselves for centralizing natural resources responsibilities:

(1) *Minimum*—Minimum transfer of principal resource agencies and programs now in other departments to the Department of the Interior with the exception of the *construction* functions of the Army Corps of Engineers. (The planning and water research functions would, however, be transferred to a water development bureau in the Interior.)

This approach would be simply a recognition of the political power of the Corps of Engineers and a means of avoiding their bare-knuckled pressures. It would leave unresolved the problem of coordination of water management and development programs. Although the planning function would be transferred, the Corps would soon find a way to revive this power. In any case the division of responsibilities between the two departments would continue to result in waste and friction, and inhibit realistic programming in this vital field.

(2) *Coordinating Committees*—Another possibility is to have a Council of Resource Advisers and a River Basin Coordinating Council. These are attempts to obtain unification through compromise by establishing another "coordinating" layer between the President and his executive action agencies. Presumably, planning, research, and reconciliation of conflicts would be assigned to river basin groups. The resource advisers would be similar to the Council of Economic Advisers in make-up and duty and therefore largely advisory and without line authority.

Efforts to coordinate through committees have failed in the past because there has been no central cabinet responsibility for program development and execution. The greatest good will is no substitute for authority and responsibility in one cabinet officer. This is particularly important in the formulation of new programs.

(3) *Complete*—A complete reorganization would require transfer by executive order of all resource agencies from other Departments to Interior, including the Army Corps of Engineers, and a request to the Congress to create a Department of Natural Resources.[5]

The cleanest and most effective procedure would be to transfer all resource functions to Interior and then to concentrate all efforts to gain Congressional acceptance. Offsetting the pressure groups opposed to this transfer will be several hundreds of conservation and other organizations which will support complete reorganization. This will take generalship, strategy, and an effective information effort during the 60-day period of grace during which Congress may deny the President's action.[6]

The Reorganization Act of 1949[7] gives the President power to transfer outside agencies to Interior by executive order. Legislative authority would be needed to change the name of Interior to Department of Natural Resources.

The organization of resource activities resulting from these proposed changes would centralize all responsibility for development and management of natural resource programs (except for the T.V.A.) in a Secretary of Natural Resources. The Secretary would have an Under Secretary and staff assistants for program coordination, public affairs, and so forth. There would also be an advisory board on natural resource policy with the Secretary as chairman. Regional or river basin planning committees in the field would report directly to the advisory board.

Resource activities would be divided into six groups, each supervised by an Assistant Secretary. This grouping would be basically along resource lines; minerals, electric power, water, parks and wildlife, land,

and Indian affairs. Bureau responsibilities and organization also would be redefined with the objective of eliminating duplication of effort.

Primary responsibility for program development and management would remain, as at present, with the various bureaus. However, there would be two, and only two, coordinating levels below the President's level. These would be at the Assistant Secretaries' level and at the Secretary's level.

An organization such as this one would not automatically solve all natural resource policy problems. It would, nevertheless, simplify authority and focus responsibility. It would provide the possibility—now lacking—to develop consistent and coherent resource policies and programs. In the absence of such a change, we can expect nothing better than the present inconsistency, confusion, and deadlock. Change is never easy but considering the challenge to public policy presented by our future needs for natural resources it is essential. The time is past due for acceptance by the federal government of its responsibility to provide clear and decisive leadership in the conservation and development of natural resources. The first and most vital step is to organize a Department of Natural Resources.

Richard M. Nixon

Environmental Quality

February 10, 1970

To the Congress of the United States:

Like those in the last century who tilled a plot of land to exhaustion and then moved on to another, we in this country have too casually and too long abused our natural environment. The time has come when we can wait no longer to repair the damage already done, and to establish new criteria to guide us in the future.

The fight against pollution, however, is not a search for villains. For the most part, the damage done to our environment has not been the work of evil men, nor has it been the inevitable by-product either of advancing technology or of growing population. It results not so much from choices made, as from choices neglected; not from malign intention, but from failure to take into account the full consequences of our actions.

Quite inadvertently, by ignoring environmental costs we have given an economic advantage to the careless polluter over his more conscientious rival. While adopting laws prohibiting injury to person or property, we have freely allowed injury to our shared surroundings. Conditioned by an expanding frontier, we came only late to a recognition of how precious and how vulnerable our resources of land, water and air really are.

The tasks that need doing require money, resolve and ingenuity— and they are too big to be done by government alone. They call for fundamentally new philosophies of land, air and water use, for stricter regulation, for expanded government action, for greater citizen involvement, and for new programs to ensure that government, industry and individuals all are called on to do their share of the job and to pay their share of the cost.

Because the many aspects of environmental quality are closely interwoven, to consider each in isolation would be unwise. Therefore, I am today outlining a comprehensive . . . program . . . in five major categories:

—Water pollution control.
—Air pollution control.
—Solid waste management.

—Parklands and public recreation.

—Organizing for action.

As we deepen our understanding of complex ecological processes, as we improve our technologies and institutions and learn from experience, much more will be possible. But these . . . measures represent actions we can take *now*, and that can move us dramatically forward toward what has become an urgent common goal of all Americans: the rescue of our natural habitat as a place both habitable and hospitable to man.

WATER POLLUTION

Water pollution has three principal sources: municipal, industrial and agricultural wastes. All three must eventually be controlled if we are to restore the purity of our lakes and rivers.

Of these three, the most troublesome to control are those from agricultural sources: animal wastes, eroded soil, fertilizers and pesticides. Some of these are nature's own pollutions. The Missouri River was known as "Big Muddy" long before towns and industries were built on its banks. But many of the same techniques of pest control, livestock feeding, irrigation and soil fertilization that have made American agriculture so abundantly productive have also caused serious water pollution.

Effective control will take time, and will require action on many fronts: modified agricultural practices, greater care in the disposal of animal wastes, better soil conservation methods, new kinds of fertilizers, new chemical pesticides and more widespread use of natural pest control techniques. A number of such actions are already underway. We have taken action to phase out the use of DDT and other hard pesticides. We have begun to place controls on wastes from concentrated animal feed-lots. We need programs of intensified research, both public and private, to develop new methods of reducing agricultural pollution while maintaining productivity. I have asked The Council on Environmental Quality to press forward in this area. Meanwhile, however, we have the technology and the resources to proceed *now* on a program of swift clean-up of pollution from the most acutely damaging sources: municipal and industrial waste.

Municipal Wastes

As long as we have the means to do something about it, there is no good reason why municipal pollution of our waters should be allowed to persist unchecked.

In the four years since the Clean Waters Restoration Act of 1966 was passed, we have failed to keep our promises to ourselves: Federal appropriations for constructing municipal treatment plants have totaled only about one-third of authorizations. Municipalities themselves have faced increasing difficulty in selling bonds to finance their share of the construction costs. Given the saturated condition of today's municipal bond markets, if a clean-up program is to work it has to provide the means by which municipalities can finance their share of the cost even as we increase Federal expenditures.

The best current estimate is that it will take a total capital investment of about $10 billion over a five-year period to provide the municipal waste treatment plants and interceptor lines needed to meet our national water quality standards. This figure is based on a recently-completed nationwide survey of the deficiencies of present facilities, plus projections of additional needs that will have developed by then—to accommodate the normal annual increase in the volume of wastes, and to replace equipment that can be expected to wear out or become obsolete in the interim.

This will provide every community that needs it with secondary waste treatment, and also special, additional treatment in areas of special need, including communities on the Great Lakes. We have the industrial capacity to do the job in five years if we begin now.

. . . .

Providing money is important, but equally important is where and how the money is spent. A river cannot be polluted on its left bank and clean on its right. In a given waterway, abating *some* of the pollution is often little better than doing nothing at all, and money spent on such partial efforts is often largely wasted. Present grant allocation formulas— those in the 1966 Act—have prevented the spending of funds where they could produce the greatest results in terms of clean water. Too little attention has been given to seeing that investments in specific waste treatment plants have been matched by other municipalities and industries on the same waterway. Many plants have been poorly designed and inefficiently operated. Some municipalities have offered free treatment to local industries, then not treated their wastes sufficiently to prevent pollution.

. . . .

Industrial Pollution

Some industries discharge their waste into municipal systems; others discharge them directly into lakes and rivers. Obviously, unless we curb industrial as well as municipal pollution our waters will never be clean.

Industry itself has recognized the problem, and many industrial firms are making vigorous efforts to control their water-borne wastes. But strict standards and strict enforcement are nevertheless necessary—not only to ensure compliance, but also in fairness to those who have voluntarily assumed the often costly burden while their competitors have not. Good neighbors should not be placed at a competitive disadvantage because of their good neighborliness.

Under existing law, standards for water pollution control often are established in only the most general and insufficient terms: for example, by requiring all affected industries to install secondary treatment facilities. This approach takes little account of such crucial variables as the volume and toxicity of the wastes actually being discharged, or the capacity of a particular body of water to absorb wastes without becoming polluted. Even more important, it provides a poor basis for enforcement: with no effluent standard by which to measure, it is difficult to prove in court that standards are being violated.

The present fragmenting of jurisdictions also has hindered comprehensive efforts. At present, Federal jurisdiction generally extends only to interstate waters. One result has been that as stricter State–Federal standards have been imposed, pollution has actually increased in some other waters—in underground aquifers and the oceans. As controls over interstate waters are tightened, polluting industries will be increasingly tempted to locate on intrastate lakes and rivers—with a consequently increased threat to those waterways—unless they too are brought under the same strictures.

I propose that we take an entirely new approach: one which concerts Federal, State and private efforts, which provides for effective nationwide enforcement, and which rests on a simple but profoundly significant principle: that the nation's waterways belong to us all, and that neither a municipality nor an industry should be allowed to discharge wastes into those waterways beyond their capacity to absorb the wastes without becoming polluted.

. . . .

AIR POLLUTION CONTROL

Air is our most vital resource, and its pollution is our most serious environmental problem. Existing technology for the control of air pollution is less advanced than that for controlling water pollution, but there is a great deal we can do within the limits of existing technology—and more we can do to spur technological advance.

Most air pollution is produced by the burning of fuels. About half is produced by motor vehicles.

Motor Vehicles

The Federal Government began regulating automobile emissions of carbon monoxide and hydrocarbons with the 1968 model year. Standards for 1970 model cars have been made significantly tighter. This year, for the first time, emissions from new buses and heavy-duty trucks have also been brought under Federal regulation.

In future years, emission levels can and must be brought much lower.

. . . .

With . . . changes, we can drastically reduce pollution from motor vehicles in the years just ahead. But in making and keeping our peace with nature, to plan only one year ahead or even five is hardly to plan at all. Our responsibility now is also to look beyond the Seventies, and the prospects then are uncertain. Based on present trends, it is quite possible that by 1980 the increase in the sheer number of cars in densely populated areas will begin outrunning the technological limits of our capacity to reduce pollution from the internal combustion engine. I hope this will not happen. I hope the automobile industry's present determined effort to make the internal combustion engine sufficiently pollution-free succeeds. But if it does not, then unless motor vehicles with an alternative, low-pollution power source are available, vehicle-caused pollution will once again begin an inexorable increase.

Therefore, prudence dictates that we move now to ensure that such a vehicle will be available if needed.

I am inaugurating a program to marshal both government and private research with the goal of producing an unconventionally powered, virtually pollution-free automobile within five years.

. . . The immediate task . . . is to see that an intensified program of research and development begins at once.

One encouraging aspect of the effort to curb motor vehicle pollution is the extent to which industry itself is taking the initiative. For example, the nation's principal automobile manufacturers are not only developing devices now to meet present and future Federal emission standards, but are also, on their own initiative, preparing to put on the market by 1972 automobiles which will not require and, indeed, must not use leaded gasoline. Such cars will not only discharge no lead into the atmosphere, but will also be equipped with still more effective devices for controlling emissions—devices made possible by the use of lead-free gasoline.

This is a great forward step taken by the manufacturers before any Federal regulation of lead additives or emissions has been imposed. I am confident that the petroleum industry will see to it that suitable non-leaded gasoline is made widely available for these new cars when they come on the market.

Stationary-Source Pollution

Industries, power plants, furnaces, incinerators—these and other so-called "stationary sources" add enormously to the pollution of the air. In highly industrialized areas, such pollution can quite literally make breathing hazardous to health, and can cause unforeseen atmospheric and meteorological problems as well.

Increasingly, industry itself has been adopting ambitious pollution-control programs, and state and local authorities have been setting and enforcing stricter anti-pollution standards. But they have not gone far enough or fast enough, nor, to be realistic about it, will they be able to without the strongest possible Federal backing. Without effective government standards, industrial firms that spend the necessary money for pollution control may find themselves at a serious economic disadvantage as against their less conscientious competitors. And without effective Federal standards, states and communities that require such controls find themselves at a similar disadvantage in attracting industry, against more permissive rivals. Air is no respecter of political boundaries: a community that sets and enforces strict standards may still find its air polluted from sources in another community or another state.

Under the Clean Air Act of 1967, the Federal government is establishing air quality control regions around the nation's major industrial and metropolitan areas. Within these regions, states are setting air quality standards—permissible levels of pollutants in the air—and developing plans for pollution abatement to achieve those air quality standards. All state air quality standards and implementation plans require Federal approval.

This program has been the first major Federal effort to control air pollution. It has been a useful beginning. But we have learned in the past two years that it has shortcomings. Federal designation of air quality control regions, while necessary in areas where emissions from one state are polluting the air in another, has been a time-consuming process. Adjoining states within the same region often have proposed inconsistent air quality standards, causing further delays for compromise and revision. There are no provisions for controlling pollution *outside* of established air quality control regions. This means that even with the designation of hundreds of such regions, some areas of the country with serious air pollution problems would remain outside of the program. This is unfair not only to the public but to many industries as well, since those within regions with strict requirements could be unfairly disadvantaged with respect to competitors that are not within regions. Finally, insufficient Federal enforcement powers have circumscribed the Federal government's ability to support the states in establishing and enforcing effective abatement programs.

It is time to build on what we have learned, and to begin a more ambitious national effort. I recommend that the Clean Air Act be revised to expand the scope of strict pollution abatement, to simplify the task of industry in pollution abatement through more nearly uniform standards, and to provide special controls against particularly dangerous pollutants.

—*I propose that the Federal government establish nationwide air quality standards, with the states to prepare within one year abatement plans for meeting those standards.*

This will provide a minimum standard for air quality for all areas of the nation, while permitting states to set more stringent standards for any or all sections within the state. National air quality standards will relieve the states of the lengthy process of standard-setting under Federal supervision, and allow them to concentrate on the immediate business of developing and implementing abatement plans.

These abatement plans would cover areas both inside and outside of Federally designated air quality control regions, and could be designed to achieve any higher levels of air quality which the states might choose to establish. They would include emission standards for stationary sources of air pollution.

. . . .

In the first instance, national standards are needed to guarantee the earliest possible elimination of certain air pollutants which are clear health hazards even in minute quantities. In the second instance, national standards will ensure that advanced abatement technology is used in constructing the new facilities, and that levels of air quality are maintained in the face of industrial expansion. Before any emissions standards were established, public hearings would be required involving all interested parties. The States would be responsible for enforcing these standards in conjunction with their own programs.

. . . .

SOLID WASTE MANAGEMENT

"Solid wastes" are the discarded left-overs of our advanced consumer society. Increasing in volume, they litter the landscape and strain the facilities of municipal governments.

New packaging methods, using materials which do not degrade and cannot easily be burned, create difficult new disposal problems. Though many wastes are potentially re-usable, we often discard today what a generation ago we saved. Most bottles, for example, now are "non-returnable." We re-process used paper less than we used to, not only adding to the burden on municipal sanitation services but also making wasteful use of scarce timberlands. Often the least expensive way to dispose of an old automobile is to abandon it—and millions of people do precisely that, creating eyesores for millions of others.

One way to meet the problem of solid wastes is simply to surrender to it: to continue pouring more and more public money into collection and disposal of whatever happens to be privately produced and discarded.

This is the old way; it amounts to a public subsidy of waste pollution. If we are ever truly to gain control of the problem, our goal must be broader: to reduce the volume of wastes and the difficulty of their disposal, and to encourage their constructive re-use instead.

To accomplish this, we need incentives, regulations and research directed especially at two major goals: (a) making products more easily disposable—especially containers, which are designed for disposal; and (b) re-using and recycling a far greater proportion of waste materials.

As we look toward the long-range future—to 1980, 2000 and beyond—recycling of materials will become increasingly necessary not only for waste disposal but also to conserve resources. While our population grows, each one of us keeps using more of the earth's resource. In the case of many common minerals, more than half those extracted from the earth since time began have been extracted since 1910.

A great deal of our space research has been directed toward creating self-sustaining environments, in which people can live for long periods of time by re-processing, re-cycling and re-using the same materials. We need to apply this kind of thinking more consciously and more broadly to our patterns of use and disposal of materials here on earth.

Many currently used techniques of solid waste disposal remain crudely deficient. Research and development programs under the Solid Waste Disposal Act of 1965 have added significantly to our knowledge of more efficient techniques. . . .

. . . .

Few of America's eyesores are so unsightly as its millions of junk automobiles.

Ordinarily, when a car is retired from use it goes first to a wrecker, who strips it of its valuable parts, and then to a scrap processor, who reduces the remainder to scrap for sale to steel mills. The prices paid by wreckers for junk cars often are less than the cost of transporting them to the wrecking yard. In the case of a severely damaged or "cannibalized" car, instead of paying for it the wrecker may even charge towing costs. Thus the final owner's economic incentive to deliver his car for processing is slight, non-existent or even negative.

The rate of abandonment is increasing. In New York City, 2,500 cars were towed away as abandoned on the streets in 1960. In 1964, 25,000 were towed away as abandoned; in 1969, more than 50,000.

The way to provide the needed incentive is to apply to the automobile the principle that its price should include not only the cost of producing it, but also the cost of disposing of it.

. . . .

The particular disposal problems presented by the automobile are unique. However, wherever appropriate we should also seek to establish incentives and regulations to encourage the re-use, re-cycling or easier disposal of other commonly used goods.

.   .   .   .

PARKS AND PUBLIC RECREATION

Increasing population, increasing mobility, increasing incomes and increasing leisure will all combine in the years ahead to rank recreational facilities among the most vital of our public resources. Yet land suitable for such facilities, especially near heavily populated areas, is being rapidly swallowed up.

Plain common sense argues that we give greater priority to acquiring now the lands that will be so greatly needed in a few years. Good sense also argues that the Federal Government itself, as the nation's largest landholder, should address itself more imaginatively to the question of making optimum use of its own holdings in a recreation-hungry era.

> —*I propose full funding in fiscal 1971 of the $327 million available through the Land and Water Conservation Fund for additional park and recreational facilities, with increased emphasis on locations that can be easily reached by the people in crowded urban areas.*
>
> —*I propose that we adopt a new philosophy for the use of Federally-owned lands, treating them as a precious resource—like money itself—which should be made to serve the highest possible public good.*

Acquiring needed recreation areas is a real estate transaction. One third of all the land in the United States—more than 750,000,000 acres— is owned by the Federal Government. Thousands of acres in the heart of metropolitan areas are reserved for only minimal use by Federal installations. To supplement the regularly-appropriated funds available, nothing could be more appropriate than to meet new real estate needs through use of presently-owned real estate, whether by transfer, sale or conversion to a better use.

Until now, the uses to which Federally-owned properties were put has largely been determined by who got them first. As a result, countless properties with enormous potential as recreation areas linger on in the hands of agencies that could just as well—or better—locate elsewhere. Bureaucratic inertia is compounded by a quirk of present accounting procedures, which has the effect of imposing a budgetary penalty on an agency that gives up one piece of property and moves to another, even if the vacated property is sold for 10 times the cost of the new.

The time has come to make more rational use of our enormous wealth of real property, giving a new priority to our newly urgent concern with public recreation—and to make more imaginative use of properties now surplus to finance acquisition of properties now needed.

> —*By Executive Order, I am directing the heads of all Federal agencies and the Administrator of General Services to institute a review of all Federally-owned real properties that should be considered for other uses. The test will be whether a particular property's continued present use or another would better serve the public interest, considering both the agency's needs and the property's location. Special emphasis will be placed on identifying properties that could appropriately be converted to parks and recreation areas, or sold, so that proceeds can be made available to provide additional park and recreation lands.*

. . . .

This would allow a part of the proceeds from the sales of surplus properties to be used for relocating such installations, thus making more land available.

. . . .

The net effect would be to increase our capacity to add new park and recreational facilities, by enabling us for the first time to use surplus property sales in a coordinated three-way program: (a) by direct conversion from other uses; (b) through sale of presently-owned properties and purchase of others with the proceeds; and (c) by sale of one Federal property, and use of the proceeds to finance the relocation and conversion costs of making another property available for recreational use.

. . . .

As one example of what such a property review can make possible, a sizable stretch of one of California's finest beaches has long been closed to the public because it was part of Camp Pendleton. Last month the Defense Department arranged to make more than a mile of that beach available to the State of California for use as a State park. The remaining beach is sufficient for Camp Pendleton's needs; thus the released stretch represents a shift from low-priority to high-priority use. By carefully weighing alternative uses, a priceless recreational resource was returned to the people for recreational purposes.

Another vast source of potential parklands also lies untapped. We have come to realize that we have too much land available for growing crops and not enough land for parks, open space and recreation.

. . . .

ORGANIZING FOR ACTION

The environmental problems we face are deep-rooted and widespread. They can be solved only by a full national effort embracing not only sound, coordinated planning, but also an effective follow-through that reaches into every community in the land. Improving our surroundings is necessarily the business of us all.

At the Federal level, we have begun the process of organizing for this effort.

The Council on Environmental Quality has been established. This Council will be the keeper of our environmental conscience, and a goad to our ingenuity; beyond this, it will have responsibility for ensuring that all our programs and actions are undertaken with a careful respect for the needs of environmental quality. I have already assigned it major responsibilities for new program development, and I shall look to it increasingly for new initiatives.

The Cabinet Committee on the Environment which I created last year acts as a coordinating agency for various departmental activities affecting the environment.

To meet future needs, many organizational changes will still be needed. Federal institutions for dealing with the environment and natural resources have developed piecemeal over the years in response to specific needs, not all of which were originally perceived in the light of the concerns we recognize today. Many of their missions appear to overlap, and even to conflict. Last year I asked the President's Advisory Council on Executive Organization, headed by Mr. Roy Ash, to make an especially thorough study of the organization of Federal environmental, natural resource and oceanographic programs, and to report its recommendations to me by April 15. After receiving their report, I shall recommend needed reforms, which will involve major reassignments of responsibilities among Departments.

For many of the same reasons, overlaps in environmental programs extend to the Legislative as well as the Executive branch, so that close consultation will be necessary before major steps are taken.

No matter how well organized government itself might be, however, in the final analysis the key to success lies with the people of America.

Private industry has an especially crucial role. Its resources, its technology, its demonstrated ingenuity in solving problems others only talk about—all these are needed, not only in helping to curb the pollution industry itself creates but also in helping devise new and better ways of enhancing all aspects of our environment.

I have ordered that the United States Patent Office give special priority to the processing of applications for patents which could aid in curbing environmental abuses.

Industry already has begun moving swiftly toward a fuller recognition of its own environmental responsibilities, and has made substantial progress in many areas. However, more must be done.

Mobilizing industry's resources requires organization. With a remarkable degree of unanimity, its leaders have indicated their readiness to help.

I will shortly ask a group of the nation's principal industrial leaders to join me in establishing a National Industrial Pollution Control Council.

The Council will work closely with the Council on Environmental Quality, the Citizens' Advisory Committee on Environmental Quality, the Secretary of Commerce and others as appropriate in the development of effective policies for the curbing of air, water, noise and waste pollution from industrial sources. It will work to enlist increased support from business and industry in the drive to reduce pollution, in all its forms, to the minimum level possible. It will provide a mechanism through which, in many cases, government can work with key leaders in various industries to establish voluntary programs for accomplishing desired pollution-control goals.

Patterns of organization often turn out to be only as good as the example set by the organizer. For years, many Federal facilities have themselves been among the worst polluters. The Executive Order I issued last week not only accepts responsibility for putting a swift end to Federal pollution, but puts teeth into the commitment.

I hope this will be an example for others.

At the turn of the century, our chief environmental concern was to conserve what we had—and out of this concern grew the often embattled but always determined "conservation" movement. Today, "conservation" is as important as ever—but no longer is it enough to conserve what we have; we must also restore what we have lost. We have to go beyond conservation to embrace restoration.

The task of cleaning up our environment calls for a total mobilization by all of us. It involves governments at every level; it requires the help of every citizen. It cannot be a matter of simply sitting back and blaming someone else. Neither is it one to be left to a few hundred leaders. Rather, it presents us with one of those rare situations in which each individual everywhere has an opportunity to make a special contribution to his country as well as his community.

Through the Council on Environmental Quality, through the Citizens' Advisory Committee on Environmental Quality, and working with Governors and Mayors and county officials and with concerned private groups, we shall be reaching out in an effort to enlist millions of helping hands, millions of willing spirits—millions of volunteer citizens who will put to themselves the simple question: "What can *I* do?"

It is in this way—with vigorous Federal leadership, with active enlistment of governments at every level, with the aid of industry and private groups, and above all with the determined participation by individual citizens in every state and every community, that we at last will succeed in restoring the kind of environment we want for ourselves, and the kind the generations that come after deserve to inherit.

This task is ours together. It summons our energy, our ingenuity and our conscience in a cause as fundamental as life itself.

Part Four

The Public Interest

"*C*onservation" is one of the great value words in applied politics. Basically it has come to mean the attitude that *I*—or individuals like me—have toward natural resources. No one is opposed to conservation—only to certain policies pursued in accordance with *unacceptable* definitions of the word. You will note that the articles reprinted in this part have such words and phrases in their titles as "standards" "policy goal" and "public interest." This is the company which conservation keeps.

Much of the debating in natural resources is over how to define the term "conservation." If a definition could be agreed upon, much of the wrangling would be taken out of the struggles to establish resource policies.

Of course, I can say that *I* know what conservation *really* means—which makes this entire book reflect ideas which support *my* point of view. But that is the nature of the debate: People only believe those with whom they agree and trust those whose ideas they know.

The battles over "conservation" are emotional ones. No one is objective. If one is neutral, he is opposed—for lack of support could lead to a loss. And often in environmental politics a loss is seen as final with no turning back, while a win is regarded as only temporary. Consumer demands, national emergencies, changes in party control or industrial disasters are seen as opportunities to turn the tables or reinforce a current policy.

Conservation is also a complicating factor because an attitude toward the environment is seldom applied generally. One's attitude toward that from which he derives pleasure or economic gain may often differ from the way he feels about that which affords him other satisfactions. Thus, Mr. A may not mind oil drilling off Santa Barbara because he is a company stockholder or does not expect to visit Santa Barbara; but do not disturb the woods behind his house by building a freeway. Or Mrs. B could be deeply involved in protecting a local scenic sight while being oblivious to pelagic sealing.

There are few who hold a consistent point of view toward nature and its resources. A wealthy industrialist who is generally regarded as an "exploiter of nature" by his opponents can at the same time be a fierce and influential protagonist to preserve the pristine beauty surrounding his summer home.

There are few Hindus amongst us who wish to preserve all life and all nature; nor are there many, if any, of those who have complete disregard for the future of the earth's riches.

Orris C. Herfindahl discusses the nature of the conservation argument in the following selection. Then George R. Hall, who has written widely on translating conservation into public policy, outlines the broad schools of conservation thought. The need for refining the information which defines the criteria upon which resource policies are decided is discussed in Norman Wengert's article, and Gerald F. Vaughn writes on the problems of setting standards for a specific policy goal. John Kenneth Galbraith closes this part by calling for a discussion of consumption policy; he asserts that there is a need to determine the nature of demands on resources so as to more rationally approach the required divisions. This section as a whole indicates that whatever the resource policy goal, there are diverse arguments and forces which are eligible for enlistment.

Orris C. Herfindahl

*What is Conservation?**

A discussion between two conservationists who are interested in conserving different things often degenerates into polite name-calling or worse. Smith will tell Jones that he doesn't know what *true* conservation is. And Jones will reply acidly that what Smith proposes—far from being conservation—is profligate waste. Finally the discussion ends from boredom or exhaustion, with each conservationist walking away shaking his head and saying to himself that he doesn't see how anyone could hold such inane views. The outsider viewing this fruitless exchange is puzzled. If both parties are for conservation, which everybody seems to think is a good thing, what are they quarreling about?

One of the difficulties is that the word conservation is used with varying meanings, often without telling the other party to the discussion what one's definition is. But the confusion is not simply a matter of failing to let the other fellow in on one's private definition, for many users of this term seem to have no clear definition of their own and seem to prefer the ambiguity that results.

The imprecision surrounding use of the word, conservation, has been associated with widespread attempts to appropriate its persuasive sound for special interests. If a certain proposal is labeled a conservation proposal, or to go even further, if the proposal is said to represent *true* conservation—implying that there is a subtle but compelling case for its adoption—there is probably a tendency for more favorable reaction than if a less emotive term is used. After all, if a person is asked whether it is better to conserve or not conserve, he no doubt will vote for conservation. Of course it would be unthinking of him to vote at all since he didn't ask the questioner what meaning was to be given to conservation, but the point is that the mere mention of the word tends to stimulate favorable response rather than a search for meaning.

The confusion surrounding use of the term conservation and the attempt to appropriate favorable reaction to it for special interest proposals and programs is readily apparent to even the most cursory examination. It is an interesting exercise to go over speeches or writings

*Reprinted by permission from *Three Studies in Mineral Economics* (Washington: Resources for the Future, 1961), 1–12.
(Notes to this selection will be found on p. 416.)

on conservation matters and to ask what definition of conservation the person might have in mind. Quite often it turns out that he believes his policy should be adopted *because* it will conserve (that is, save for future use or preserve for use) a *particular* resource product, for example, water for irrigation. But confusion arises when the city dweller insists that the water should go to the city for drinking, cooling, etc., because *that* is really conservation.

Sometimes general definitions are given. A widely favored one is the following: "Conservation is the use of natural resources for the greatest good of the greatest number for the longest time." This is the definition that Gifford Pinchot, the founder of what historians are wont to call the Conservation Movement, was fond of using. Pinchot credits the definition to W J McGee (who insisted on no periods after the initials), a freewheeling intellect of very wide interests and great ability who worked with John Wesley Powell and later with Pinchot.[1]

When this definition is read off rapidly—conservation is the use of natural resources for the greatest good of the greatest number for the longest time—the three superlatives have a delightful ring. If this is conservation, how could anyone be opposed to it? No one could be, of course, unless he stops to ask himself how three variables can be maximized at the same time. Imagine a father trying to distribute a bag of candy to his children so as to maximize the amount of candy received by each child who gets candy *and* the number of children receiving candy *and* the length of time the candy will be visible.

Still another general formulation has enjoyed great popularity with politicans for over half a century, and with others whose audiences are of opposing minds. Again let us take Pinchot's formulation, which may have been fathered by him: "Conservation implies both the development and the protection of resources, the one as much as the other. . . ."[2] On the surface, this should command general assent, for who among us is opposed to development? Who is opposed to the protection of resources? The trouble comes when the blanks are filled in. Suppose that development means covering a canyon with a lake for purposes of power and irrigation while preservation means leaving the canyon alone so that its beauty can be seen. An excellent example is provided by the Echo Park controversy. It was indeed impossible both to develop the dam site and at the same time preserve one of the products of this natural resource, namely, the beauty of Echo Park and the nearby canyons. Unfortunately, a verbal incantation that reconciles the irreconcilable does not in fact resolve the very real conflict between development and preservation. There is no inconsistency between development and preservation, however, if one's objective is the "conservation" of only one of the uses of the resource.

In the case of mineral resources, the stock of which is used up in the act of consumption—perhaps with some recirculation—the injunction to develop and preserve simultaneously is even more mystifying than it was in the preceding case. Development in the case of minerals means production, but preservation presumably means postponement of consumption. How can both be done simultaneously except by accumulating an ever larger inventory of metal above the ground?

Pinchot's casual approach to the problem of definition is even further illustrated on the same page where we are admonished both to develop and to preserve. For example, "The essence of conservation is the application of common sense to the common problems for the common good." Or, "Conservation is simple, obvious and right." Comment would be superfluous.

Slackness and confusion in definition, so clearly exemplified in the writings of Pinchot and his contemporaries, have continued down to the present. It is only the exceptional writer on conservation whose use of the word is not self-contradictory or a mere camouflage, whether deliberate or not, for the promotion of some special interest such as special wilderness areas, irrigation, power, and so on. The definitions of Pinchot's time, perhaps better called slogans, have been repeated ever since. "The greatest good for the greatest number for the longest time" will be with us for a long time to come. And almost any speech on natural resources coming out of the Department of the Interior contains the contradictory admonitions to develop and to preserve within the same sentence.

What is the origin of this confusion in definition? Why has it continued for so long? In my view this indifference to clarity of definition rests in considerable part on the existence of deep underlying conflicts among various interest groups in the area of conservation policy, by which I mean the policy problems involved in determining how natural resources are used. Proponents of special conservation interests, in their zeal to alter governmental policy, have made clarity and consistency of definition a secondary consideration. Indeed, clear definition might lose all the advantage to be gained from using so fine sounding a word as "conservation" or the related "develop and preserve." Clarity about real intentions might unnecessarily antagonize those who otherwise would not press home to the real meaning behind generalities.

Certainly one of the dominant conflicts in the field of conservation was and is the conflict between development and what I shall call nature preservation. By development is meant the use of natural resources in such a way as to involve the construction of auxiliary capital goods such as dams, roads, processing plants, hotels, etc. "Nature preservation" is a term which embraces the whole spectrum of groups interested in preserving various aspects of nature as she is (Or is it with some "development"?) for the direct enjoyment of individuals. Such diverse things are involved as birds (to be preserved for eye, ear, and palate), solitude, scenery, trees, flowing water, naturally still water (that is, natural lakes), etc. This is sometimes said to constitute the birds and bees school of conservation, a phrase that can be uttered with a tone of either affection or derision, depending on whether one is in or out of the group.

The antagonism between development and nature preservation has always been present in the field of conservation. Even the founder of the movement in the United States, Gifford Pinchot, was not disposed to ride both these horses at the same time. It is quite clear on reading his writings that he was a developmentalist first and a preservationist only secondarily, if at all.

For example, in 1903 Pinchot made the following statement in an address to the Society of American Foresters:

The object of our forest policy is not to preserve the forests because they are beautiful . . . or because they are refuges for the wild creatures of the wilderness . . . but . . . the making of prosperous homes . . . . Every other consideration comes as secondary.[3]

It is not surprising that the nature preservationist groups became increasingly dissatisfied with Pinchot's views on what conservationists should be doing, and that they came to feel he was using the Conservation Movement to promote policies to which they were strongly opposed. This divergence in points of view was an important factor in bringing about the disintegration of the Conservation Movement.[4]

The conflict between development and nature preservation has erupted from time to time in pitched battles. For example, New York's constitutional provision requiring the Adirondack State Park lands to be kept "forever wild"—that is, with no lumbering—was the subject of intense controversy in the constitutional revisions of 1895 and 1915, and there are always attempts to nibble away at it. Most recently the nature preservationists tilted with developmentalists who wanted a thruway constructed to pass through the eastern part of the park. This controversy is especially interesting for our purposes because it also provided an example of the conflict between development and preservation *within* the ranks of the preservationists. That is to say, the preservationists were divided, with one group, whose *bona fides* is not open to question, supporting the thruway partly on the ground that it would not prevent the preservation of anything worth preserving. The Constitutional amendment required to allow construction of the thruway (called the Northway) was passed, and construction is in progress.

The Hetch–Hetchy controversy, involving construction of a dam across a beautiful valley to supply water for San Francisco, is still remembered by many. The establishment and the regulations governing the uses of wildlife refuges, national parks, and national forests have been and continue to be the source of controversy between the two groups. Recently an intense struggle has been going on over a bill that would establish wilderness areas on certain parts of federal land holdings.

These few brief references give only a hint of the depth and pervasiveness of the perennial conflict between development and nature preservation. It should be emphasized again, however, that this is not the only controversy within the groups who call themselves conservationists. Various types of development often turn out to be incompatible with each other: irrigation versus urban water supply, for example. And within the nature preservation group there are latent conflicts that come into the open every now and then. The split over construction of the Northway has been mentioned, but there are many more. For example, the National Park Service—certainly a nature preservationist organization—frequently comes under fire because it concedes too much to development in the form of roads, accommodations, and so on. Struggles within the preservationist group frequently involve a difference of view in the amount and type of development in the form of facilities that should accompany "preservation."

It is these conflicts, then, which are an important source of uncritical or intentional usage according to which the statement that a certain action or policy is conservative in nature (in the everyday meaning of conserve) is meant to imply the desirability of that action or policy. "Build the dam, because that will *conserve* water and prevent its waste in spring floods." Or, "It is only by not building the dam that the natural beauties of the valley can be *conserved*." Each side has tried to wrap itself in the favorable reaction surrounding the word conservation.

Broadly speaking, there are two ways by which usage can be brought to heel so that it will aid rather than hinder understanding. One way is to say that the goal of conservation policy is to adjust outputs through time in such a way as to maximize the return from *all* resources at the disposal of society. In the process of doing this, some resources will be used up, perhaps "completely," and there may be a gradual transformation of "natural" resources into man-made capital "goods" of many different types. To put it differently, this view of conservation policy equates it with "wise use of resources."

This is a view that enjoys considerable currency. If carefully adhered to, it avoids what we have called the main difficulty in usage, for on this view you cannot say that a certain policy represents "true conservation" until a *complete* economic analysis of its effects has been attempted, and no reasonable person can ask for more than that. But to equate conservation with "wise use" is to attain a defensible usage only by assimilating the problem of conservation completely into the general economic problem of maximizing output and by departing radically from the everyday meaning of the word "conserve."

It is preferable, in my opinion, to preserve common usage and to agree that a conservative act is one which saves something for future use instead of present use or which saves something for use instead of nonuse. This usage leaves open the possibility that the conservation of one resource may entail the sacrifice of another resource which others may want to conserve. Thus there is *no* justification for concluding that a certain policy should be adopted simply because it conserves some resource, for it may involve so much cost either in the form of current productive services required (e.g., to build a dam) and/or in the destruction of *other* resources that it is not justified. A proper usage, if the everyday meaning of "conserve" is retained, should *not* involve the implicit view that conservation is always desirable. Sometimes it is, but sometimes it is not. The question always is whether the gains outweigh the costs.

If this obvious but important point is neglected, the way is open to advocate policies that make no economic sense at all. An extreme example is provided by those who have been able to conclude—without examining costs—that government policy should be directed to the *full* regulation of nearly all the nation's streams over the long run. (Full regulation means the complete or nearly complete evening out of flow on a stream. The usual means for doing this is to build storage capacity behind dams.) Other cases of error resulting from neglect of costs may be more subtle. For example, no satisfactory argument can be constructed for an indiscriminate policy of maximum sustained yield from "forest lands." Nor can a satisfactory argument be made for a policy to conserve coal by requiring coal operators to mine 100 per cent or any other percentage of the coal in a deposit. Such questions cannot be discussed usefully without reference to costs.

Conflicts within the conservation area will not be eliminated even if the term conservation is used in a proper way; that is, without pretense that a particular conservation policy is desirable, *ipso facto*, without reference to costs. But clear usage is a tool which at least will not hinder—and probably will aid—the resolution of conflicts over the use of resources. It is likely that a clear usage, always with the realization that conservative action is desirable only if benefits exceed costs, will be of increasing importance, for the intensity of conflicts over the use of certain resources probably will increase as time goes on.

In the future as in the past, however, many conservation problems will continue to be settled for us by the working of the private market system. This is especially true of the minerals industries. By and large, we accept the price system as the arbiter between the present and the future, and there is little prospect that this practice will be abandoned.

We do not, for example, impose a tax on the production of copper in order to save copper for use by future generations. The problem of the level of recovery is left to the mining company, the smelter, and the refiner. The reason why the price system can be trusted to yield a suitable solution to many of the conservation problems involving minerals is that costs and benefits involved in mining and related activities effectively enter into the calculations of private firms to a greater extent than is true for the exploitation of other natural resources.

The petroleum industry in the United States constitutes a notable exception, of course. The fact that single ownership was not coextensive with oil pools required some sort of action to prevent the needless multiplication of oil wells and to prevent economically wasteful loss of oil underground. Our attempts to cope with these problems seem to be running into increasing difficulty, however, not because the problem of rational exploitation of an oil pool has suddenly become more difficult from a technical point of view, but because the particular method of control in vogue is yielding some undesired results.

The elements of our control system are, first, control (actually only partial) of total production of the industry. The objectives are mixed, of course, being both conservation and control of price. If control of price were not involved there would be no restriction of production of individual wells below "efficient capacity" or perhaps MER (maximum efficient rate). The second element of the system is spacing regulation. A third element is limitation of imports. An additional point, so important it must be called a fourth element of the system, is that there is essentially no restriction on the development of new producing capacity other than the test of profitability. The combined effect of these factors is the development of capacity to produce far in excess of current production, as could easily have been predicted.

The difficult conservation problems—and this includes U.S. petroleum production—arise in those cases where relevant costs and benefits are not united in the calculations of a single economic unit. In some cases, the benefits from a certain action cannot be appropriated by the business that would have to pay for the action. Elimination of stream pollution is a case in point. Or the benefits from a certain action may be worth the cost to a firm, but perhaps this action imposes costs on others for which the firm does not have to pay. Logging and grazing may increase the rapidity of runoff, for example, an effect that may be of no concern to the logger or grazer but which may be of prime importance to downstream users of the water. Sometimes a governmental decision-making unit may neglect certain costs or benefits because it is engaged in stimulating one type of resource use. This may even be viewed—in practice if not legally—as its official mission. Sometimes certain costs or benefits are not brought to bear on a decision because they cannot be quantified in money terms or can be described only in vague nonquantitative terms.

It is likely that in the natural resource area this type of problem will become more pressing as time goes on, both because demands for each of the possible uses of some resources are growing relative to supply, and because new rival demands are rising rapidly whereas before they may have been inconsequential.

Consider, for example, just a few of the various parties with at least partially conflicting interests in the way land and streams are used. There is irrigation vs. power; irrigation vs. domestic and industrial water use; uses requiring dams vs. the scenery, fishing, etc., associated with flowing streams; in particular the whole complex of benefits associated with flowing streams vs. domestic and industrial water use. There is the sand and gravel pit or the clay pit, with its ugliness and sometimes dangerous pools of water, vs. the residential area with its small children; logging vs. scenery; highways bringing a greater density of people to remote areas vs. solitude; logging and grazing vs. the people downstream who want a slower runoff; and so on.

There are two factors that will tend to intensify these conflicts as time goes on. One is the increase in population, with its obvious effects on the demands for the many different uses of water and on the supply of open space. The other factor is what appears to be an increasing per capita demand for many particular forms of outdoor recreation and for outdoor recreation in general. A number of these forms of recreation do require extensive space and a low density of people. The changing structure of demands for services of resources arising from these two factors suffices to insure no easing of problems in the conservation area.

Exploitation of minerals may be less affected than will be the use of other natural resources, but even here the increased density of population will have its effect—by zoning or otherwise—especially on the ubiquitous minerals. And even in areas where population density remains low, mineral operations will experience more frequent collisions with the various forms of outdoor recreation activity. This will not be a new problem, but it will arise more frequently.

How are the conflicts to be resolved? A first step has already been suggested; namely, to stop pretending that a policy is desirable just because it entails the conservation of something.

Some conflicts can be solved easily since they involve situations in which all the potential users of a resource can *effectively* voice their demands in a monetary form. In such cases the presumption in our society (but perhaps rebuttable in some instances!) is that the highest bidders should win, whether the resource is in public or private ownership. It is highly desirable that an effort be made to develop new forms of organization and procedure to permit more extensive use of the market to resolve questions of resource use.

But in many cases there are serious difficulties standing in the way of a thoroughgoing market solution of the problem of rival demands. While interference with and modification of the market's solution will not necessarily yield a better result, the possibility is open. Regulation of the way a resource is used may be desirable where the private user does not take account of significant costs or benefits that his action imposes or gives to others. Some decisions have long-lasting consequences requiring an estimate of demands and costs far into the future, with some cases involving social penalties for underestimate (or overestimate) that may not effectively enter into the private decision. Some benefits and costs do not yield easily, if at all, to valuation in terms of money even for current flows of benefits and costs, let alone those of the future. Here we must analyze and calculate as best we can, trying to search out *all* benefits and costs, some of which may have to be measured and described in nonmonetary terms. It should be recognized that there *are* benefits flowing from natural resources for which individuals cannot express their preferences in money terms simply because there is no feasible way for this to be done. In particular, it will not do to argue that society "needs" lumber or minerals but that scenery, etc., can always be dispensed with. This is an unreal choice, for the problem always involves a specific location. If consumers could express their preferences in economic terms, they might well indicate they want a particular slope to be forested rather than bare.

A consequence of the fact that some flows of benefits and costs do not receive effective expression in monetary terms is that some of the decisions about the use of natural resources inevitably involve substantial redistributions of real income. The losers from the destruction of the beauties of nature are rarely compensated. The point is not that they should be compensated or that "nature" must always be preserved. The point is that, at a minimum, those whose responsibility it is to make decisions on the use of certain resources should be aware that attention to total costs and benefits may not be enough, for the effects on the real incomes of particular individuals may be substantial.

Unfortunately there is no magic formula that will resolve these problems. The "multiple use" solution, for example, is certainly applicable in many cases, but in some cases it turns out to be just a slogan serving to camouflage the complete sacrifice of one use to others. For example, a reservoir may yield multiple uses including certain forms of recreation, but it is also true that construction of a reservoir entails the complete sacrifice of all uses that depend on the presence of a flowing stream. Once again the lesson is that no slogan, not even one so appealing as multiple use, can resolve all the conflicts present in resource use. Some uses are simply inconsistent with some other uses.

In any particular decision involving incompatible uses, one or the other must be sacrificed, of course. But for a group of decisions involving different projects, uses need not be inconsistent for all projects in an area taken together. It is only by paying close attention to the evolving pattern of use decisions that it is possible to give recognition and at least partial satisfaction to incompatible demands. An indiscriminate application of a multiple-use slogan runs the danger that certain uses which are inconsistent with "multiple use" will get neglected in decision after decision, thus securing no recognition in the final picture that emerges.

In many cases the instrument for resolution of conflict will have to be the political process. The participants include not only those ordinarily thought of as politicians, but the varied types of participants in any significant political problem such as interested voters, government employees, lobbyists, journalists, and so on. Obviously *some* sort of resolution comes out of the process, but the question is how to make the results better. Certainly information and understanding of effects are necessary. Apart from this we need ingenuity and imagination in the formulation of new or variant solutions—new compromises, if you like. And in this area, as in many others, the majority ought to take very seriously its obligation not to trample unheedingly over the minority. In the case of nature preservation issues, especially, certain segments of the population may receive an important part of their real income— measured in satisfaction—from publicly or privately owned resources in which they have no legal interest.

If this advice is taken to heart by the participants in these conserva- tion problems, a change in posture will be required in some cases. While it may seem tactically wise—and may even be pleasant—to oppose all dam construction or to damn the wilderness enthusiasts as a minute nonworking portion of the population with perverted tastes, any progress toward a more suitable resolution of conflicts as they arise is going to be made by those who are less inflexible. An abandonment of fixed positions would be helpful.

The main burden of this discussion perhaps will not be attractive to those who believe that greater conservation of some one thing is always desirable, whether that be songbirds, irrigation water, trees, or grass for sheep, for we have downgraded the term. As often used, it is taken to imply sufficiency for action. The view suggested here, on the other hand, is that a conservative act may or may not be desirable, depending on all the associated benefits and costs and perhaps on the redistribution of real incomes involved. But this downgrading of the term, if it should be called that, does not carry with it any implication that conservation issues are unimportant. Rather, insistence that acts of conservation should not be undertaken simply because something is conserved reflects a view that conservation problems are so important that it is unwise to deal with them on the basis of slogans.

George R. Hall

Conservation as a
Public Policy Goal*

Conservation, like patriotism, motherhood, and the flag, is good by definition, but any specific conservation policy is likely to give rise to the bitterest disagreement. The trouble arises because there are three basic groups of conservationists, each claiming to be the only spokesmen for conservation. Although each of these groups has important insights into problems of using natural resources, they differ fundamentally with respect to objectives. Consequently, conservation as a political force has suffered from internal conflicts and schisms.

An illustration of the diversity of viewpoints on conservation is provided by the $27\frac{1}{2}$ per cent depletion allowance for oil wells. This provision gives the petroleum industry a profit advantage over other industries and is usually justified as increasing oil production and thereby promoting conservation. Production is limited, however, by the Texas Railroad Commission and similar regulatory boards which set monthly production allowances for each well. Yet this limitation is also defended as eliminating waste and thereby promoting conservation. Thus in the name of conservation we both encourage and discourage oil production. To complicate the picture, in 1957 limitations were imposed on oil imports in order to increase domestic production and thereby, so it was claimed, promote conservation. Depletion allowances and import quotas increase domestic production, but the monthly production allowances decrease output. Yet each policy has sincere defenders who feel that their policy is the only way to conserve petroleum resources. In terms of the different conservation ideologies, each position has some justification.

A further example is provided by the serious political dispute over the effect of the proposed Echo Park Dam on the Dinosaur National Monument. The argument was largely between two groups, each claiming to speak in the name of conservation. The first group argued that unless the Echo Park Dam was constructed, potential hydroelectric power would be wasted. The second group argued that to build a high dam in the area would violate conservation principles by destroying

*Reprinted by permission from *The Yale Review*, LI (1962), 400–413. Copyright Yale University Press.

priceless natural scenery. Again, each group could claim to be speaking for conservation.

A long list of disputes in which each side claimed to be for conservation could be drawn up. There have been arguments over timber, irrigation, soil, wilderness, recreation facilities, and other resources. However, these two cases demonstrate that conservation intrudes in many different types of political decisions and that there is no settled and clear consensus on what the conservation of natural resources requires.

Conservation as a policy goal needs to be given a specific meaning. Among the economic objectives considered most important today are growth, price stability, efficiency, freedom of decision-making, and conservation. There are problems for each of these goals, but for most of them the semantic issues are of secondary significance. With conservation that semantic problem is paramount and requires investigation.

On the basis of political and social goals there are three different conservationist positions. Let us call these positions the neo-Malthusian, the technician, and the naturalist.

Increased attention to the problem of economic growth has re-awakened interest in the basic Malthusian question of whether population will tend to outstrip the resource base of an economy. Since World War II a number of books, such as those by Harrison Brown, Fairfield Osborn, and Samuel H. Ordway, Jr., have examined current population trends in relation to the resources required to maintain current standards of living. Neo-Malthusians point to the doubling of the United States population in exactly fifty years and the staggering amounts of raw materials consumed each year. Classical Malthusians argued that food was the factor limiting expansion, but the neo-Malthusians stress that many inorganic materials are also in short supply. They point out that even if we do not face starvation, there is a real question as to our ability to maintain present standards of living. They point out that millions of dollars are spent annually to search for new deposits of raw materials and for substitutes, but that there is no certainty that new replacements will continue to be found. Neo-Malthusians are pessimists about the ability of mankind to maintain present standards of consumption. Unless man adjusts to nature, they feel that the results will be disastrous.

To the optimistic assertion that science and technology will continue to increase our resource base as in the past, neo-Malthusians reply that such a procedure becomes increasingly difficult and that substitutes for new materials will themselves become as scarce as the materials for which they are to substitute. As a clinching argument members of this group frequently state that even if substitutes can be found they will undoubtedly be grossly inferior to present supplies in quality. Even if we can make steaks from sawdust or plankton, it is hard to imagine that they will be an adequate replacement for prime sirloin.

If one accepts this vision of the conservation problem, two lines of attack are open: Either the growth of population must be limited, as classical Malthusians emphasized, or our views about the desirability of a continued expansion of the standard of living must be revised. Samuel H. Ordway, Jr., in his very persuasive book, *Resources and the American Dream*, suggests the second route. His reasoning about industrial growth is that sooner or later industrial expansion will have to halt because of the limited resource base. If this limit is reached unexpectedly and abruptly it is likely that the social order and civilization as we know it would not recover. To him the obvious answer is to slow down on our growth rate and spread out our use of resources over a longer period of time.

The idea of limiting the improvement in the standard of living runs directly counter to prevailing thought in official and private circles. Acceptance or rejection of continual economic expansion as a policy objective depends not only upon economic but also many social and political considerations. It is clear, however, that on this question, neo-Malthusians are in the minority.

There is a more serious objection to the neo-Malthusian view than its minority status. The basic error in the position is that an economy does not suddenly run out of resources; it merely becomes more difficult and expensive to obtain them. This means that a country would never experience an *abrupt* halt to growth due to a lack of resources. The rate of growth would just slow down or be more difficult to maintain.

To demonstrate the proposition that lack of resources would not lead to a sharp halt in growth, let us imagine a fantastic situation. Let us posit that all fossil fuels (oil, coal, gas, etc.) were suddenly destroyed. With present technology we could use atomic power for stationary and large mobile power units. Cars could be run on storage batteries; solar heat could be used for homes in many areas. Numerous other changes could be made to substitute nonfossil fuels or to cut down on the amount of fuels required. Despite all the changes we would continue to transport ourselves, operate our industry, and heat our homes. Of course, the cost of power would be much greater. Production and consumption in the United States is organized on the basis of low-cost fuels. The hypothetical case assumed would require startling changes in the way we live and work. People would build houses with low ceilings, fewer windows and more insulation. Industry would have to depend on atomic or other expensive types of power. The industrial revolution was, in essence, the discovery of new and cheap power sources and expensive power would produce changes just as startling.

Of course in reality fuels or any resource are not all destroyed at once; they gradually become scarce or difficult to obtain. Changes in production and consumption, therefore, are gradual, unspectacular, and generally unnoticed. High-priced resources usually stimulate scientific and engineering efforts so that new inventions cut down the cost of raw materials. But even considering only present technology, shifts in production and consumption occur gradually as resources become scarce.

The point is that a nation's resource base is not a fixed sum. In large degree the amount of resources we have is determined by costs and prices. Costs and prices in turn have two functions. They reflect the effort required to obtain resources or the scarcity of the resources relative to demand. And costs and prices serve as incentives for people to economize on the use of scarce resources by adjusting the types of materials consumed.

Thus the neo-Malthusians' emphasis on running out of resources is somewhat misplaced, although they are correct in asserting that large price changes would have substantial social effects. An America based on high-cost resources would be a very different society from today's, even though civilization would not be destroyed.

Although the neo-Malthusian approach to conservation is becoming more popular it remains a minority position. The dominant position on conservation, particularly in government circles, is what we may call the technological–conservationist. Unlike the pessimistic neo-Malthusians, technicians are very optimistic about the ability not only to maintain but to expand living standards. The identifying characteristic of the technological–conservationist position is an emphasis upon improving efficiency through the application of scientific techniques.

Technological–conservationists would pose to neo-Malthusians the following argument. If we need more resources to maintain or increase our standard of living, the appropriate answer is to invest more money in forests, water resources, minerals, etc. To be sure, more attention to science would also be needed to eliminate waste and to discover new sources of supply. Science has prevented the fulfillment of the predictions of 50 years ago that we would run out of raw materials and there is no reason to expect that we will not have further inventions, innovations, and discoveries. The problem is to use our resources in an efficient manner and to prevent waste. Mr. Thomas B. Nolan summarized this position succinctly in a speech on conservation sponsored by Resources for the Future. He said:

I suppose there will be always a tendency to accept a concept of conservation that is based on exhaustion and that proposes restriction in the use of resources, simply because it is so easy to project the present. But I cannot concur that such a concept can prevail, since it ignores the fact that continual change, rather than a permanent stability, is characteristic not only of the earth, but of its inhabitants. I believe that the prospect of impending shortages or unsuitable supplies will continue to inspire the research and technical advances that will make it possible to resolve such problems well in advance of the doom we often are prone to foresee.

This is not the place to resolve the question whether science can offset any scarcity of raw materials and maintain economic growth. But technicians do have an optimistic faith that the raw material problem is not scarcity, but prevention of waste. The term waste plays such a large part in the vocabulary of conservation that careful consideration must be given to definining it.

In the literature on natural resources, waste had not one but three definitions. Waste, first, is sometimes used in a technological sense to mean any product which is not at present used but for which there are existing or prospective methods of conversion into more valuable commodities. In this sense there is a fantastic waste of all resources. Pine needles and sawdust, for example, could be converted into valuable products; much oil is left in the ground which could be pumped and refined; many rivers do not now produce hydroelectric power; and the list could be extended indefinitely.

The second definition of waste is more common in the literature on resources. Waste is defined to mean that the maximum *amount* of some product is not being produced given present technology. Foresters and forest economists, for example, often regard forest land as wasted if less capital is applied than the land will support—that is, if the land is not being used to maximum intensity in the production of wood.

The third definition of waste, more common in economic literature, is that waste occurs whenever the maximum economic benefit of all resources is not being produced given the existing technology, consumers' tastes, and the quantity of resources available—that is, when it would be possible to produce a product which could sell for more than the cost of production.

An example may serve to clarify the differences. In some Western states there are rivers which could be developed for irrigation purposes. Some economists and scientists would regard this water as wasted because there are technological possibilities for converting these rivers to irrigation. Most of those who apply the second definition of waste also regard the water in these rivers as wasted. They would argue that the economy must produce the maximum amount of water it can as long as water is scarce. Nevertheless, most economists do not regard these rivers as being wasted. This is because the value of the water produced from developing them for irrigation purposes would be less than the cost of the development. In other words, given the expected benefits and costs, resources will be better utilized in other sectors of the economy rather than in developing these rivers for irrigation purposes.

The popularity of the second or maximum physical output definition of waste comes about because most experts in the area of natural resources have (with apologies to Marx) a "raw materials theory of value." That is, they consider only the benefits from utilizing resources but not the costs. Anthony Scott has referred to this type of argument as "wartime economics." In his study, *Natural Resources: The Economics of Conservation*, he refers to the usual argument by forest policy makers as follows:

What it [forest policy] seems to imply . . . is something like this: forest lands should not be left bare, but should be protected and used (and planted if necessary) so that we can never say that a "shortage" of wood arises from not using the available land to sufficient intensity. Furthermore, it seems to be implied that this end should be given a high priority in the legislative programme. . . . In peacetime, income in general is scarce and is allocated by users for various ends. But in wartime, there is one scarcest resource, transport or fuel or food, in any one period; and in the allocation of this resource is registered the priorities of the planning ministry. . . . The problem of allocation can be reduced in final analysis to the allocation of this one resource. Now the objective that, no matter what else happens, our forest land should be covered with trees, amounts to giving to forestry the same priority that food supply had in war.

This stress on obtaining the maximum physical output of raw materials is the hallmark of technological–conservationists' thought. For most of the most essential influential conservationists it has been use, not saving, that is the essence of conservation. Most advocates of this position define conservation as "wise use" and implicitly equate maximum output with wise use. The difficulty with this position is that it slights the demand for the materials and the costs of obtaining maximum output. In the United States all commodities and services are scarce, not just raw materials. Wise public policy will try to maximize the total of all goods and services produced and not just maximize the use of natural resources.

The third type of conservationist is the naturalist. Like the neo-Malthusian he opposes the transformation of raw materials and supports preservation. But like the technician and unlike the neo-Malthusian he is not pessimistic about economic growth; naturalists just prefer nature in its original state. The distinguishing characteristic of naturalist–conservationists is an emphasis on the need to change consumer tastes. Twentieth-century life, they argue, places too high a value on manufactured commodities and too low a value on scenery, wilderness, virgin forests, etc. It is the *natural* in natural resources that this group finds important while for the technician–conservationists it is the *resources* that are the vital part of the expression. Naturalists do not want to see resources used; effectiveness in the harvesting and extraction of resources is exactly what they do not want.

Unlike neo-Malthusian conservationists, naturalists are not fundamentally worried about the problem of maintaining our present standards of living. What this group wants is to change the composition of the national income so that we consume or maintain more goods in their natural state and consume less manufactured goods. More parks and fewer fancy six-lane highways are the objective. This line of thought has a number of illustrious progenitors. John Muir and the pioneers of the National Park System are early examples. Recently there has been a substantial increase of interest in this position. We hear much today about the need to preserve the remaining wilderness areas, the need to protect fish and wildlife, the need for more parks and recreation areas.

Although the aims and objectives of neo-Malthusian conservationists, technician-conservationists, and naturalist–conservationists are dissimilar, often some project will appeal to two or all groups. Both the naturalist–conservationist and the technician–conservationist are interested in forests. But the naturalist often has a "woodman-spare-that-tree" attitude while the technician–conservationist wants to cut down the virgin trees and put in a management plan that would be the most effective for producing timber. Since neither group likes bare land, reforestation programs command the support of both.

As a political force or movement, conservation has basically represented an uneasy alliance between the various types of conservationists. This alliance has frequently been broken by conflicts of surprising violence. For example, in 1914 Gifford Pinchot and John Muir split over a reservoir site in the Hetch-Hetchy valley in Yosemite National Park. The technician believed that the development of a water source for San Francisco and hydroelectric power was more important than damage to the scenery and recreation facilities. In our own day, much of the dispute over the Echo Park Dam Project was caused by the different views of conservation held by technicians and naturalists. For the former it was the development of water power, flood control, and navigation that was important. For the latter, a physical transformation of the Upper Colorado was exactly what was not needed.

From its earliest days the conservation movement has revealed this diversity of viewpoints. The phrase "conservationist" was coined by Gifford Pinchot in 1907 to cover a complex of political and social ideas. The early conservation movement, usually dated from 1890 to 1920, presented a response to the closing of the frontier and the industrialization of the United States. These structural changes in the economy focused attention on the adequacy of the resource base to support continued economic growth. Conservationists were agreed that "something had to be done," but what was to be done was a source of much argument.

During the 1870's and 1880's some spokesmen had advocated preserving unused various commodities and areas before they were consumed or transformed in the process of settlement and industrialization. Areas such as the Hot Springs Reservation and the Yosemite Valley were set aside as parks to be maintained untouched as a form of museum. Also during this period interest developed in protecting the government's timber and mineral interests on the public lands. The public domain was almost entirely unprotected from trespass and several laws were passed to try to safeguard the public property. Nevertheless, interest in natural resources was slight. Governmental activity was scattered, lacked unity of purpose, and frequently laws were unenforceable given the scope of the task, the appropriations, and the administrative facilities.

It was land policy which earlier occupied the attention of the country. Raw materials questions were regarded as minor issues, subsidiary to the problem of how to dispose of a continent. The triumph of Jeffersonian and Jacksonian ideas committed the federal government to the rapid transfer of public land to private citizens in family-sized plots and little consideration was given to the resources of the land. Converting the land to agricultural uses was the major goal of most settlers, and timber and minerals were for the most part regarded as either worthless or as a barrier to farming. In some cases raw material sources were prized but as a lure to attract industry and capital to the frontier. Much of the fraud and exploitation that receives attention in the history books under headings such as "The Rape of the Continent," is due to the general attitude that resources were of little value. Easterners protested the cutting of Western forests or destructive mining practices; Westerners attributed these complaints to jealousy over Western growth. To the Westerner minerals and forests were only valuable if they helped the West develop, and if the West was expanding, what was all the fuss about?

A corollary to this lack of concern with raw materials was a lack of interest in scientific techniques for the care, preservation, or utilization of natural resources. Until the latter part of the nineteenth century work in this area was almost entirely European. The structural changes in the economy following the Civil War had a substantial effect on both the supply and demand for raw materials. Industrialization involved an unprecedented drain on raw material stocks. Commodities such as timber, land, coal, had formerly been so abundant relative to demand that they were either free goods or sold for very low prices. America's new industrial capacity vastly increased demand for materials, and prices doubled and redoubled. Resources became valuable, and men who through foresight or luck took advantage of these changes became "timber barons," "coal barons," etc.

The effects of increases in demand on the resource base were generally recognized in the late nineteenth century, but the effects of industrialization on the supply of raw material, which were just as important, were not generally recognized. The industrial revolution provided new techniques for harvesting, extracting, and managing resources. As an illustration, consider the harvesting of virgin timber on the East Coast and in the Midwest; the former before the Civil War, the latter after the Civil War. In the East the timber was logged with oxens or horse teams. Usually only the best trees were cut at any one time and small trees were always left. As a result forests reseeded themselves naturally with valuable species. In the Midwest the timber was logged by steam railroads. A railway would be laid into a timber section; all the trees, big and small, were cut; the tracks were removed and the process repeated on another section. As a result Midwestern forests did not reseed themselves naturally to valuable species; the trash left in the logging encouraged destructive fires; and there was a "boom and bust" economy in the forest regions. Lumbering by steam railroad was cheaper and more effective than by oxen or horses but there were socially undesirable effects on the forests and on regional development.

Engineering and scientific advances affected every resource industry: new mining techniques, advances in irrigation engineering, hydroelectric discoveries; there were numerous scientific "breakthroughs." The key to understanding the conservation movement is that it was the changed production conditions in the late nineteenth century that provided the major stimulus to early conservationist thought. Pioneer conservationists, such as Gifford Pinchot, W J McGee, Frederick H. Newell, and Major John Wesley Powell were usually engineers, scientists, or had been technically trained. It was the possibility of increasing supplies of raw materials by rationalizing production that fascinated these pioneers.

This is not to say that early conservationists ignored the increasing demand for raw materials. Some of the most violent scare literature forecasting the exhaustion of our raw materials was produced by these leaders. But in the main, this represented an attempt to obtain popular support by appealing to the intuitive fears of the general public. Their first concern was that production or extraction of raw materials be done in an "efficient" manner. They were an advance guard of what was later called the "scientific management movement."

These technological conservationists were able to attract to the banner of conservation the neo-Malthusians and the naturalists, since all three groups were concerned with the natural resource usage. But the inherent differences in aims and objectives meant that, as over the Hetch-Hetchy Dam, there were internal divisions and arguments as to who had the right to call himself a conservationist. The schisms in the first conservation movement were important reasons for the decline of conservation as a political force. And since that time lack of agreement on the goals to be achieved has decreased the political popularity of conservation as a goal of public policy.

Despite conflicts and ideological splits there is a common unifying factor among conservationists. This factor is a recognition that economic growth depends upon natural resource usage. Public opinion tends to be myopic and those rare people concerned with long-range questions have a common interest. In an age when optimism about economic growth is all but unanimous it is very desirable to be reminded that economic expansion requires raw materials. A distinguishing characteristic of all types of conservationists is a distrust of the effectiveness of unregulated markets to direct natural resources into the uses which will maximize the benefits to both present and future citizens. Although conservationists have been concerned with specific problems of resource usage and investment rather than theory, two general problems have emerged to dominate discussion. In the first place, conservationists have stressed that the production of one commodity or service from a natural resource usually affects the production of other commodities or services. In the conservation literature this is referred to as multi-use; economists call this external economies. For example, in the Hell's Canyon development the type of hydroelectric dams constructed affect the amount of flood control and navigation services which could be provided. Another typical case is in forestry where the amount of timber produced affects the amount of wildlife and watershed protection. In the second place, conservationists have questioned whether the present generation of consumers give enough consideration to the needs of future consumers. This has several aspects. One that has long been emphasized is whether, in the absence of subsidies or special inducements, enough money will be spent on scientific search for new sources of materials. Another is whether present consumers will not squander the rightful heritage of our descendants on trivial uses. In the oil industry, for example, many conservationists believe that without depletion allowances and import quotas the effort devoted to exploration and wildcat drilling would cease. Another example often mentioned by conservationists is our lead supplies. Many believe that we should limit octane rating of gasoline or horsepower of cars in order to cut down on present lead consumption. Future generations, it is argued, will be deprived of lead for essential uses because of our frivolous consumption of high octane fuels.

The basic issue is the efficacy of markets in directing resources among present wants and between generations; a problem much studied by economists. Of course, as long as future consumers have no voice in present decisions, one can never be sure that the best intertemporal distribution of resources will be achieved, but this is true of all public action and not just of resource policy. Economists also recognize that external economies and research and innovations require special consideration and may pose difficulties for the operation of unregulated markets. But in general, theoretical analysis and historical experience indicate that free markets are reasonably satisfactory in satisfying consumer demands and in allocating resources—including raw materials—to their best uses.

Conservationists, however, disagree. In the past they feel there has been a failure of free markets to protect the public interest and this is likely to be true in the future. But each of the different groups of conservationists sees the market failure in a different light. To the neo-Malthusian the problem is that there is no control over population increase. This, plus a desire for a rising standard of living results in the present generation's depriving future consumers of their just inheritance of raw materials. To the technician the problem is that the market does not generate enough new technology or insure that ignorance or habitual patterns which serve as barriers to the introduction of new technology will be overcome. Naturalists believe that the failure of the market comes about because many goods such as scenery, wildlife, etc. are collective goods and under present institutions cannot or should not be sold through markets.

Population, scientific invention, and collective goods all pose substantial problems for an economy based on free, unregulated markets. Conservationists, therefore, are serving a vital function in pointing out these issues. On the other hand, if we are to have a sensible public policy for the conservation of natural resources it is vital that we separate the viewpoints of the different types of conservationists. Each particular position must be considered on its own merits and not just because the spokesman claims to be advocating conservation or opposing waste.

To show the difference that separation of viewpoints can make, let us return to the oil industry. Here a technician might argue that high and stable domestic oil prices provide necessary incentives to increase the amount of oil reserves, to promote research into the uses of shale and other sources, and to maintain a strong petroleum industry as a basis for industrial expansion. A neo-Malthusian conservationist might argue that present policies lead to the unnecessary current consumption of irreplaceable American stocks. In an industry based on nonreplaceable resources the neo-Malthusian view seems to have the better of the argument, particularly if we consider that other incentives besides restrictive quotas are available to encourage exploration if this is desired. The moral of the story is that conservation poses vital problems for public policy-makers but that the label of conservationist covers too many contradictory positions to give much guidance for public action. In decisions on specific programs affecting natural resources, it is necessary to distinguish between the varieties of conservationists if the search for effective conservation measures is to be more than a matter of ritual.

Norman Wengert

Resource Development and the Public Interest: A Challenge for Research*

It seems axiomatic that government cannot in any single fiscal period undertake all of the programs and activities that might be justified as worthwhile. Even where ideological questions as to the scope and direction of government programs do not obtrude, schedules and time-tables must be set, since scarcities of money and manpower determine feasibility limits at any particular time. Thus a fundamental problem of government is the allocation of resources, the setting of priorities, the determination of emphasis, the making of choices.

It also seems axiomatic that those who espouse and support new government action generally assert that the course they oppose is in the public interest. Obviously, no one is likely to sponsor programs which he admits are against the public interest.

Yet there is widespread disagreement over the general content, scope and direction of government programs, and even more over specific details. There is little consensus as to what government should do or why. There is much disagreement as to when and how government should act. And questions of who should benefit, who should pay, and how benefits would be distributed among various sections of the nation are often ignored or avoided. Typically, the nature of the public interest in some program or activity is assumed or inferred. Rarely is it specifically proved or articulated.

The problem of providing standards for appraising public programs and determining the public interest presents a double challenge—to *administration* to develop mechanisms, procedures and institutions for making more rational choices and for setting wise priorities, and to *scholarship* to probe and analyze public programs in order to determine their consequences and to assess the extent to which they fulfill needs

*Reprinted by permission from *Natural Resources Journal* (School of Law, University of New Mexico), I (1961), 207–223.
(Notes to this selection will be found on pp. 417–419.)

and expectations. With respect to resource programs, these challenges are particularly significant.

A. The Problem Stated—A recent headline in the *New York Times* announced

"Walden Pond Saved"

and the story went on to state:

The final skirmish in a legal war to preserve Walden Pond in its natural state brought victory this week. . . . The dispute arose three years ago when the [county] commissioners leveled an acre of woodland to provide better access to a public beach area where Red Cross safety programs are conducted in the summer. A group known as the Save Walden Committee took legal action to halt the work. . . .[1]

To those who value America's historic heritage, who regard Walden Pond as a symbol of wilderness solitude, and who yearn for a simpler agrarian America, the saving of Walden Pond from intensive use was a victory for the public interest. Yet what of the interests of those who want to swim, who want to learn Red Cross life-saving techniques, who want a place where they and their families can picnic and play? To them, perhaps, this action was a defeat for the public interest, reflecting typical judicial bias favoring the few against the many.[2]

Although purporting to rest upon determinations of the public interest, more typically than not, legislative enactments reflect mere assertions, the phraseology hiding many problems and obscuring difficult choices that are then left to those who administer the statute. For example, when Congress created the Outdoor Recreation Resources Review Commission the preamble of the statute stated its goals to be:

To preserve, develop, and secure accessibility to all American people of present and future generations such quality and quantity of outdoor recreation resources as will be necessary and desirable for individual enjoyment, and to assure the spiritual, cultural, and physical benefits that such outdoor recreation provides.[3]

But what does it mean to preserve and develop? How is accessibility to be measured, especially in contemplation of *all* the people now and in the future, a future which within a century could involve a population of 600 million at present growth rates. How take into account the tremendous range in population densities among the various sections of the nation? What about travel and vacation habits and preferences, income and other determinants of recreation patterns. What resources are necessary? Which ones desirable? How are they to be compared? By what criteria? Where should recreation developments be located? How are spiritual, cultural, and physical benefits measured? How assured? What if they conflict, as in the case of Walden Pond where cultural benefits and access benefits apparently cannot be reconciled?

On Feb. 23 [1961], President Kennedy sent to Congress proposals for a vast expansion of programs to develop America's natural resources, asserting that the policies of the previous administration has been inadequate and had resulted in the postponement of many necessary and desirable projects. The President's message was remarkable because of the range of proposals after but one month in office. Clearly these were not the result of careful planning and judicious determination of need by the new administration. They could hardly have reflected an integrated and coordinated approach either to the nation's economic or resource problems. There is every reason to suspect, rather, that items listed by the President were the pent-up requests of agencies and interest groups that in the preceding years had not received what they felt was their due. A cynic might perhaps have commented that the message seemed to have in it something for everyone—at least for everyone among those groups and interests which in past decades have been concerned with resources and conservation activities.

Thus, although asserting that the proposals were in the public interest, the President's message, too, raises the question of how the public interest is determined. What standards are available by which to measure the desirability and appropriateness of particular policy and program proposals? How can questions of timing, of costs, of benefits be appraised?

B. *The Political Process in America*[4]—It is generally recognized that American political action is pragmatic and expedient, rather than idealistic and principled. The political struggle is typically concerned with urgent problems and immediate solutions, though these may sometimes be portrayed in generalized terms. Government programs thus reflect particularized responses to the demands of those who have access to points of decision. They frequently incorporate practical judgments of men of affairs who project and interpret their often limited personal experiences as operational universals.[5] Usually absent are long-range, comprehensive conceptions resting on systematic appraisal of data, or rigorous analysis of causes, effects, impacts and interrelationships.

This brief characterization of the American political system and the decisions it produces, leads to several corollaries significant to an understanding of governmental processes in the field of natural resources:

(1) The pragmatic emphasis in American politics intensifies the struggle for influence and favor at the points in the governmental structure where decisions are made, and contributes to the importance and strength of lobbies and pressure groups. But the fact of this struggle often encourages a cynical attitude in which the pork-barrel takes the place of the cracker barrel as the symbol of grass-roots politics.

(2) This pragmatic emphasis contributes to a fragmentation of the public interest, and inhibits development of meaningful standards, mechanisms and institutions for determining that interest. Undoubtedly, this partially explains why American political parties are not program- or issue-oriented, and frequently express only generalities or platitudes on many questions. Responsible programmatic parties can hardly develop so long as the political environment encourages pragmatic, even expedient, responses to short-range pressures of special and local interests, and discourages definition and clarification of comprehensive and long-range objectives.

(3) This pragmatic emphasis leads to the convenient assumption that the whole public interest is equal to the sum of partial, articulate, individual, local or other special and particularized interests. In the absence of institutions and traditions stressing public interest conceptions, it is probably not surprising that groups or individuals equate their own advantage and prosperity with that of the nation. But it seems logically dubious to assume an automatic and inevitable coincidence among individual, group and national interests.

(4) Finally, this pragmatic emphasis in American politics has led to the assertion that the concept of the public interest is not useful. Since there are so many conflicting interpretations of the public interest, it is argued that the term merely reflects a common tendency to clothe personal preferences in the mantle of high purpose. It is therefore concluded that objective standards are not available and that government programs and policies will ultimately be the net result of interaction among the groups that make up the American polity.

The point of view identified in this last corollary has recently been comprehensively restated in a monograph by Professor Glendon Schubert entitled, simply, *The Public Interest*. After a detailed analysis of discussion and writing about the public interest, Schubert concludes:

[O]ur investigation has failed to reveal a statement of public-interest theory that offers much promise either as a guide to public officials who are supposed to make decisions in the public interest, or to research scholars who might wish to investigate the extent to which governmental decisions are empirically made in the public interest.[6]

Unquestionably, this conclusion will be disturbing to officials and scholars alike simply because the idea of the public interest is so deeply imbedded in our rationalization of government action.

The justification of judicial action in terms of the public interest is common. Many statutes instruct regulatory agencies to act after determining the public interest. And policies followed by the executive branch are generally assumed to be in the public interest.[7]

In the normal course of everyday life, too, it is generally believed that what is said and done obviously adds up to the general welfare, and here, of course, a century and a half of economic theory bolsters the idea of an unseen hand guiding individual action automatically along a course which coincides with the public interest.

I. PUBLIC INTEREST AND RESOURCE POLICY

Public resource programs and policies rest on inarticulate premises that they are in the public interest. The mere fact of authorization, almost by definition, is believed to prove the point. Through most of the 19th century, even before conservation or resource policies were clearly identified as such, public action with respect to the public domain, timber resources and minerals were *presumed* to be sound, the concern, more often than not, being with the manner in which these policies were administered, rather than with basic objectives or consequences. Neither administration nor scholarship was concerned with appraisal of these policies and programs.

As the conservation movement became a rallying point for liberals and progressives, Gifford Pinchot, stimulated by his co-worker W J McGee, proposed "The greatest good of the greatest number for the longest time" as the standard by which to measure the public interest in conservation.[8] Effective slogan though this may have been, it did not indicate how "the good" was to be measured or determined, how one good might be compared with another, how the greatest number might be identified, whether benefits should be direct or indirect, nor the length of the time span. Pinchot and the conservation leaders at the turn of the century were not particularly concerned with these questions because they felt assured that they knew the answers.[9] The actions they were taking and the programs they were proposing would obviously, in their view, result in the greatest good for the greatest number over time. In any case, Pinchot himself was more concerned with political action than with analytical and philosophical questions. And again neither administrator nor scholar was particularly concerned with program appraisal. It should be noted, however, that in the first decade of the century techniques for analyzing and measuring the consequences of particular programs and data relevant to this purpose were primitive.

A. Physical or Technical Criteria of Public Interest—As the role of government with respect to the conservation and development of resources became accepted, particular programs were often justified in physical or technical terms.

Because natural resource programs deal with the physical universe—the stuff of nature—and because program formulation and leadership has often been in the hands of scientists and engineers, physical or engineering criteria have frequently been applied as measures of the public interest, with only slight attention to social, economic, or other factors. A brief examination of two areas, in which the development of public resource programs has been extensive, illustrates this tendency to rely on physical standards and suggests some of their limitations as determinants of the public interest. These program areas are soil conservation and flood control.

Although the facts are much more complex, most soil conservation activities are popularly justified in terms of stopping all erosion and saving every ounce of soil.[10] The implied measure of effectiveness is the quantity of soil that is or should be prevented from moving from one place to another. But several qualifying facts should be considered.

A substantial amount of erosion can not and probably should not be stopped. It is a process of nature, essential to productive soils. So long as rains fall and winds blow, mountains and hills will be worn down and valleys filled up.[11] Yet the factor of geologic erosion is often ignored in discussions of soil conservation programs.

It is common, for instance, to deplore that so much of the rich Mississippi Valley is annually being carried to the Gulf of Mexico.[12] But after all, the Mississippi Delta was built up long before white men reached the valley, and the Missouri River, called the "Big Muddy" by Indians who had used no plows to break the plains and grazed no cattle on the virgin prairie, was dumping its silt load into the Mississippi long before 1492. Scouts and early residents of the Great Plains have also testified to the dust storms which plagued the region when the only land use was that of the buffalo and the antelope.

No one defends land-use practices which encourage gullying, sheet erosion or soil blowing, *where practicable alternatives exist.* But this is just the point at which the physical measures of erosion and its cure are inadequate, for the tests of practicability are not simply physical but also economic and social.

In the humid portion of the United States the physically best cover from the point of view of water retention and erosion control would generally be the forest cover which originally blanketed most of this region. Agricultural use, by definition encourages erosion and water losses in some degree, for it means clearing some timber and often also plowing and cropping. Further, commercial agriculture and urban consumption mean depletion of plant nutrients by the quantity in the products that leave the farm. The real problem, thus, is determining just how much erosion and how much mineral and water loss to control at any given place and in any given period. The physical facts must be known, but the criteria that govern are also social and economic.[13]

An oversimplified illustration suggests some questions that require consideration. Imagine a 40-acre farm on a steep hillside in the southern Appalachians. On purely physical standards of soil preservation it should have been left in trees. At its highest level of productivity it does little more than feed a mountain family at nutritional standards below those considered desirable. After a number of years of cropping, erosion takes it toll, the farm is abandoned, the family moves to Detroit, and the land returns to trees. How much has been lost from the productive base of American agriculture by this process? Certainly there are complex human costs and social problems involved. But current soil conservation programs neither deal with these, nor are their justifications put forward in these terms. From the point of view of land policy, how much effort, how many public dollars should be spent to conserve the soil on this hypothetical 40-acre farm? Should it be kept in farm use or abandoned? Physical data can supply only a small part of the answers to these and similar questions which become critical in relation to allocation of public resources (money and manpower) and setting priorities for public activities.

Another program area which illustrates some of the limitations of physical criteria as guides to public action is flood control, where concepts of engineering feasibility have tended to dominate public policy decisions, and where the idea of an Engineering Board of Review in the Office of President is often proposed as a mechanism for resolving policy conflicts.

In the midst of a flood it is easy to resolve that "it shall not happen again" and to trade political support with other communities for more and better flood control appropriations. The analogies of disease prevention, of fire fighting, of social service are marshalled. And thus stress on the simple problem of eliminating floods by re-engineering the watershed leads to a pattern of policy that says, in effect, everyone is entitled to flood protection, no matter where he lives or works nor how sensible it is for him to be there. The only question is "Do you get flooded"—a physical, engineering standard. In the absence of more discriminating standards, it is not surprising that flood control continues, in the opinion of many, to be the biggest pork-barrel operation this country has yet seen.[14]

But like erosion, floods are natural phenomena, and contrary to popular impressions, there is no evidence to suggest that floods are worse today than they were 100 or 200 years ago, except perhaps on small, localized watersheds.[15] What has increased, of course, is the economic loss from floods. This reflects the growth of our economy and the fact that cities have been built in flood plains, industries located in flood plains, and railroads and highways constructed in flood plains. Sometimes there have been no alternatives; but often risks have been ignored.[16]

The record of unwise allocation of public resources in the area of urban flood protection is discouraging. But even more serious misallocations may occur under the Watershed Protection and Flood Prevention Act[17] which seems to combine the policy that every ounce of soil should be conserved with the policy that every rural resident is entitled to flood protection. As the promotional literature for this program has asserted: "Wherever you live, you are within a watershed."

Some may shrug and say "So what? So every congressional district gets a flood protection project, or two or three?" Because of allocation of public investment funds to flood control, investment in possibly more desirable and more necessary projects may be curtailed. This again raises the issue of policy standards and how these may be determined.[18]

B. *Economic Criteria of Public Interest*—Resource allocation is the fundamental question of economics and a great deal of economic literature deals with this subject. In the private enterprise sectors of a free economy, allocation decisions tend to be made on a decentralized basis as a result of the working of the price system, the interplay of competitive forces and the assessment of individual advantage. But when allocation decisions are made in the public sector of the economy, price mechanisms, profit motives, automatic selective processes, are of limited significance.[19]

Some writers have suggested that the political process operates analogous to the economic, voting being comparable to the expenditure of money.[20] It is also suggested that the political struggle among diverse interest groups is like competition among buyers and sellers. Such analogies are useful, but only of limited applicability because the subject matter with which the two processes deal is different. The processes are similar, but the end product is not. Politics is not just another way for making the same decisions. It is not enough to say that the interaction and struggle among political groups will result in a reasonable allocation of resources, for after resources are allocated politically, by government, the economic efficiency question remains.

So long as government plays only a minor part in the total economy, questions of the misallocation of resources are probably not of major concern. But today it is no longer possible to dismiss this problem as being of small consequence. The role of government is particularly important in relation to investment, and it is at this point that resource programs become significant because they involve substantial capital investments. It is not size alone, but location, type and purpose of the investment that is important. Some, stressing the group struggle, assume a countervailance among those seeking public benefits, and pay little attention to costs and still less to who bears them, in the expectation that somehow, over time, the equities will work themselves out.

In an earlier period, the amount of revenue available from taxation tended to force a kind of *ad hoc* allocation among competing demands. This control still operates at local and state levels. But at the national level, with deficit financing automatic, program decisions tend to be made in response to pressure demands rationalized in terms of *problems* and *needs*, rather than in relation to tax income. The result is a constant pressure to expand public programs, justified, not in terms of their impact upon the total community, but largely in terms of the *problem* or *need* to which they are the response, the reality of which is often beyond cavil.

The emphasis on *need* and on *problem-solving* has a great deal of appeal, but it avoids the issues of allocation, of priority among activities and programs, simply because the problems pressing for solution are endless. Where is there a research worker who could not justify expanding his program tenfold? Who can say that we will ever have all the highways, schools, hospitals, etc. that we need, or that those we now have cannot be improved? Where is there a park that could not be bettered, a forest that could not be more effectively managed, a river course that could not be made more beautiful and useful?

It is sometimes argued that other than economic values govern resource policies, and that therefore economic criteria are irrelevant. Objectives of water development, for example, include social and strategic elements as well as short-range goals of operating efficiency. A dominant purpose of federal irrigation programs has always been the creation of new homes (family farms) in arid states. Activities labeled "regional development" have been similarly justified not in terms of their contributions to national welfare and economic growth, but on the basis of the stimulus to the particular regional economy.[21] Substantial parts of current agricultural programs are also rationalized as maintaining an essential occupation, providing homes, encouraging redistribution of wealth, and not simply as contributing to national economic growth.

But labeling something as justified for noneconomic reasons does not eliminate its cost to the economy, although the argument that benefits or purposes are social or strategic often has the effect, in fact, of precluding an examination of costs or of alternatives. It is important to know what part of the economy bears the cost, and what benefits are foregone in order to absorb such costs. Also relevant is the efficiency question of whether the cost is balanced by the noneconomic benefits, and the equitable question whether cost burdens are properly allocated. The criticism here is not with the fact of noneconomic goals, nor with the desire to redistribute burdens in a way that may not coincide with benefits, but rather with the fact that the cost issues are often not faced deliberately, if at all, in many resource programs.

C. *Popular Concepts and Political Action*—The popular literature dealing with resource policy abounds in such phrases as "wise resource use," "resource waste," "balance of nature," "multiple purpose use," and many others. Often, too, public policies and government programs have been justified by the assumed criteria implicit in terms like these. Many phrases of this type are, at best, vague and ambiguous, shifting in meaning as the user or hearer desires. And their use, over the years, has rarely given them greater precision and intellectual content.[22] At the same time, many of these terms have strong moral and emotional connotations which may make them effective weapons in the political struggle, but do not add to their analytical usefulness.

Take as an example the concept "waste". Everyone is against resource waste, but what is waste? Clear cutting of a timber lot, leaving a great quantity of wood in the branches and stumps, failing to salvage bark and sawdust—is this waste? But does it really make any difference if the end product of the harvested timber is a comic book, or even a Sunday newspaper which is read and then cast into the fire? Who in this chain of events committed the waste? Or is it waste to plant corn in contour furrows in order to get bigger yields in order to add to corn surpluses already filling federal storage bins? The point, of course, is that a concept like resource waste by itself is nonoperational as a guide for public policy.

Many of these popular phrases are rooted in deep-seated fears and anxieties, related to Malthusian worries about the adequacy of resources. Malthus was, of course, primarily concerned about food, and neo-Malthusians continue to write books with scare titles such as "Food Enough," "Food or Famine," and some, who have broadened their perspective, talk about "Our Plundered Planet" and "The Road to Survival."

In all of this literature there is an immediacy—an urgency—which the facts do not warrant.[23] From the viewpoint of public policy, this urgency has, however, become part of the frame of reference of many pressure groups seeking conservation action.

Problems of resource adequacy cannot be disregarded. But they are far less immediate than many suggest. The world is not going to wake up some morning and, like Mother Hubbard, find the resource cupboard bare.

In this connection, resource and conservation literature stresses preserving resources for future generations. Yet rarely is there any indication of how far into the future such responsibility extends. Skills for looking 25 to 50 years into the future have improved, and there is little evidence that resource shortages are going to be a major factor limiting U.S. economic growth in this period. But what about 100 or 200 years from now? No techniques now available permit a forecast of the shape of the world that far into the future.

In any case, most proposals for conservation of particular resources would really add only infinitesimal quantities to the long-run future supply. If conservation of a particular mineral would add ten years to its availability, is this significant? The American supply of natural petroleum may run out in 15 to 100 years. So what to do? Travel less? Increase fuel efficiency of gasoline engines? Cut down horse power and prohibit Lincolns and Cadillacs? Institute a rationing program? How much petroleum would thus be saved? And saved for what end? Where in the picture do synthetic fuels fit and where atomic energy? Would it be better to seek substitutes, developing technology and science, than to spend energy trying to restrict oil use?

Because most resource problems in the United States have *not* been immediate nor pressing, public attention has been low. Hence a perennial question has been how to gain public support of resource programs. The pragmatic character of the political process itself and the fact that the support base for most resource programs is narrow, the size of the groups immediately affected small, and the clientele interest particularized, has intensified this support problem.

It is normal in a democratic society to use generalized and evocative symbols to stimulate group support. In the process of political communication, precise, scientific terms often take on symbolic overtones, and colorful phrases are loosely applied. In the area of resource policy these tendencies may perhaps be exaggerated. But recognizing this situation certainly does not solve the problem of defining the public interest or of program evaluation.

II. WHAT OF THE PUBLIC INTEREST?

The analysis to this point has suggested that the label "public interest" is often loosely used and uncritically applied. In many cases, it merely serves as a rationalization of personal preferences or group advantage. It has also been suggested that many standards and criteria applied to resource programs are inadequate and often partial and overgeneralized, serving more to rationalize particular actions than to provide a basis for appraisal and evaluation. Doubts have also been expressed as to the viability and operational validity of concepts of public interest, particularly as applied to natural resources programs and activities.

Should the concept of the public interest, therefore be rejected? Is it impossible to develop standards for choosing between alternatives, for assessing consequences? What is the role of the scholar in this regard?

It is one thing to admit that efforts to date to give meaningful content to concepts of public interest have not been successful. It may be conceded that standards for appraising resource programs have not been adequate. But to deny that government programs have effects which can be studied, measured and evaluated in terms of advantage and disadvantage to the nation generally, is to deny the possibility of any scholarship.

By means of logical analysis and rational calculation, costs and benefits can, in fact, be identified, and impacts and consequences of particular programs assessed. Sometimes only inferences or approximations are possible. But to deny that there may be better decisions and poorer decisions, that some actions might affect the nation adversely and others favorably, and that these facts can be determined, would seem to leave nothing but a trust in benevolent fate or victimization by inexorable processes of history.

To be sure, analyses are only as good as the data on which they are based.[24] Selections and interpretations must be made; and these may be in error. They may be distorted by the values and personality of the analyst. But personality is neither a random factor nor is it uncontrolled. Values involve intensity ranges; some held more firmly than others; some having greater influence than others; some more widely recognized than others. And values too may be altered by reason as well as by propaganda. In varying degrees, of course, analyst and decision-maker both are system-bound. There are built-in conditions that set limits to or distort appraisals of government programs. But here, too, we are dealing not with infinity, but with a range of possible alternatives.

Those who argue that the concept of public interest is meaningless have been caught in a nihilistic trap which destroys by implication the value and validity of *any* standards and of knowledge itself. If the public interest is meaningless then the idea of group or individual interest also is meaningless and for similar reasons. There is, of course, a distinction between what an individual thinks is in his interest and what is in fact in his interest, given his values and desires. But the problems of measurement, of data availability, of precision, of foreseeing the future, should not be confused with the viability of the concept, or the necessity of making choices on the best possible (most rational) basis.

The operational definition of the public interest will never be an easy task. It is not something that can be settled once and for all. It is not an idealized concept, the meaning of which can be captured in a few general phrases. Rather, it is a changing concept, for values and goals of society do not remain the same, and the knowledge and ability to analyze programs and policies grow. The concept is nevertheless a conservative one, for it assumes a stable system resting upon generally accepted core values and contemplating only gradual changes, neither drastic nor revolutionary in character. It deals with changes at the margins.

The usefulness of a concept like the public interest lies perhaps in the search for it,[25] in the effort by administrator and scholar to make explicit the data and the rationale behind particular decisions that are or have been urged as being in the public interest. This permits, among other things, corroboration of the analyses by others, so in place of bald assertions that a course of action is in the public interest, the statement really becomes that a course of action has these impacts (costs and benefits) or those effects, which are consistent with or contrary to the identified aims and expectations. If this view is valid, then the concept of the public interest can be useful to the extent that institutions and agencies are struggling with its identification and specification, and groups and individuals feel it necessary to justify proposed policies and programs in terms of their effects upon the larger public.

Like justice, the public interest is given meaning in the constant striving to achieve it, in the on-going effort to assess the impact of particular facts and to determine effects of particular situations. And similar to justice, the significance of the public interest lies not in the fact that one can state unequivocally the idea of the public interest, but in analysis of programs and appraisals of policies, in critical review of alternatives and systematic assessment of consequences, costs and benefits, causes and effects, so as to permit careful identification and rational weighting of factors considered relevant. In this connection the scholar plays a particularly significant role.

While one may concede that the interplay of power groups is a dominant aspect of the governmental process, it does not seem to follow that the participants in the political struggle are without choice, unable to rise above the narrow limitations of group interests. More reasonable is the assumption that choices for good or ill of the larger society (the nation) and even against the immediate and particular interests of individual group or community, can be made. No doubt such choices are facilitated by conflicting interests and overlapping memberships. But groups too can respond to reason; they may be persuaded by logical analysis and rational calculation as well as by emotional factors like patriotism. To regard group motivations as solely limited to narrowly conceived interest stimuli is to overlook a great deal of human experience.

Economic welfare is certainly an important element in defining the public interest, and more systematic attention has been given to measuring the economic impact of public programs than to most other factors and elements. Because useful data has been accumulating, and techniques have been developed, it is possible to appraise some economic effects of public programs and thus to decide their advantages and disadvantages, costs and benefits.

Economic assessment is particularly important to resource programs since a dominant objective of such programs is, by definition, economic welfare. In many respects, too, economic costs and benefits provide a kind of common denominator for program choices. Other dimensions may of course also be significant. For example, esthetic values may be of considerable importance to some resource programs, although esthetic values are difficult to measure.

One can accept the fact that it is not unusual to clothe personal action in the cloak of public interest. But this process of rationalization says nothing as to whether the action may, in fact, be in the public interest.

One can recognize that public decisions are the resultant of group interaction and struggle, without settling the question of whether the consequences are good or bad. One need not, however, posit the public
interest as some esoteric, eternal principle or set of principles, in order
to determine consequences, to assess impacts, to study effects.

Some distinctions may aid in clarifying the problem. One distinction
is that of *time*. It is one thing to assess the impact of past action; it is
quite another to assess the impact of proposed action. Hindsight is often
better than foresight. In both cases the precision of assessment will be
influenced by the data available and the technology available for assessment.
Both will also be affected by the length of time span over which assessment
is made. Immediate consequences are easier to assess than long-run
consequences. Advantages or disadvantages in terms of the day, the year,
or the decade may, in the perspective of a century, appear in the
opposite light.

Another distinction concerns the *purpose* of appraisal. Analysis of
consequences in an action or decision-making context may be different
from analysis in a scholarly or research context.

The policy-maker, the government employee, is daily confronted with
the necessities for decision. Problems of all kinds converge on him, and
while he may at times engage in program research, more often than not
he must act before all the facts are in or can be gathered. And his frame of
reference for decision must include the culture and organization of which
he is a part, its history and traditions, and the political and other pressures
that have grown up around the programs he is administering. Although
he may be dedicated to wise decision-making, rationality for him must
include the context within which he operates. Among the important
factors in that context is survival for him and his agency. His own
personal heredity and environment, values and beliefs, may also be relevant.

The scholar and researcher, in contrast, seeks through research to
contribute to the potential rationality of governmental decision. The
scholar studying governmental natural resource programs and activities
is particularly interested in accounting for existing conditions and events
and in suggesting relationships between thought and action, means and
ends, causes and effects, conditions and consequences. From such effort
may come greater insight with respect to the nature of the political–
governmental process and perhaps a basis for understanding, if not
predicting, the course of future events. The concern of the scholar is
thus, to use the words of Thomas Hobbes, to impart "knowledge of
consequences, and dependence of one fact upon another."[26]

To be sure, the scholar and researcher also have values; they have
commitments which shape their views and determine their approaches.
This is the perennial dilemma of social science research. Yet, in part, the

scholar is dedicated to overcoming or controlling these biases by explicitly stating his premises and forthrightly identifying the problems with which he seeks to deal. The study of politics must thus be conceived of as a question-posing and question-answering activity. Scholarship not dedicated to improving the rational basis for action is dilletantism or nonsense.

What has, perhaps, misled some of those who despair of determining the public interest is implicit in the principle stated by F. C. S. Schiller in his work on logic:

> Whenever an attempt is made to point out that in every step in actual thinking a person intervenes and directs the course of thought in accordance with his interests and ideas, and that therefore to understand the sequence and connection of thought this fact must be taken into account, the cry is raised that this is psychology, and an attack upon the dignity and integrity of logic. It may be so, but it does not follow that the fact can therefore be disregarded.[27]

And one might add that it does not follow that it cannot be studied.

III. THE RESEARCH CHALLENGE

The premises of this article are that operationally useful standards for program evaluation, for setting priorities, for choosing desirable rather than less desirable courses of action theoretically can be developed. At the same time, it has been suggested that, to date, only a start in developing a methodology for evaluating resource programs has been made, and this largely with respect to resource economics. This is the challenge to those interested in research in this field.

Space does not permit the development of a comprehensive scheme for such research, but several significant factors may be identified and a few caveats expressed.

The person studying resource programs has a major responsibility to lay bare the objectives of the programs and to identify the values, motives and motivations of those supporting them. In addition to analyzing costs and benefits, those who pay and those who gain should be considered. Attention should also be paid to alternative ways of attaining the same or similar objectives. Care must be taken to consider actual consequences as well as simply stated consequences.

In many cases, a decision-making framework of analysis might prove useful, consideration being given to the actors in the particular decision, the environment of the decision including the occasion which gave rise to it, the values involved, the alternatives available, the status of knowledge and information, and the general context within which the decision was made. While such analysis obviously will not determine whether particular decisions or programs are good or bad, it will provide data essential to the analysis of consequences and impacts of the decisions or programs and of appraising results against expectations.

Finally, research needs to be directed to identifying values and articulating goals. In this connection, the easy distinction between facts and values must be avoided. More realistic and useful is the concept of the means–end chain which recognizes that particular ends "are often merely instruments to more final objectives."[28] In this connection Herbert Simon has stated: "The function of knowledge in the decision-making process is to determine which consequences follow upon which of the alternative strategies. . . ."[29] He has emphasized, moreover

> The fact that consequences usually form "isolated" systems provides both scientist and practitioner with a powerful aid to rationality, for the scientist can isolate these closed systems in his experimental laboratory, and study their behavior, while the practitioner may use the laws discovered by the scientist to vary certain environmental conditions without significantly disturbing the remainder of the situation.[30]

Too often, perhaps, research into resource programs has involved advocacy and persuasion, the participant observer too readily forgetting that to remain an observer he must not become a committed participant. Yet, if the goal of scholarship is to contribute ultimately to more rational decision, research that deals with resource programs and policies must avoid mere promotion. It must develop effective techniques for programmatic research which in turn will permit the application of useful standards for program evaluation and appraisal.

Gerald F. Vaughn

In Search of Standards for Preserving Open Space*

The New York electorate, in November 1960, authorized by a three-to-one majority a $75 million bond issue to finance a new program for preserving "open space" in that state. The New York Open Space Act, legislative framework for this program, previously emphasized the urgent need to acquire land for open space:

The disappearance of open and natural lands, particularly in and near rapidly growing urban and suburban areas is of grave concern to the legislature and to the people of the state. Once such lands are used for residential or commercial purposes, they are often permanently rendered unsuitable for parks, conservation, or other recreation purposes. The present and future needs of the growing population of the state require the immediate acquisition of such lands for park, conservation, and other recreation purposes.[1]

Following New York's lead, the citizens of New Jersey in 1961 approved a similar bond issue for a $60 million open space preservation program, and voters in Wisconsin approved an increase in the state cigarette tax to finance a $50 million open space program.

In quick succession, Pennsylvania residents authorized a $70 million open space program and bond issue, and New York voters approved an additional $25 million for their program. California voters sanctioned a $150 million bond-supported program in Nov., 1964's general election. Several comparable programs are currently in various stages of formulation and activity throughout the United States.

The open space movement initiated in New York, New Jersey, and other states soon will spread to the majority of states with large urban populations. Metropolitan regions increasingly are seeking the potential benefits of effective open space preservation:

Open space can provide room for service facilities, such as parks and recreation

*From *Public Administration Review*, XXIV (Dec., 1964), 254–258. Reprinted by permission of the American Society for Public Administration. (Notes to this selection will be found on p. 419.)

areas, institutions, and other extensive land using activities. . . . Open space can provide amenities, such as fresh air, quiet, and a change from the monotony of cityscapes. It can provide the required physical conditions for watershed protection, soil conservation, flood prevention, and preservation of wildlife and other natural resources, including preservation of the best lands for crops and forests in economically significant acreage. Permanent open spaces can be used to separate neighborhoods, communities, towns or cities, metropolitan areas, and regions. By providing a framework for development, open space is a means of controlling urban sprawl. Properly planned open spaces can serve all these purposes simultaneously."[2]

AMBIGUITY IN LAND-USE STANDARDS

Thus, the main public policy issue is, "Do the governmental units embarking on these programs have any reliable standards or criteria to guide open space preservation programs?" Is there a clear idea how the millions of dollars allocated to these programs should be spent, for considerable public expenditures are both being made and planned?

Lacking projections of open space requirements and even a generally accepted definition of open space,[3] those administering open space programs are pressed to achieve the benefits necessary to justify the program's existence. Recreation and urban planning agencies, civic groups, and our state and federal legislatures are now guided by standards that have little basis in long-range demand projections.

The inadequacy of current criteria for open space preservation can be illustrated by examining the standards for a major type of open space land use—outdoor recreation areas.

Open Space Area Standards

In 1961, the Outdoor Recreation Resources Review Commission (ORRRC) reviewed outdoor recreation area standards then used by planning agencies throughout the country. For nonurban local recreation areas, the number of acres per thousand persons varied from 10 to 20.[4] For state recreation areas, the standards varied from 31 to 45 acres per thousand persons. For nonurban reservations less than 60 minutes of travel-time from point of residence, standards varied from 17 to 500 acres per thousand persons.

The study group reported:

The very wide range of such land–man ratios among public authority attests to its lack of scientific foundation and broad applicability.[5]

A standard frequently cited for urban park and playground areas has been the National Recreation Association's (NRA) recommendation of one acre per hundred persons in the population. Developed at a time when public agencies had virtually no guides for recreation planning, it was a notable step. Many years later it still remains the principal guide for many recreation and urban planning agencies. The American Public Health Association's most recent (1960) edition of *Planning the Neighborhood: Standards for Healthful Housing*—the classic reference in environmental standards for use by planning agencies—continues to accept this NRA standard.[6]

However, the NRA standard, even when developed, did not represent *optimum* conditions with respect to health or aesthetic considerations. As George D. Butler of NRA has indicated:

The standards that have been suggested for a city's recreation area are not ideal or theoretical objectives, but they are practically attainable. A study of municipal parks in 1940 revealed the fact that 379 cities of varying sizes, or about one-fourth of those reporting, had acquired more than 1 acre of park for each 100 of the population.[7]

Certain vagaries also surround the NRA standard. It referred to *publicly* owned recreation areas but stated no assumption as to (1) the amount of available private recreational facilities or (2) to the intensity of use in both private and public areas. The Institute of Public Administration, in its study for ORRRC, noted that in the New York–New Jersey–Philadephia region many public recreation areas are underused and that "the need to develop [existing] facilities looms larger than the need to buy additional land."[8]

Finally, ORRRC has emphasized that an individual's demand for outdoor recreation (with states and preferences held constant) essentially is dependent upon his disposable income, his amount of leisure time, and his mobility—all of which typically have shown marked increases since World War II.[9] As a result, changing per capita recreation demand has made the NRA standard outmoded.

Outdoor recreation areas for intensive use generally have been described as being only part of our total open space requirements. How much land should be set aside for hunting, fishing, hiking, and other extensive forms of outdoor recreation? What is the need for land held permanently from development simply to serve as "buffer zones" or "separator strips" between urban centers, and land reserved for future *planned* suburban development?

Leading standards for extensive-use open space are those of the Baltimore Regional Planning Council. In 1958, the Council produced a set of criteria designated as "desirable standards for green spaces." These standards—in part—are as follows:[10]

Type of Use	*Acres per 1,000 Population*
Regional and state parks, parkways, etc.	10
Greenbelt-type open spaces (buffer zones)	33
Hunting and fishing areas	20
Total	63

How were these standards derived? To its credit, the council freely stated that:

After having reviewed local conditions as well as standards suggested in other sections of the United States, the Committee arrived at the standards outlined below on the basis of the best judgment of its members.[11]

Furthermore, the council cautioned:

As has been pointed out, the recommended standards are based on the best judgment of the committee members and must be considered in that light. The committee felt very strongly the need for much more detailed study of desirable standards.[12]

In 1960 the council developed a markedly improved set of open space standards, based upon the following assumptions:

(a) Present trends toward larger lot sizes and somewhat more emphasis on aesthetic considerations will continue; (b) in properly planned and developed areas, a much more effective use of open space could be made, as compared with present development, and (c) on a regional basis, at least, the private sector of our economy may provide facilities that the public sector has been unable to furnish.[13]

The new standards suggested that 78 acres per thousand persons should be maintained as regional and local open space areas. However, these standards pertain only to public parks and recreation areas, private recreation facilities, and other public or quasi-public "green space" (primarily institutional properties such as hospitals and colleges, but also including reservoirs and airports). No standards were offered for preservation of agricultural and forest land (the most prevalent forms of open space land use) other than to indicate the relatively small acreage of such land that was recommended for incorporation into two proposed separator strips or green-belts to surround Baltimore, having variable widths ranging from three-fourths to five miles.

General standards of land retention for planned future suburban development still have serious gaps. Although land requirements for residential and commercial purposes can be projected with reasonable accuracy, the reservation of open space for eventual industrial use—of vital economic importance to communities—is more nebulous. F. Stuart Chapin, Jr., author of the major reference in land use planning techniques, indicates:

There is no standard practice in estimating space requirements in this category [industrial reserves]. It is largely a subjective matter, tempered somewhat by the supply of land in fringe and dispersed locations appropriate for industrial use.[14]

FUTURE DEMAND AND RECREATION PREFERENCES

Outdoor Recreation Resources Review Commission surveys have presented a reasonably definitive picture of the existing balance of recreation activity requirements. But the balance is everchanging, and open space preservation programs pertaining to outdoor recreation, geared to today's preferences, may lead us far astray, resulting in horrendous wastes of money.

The University of California, in a study report prepared for ORRRC, has recognized this dilemma:

The acceptance of the utility concept of outdoor recreation demand provides a serious challenge to the argument that certain lands should be reserved now for future outdoor recreation activities. The strength of this argument is weakened to a considerable extent by the relative rapidity with which tastes in outdoor recreation activity change and our inability to anticipate these changes. For example, who in 1940, just 20 years ago, could have predicted the emergence of skin diving and motor boating as major outdoor recreation activities. Thus, there is a very strong possibility that any attempt to reserve lands now for future generations is liable to result in serious errors in future supply.[15]

Today's unprecedented open space preservation programs are being proposed, set up and guided by adults in responsible positions—public officials, civic leaders, and legislators. By virtue of their positions, they may be assumed to be at least 40 years of age. In 1930, likely during these adults' childhoods, 48 per cent of our people still lived in rural areas or small towns containing less than 5,000 people, with 25 per cent living on farms. Will the children of today—born into a highly urban society— retain their parents' compelling desire for open space, which for the parents may be in part a nostalgic yearning for a return to their childhood environment?

What effect will the changing age structure of our population have upon open space requirements? Currently, the percentage of senior citizens (age 65 and over) is rising. Certainly, the open space demands of a population with increasing proportions of older persons seeking passive recreation facilities (nature photography, quiet mountain retreats, etc.) can be expected to differ from the demands of a generally younger population wanting more active forms of recreation (swimming, hiking, etc.).

Similarly, what effect will the increasingly prevalent "cluster" pattern subdivisions or the "new towns" have upon our open space requirements? Conceivably, the availability of greater open space in the immediate vicinity of a family's house, i.e., the cluster advantage, could reduce the potential demand for outlying recreation areas, regional parks, and "breathing room" in general. Plans for numerous "new towns" under development—which may account for one fifth of the United States' annual housing production by 1975—are highlighted by their built-in open space features.

Leading away from New York City and stretching up into Connecticut is the pleasant Merritt Parkway. The Merritt Parkway seemingly is bounded by open countryside, but actually intensive suburban development often lies only a few hundred yards on either side of the parkway— hidden by the dense foliage of trees, shrubs, and flowers. The psychological effect sometimes received while driving on the attractively landscaped parkway, in the midst of suburban development, approaches that of the familiar leisurely Sunday afternoon ride out in the country. An *illusion* of boundless open space has been created. It may be that future highway systems—if constructed in the form of parkways, even through the centers of cities where urban renewal is occurring—could provide the aesthetic *semblance* of open space which might satisfy a great portion of our children's open space desire when they have reached maturity.

Planning Future Programs

In the absence of any but the most general types of guides, today's open space preservation programs *are proceeding without sufficient direction.* Proposed open space programs are not primarily intended to meet current needs but rather hope to provide for future generations. Yet, we have only the barest understanding of today's needs, and our knowledge of future needs may not be, in statistical terminology, "significantly different from zero." Even Ann Louise Strong, as she competently pleads the cause of open space preservation, must warn:

Unfortunately, no standardized method exists for calculating an urban area's open space requirements. . . . Cost and availability of land always will be among the factors limiting and shaping choice.[16]

Many advocates of the open space preservation movement believe that it makes little difference whether or not these programs are focused upon specific goals. They emphasize that land currently acquired for open space uses can be resold if real need for the land does not long remain evident. Since specific future needs cannot be more reliably identified, the long-term cost to society might be lower by permitting widespread intensive urban development now—and later "de-building", i.e., urban renewal. Resources would not be expended until the need for open space can be better identified, an important consideration in view of our current needs for funds in education, medicine, and other basic areas of human concern.

The urgency of open space preservation may be so immediate that we cannot wait for precise, exact standards. However, without more complete information than we possess at present, many decisions involving huge expenditures of money in open space programs will be based upon little more than emotion and value judgment.

Open Space Research Requirements

Research in the subject of open space—or even in its primary subfield, outdoor recreation—has been one of the most neglected areas of concern in contemporary urban society. ORRRC observed that:

Perhaps no other activity involving so many people and so basic a part of our life has received less attention from qualified investigators and scientists [than has outdoor recreation].[17]

A vital, concerted research effort into open space requirements at this time might reduce the number of imponderables that exist and provide a factual base for decisions on open space preservation policy.

Research into future open space demand could resemble the continuous "consumer preference" analyses. Market research organizations often utilize panels numbering 25,000 or more families, comprising a stratified sample of the national population; such a firm could be employed to survey its own panel of families. Though they would have to overcome methodological and conceptual difficulties, a team of specialists from the fields of medicine, psychology, sociology, economics, geography, recreation, urban planning, and public administration could develop questionnaires designed to determine, in depth, the attitudes of representative families about open space needs. Alternative public policies and programs (including *no* program) could be considered.

Socioeconomic information—particularly an identification of family members as either rural- or urban-reared—could be correlated with responses. Panels associated with leading market research firms generally consist of families who regularly participate in such surveys as part of the firm's operations, and thoughtful responses should be obtainable. A central hypothesis could be that urban-reared families do not feel as great a need for open space as do rural-reared families. If the data permit acceptance of this hypothesis, the fact that family formation now occurs predominantly in urban areas has pronounced open space policy implications.

As a point of departure these research results when supplemented by other studies could be used by the interdisciplinary research team to produce a contemporary report on open space standards similar to the American Public Health Association's *Planning the Neighborhood: Standards for Healthful Housing*, previously mentioned. Thus, new, flexible standards with mechanisms for adjusting to changing community population characteristics, economic base, and terrain (rather than rigid standards that are soon outmoded) could be formulated.

At present, only a handful of scattered researchers are conducting investigations on this order. Financial support to expand and coordinate these efforts is needed. The research should seek a national perspective through the establishment of study priorities. The coordination of this broad open space research program could best be accomplished by a single governmental agency. Since the U.S. Housing and Home Finance Agency is now both administering grant-in-aid programs for urban planning assistance and open space land acquisition, and financing exploratory studies of open space needs, it seems best equipped to provide this program direction.

The recent passage of the monumental Land and Water Conservation Fund Act will provide about $180 million annually over its first ten years for planning, acquisition, and development of outdoor recreation areas. This is indicative of the public expenditures for environmental and recreational purposes which lie ahead. Perhaps it is too pragmatic or even whimsical to suggest that we can develop a sufficient understanding of our environment and open space requirements to improve the legislative and administrative decisions in this critical public policy area. Yet, the preservation of land for social amenities and the conservation of scarce public financial resources for other areas of human concern make the effort essential.

John Kenneth Galbraith

How Much Should
a Country Consume?*

Conservationists are unquestionably useful people. And among the many useful services that they have recently rendered has been that of dramatizing the vast appetite which the United States has developed for materials of all kinds. This increase in requirements we now recognize to be exponential. It is the product of a rapidly increasing population and a high and (normally) a rapidly increasing living standard. The one multiplied by the other gives the huge totals with which our minds must contend. The President's Materials Policy Commission[1] emphasized the point by observing that our consumption of raw materials comes to about half that of the non-Communist lands, although we have but 10 per cent of the population, and that since World War I our consumption of most materials has exceeded that of all mankind through all history before that conflict.

This gargantuan and growing appetite has become the point of departure for all discussions of the resource problem. In face of this vast use what is happening to our domestic reserves of ores, to our energy sources, to the renewable resources? Are we being made excessively dependent on foreign supplies? How can we ensure that they will continue to flow in the necessary volume and with the necessary increases to our shores? How is our security affected?

The high rate of use has catalyzed conservationist activity on many other fronts. Because of it we have been busily assessing reserves of various resources and measuring the rate of depletion against the rate of discovery. We have become concerned with the efficiency of methods of recovery. As a result, for example, of the meteoric increase in natural gas consumption, the prospect for further increase, and the limited supplies at least within the borders of continental United States, we have had an increasing concern over what was flared or otherwise lost. The large requirements and the related exhaustion of domestic reserves

*Reprinted by permission from *Perspectives on Conservation*, Henry Jarrett, ed. (The Johns Hopkins Press, 1966), 89–99. © 1958, The Johns Hopkins Press, for Resources for the Future.
(Notes to this selection will be found on pp. 419–420.)

support the concern for having ready stocks of materials in the event of national emergency. (Support for this also comes from the not inconsiderable number of people who, in this instance, find prudence a matter of some profit.) Our large fuel requirements have deeply affected our foreign policy even though it remains a canon of modern diplomacy that any preoccupation with oil should be concealed by calling on our still ample reserves of sanctimony.

Finally, and perhaps most important, the high rate of resource use has stirred interest in the technology of resource use and substitution. Scores of products would already have become scarce and expensive had it not been for the appearance of substitute sources of materials or substitute materials. We still think of innovation in terms of the unpredictable and fortuitous genius which was encouraged by the patent office. In fact, input/output relationships for investment in innovation, not in the particular case but in general, are probably about as stable as any other. And investment in such innovation may well substitute, at more or less constant rates, for investment in orthodox discovery and recovery. This means, in less formidable language, that if a country puts enough of its resources into researching new materials or new sources of materials, it may never be short of the old ones. We cannot necessarily rely on the market for this investment—market incentives did not get us synthetic nitrogen, synthetic rubber, or atomic energy—to mention perhaps the three most important new materials substitutes or sources of this century. We shall have to initiate publicly much of the needed innovation, and much of it will have to be carried to the point of commercial feasibility by public funds. We shall have to be watchful to anticipate needed investment in innovation. We will be making another of our comfortable and now nearly classic errors if we assume that it will all be taken care of automatically by the free enterprise system.

But the role of research and innovation is not part of this story. I cite it only because one must do so to keep the resource problem in focus. In the future, as in the past, substitution nurtured by science will be the major hope of the conservationist. I am not unimpressed with the importance of what I have now to say. But I would not wish it thought that I identify all resource salvation therewith.

II

In my opening sentences I spoke agreeably about the conservationist as a citizen. May I now trade on those graceful words and be a trifle rude? Any observer of the species must agree that he is also frequently capable of marked illogicality combined with what may be termed selective myopia. There are many manifestations of this. Nothing, for example, is more impressive than the way the modern conservationist rises in awesome anger—particularly, I think, along the Eastern Seaboard—at a proposal to dam and thus to desecrate some unknown stream in some obscure corner of some remote national park, and at the same time manages to remain unperturbed by the desecration of our highways by the outdoor advertising industry. Were the Governor of New York, in some moment of political aberration to propose a minor modification of the state's "forever wild" proviso as it applies to the state parks, he would be jeopardizing his future. When he seeks to make the highways of his state less hideous, he can hope, at most, for the applause of Robert Moses, the *New York Times*, the most determined garden clubs, and a few eccentrics. One may formulate a law on this: The conservationist is a man who concerns himself with the beauties of nature in roughly inverse proportion to the number of people who can enjoy them.

There is, I sense, a similar selectivity in the conservationists' approach to materials consumption. If we are concerned about our great appetite for materials, it is plausible to seek to increase the supply, to decrease waste, to make better use of the stocks that are available, and to develop substitutes. But what of the appetite itself? Surely this is the ultimate source of the problem. If it continues its geometric course, will it not one day have to be restrained? Yet in the literature of the resource problem this is the forbidden question. Over it hangs a nearly total silence. It is as though, in the discussion of the chance for avoiding automobile accidents, we agree not to make any mention of speed!

I do not wish to overstate my case. A few people have indeed adverted to the possibility of excess resource consumption—and common prudence requires me to allow for discussion which I have not encountered. Samuel H. Ordway in his *Resources and the American Dream*[2] has perhaps gone farthest in inquiring whether, in the interests of resource conservation, some limits might be placed on consumption. He has wondered if our happiness would be greatly impaired by smaller and less expensive automobiles, less advertising, even less elaborate attire. And he argues, without being very specific about it, that the Congress should face the question of use now as against use by later generations.

By contrast, The Twentieth Century Fund in its effort to match materials and other resource requirements to use, takes present levels of consumption and prospective increases as wholly given. It then adds to prospective needs enough to bring families at the lower end of the income distribution up to a defined minimum. While the authors are, on the whole, sanguine about our ability to meet requirements, they foresee difficulties with petroleum, copper, lead, zinc, and the additive alloys for steel.[3] I would say on the whole that The Twentieth Century Fund's approach represents a kind of norm in such studies.

The President's Materials Policy Commission took a similar although slightly more ambiguous position which is worth examining in some slight detail. It began by stating its conviction that economic growth was important and, in degree, sacrosanct. "First, we share the belief of the American people in the principle of Growth."[4] (It is instructive to note the commission's use of a capital G. A certain divinity is associated with the word.) *Growth* in this context means an increasing output of consumers' goods and an increase in the plant by which they are supplied. Having started with this renunciation, the commission was scarcely in a position to look critically at consumption in relation to the resource problem, and it did not.

Yet the PMPC could not entirely exclude the problem of consumption from consideration. In the course of its formal recommendations it asked that the armed services in "designing military products, and in drawing up specifications, focus on using abundant rather than scarce materials, and on using less of any material per unit of product where this can be done without significantly affecting quality or performance." And it asked for "greater emphasis on care and maintenance of military equipment and conservation in use and increase[d] scrap recovery of all kinds."[5] But it almost certainly occurred to the able members of the commission that this was straining furiously at the gnat. Why should we be worried about the excess steel in a tank but not in an automobile? What is gained from smaller radar screens if the materials go into larger TV screens? Why should the general be denied his brass and his wife allowed her plumage? There is an obvious inconsistency here.

As a result the PMPC did venture on. Although it did not support the observation with any concrete recommendation, it did comment with some vigor on present tendencies in consumption. "The United States," it observed, "has been lavish in the use of its materials. . . . Vast quantities of materials have been wasted by overdesigning and overspecification. We have frequently designed products with little concern for getting maximum service from their materials and labor. We drive heavier automobiles than is necessary for mere transportation, and we adorn them with chromium. . . . We blow thousands of tons of unrecoverable lead into the atmosphere each year from high octane gasoline because we like a quick pickup. We must become aware that many of our production and consumption habits are extremely expensive of scarce materials and that a trivial change of taste or slight reduction in personal satisfaction can often bring about tremendous savings."[6]

The captious will want to inquire, if the losses in satisfaction here are trivial and the savings are tremendous, why the commission did not seize the opportunity to urge savings. Why did it make no recommendations? But given its position on growth and the meaning of growth, it could in fact go no further. At first glance it does not seem impossible to pick out kinds of consumption which seem especially wasteful—things which reflect not use but wasteful use. Surely the utility of an automobile is not diminished if it is lighter or if its gasoline contains less lead. But this is a distinction that cannot be made. Consumption, it quickly develops, is a seamless web. If we ask about the chromium we must ask about the cars. The questions that are asked about one part can be asked about all parts. The automobiles are too heavy and they use irreplaceable lead? One can ask with equal cogency if we need to make all the automobiles that we now turn out. This question gains point when we reflect that the demand for automobiles depends on that remarkable institution called planned obsolescence, is nurtured by advertising campaigns of incredible strategic complexity, and on occasion requires financial underwriting that would have seemed rather extravagant to Charles Ponzi.

As with automobiles so with everything else. In an opulent society the marginal urgency of all kinds of goods is low. It is easy to bring our doubts and questions to bear on the automobiles. But the case is not different for (say) that part of our food production which contributes not to nutrition but to obesity, that part of our tobacco which contributes not to comfort but to carcinoma, and that part of our clothing which is designed not to cover nakedness but to suggest it. We cannot single out waste in a product without questioning the product. We cannot single out any one product without calling into question all products. Thus having specifically endorsed ever more luxurious standards of consumption—for this is what is meant by growth—the PMPC obviously could not pursue the notion of wasteful consumption without involving itself in a major contradiction. It made its gesture against the automobiles and then, wisely, it stopped.

III

There are several reasons why our consumption standards have not been called in question in the course of the conservation discussion over the last 50 years. There is also some divergence between those that are given, or which come first to mind, and those that are ultimately operative. Thus, to recur once more to the PMPC, it simply stated its belief that economic stagnation is the alternative to growth, meaning uninhibited increases in consumption. No one, obviously, wants stagnation. But does this argument really hold? Clearly we can have different rates of growth of consumption. In other contexts we are not nearly so committed to the notion of all-out increase in consumption. In 1957 economic output was virtually constant. This leveling-off of output—stagnation if I may use the pejorative term—was, more or less, a goal of public policy. The purpose of the tight money policy was to reduce the rate of investment spending and thus of economic expansion in order hopefully to win a measure of price stability. In this context we weren't so appalled by the idea of a lower rate of growth—something approaching what the PMPC would have had to call stagnation. As I write, in the first quarter of 1958, we have had something more than a leveling-off; we have experienced a rather sharp reduction in output. But even this, at least in some quarters, has not been regarded with great alarm. We are being told that breathing spells are inevitable in the free enterprise system.

Also, as I shall suggest in a moment, we can have patterns of growth which make heavy drafts on materials and other patterns which are much more lenient in their requirements.

In any case, if our levels of consumption are dangerously high in relation to the resource base, or are becoming so—and the PMPC at least expressed its concern—it would obviously be better to risk stagnation now than to use up our reserves and have not stagnation but absolute contraction later on. Those who sanctify growth but also say that the resource position is serious are, in effect, arguing that we have no alternative to having our fling now even though, more or less literally, there is hell to pay later on. This is an odd posture for the conservationist.

It is also suggested that uninhibited consumption has something to do with individual liberty. If we begin interfering with consumption, we shall be abridging a basic freedom.

I shan't dwell long on this. That we make such points is part of the desolate modern tendency to turn the discussion of all questions, however simple and forthright, into a search for violation of some arcane principle, or to evade and suffocate common sense by verbose, incoherent, and irrelevant moralizing. Freedom is not much concerned with tail fins or even with automobiles. Those who argue that it is identified with the greatest possible range of choice of consumers' goods are only confessing their exceedingly simple-minded and mechanical view of man and his liberties.

In any case, one must ask the same question as concerns growth. If the resource problem is serious, then the price of a wide choice now is a sharply constricted choice later on. Surely even those who adhere to the biggest supermarket theory of liberty would agree that their concept has a time dimension.

Finally it will be said that there is nothing that can be done about consumption. This of course is nonsense. There is a wide range of instruments of social control. Taxation; specific prohibitions on wasteful products, uses, or practices; educational and other hortatory efforts; subsidies to encourage consumption of cheaper and more plentiful substitutes are all available. Most have been used in past periods of urgency.

And here, indeed, is the first reason we do not care to contemplate such measures. The latter forties and the fifties in the United States were marked by what we must now recognize as a massive conservative reaction to the idea of enlarged social guidance and control of economic activity. This was partly, no doubt, based on a desire to have done with the wartime apparatus of control. In part, it was a successful conservative reaction to the social intervention of the New Deal. In part, it was the resurgence of a notably oversimplified view of economic life which seized on this moment to ascribe a magical automatism to the price system (including the rate of interest) which, as we are again gradually learning, it does not have. Euphemisms have played a prominent part in this revolt. Many have found it more agreeable to be in favor of liberty than against social responsibility. But the result has been to rule out of discussion, or at least to discriminate heavily against, measures which by their nature could be accomplished only by according increased responsibilities to the state.

Since consumption could not be discussed without raising the question of an increased role for the state, it was not discussed.

However, tradition also abetted this exclusion of consumption levels from consideration. Economics is a subject in which old questions are lovingly debated but new ones are regarded with misgiving. On the whole it is a mark of stability and sound scholarship to concern oneself with questions that were relevant in the world of Ricardo. In the Ricardian world, to be literal about it, goods were indeed scarce. One might talk, although without courting great popularity, about redistributing wealth and income and thus curbing the luxurious consumption of the classes. But the notion that people as a whole might have more than a minimum—that there might be a restraint on the consumption of the community as a whole—was unthinkable. In modern times this has, of course, become thinkable. Goods are plentiful. Demand for them must be elaborately contrived. Those who create wants rank among our most talented and highly paid citizens. Want creation—advertising— is a ten billion dollar industry. But tradition remains strongly against questioning or even thinking about wants.

Finally, we are committed to a high level of consumption because, whether we need the goods or not, we very much need the employment their production provides. I need not dwell on this. The point is decidedly obvious at this witing in early 1958. We are not missing the cars that Detroit is currently not producing. Nor are we missing the steel that Pittsburgh and Gary are currently not making. The absence of these products is not causing any detectable suffering. But there is much suffering and discomfort as the result of the failure of these industries to employ as many men as in the recent past. We are chained to a high level of production and consumption not by the pressure of want but by the urgencies of economic security.

IV

What should be our policy toward consumption?

First, of course, we should begin to talk about it—and in the context of all its implications. It is silly for grown men to concern themselves mightily with supplying an appetite and close their eyes to the obvious and obtrusive question of whether the appetite is excessive.

If the appetite presents no problems—if resource discovery and the technology of use and substitution promise automatically to remain abreast of consumption and at moderate cost—then we need press matters no further. At least on conservation grounds there is no need to curb our appetite.

But to say this, and assuming that it applies comprehensively to both renewable and nonrenewable resources, is to say that there is no materials problem. It is to say that, except for some activities that by definition are noncritical, the conservationists are not much needed.

But if conservation is an issue, then we have no honest and logical course but to measure the means for restraining use against the means for insuring a continuing sufficiency of supply and taking the appropriate action. There is no justification for ruling consumption levels out of the calculation.

What would be the practical consequences of this calculation—taken honestly and without the frequent contemporary preoccupation not with solution but with plausible escape—I do not pretend to say. As I suggested at the outset, I am impressed by the opportunities for resource substitution and by the contribution of technology in facilitating it. But the problem here is less one of theory than of technical calculation and projection. As such it is beyond the scope both of this paper and my competence. It has been my task to show that at any time that the calculation is unsanguine, restraint on consumption can no longer be excluded as a remedy.

However, let me conclude with one suggestion. There may be occasions, in the future, when in the interest of conservation we will wish to address ourselves to the consumption of particular products. (This, as noted, can only be in the context of a critical view of all consumption.) The modern automobile may be a case in point. I share the view that this is currently afflicted by a kind of competitive elephantiasis. As a result, it is making a large and possibly excessive claim on iron, petroleum, lead, and other materials; but much more seriously it is making excessive inroads on urban and rural driving and standing space and on the public funds that supply this space.

But in the main it would seem to me that any concern for materials use should be general. It should have as its aim the shifting of consumption patterns from those which have a high materials requirement to those which have a much lower requirement. The opportunities are considerable. Education, health services, sanitary services, good parks and playgrounds, orchestras, effective local government, a clean countryside, all have rather small materials requirements. I have elsewhere argued that the present tendency of our economy is to discriminate sharply against such production.[7] A variety of forces, among them the massed pressures of modern merchandising, have forced an inordinate concentration of our consumption on what may loosely be termed consumer hardware. This distortion has been underwritten by economic attitudes which have made but slight accommodation to the transition of our world from one of private to one of opulence. A rationalization of our present consumption patterns—a rationalization which would more accurately reflect free and unmanaged consumer choice—might also be an important step in materials conservation.

Part Five

Public Perception

*E*veryone is a potential policy participant. Many may never become involved, but, more importantly, many will, and are involved in the process of determining and reshaping political policies concerning our natural resources. Some participants are involved in virtually every decision concerning a particular resource. Others are concerned with a few decisions about several resources. Some are deeply interested in issues; others, only peripherally. Some have great influence; others, very little. And the roles and interests of participants, of course, change from time to time.

There may be, and often is, an internal process within an organization which guides or specifies the participation. The degree of participation and cast of participants can usually be predetermined by assessing the roles, both formal and informal, which individuals and groups play, and by judging the degree of saliency others have for the issue.

The saliency of a participant is determined in a large part by his awareness of the issue and his interest in it. Since both awareness and interest can be increased, decreased, or altered as the result of either internal or external causes, the salience of an issue can be changed. Sometimes the change is only relative as regards the issue itself, as when interest or information concerning another related or entirely different subject becomes more prevalent and demanding. There is continual competition among issues for attention from the public and the policy-maker.

For example, established interest and awareness in an issue, such as water pollution, may have propelled it to a point of active consideration. But a new or different issue may displace the old from preeminent consideration. An air pollution crisis could put that issue in a higher priority, though none of the old supporters may have changed his mind on the basic importance of the water pollution. Only its relative importance has changed, not necessarily the nature of the problem.

Nor is the competition limited to other ecological issues. When crises in foreign policy, national defense, or poverty amass an accumulation of interest, awareness, and resources, we may again see the virtual abandonment of other issues (though the substance of the problems still basically remain the same).

The selections in this chapter illustrate different aspects of public perception. Ashley Schiff has written on how different values are perceived in the decision-making process. Gilbert F. White discusses the involvement of the public in resource issues, and Thomas Saarinen reports an attitudinal survey on the issue of weather modification. Finally, H. George Frederickson and Howard Magnas compare attitudes toward water pollution in a metropolitan area.

Ashley L. Schiff

Outdoor Recreation Values in the Public Decision Process*

Few covet the inferior status connoted by such terms as "residual claimants" and "incidental by-products." Yet, to the chagrin of many conservationists, outdoor recreation has traditionally been the recipient of this low-priority rating. It is therefore understandable that they have recently been trying to stimulate greater interest in the value of recreational resources. Seeking to assure outdoor recreation its proper share of the public purse, conservationists endorsed broad-gauged recreational analyses conducted within a framework of comprehensive resources planning. In their view, past indifference was a result of a chronic inability to formulate an integrated and harmonized set of recreational proposals. If only officials concerted their energies to this end, they reasoned, the chaos of responsibility which plagued existing programs might be eliminated. Thus, one Outdoor Recreation Resources Review Commission (ORRRC) report argued that "lack of anything resembling a National recreational policy is therefore at the root of most of the recreation problems of the Federal Government. But the recreationists exist even if the policy does not."[1] In like manner, Sigurd Olson sought comforting reassurance from Robert Weaver of the Housing and Home Finance Agency that some grand vision inspired the open space program:

Could you enlighten me by a sort of a thumbnail sketch of what your hopes and ideas would be regarding the development of any typically urban area? I know there are the parks. I know there will be breathing space. I know the transportation business will have to be licked somehow, but in the back of your mind, I am sure is an ideal of a perfect situation to which you have given some thought.[2]

Secretary Stewart Udall pledged Congress: "Definite overall plans are essential if there is to be adequate provision for open spaces and public

*Reprinted by permission from *Natural Resources Journal* (School of Law, University of New Mexico), VI (Oct., 1966), 542–559.
(Notes to this selection will be found on pp. 420–421.)

use areas without duplication of effort between Federal, State and local governments."[3] Similarly, the Bureau of Outdoor Recreation (BOR) instructed planning officials: "The Nationwide Outdoor Recreation Plan will encompass all forms of outdoor recreation."[4]

I

THE APPEAL OF RATIONALITY

To students of natural resources administration, this diligent "grail-like" search for clarity, neatness, and order is familiar, because a record of repeated failures marks past attempts to unify and rationalize water resources organization. Despite these efforts, Irving Fox has noted, with apparent unconcern, the tendency toward greater fragmentation of governmental authority.[5] The loose-jointed, multifaceted decisional process implied by this development defeats the possibility of central direction or control. Yet, the contrary approach, represented by a pluralistic pursuit of the public good, does not necessarily involve the sacrifice of collective interests to private avarice.

It is erroneous to believe that the requisites for public policy integration are analogous to the role played by conductors before symphony orchestras. As Will Rogers, with earthy aptness stated, "[E]verybody is ignorant, only on different subjects." Neither prescient nor omniscient, our power to comprehend reality—to acquire, process, and assimilate knowledge—is subject to considerable limitation. Customarily, organizations, like people, content themselves with performance meeting certain minimum standards. Moreover, organizations are prisoners of experience. What facts they obtain are interpreted in the light of their own goals and value commitments. It is vain to expect even super-coordinating mechanisms to embrace within their purview a sufficiently wide spectrum of orientations and biases. Paul Diesing, in examining the nature of "political rationality," observes that:

If one man knew the whole truth his predictions would always be correct; but since all existing theories are incomplete and partly false, it is better to bring together a variety of partial theories to better approximate the whole truth. To some extent this is correct; ideological variety is necessary as a corrective to partiality. But in some respects partiality and bias are even helpful. Partiality makes possible a division of labor in describing and interpreting, in that each person will look at a problem from the standpoint of his own beliefs and values. His standpoint will enable him to see and predict things that others would not be able to see or expect, and to exaggerate things that others can just barely see. . . . A vigorous opponent can be relied on to bring out all possible shortcomings of a proposal including some that are not there but may yet come about with bad luck. And when a program is being carried out, a vigorous opponent will be alert to the first small signs of failure which zealous advocates of a program would not notice or would brush aside.[6]

In a world of great complexity and uncertainty (and one in which policy views are strongly held), it may be reasoned with some cogency that the partial view of the public interest approach is more sensitively attuned to reality than its traditional foil—the total view of the public interest orientation. Altered to his limitations, man may better devise strategies to transcend them.

Having said this much, it would be absurd to contend that the claims for comprehensiveness were, in fact, meant to be taken at face value by officials associated with the outdoor recreation program. Rhetoric functions as balm to the uneasy public mind yearning for coherence and structure in an otherwise disorganized world. Moreover, rhetoric justifies the demand that another member be admitted to the bargaining table of politics. It also furnishes ideological support necessary to rally one's own forces. In the process many have been seduced by their own words. Yet, events would indicate that this stage for outdoor recreation has not and probably never will be reached. Administrators have been steeped too long in the tactics of pluralistic politics to jeopardize their careers by following the siren song of physical rationality.

Officials of the Bureau of Outdoor Recreation are conscious of the agency's precarious and delicate position standing across the ambitions of established agencies such as the Corps of Engineers and the Park and Forest Services. They are mindful of their absolute dependence on secretarial support. They appreciate the strategic intervention of the secretary's staff, as for example at Yosemite when Carver lectured the Park Service for being indifferent, indeed actively hostile, to the bureau's existence;[7] at the same time, they know they cannot invoke the secretary's blessings too often lest BOR become unduly identified with the interests of the Department of the Interior and therefore ineffective as an "impartial" aide to the Recreation Advisory Council. They realize they must tread cautiously to avoid exposing themselves to charges of empire building; thus, they must continually disclaim any intention to become an operating agency. With respect to their sister agencies, they must apportion land and water conservation funds so as not to alienate them. It may be significant, in this regard, that Secretary Udall once advocated a 40:40:20 per cent sharing of land and water conservation funds among the National Park Service, Forest Service, and Bureau of Sports Fisheries and Wildlife.[8] Such formulas—with adequate slack for flexibility to allow for unanticipated circumstances—may put a damper on conflict. In short, BOR must sedulously cultivate the image of counsellor, not commissar, with respect to its federal rivals.

Likewise, regarding its relations with the states and localities, BOR must profess the partnership principle, constantly reiterate faith in state potential for effective action, and emphasize the *assistance* it can proffer. There seems little reason to expect that the evolution of the outdoor recreation program *vis-à-vis* the states will differ from precedents previously set by other grant-in-aid efforts. Certainly, the state outdoor recreation planning requirements promulgated by BOR on December 30, 1964, perfectly fit the traditional mold of federal-state relations. As a recent Subcommittee on Intergovernmental Relations of the Senate Committee on Governmental Operations concluded:

Even those [programs] that foster comprehensive planning do so passively. . . . Fourteen of the forty-three [grant-in-aid] programs require only that projects assisted be "not inconsistent" with existing comprehensive plans. They do not require such planning and they do not go out of their way to see that it is effective when undertaken. They merely refrain from intentionally damaging comprehensive planning efforts.[9]

BOR is quite cognizant of the strength of American ideological attachments to states' rights and localism. The changes Congress effected in BOR's organic statute[10] hardly were needed to impress administrators with the wisdom of proceeding cautiously in order not to offend those sensibilities.

In formulating criteria for allocating resources to various programs and agencies, BOR recognizes the virtue of vagueness and ambiguity. It is intelligent enough to know that these semantic "defects" bring benefits exploitable by nimble administrators. Mr. Cliff and Mr. Wirtz (or his successor, Mr. Hartzog) have realized the difficulty (and inadvisability) of binding themselves to objective criteria. They admit that allocation questions demand a high order of judgment;[11] witness the diffuse operational meaning of the "multiple use" formula, and the "inability" of the Park Service to set down definite standards regarding proposed national park areas. The value of flexibility in an uncertain environment is much too precious to surrender to the unbending tyranny of mathematical equations. Aside from the obvious inability to assign weights to cultural, social, spiritual, and psychological factors, such formulas tend to freeze the political process to allocations based on measurable data, thereby enthroning certain value biases. Ira Gabrielson perceived this peril at the Fourth Joint Meeting of the Outdoor Recreation Resources Review Commission with its Advisory Council (1961): "It is not possible to delineate specifically the proper areas of responsibility of federal, state and local governmental jurisdictions. We must remain flexible to meet present and future needs."[12] It is also rather meaningful that the Recreation Advisory Council forced a BOR study group to discard a precise formula it had fashioned for evaluating the merit of suggested national recreation areas. Instead, the council issued rather ambiguous criteria.[13] Doubtless, the council feared that the study group criteria would have stopped it from independently passing upon projects which had excited conservationist interest. Their concern over a possible "miscarriage of justice" is dramatically highlighted by the following statement prepared in opposition to Sleeping Bear Dunes National Seashore:

Bearing in mind that the greatest need for recreation areas is near metropolitan centers and that about a third of all vacation trips are confined to within 100 miles, we then note these comparisons, or contrasts:

Within a 100-mile driving radius of Sleeping Bear there are only 2 cities of over 10,000 people. Their combined population is 28,544.

Within a 100-mile driving radius of Cape Cod National Seashore, there are 80 cities of over 10,000 people. Their combined population is 3,184,563. This is nearly 112 times as much as Sleeping Bear.

Within a 200-mile radius of Sleeping Bear there are 17 cities of 10,000 or more people. Their combined population is 990,804. The total population in cities of 10,000 or more within 200-mile driving radius of Cape Cod is 6,335,561, more than 6 times as many as for Sleeping Bear. The report of the National Outdoor Recreation Resources Review Commission . . . states that 'Michigan has a vast recreation resource in public ownership, but most of it is located just beyond the range of mass recreation use for the people of Detroit.' It might have added that half of Michigan's population lives within an hour's drive of downtown Detroit.

Now, let's see, on a per capita basis, how Michigan and Massachusetts compare in recreational resources, remembering that in density of population, Massachusetts has 618 persons per square mile, compared to 137 for Michigan. . . .

State Parks: Michigan has an acre for each 44 persons; Massachusetts has an acre for each 538 persons.

.   .   .   .

National parks and recreation areas: Michigan (Isle Royale . . .) has an acre for each 15 persons; Massachusetts (Cape Cod . . .) has an acre for each 192 persons. . . .

National forests: Michigan has an acre for each three persons; Massachusetts has no National forests, as such, only an experimental forest of 1,651 acres.[14]

Administrators prize the flexibility afforded by escape clauses and nebulous phrases. Congress insists on a direct voice in decision-making. It objects to procedures which would effectively remove it from a position of creative influence. Thus, Senator Talmadge reported his irritation over review procedures for small watershed projects:

We get a report to act on, and the areas in acres to benefit are given, the benefit ratio is given, the amount of funds to be put under Public Law 566 is given, the percent of Public Law 566 of the total cost is given, the other funds are listed, and the total cost is given. And we are asked to vote yes or no on such a project. Of course, no Senator can utilize great intelligence in voting yes or no on such a project, because he must take as evidence something that he had no part in evaluating, and he doesn't really know what he is evaluating and what he is not evaluating. And in that situation we really have to vote yes or no.[15]

If precision poses a threat to Congress, comprehensiveness may undermine its "little legislatures." Organization demands for wider jurisdiction—whether in the form of operating or clearance authority over other agencies—and may invade the existing prerogatives of congressional committees leading to bitter legislative struggles. For example, one can refer to Congressman Wayne Aspinall's pique over the Bureau of Sport Fisheries and Wildlife's claims regarding the Bureau of Land Management's administration of the public lands under the Fish and Wildlife Coordination Act:

What is involved here is that this committee has jurisdiction over all public lands of the United States, supposedly as far as the public domain is concerned, and yet we find ourselves having had a great deal of this jurisdiction apparently taken away from us. . . . When we lose a million acres of land from the public domain through the operations of another committee and an agency of Government over which we have jurisdiction, we want to know how they are coordinated.[16]

Alterations in organizational scope—its functional range—may have substantial consequences for other governmental institutions. Whirlpools of influence once agitated can exert an impact far beyond the point at which initial disturbance occurs.

II
POLITICS AND RECREATIONAL VALUES

Skeptical as we have been on the supposed advantages of, indeed possibilities for, organizational tidiness and totality of view, we do not despair in outdoor recreation's prospects for higher ranking in the future on the political agenda. Basically, political indifference and disinterest rather than uncoordinated administrative activity had accounted for conservationist alarm. Ever since the inauguration of the Outdoor Recreation Resources Review Commission, and partly because of its catalytic powers, an impressive awakening has occurred. Innumerable legislative and executive actions register this trend. In the space of less than a decade, affluence has profoundly affected resource management thinking in the form of concern for outdoor recreational opportunities and environmental quality. On every front, from every stance, the value of outdoor recreation has diffused itself and has permeated through a loosely integrated political system imposing a measure of cohesion in the midst of chaos. Admittedly, particular bureaucratic interests give a distinctive cast to each agency program. Recreation has been undeniably politicized, despite BOR statements that "National leadership which is nonpolitical in nature is a major need."[17] The sympathetic response elicited from so many governmental agencies indicates a general societal (governmental) obligation in this arena. In the past, when only a few organizations concerned themselves with providing recreational experiences, the myth of lofty noninvolvement might more easily have been sustained. Today, with expanded general governmental participation, that nonpolitical posture—whether in the form of revolving loan funds, bond sales, recreational professionalism, disinterested advisory boards, or high-minded state park commission leadership—might be useful for enlisting political support but it does not square with administrative reality.

Conflict will most assuredly persist, even intensify; its character, however, will be transformed as each organization bids for a share of a limited recreational budget. Ironically, as population expansion and spreading urbanization increase pressure on the land, limited financial, not physical, resources will generate future cleavages. Money, not land, will likely constitute the chief component of administrative power and political division. How utterly fascinating that the traditional folklore of American conservation should have inspired a movement tied so closely to a veneration of the land at the same time that a shift is occurring in the basis of influence away from the control of land towards the command of capital. Resource politics frequently exemplify politics of crisis. Its customary tendency has been to reaffirm emotional attachments deeply imbedded in the culture irrespective of their relevance to contemporary situations. Political exhortation (perhaps quite unconsciously and unintentionally as seems presently the case) has masked his metamorphosis while assuring legitimacy for programs undergoing change in the very process of their implementation. Amid a world of unceasing, accelerating change, widespread nostalgia exists for the land as a symbol of permanence and stability. As Thoreau maintained, it provides a certain balance to man's existence in the face of onrushing developments.[18] Through the preservation of wilderness, man gains perspective on himself and his place in the firmament. Similarly, Mr. Justice William O. Douglas has said that the wilderness offers spiritual sustenance as it enables man to "come to know both himself and God."[19] Aldo Leopold contended that from a knowledge of nature, man comes to a realization of his utter

234 Ashley L. Schiff

dependence on the environment. Hence, humility would replace arrogance in one's approach to life.[20] In a philosophic and poetic vein, Sigurd Olson, quoting Trevelyan's "we are children of the earth and removed from her our spirits wither," went on to say that a national parks experience could put man in contact with "some of the ancient earth wisdom of the race."[21] Ernest Swift in a recent editorial for the National Wildlife Federation, gave outdoor recreation a more mundane and sobering rationale:

It does seem, however, that when children are brought up to enjoy the more primitive aspects of the out-of-doors they gain a better appreciation of personal and economic survival. And that is one reason why it is more necessary today than ever before. Urban types of recreation do not emphasize the origin of a loaf of bread, a glass of milk, a sirloin steak, a piece of lumber, a railroad tie or a wooden fence post; or that the metals which go into building a hot rod are renewable. The danger lies in assuming that there is no bottom to the resource barrel. Previous generations thought the resources were inexhaustible, but at least they knew their origin. A large segment of the present generation assumes that resources are inexhaustible because they do not know where they come from, and care less.[22]

The approach is rigid in the dimensions of both time and space.

On one plane, to these dedicated conservationists, undeveloped land is fundamental; it is seen as possessing intrinsic value. If the land symbolizes permanence, decisions regarding its use are also seen as irreversible, irretrievable: "Decisions we make in the next few years may well be the last ones we can ever make."[23] According to critic Arnold Green, these attitudes, taken together, explain the frenzied urgency with which efforts to save a vanishing heritage have been launched. Green notes that conservationists act as though their "own time is critically important for all time to come. . . ."[24] Overdrawn, distorted, and obviously unfair as is most of Green's caricature, he is on sound ground in this description of conservationist orthodoxy. The desire to insure forever against any possible alienation of the land might have confirmed the National Park Service in its reluctance to utilize scenic easements—in lieu of fee acquisition, for the Ozarks Scenic Riverway.

Indeed, the dogma may also explain why BOR's nationwide plan manual sought to define recreational needs in acreage terms. Interestingly, the sociologist, Amitai Etzioni, has observed that in an effort to appear rational, most organizations

are eager to measure their efficiency. Curiously, the very effort . . . often has quite undesired effects from the point of view of the organizational goals. Frequent measuring can distort the organizational efforts because, as a rule, some aspects of its output are more measurable than the others. Frequent measuring tends to encourage over-production of highly measurable items and neglect of the less measurable ones.[25]

Probably, the initial decision regarding phenomena eligible for quantification already revealed a prior organizational bias. Continued quantification only contributed to the further skewing of goals.

The Forest Service seems to have been similarly bound to an inelastic *spatial* conception. Its highway development plans for the Boundary Waters Canoe Area were influenced by the thought that wilderness begins at the officially designated limits. Thus, the organization paved roads leading up to the boundary in the belief that psychological attitudes conformed to a physical definition. Robert Lucas' study on user wilderness perception has induced changes in Forest Service designs and has had a striking influence on conservationist ideas.[26] It would also seem that conservationist predilections for examining questions of recreational supply (involving study of the resources itself) in preference to problems of demand (relating to desired activities) bespeak this same anxiety for land scarcity. Past research interest has tended to flow backward from the resource; too little attention has been devoted to the more apposite, albeit elusive, user-oriented side of the recreation market. Since many regarded preserving open space, in Whyte's words as "an almost incontrovertibly good cause—like being for motherhood and the flag,"[27] proposals for careful study of consumer satisfaction seemed unnecessary. Robert Weaver, in a gracious gesture to the newly established BOR, disclaimed any intention of immersing his agency in the recreational field. He willingly left that function to other agencies. The Housing and Home Finance Agency, Weaver pledged, would merely determine open space locations. Comprehensive planning was HHFA's task, not comprehensive recreation planning.

Stress on the distinctive value of "virgin" land as a base for recreation has led conservationists to overlook the potential contributions of commercial enterprise in serving recreation needs. First, through insistence on the fundamental worth of human identification with the natural world, this orientation fostered a belief in outdoor recreation as the vital force of a democratic society. Hence, it underscored the desirability of making these opportunities available to all at minimum cost. Second, emphasizing site in contrast to activity, it diminished the importance of capital investment in satisfying recreational interests. Yet it is in this sphere that private enterprise has most to offer. Relying chiefly on capital resources, its role is crucial to the provision of those specialized facilities which make recreational diversity possible. It is astonishing to find Disneyland unlisted in that swansong report of the National Park Service—*Parks for America*. Would Marineland, or the Mission Bay enterprise in San Diego, qualify as outdoor recreation?

To cite but a few, would the following "amusements" be eligible—the chute flume ride at the New York World's Fair (for example, if established in New England or the Lake States), Greenfield Village, the Seattle Space Needle, drive-in theaters, mine tours, or the automobile exposition center proposed by Professor Richard Meier of the University of Michigan for the Detroit metropolitan area?

This fondness for the land often is linked with a rejection of urban civilization. It is revealing that despite protests from such eminent park officials as Robert Moses, the Outdoor Recreation Resources Review Commission study mandate stopped "at the city line." For this reason, "outdoor recreation resources" were defined to exclude "facilities, programs, and opportunities usually associated with urban development such as playgrounds, stadia, golf courses, city parks and zoos."[28] Reflecting kindred values, the federal and state open space programs generally describe open space as "undeveloped or predominantly undeveloped land."[29] To encourage a feeling of liberation, some states, in fact, required that areas be at least fifty acres in size. For many years planners have endorsed green belt parks. Implicitly, they were to function as *cordons sanitaires* protecting the countryside from contamination by urban encroachment and affording urbanites a place of occasional escape from the torment of civilized existence.

Toward parkways, the conservationists were ambivalent. Certainly, these roads represented an aesthetic advance over miles of highway bordered by tawdry honky-tonks. On the other hand, they stood for abject surrender to those "insolent chariots" of a mobile age, as Lewis Mumford has stigmatized them. It galled conservationists that man could be deceived into accepting such counterfeit contacts with nature as rewarding experiences. Yet for all their limitations, scenic roads did introduce a measure of order and beauty to the urban setting and thus met with conservationist acceptance. Their extension as integral parts of the national park system, however, raised preservationist hackles. Conservationists reasoned that another Baltimore–Washington Parkway would cause irreparable impairment to the meaning of national park standards. It appears significant that not until 1961 did the National Park Service's Advisory Board rescind an earlier resolution stating, "it is not a proper function of the National Park Service to participate in the construction or administration of future parkways unless they are within National Park areas."[30] Moreover, among the noteworthy omissions in the recommendations of ORRRC was one calling for a nationwide network of scenic roads. Perhaps, failure specifically to designate the Secretary of Commerce as one of the members of the Recreation Advisory Council was attributable in part to the attitude toward these creations of an industrial era.

Admittedly, it would be false to contend that ORRRC entirely ignored the areas mentioned above. It did point to the need, not simply for more parks, but for "building recreation into the environment."[31] Again, it spoke not of the "number of acres but of *effective* acres."[32] *Outdoor Recreation For America* even proposed a search to discover "substitutes for outdoor recreation." Nonetheless, its overriding thrust and, indeed, that of HHFA's open space program, was in terms of acquisition, not development; on "lost opportunities," not future promises; on open spaces and communion with nature, not urban aesthetics and the excitement offered by city life.

These deficiencies did not escape notice. Recognizing them, Mayor Richard Lee of New Haven claimed the Open Space Act

will actually benefit—at least in New England—. . . the small towns far more than it would the larger cities, because all of the cities that I know of in New England have been planned decades, as a matter of fact, several centuries ago and we have our parks and we have our green spaces and we have our open areas and actually the problem in New England is with the growth of the small towns. . . .[33]

Luther Gulick addressed himself to the same point: "we are going to have very heavy demands for leisure time activities and cultural activities in the urban areas. . . . Now, you left their problems out of these internal needs. So don't lean on their money unless you are going to fulfill their total requirement."[34] The crusade for open space had too readily assumed that the values which dominated a rural America would continue to exert equal force in a transformed setting. This view received apparent corroboration from a commission finding that: "At present, it is the simple pleasures Americans seek most."[35] But extrapolation of these behavior patterns into the future may be most unwise as Perloff and Wingo have argued:

Conserve our natural recreation and landscape resources, yes; but do not confuse this conservation objective with the powerful objective of meeting the recreation needs of the Nation. What is needed is a new strategy for recreation policy which is urban-oriented—that is, oriented toward serving the great majority of the national population—in its articulation with urban needs, developmental in its constantly improving levels of performance, and carefully integrated with the whole array of public activities which afford a joint pay off for the production of recreation services.[36]

Significantly, within the short span of three years, signs of adjustment to urban growth and influence have become increasingly evident. Repercussions from *Baker v. Carr*[37] may intensify the value struggle leading to an acceleration of these changes. Despite its previous orientation,

BOR may well be capable of making the shift. Lacking its own areas to manage, the psychological burden might not prove too onerous. Further, the Forest Service, even with its vast reserves, has shown some indications that it recognizes the nature of the problem. To the dismay of such former service officials as R. E. Marsh, C. M. Granger, and Thornton Munger, the organization refrained from competing aggressively for the Ozark Scenic Riverway and the Oregon Dunes Seashore.[38] Aware of its limited capital funds, it much preferred to earn Land and Water Conservation Fund support blocking existing holdings. If it is to make an impact, to forge a new recreation image, the agency realizes that it must concentrate investment on more highly patronized facilities. Doubtless, this new attitude also is partly the product of western land acquisition restrictions in the Land and Water Conservation Fund Act.[39] Still another factor which seems responsible for this policy change is traceable to the increased influence of economists in the service who have emphasized the meaning of capital scarcity. The result is apt to stimulate interest in specialized intense use developments instead of more uniform allocations to most administrative districts.

No doubt, the chief pressure for policy alterations will come from urban centers. Already, for example, it appears likely that New York City will be successful in adding the following amendments to a proposed state open space bond issue: (1) 50 per cent state cost-sharing for construction purposes (an earlier issue had earmarked no money for development); (2) elimination of acreage restrictions in order to permit creation of vestpocket parks, and the like, and (3) 50 per cent state cost-sharing for acquisition (as compared with 25 per cent state grants under the present formula). The city also hopes to secure increased funds from BOR by urging the adoption of usage criteria in apportioning Land and Water Conservation appropriations. Finally, Gotham officials endorse higher federal open space grant incentives to facilitate greater local participation. Regarding this last program, demands for repealing a clause[40] prohibiting federal grant assistance in acquiring and clearing completely developed property have issued interestingly enough, from the Advisory Committee on Intergovernmental Relations, on which are represented officials of HEW and HHFA.[41] Neither Agriculture nor Interior spokesmen served on this body.[42]

Thus, it is within the realm of possibility that outdoor recreation might yet be defined to permit the development of play areas on rooftops, a pedestrian and bicycle path across the Verrazano bridge,[43] the acquisition of public rights in private cemeteries to encourage multipurpose utilization for bird-watching and botanical gardens,[44] cantilevered promenades as in Quebec and Brooklyn, additional park police patrols and lighting to encourage public utilization, air-conditioned edifices where vegetative displays might be enjoyed during bleak winter months and torpid summer days, electronic parkways to promote scenic appreciation without endangering life, water fountains, and portable stands for festival parades.

III

CONFLICT AND INNOVATION

Conflict can function as the craftsman of creativity. Coordination by friction is a time-honored management technique. It may be turned to the service of outdoor recreation by promoting the confrontation of disparate value systems. It must be remembered that the verb "articulate" has two meanings: The first conveys the idea of joining; the second refers to an act of expression. Through the process of interest articulation, innovation and integration can proceed simultaneously. The conditions of political rationality will thereby be satisfied. The result will certainly be conducive to a more interesting and dynamic environment. While the basic stimulus to the clash of values is patently grounded in growing urban populations as evidenced by recent steps to rectify political imbalance, various devices might be employed to channel those forces toward constructive change. Agencies responsible for outdoor recreation should be encouraged to recruit specialists with diverse educational backgrounds, particularly in non-land management fields. The object here is *not* to foster coordination by making professionals of the bureaucracy.[45] Rather, the intent is to infiltrate organizations with the heterodoxies spawned by differing orientations. Second, interagency commissions, despite the risk of clumsiness and cost—might open their deliberations to active participation by additional parties. Third, review and clearance requirements similar to those in effect under the Fish and Wildlife Coordination Act,[46] the Interior–Agriculture agreements,[47] and the Bureau of Public Roads directive[48] should be increased and expanded. These may constitute more than meaningless gestures, mere perfunctory service to enlightened administration. Under the Fish and Wildlife Coordination Act, the Bureau of Sport Fisheries and Wildlife acted as a broker in arranging for cooperative management areas between the State of California and the Bureau of Land Management. It has also succeeded in persuading the Federal Power Commission to insert provisions in 30 licenses to protect or enhance habitat. Where backed by vocal and persistent support, flagrant transgression of these compacts may seem politically inexpedient. Conversely, to expect them to "work" in all cases is unrealistic and perhaps undesirable in a society prizing diversity. If handled discreetly, efforts commenced by fiat may, in some instances, lead to a genuine sharing of perspectives. For example, highway engineers mindful that the interstate system "is showing good progress toward resolving the transportation problems between our major population centers"[49] may favor a national system of scenic highways. Continued exposure to the critical advice of landscape architects would enable them to understand the importance of acquiring unusually wide rights-of-way, limited access designs, indirect routings, and the avoidance of "cut-throughs." Another illustration is supplied by a recent decision of New Jersey's Garden State Parkway Authority to construct an impressive cultural center with direct access from its artery. The development will mostly be financed out of toll revenues from increased use of the road. Bilateral review agreements or dual agency committees in the highway sphere might profitably be extended to include other organizations. For example, Marion Clawson has related that improvements to back country farm roads which currently are threatened with disuse may prove a fruitful resource for investment.[50] Unless Department of Agriculture representatives were participants, along with engineers and landscape architects, in a scenic highways program, this mine could very well be overlooked. The character of administrative planning will also influence allocation decision. Attention to the need for specialized facilities, as John Shanklin has concluded, is dependent on the adoption of a proper planning perspective.[51] To the extent that assessment of recreation needs is entrusted to the lowest hierarchical echelons, diversity will likely be sacrificed to drab uniformity. Conversely, optimal treatment of homogeneous resources may best be realized by upward devolution of responsibility for location and development of a specialized undertaking. In this regard, the appointment of economists might improve the evaluation of alternatives.

Further, restrictions on use of grant funds, either in terms of the size of the subvention or the population of the communities involved, tends to discourage collaboration for planning or administration. Removal of these limitations would appear desirable. Finally, were state or county assistance available as a sweetener, and local residents guaranteed access, peripheral communities might more readily consent to the repeal of an open space program ban on grant financing for municipal land acquisition projects outside their traditional jurisdictions. Under the present statute,[52] cities cannot look to federal support (except in the West) for purchasing, or leasing, recreational tracts beyond their borders.

The key to comprehensiveness, then, is to be found in the availability of choice. But the search for options often is most effective when alternatives are juxtaposed, set against each other, to allow comparisons and establish priorities. As the number of values so weighed and balanced increases, the system may be said to approach rationality. Conflict, or if one prefers, competition, tests the mettle of each value position in a manner no substitute procedure has been able to surpass. The chief flaw, of course, is the inherent limitation of any adversary contest. Preserving an open political order by structuring conflict to encourage participation of dissenters at the bargaining table probably compensates for much of this deficiency. As Aaron Wildavsky notes:

A partial adversary system in which the various interests compete for control of policy (under agreed-upon rules) seems more likely to result in reasonable decisions—that is decisions that take account of the multiplicity of values involved—than one in which the best policy is assumed to be discoverable by a well-intentioned search for the public interest for all by everyone.[53]

If organization is the "mobilization of bias," I favor pluralizing prejudice.

Gilbert F. White

Formation and Role of
Public Attitudes*

At the heart of managing a natural resource is the manager's perception of the resource and of the choices open to him in dealing with it. At the heart of decisions on environmental quality are a manager's views of what he and others value in the environment and can preserve or cultivate. This is not a conclusion. It is a definition: Natural resources are taken to be culturally defined, decisions are regarded as choices among perceived alternatives for bringing about change, and any choice presumes a view of the resource together with preferences in outcome and methods.

Little can be said by way of conclusion as to how the public's evaluation of environment and methods does in fact affect the decisions which are reached in polluting air and water, or defacing the terrain, or destroying habitat or in efforts to prevent or repair such damage. The terms themselves are slithery. Pollution or defacement of a physical landscape can only be measured against a human preference. Human perception and preference are related to environment and personality in ways which are not well explored. Much of the public discussion is masked by a rough plaster of horseback judgments that hide the structure of action and opinion formation. The difficulties, pitfalls, and opportunities are illustrated in a recent decision by a community of 50,000 people.

The voters of Boulder, Colorado, went to the polls in July, 1965, to cast their ballots for or against two proposals certain to alter the environment which they will occupy in the years ahead. One was authorization for a bond issue to pay for construction of an additional sewage disposal plant to reduce the waste that the rapidly growing city pours into Boulder Creek below its municipal limits. The second was to approve an agreement under which city water would be delivered to a mesa south of the city, and thus permit residential invasion of a high, scenic sector of the piedmont adjoining the Rocky Mountain front. Voting

*Reprinted by permission from *Environmental Quality in a Growing Economy*, Henry Jarrett, ed. (The Johns Hopkins Press, 1966). © 1966, The Johns Hopkins Press, for Resources for the Future.
(Notes to this selection will be found on pp. 421–425.)

was desultory, the totals were close, but the practical outcome was plain. The treatment plant gained approval; the water extension met defeat.

To understand how these decisions were reached and how public attitudes influenced them would require answers to a series of questions beyond the voting returns. The answers needed for Boulder exemplify those needed wherever public agencies alter environment. What is the decision-making network in Boulder, not only as it shows in the electoral decision but in the public and citizen agencies that framed the issues and sought to influence public action? What attitudes toward water quality and landscape enjoyment were held by those who took any part in the decision? How did their attitudes shape the public choice? What factors affect these attitudes? To what extent and in what circumstances are the attitudes subject to change? These questions will be reviewed in a broader context at the close of this paper.

The Boulder decisions were relatively simple in the concreteness of the issues, the number of people taking part, and the narrow area affected.

Consider the difficulty of trying to understand the genesis and implications of a declaration from the Department of the Interior that:

> Slowly, there is dawning in man an understanding of the intertwined cause and effect pattern which makes him subject, in some small way, to every slightest tampering with his total environment. If he is to enjoy the fruits of a truly Great Society, he must be willing to work for quality everywhere, not just in his own back yard; he must consider not just the fumes from his own car, but the total exhaust cloud from the Nation's vehicles; he must wonder not just where the next drink of water is coming from, but what is being done to keep the world's taps from going dry.[1]

How is it known what is dawning on man, and what is the quality he enjoys? Some observers argue that a consensus is emerging as to what is good quality in the environment. Looking to problems of policy formation, Caldwell argues:

> The need for a generalizing concept of environmental development that will provide a common denominator among differing values and interests is becoming clearer. And the concept of "good" environment, however one defines it, is certainly no less concrete, tangible, and specific than the concepts of freedom, prosperity, security, and welfare that have on various occasions served to focus public policy.[2]

How can these felt needs be recognized and weighed? How do they or should they affect public decision? In what ways may they be expected to change?

The number of people and organized groups directly involved in decisions that affect the quality of environment can be stated with some accuracy for any area. Water management to alter the water cycle in the United States provides one example. It is known that approximately 306,000 farmers irrigate land independently or through 8,750 districts, that farmers organized in 8,460 districts drain off excess water from the land, that 18,150 incorporated urban governments provide water and dispose of it for their residents, that each of 7,720 manufacturing plants withdraw on the average more than 20 millions of gallons of water daily for industrial purposes, that agencies and organizations generate hydroelectric power at 1,600 plants, that at least 3,700,000 rural homeowners provide their own water and waste disposal facilities, that every one of the farmers affects the movement of water on and in the soil, and that numerous state and federal agencies exercise some kind of influence over these choices.

For each of the direct decisions to make or not make one of these alterations in hydrologic systems there may be presumed to be a network of relationships. Where one manager is directly involved, as with a farmer who decides to install his own septic tank, his choice may be influenced only by a county sanitary requirement, by technical information supplied by state agencies and local merchants, and by the expressed preferences of his neighbors. Where an organization is involved, the whole process is complicated by the character of internal choice and by the number of exterior conditions that influence the process. Networks for decisions to modify air, vegetation, and urban landscape are even more complex.

Adequate models are lacking to describe the intricacies of decision-making and, thereby, to indicate critical points in the process. There seems no doubt that an individual manager of a sector of the environment takes into account in some fashion the range of possible uses, the character of the environment itself, the technology available to him for using the environment, and the expected gains and losses to himself and others from the possible action. His perception and judgment at each point is bound to occur in a framework of habitual behavior and of social guidance exercised through constraints or incentives. When the decision is lodged in an organization there is added the strong motivation of its members to seek equilibrium and to preserve the organization while accommodating its structure to changes required by shifts in preferences, environment, or personnel.[3]

Just how much of a role attitudes play in the final outcome is a matter for speculation at present. Little evidence is in hand. A few case studies of decision-making suggest points at which they might be expected to be especially significant. Thus, Gore's examination of selected government operations suggests that "formal organization accounts for only a part of surface behavior," and that informal organization, with its sensitivity to motivation, communication, sanction, habituated behavior, and threat symbols, help explain the remainder.[4] Certainly, individual goals and beliefs figure importantly in the organizational behavior.

Less systematic observations of the course of environmental management show a few obviously critical situations. Early efforts to develop public water supplies in the United States encountered serious inertia because many people did not believe in the germ theory of disease: until attitudes toward disease were altered proponents of the new, more sanitary supplies had hard sledding. A large city electric utility corporation recently installed precipitators in the stacks of a thermal fuel plant because it thought conspicuous smoke plumes would impair its relations with its customers. The classic case in the water field is the decision of the Board of Water Supply of New York City in the 1950's to pass over further study of the Hudson River as a water source because of its belief that the water users would object to anything other than pure, upland sources.

Attitudes enter into decisions in three ways. First, there are personal attitudes of the people sharing in the decision. Second, are their opinions as to what others prefer. Third, are their opinions as to what others should prefer. The three need not, and rarely do coincide, although there probably is a tendency for personal and normative attitudes to merge. In Boulder, an influential citizen favored a clean stream, thought that most of his fellows did not, and urged them to adopt waste treatment. Another Boulderite regarded the mesa subdivision as an abomination, though his fellows did not, and supported a negative vote against it. In a national park not far away, a government official who would prefer to walk and camp in a sector where no roads are present or may be seen, ignored his own preferences in advocating a new highway which would gash the mountain slopes in making the landscape accessible to tourists who, he believed, like it that way. The Outdoor Recreation Resources Review Commission was the first public agency to attempt an orderly canvass of consumer demand for qualitative use of environment, and it was careful in reporting the findings as to trends in outdoor recreation to note "A projection of these trends cannot foretell the future, but there are important clues here indicating the new order of needs."[5]

The literature of resources management and conservation is rife with assertions of what the people want. These range from sweeping declarations that "So far, our history has recorded two great threats, or attitudes, with relation to our natural resources, and now we are beginning a third,"[6] to closely reasoned arguments that the government actions in a democratic society reflect the ultimate resolution of conflicting preferences.

Far more influential in the daily course of environmental modification is the assessment of public attitudes that goes unsung and largely un-recorded. This is the assessment that is lodged deep in the engineering design of a new Potomac River dam or in the administrative decision to specify standards for land use in a Cascades wilderness. An engineer judges that people will be satisfied with a given taste of water or with a certain monotony of wayside design or with a stream bank that is deprived of algae growth. Once plowed into a design or office memoran-dum, the assumption may never reappear in its original seminal form, but it may bear profuse fruit in the character of daily action.

Strictly speaking, there is no single expert opinion about attitudes toward quality of environment; there are the opinions each person holds, the opinions he thinks others hold, and the opinions he thinks they should hold. Many public administrators get mixed up about this. Per-haps the greatest confusion arises from their not knowing what others do believe and from lacking means of finding out. What follows is a preliminary attempt to outline what is known and not known about attitudes toward quality of environment and the ways in which they vary from person to person, place to place, and time to time.

Before touching on some of what is known and not known about attitudes affecting environmental decisions, caution should be offered at four points. The first and basic reservation is that the analysis is made by a geographer who, while seeking help from social psychologist colleagues, has not absorbed their scientific lore, and who reports the use of their conclusions but may not fully comprehend the grounds for them. During the past year a few social psychologists and geographers at the University of Chicago have joined under an RFF grant in an exploration of attitudes towards water.[7] Much of what follows stems from that investigation, especially the remaining cautions.

The term "attitude" is used interchangeably with "belief" or "opin-ion" to describe a preference held by a person with respect to an object or concept. It does not in itself constitute a value or mark of value; it is the result of a valuation process of some kind, and always involves a preference. Insofar as it applies to an aspect of the environment it requires perception of that environment. By perception is meant the individual organization of sensory stimulation.[8] Apparently, there is no perception which is not organized on the basis of social experience. All of the evidence indicates that the same mountain landscape may be perceived quite differently by two people, to one as lowering and ominous, to another as refreshing and uplifting; that one man honestly terms clean a stream which another labels dirty; and that the same size coin looks larger to one boy than to another.[9] A common feature of perception is distortion of unfamiliar phenomena to adjust to familiar orientation, as when a geometrically minded American sees a skewed window frame in a different perspective in order to make it appear rectilinear. Or it may obscure painful reactions, as when a loving father does not observe a marring twist in a daughter's face. The term cognitive dissonance, as used by Festinger, describes the transformation.[10] There can be no thoroughly objective perception of the environment, only degrees of distortion which are minimized in rigorous scientific description. If this is true, then there can be no absolute standards of aesthetic experience, only standards which vary with experience and personality. What is perceived as reality may differ from person to person, and it seems likely that in such elementary ways as viewing abstract designs people vary in their spatial styles, in their preference, for example, of vertical as against horizontal lines.[11]

The next caution is against equating quality of environment with quality of life. When people speak of a high quality of an environmental vista, they often mean that the stimulus which it offers has led to a perception and accompanying response by the viewer which they regard as good for the viewer. The proper test is not the landscape itself but the response of whoever is stimulated by it. The response of an ardent ecologist who is inspired by exposure to an almost wholly undisturbed ecosystem may be like that of a mathematician in reverence before a perfect proof: The object inspires joy in the recognition of something which satisfies a particular human yearning for perfection. If this is true, then it is misleading rather than helpful to distinguish between quality of natural environment and quality of social environment. Quite aside from the fact that virtually no bit of the earth's surface is wholly undisturbed by man, it is important to remember that what commonly is called natural environment has meaning solely in a social setting in which the preferences are those of man interacting with man and nature.

The suggestion that the natural–social distinction be dropped may offend a few environmental engineers, but there is not likely to be solid objection from engineers or architects who attempt to design new buildings and communities. They subscribe in principle to the idea that they are shaping the total environment. The chief difficulty arises in trying to carry out the theory. Thus far, there are no instances where this has been done through rigorous application of what is known about human environmental stimuli.

A final caution has to do with the tendency to explain part of man's use of environment as rational and part as irrational. This is an attractive and convenient dichotomy, particularly when attention is directed toward economic optimization. It is said, for example, that if farmers were rational they would adjust their operations, within whatever constraints are set by social institutions, so as to maximize their net returns. Quite aside from the baffling task of recognizing social incentives and constraints, there are two difficulties in trying to pursue the distinction of rationality. One is that human goals rarely if ever are clearly defined;

generally they are ambiguous. There is not a single program or single policy in recent United States resource management that displays a unitary, unambiguous aim. Several aims are fused, and the most ardent administrators revel in the flexibility afforded by the resulting ambiguity: flood control is to save lives and protect economically efficient development; highway beautification is to enhance the landscape and make it more accessible by concrete expressways; waste treatment is to reduce health hazards and to render streams more useful for a variety of purposes. As it is with organizations, so it is with individuals. It is sanguine to expect neat, unambiguous aims and decision criteria.

A second difficulty is that the factors of personality and environment are so complex that to speak of a rational process is to ascribe a clarity of action and observation that rarely is attained. It is enough to struggle for rational, accurate description without seeking or claiming to find rationality in the action itself.

To sum up the cautions: Do not regard this as comprehensive from the standpoint of the social sciences. Remember that every attitude toward environment involves perception that is organized by individuals. Avoid equating quality of life with quality of environment, for the latter is judged only by the former. Abandon any early claims for rationality, and look at the way in which living people behave.

Five different avenues are followed by those who would discover attitudes. They twist and sometimes cross, but rarely merge.

The first and more traditional method is to analyze the interpretations which articulate man has made of his environment. The central route here is scholarly, sensitive appraisal of what man has felt about nature through his writings and his graphic art. Lowenthal gives the most comprehensive introduction to this approach,[12] and Glacken presses it searchingly in his examinations of attitudes toward nature held by scientists and other observers.[13] Tuan has called attention to landscapes which in literature have taken on special symbolic significance.[14] Travel diaries, the notes of explorers, or rock paintings may reveal the terrain as humans observe it.

Content analysis has the same purpose and uses the same material —the written word—but applies a more rigorous method. The Boulder decision can be subjected to analysis by examining the entire printed discussion that preceded the election according to prescribed categories of form, direction, authority, and value.[15] On the water question, the supporters stressed the need for planned development and for improvements which would enhance the city's growth. They argued that the mesa service area would enlarge the tax base, and appealed to the city's reputation and the responsibility of its citizens. Opponents stressed a prospective shortage of water and higher taxes. They argued that the city officials had acted unwisely and that the citizens should concern themselves only with the welfare of the city itself. Generally, the arguments against were not the obverse of those for, and the opposition was oriented around individual cost while support was oriented around community gain. The opposition tended to place more emphasis on effects which could be stated quantitatively than on quality, and to criticize details of design. The printed statements about the sewer issue were similar in character.

An intermediate variant of content analysis is represented by Elson's investigation of more than 1,000 textbooks used in the first eight years of American schooling during the nineteenth century. It leads to the following type of conclusion as to attitudes toward nature:

> Thus the nineteenth-century child was taught that nature is animated with man's purposes. God designed nature for man's physical needs and spiritual training. Scientific understanding of nature will reveal the greater glory of God, and the practical application of such knowledge should be encouraged as part of the use God meant man to make of nature. Besides serving the material needs of man, nature is a source of man's health, strength, and virtue. He departs at his peril from a life close to nature. At a time when America was becoming increasingly industrial and urban, agrarian values which had been a natural growth in earlier America became articles of fervent faith in American nationalism. The American character had been formed in virtue because it developed in a rural environment, and it must remain the same despite vast environmental change. The existence of a bounteous and fruitful frontier in America, with its promise not only of future prosperity but of continued virtue, offers proof that God has singled out the United States above other nations for His fostering care. The superiority of nature to man-made things confers superiority on the American over older civilizations. That Uncle Sam sooner or later will have to become a city dweller is not envisaged by these textbook writers, although their almost fanatical advocacy of rural values would seem to suggest an unconscious fear that this might be so.[16]

All of these appraisals raise the problem of how representative were the artists or pedestrian textbook writers upon whose work they are based. Was Corot's view of the forest in any sense indicative of the attitude of French foresters who managed the state land? Did McGuffey speak for the tillers of soil in Indiana? Were local newspapers which said of the Indiana prairie land in 1830 that the soil was suitable for cultivation a more accurate measure of the contemporary farmer's perception of his environment than the latter day historians who spoke of avoidance of the prairies? McManis shows that they were.[17]

If the artists' interpretation is to be verified, a second course of inquiry is to go directly to the people. Here enters the opinion pollster. An expression of attitude may be solicited by questions, and this may be checked for internal consistency and structure. Beginning with the

Department of Agriculture Program Surveys in 1940,[18] the opinion surveys of the National Opinion Research Center[19] and the Center for Survey Research[20] have canvassed segments of the American population from time to time as to its preferences concerning environment. The most extensive effort, sponsored by the Outdoor Recreational Resources Review Commission, inquired into the current habits of use of outdoor lands, and attempted to forecast the likely shifts in demand which would result from changes in population, income, and transportation.[21] Several recent studies of the survey type dealt with opinions toward air pollution in the Clarkston, Washington,[22] and metropolitan St. Louis areas,[23] and toward aviation noise at an air force base.[24] From the array of responses to those surveys it is possible to describe certain articulated attitudes toward environment, ranging from air quality to juvenile delinquency, and to correlate them with social status, location, and views of the community.

Assuming that the samples are representative, complications in the use of results of opinion surveys arise from the degree to which the interview situation reflects conditions which would be at work if the respondent were faced with a decision in real life.[25] A man who, sitting in his living room, says he would favor a waste treatment plant may behave somewhat differently in a voting booth where the question is posed in terms of authorizing a bond issue, and still differently when the issue is a matter for discussion by a neighborhood group where he is open to new information and to interaction with peers and authorities. There is a lesson in the account of the professor who said he didn't know what he thought of a complex issue because he had not started to talk about it. An election with a *yes* or *no* choice lends itself especially to polling prediction and verification. Where the issue is more complex and the range of answers susceptible to wider interpretation, the procedures require supplementing, as was revealed by the forecasts of consumer preference for a paragon of a car called the Edsel. Ideally, the polling should follow after a much more searching investigation in depth which would isolate the factors of environment and personality that may be expected to figure in the final choice.

Although the polling techniques have been popular for a quarter of a century there seems to have been no attempt to find out trends in stated opinion toward the environment during that period. Nor has there been published any successful correlation of opinion survey and content analysis for environmental attitudes at the same place and time.

Akin to the opinion poll, though more concrete in its findings and more provocative in its interpretation, is the examination of actual consumer choices. This is a third avenue of study. The school of thought that argues that the public generally "gets what it wants" asks where people go for recreation in order to find their taste in recreational facilities, and asks what they are willing to pay for water as a measure of the value they place upon it.[26] Such analysis, where its use is practicable, raises basic and disturbing questions for it may well challenge accepted beliefs as to preferences. The trouble here is that so few aspects of environment are subject to free pricing, and that so few past decisions have been made without the encumbrance of extensive social guides which impose constraints and offer incentives. It is much easier to work out shadow prices and comparative valuation of uses for purposes of benefit–cost calculation than it is to trace out the effects of different value judgments along trails of practical choices that are hedged with public prods and carrots. The opportunities to refine estimates of this sort are large and increasingly recognized. Herfindahl and Kneese point out, for example, that "preferences for pollution-free air can perhaps be inferred from relative land values, expenditures for air purifiers, and commuting costs people are willing to incur to avoid polluted air."[27]

Rather than to ask the citizen what he wants or to deduce his preferences from what he ends up taking, it is possible to look into how he goes about making his choice in daily life. Because the models of decision-making are far from satisfactory and because the task of sorting out all of the factors bearing on a decision is intricate at best, this fourth avenue has been pursued only a short distance. Thus far, the studies of organization decision-making have given little attention to broad environmental considerations.[28] Geographic studies have tended to focus on perception of particular elements in the environment. Lucas traced out the concepts of wilderness, with its elements of beauty and solitude, as held by users of the Boundary Waters Canoe Area.[29] Situations of distinct hazard from natural phenomena may present problems of perception in a clear light.[30] Kates studied the perception of flood hazard as it related to adoption of loss–reduction measures and, with others, compared fresh-water and coastal situations.[31] Saarinen investigated the perception of drought hazard by Great Plains farmers.[32] Meda White examined the perception of tornado disaster by persons responsible for taking relief measures.[33] The Ohio State Disaster Research Center has pursued the problem of how group interaction affects response to a disaster situation.[34]

A fifth and possibly more revealing method of assessing attitudes is found in subjecting people to experimental situations in which they are asked to voice opinions after being exposed to a variety of information and persuasion and to interaction with peers seeking answers to the same problem. In the Chicago study of attitudes toward water, groups of young adults of relatively homogeneous education and age were given the opportunity to learn, discuss, and take positions toward a series of problems involving pollution and other conflictive uses of water. This more nearly approximates an actual decision situation, and makes it possible to observe the effects of changes in experience and in the opinions of their fellows. So far as is known, this is the first venture along that path in assessing attitudes toward environmental quality.

From the scattered evidence accumulated along all five avenues, a few conclusions seem warranted. Generalizations are difficult because there are no adequate models of personality and attitude formation to which to relate the empirical findings.

Perhaps the most obvious observation, as might be deduced from the earlier assertion as to distortion in perception, is that different people may view the same segment of the environment differently. In two neighboring Georgia towns taking water from the same stream, one group of citizens regard the taste as satisfactory, the other as unsatisfactory.[35] A landscape which seems friendly and inviting to one traveler is austere and hostile to another.[36] Perceptions of "dirty" water, "ugly" landscapes, "barren wastes," "murky" hazes, do not appear to conform to any universal aesthetic. Without commenting on how these perceptions differ or how their variance is related to other factors, a few other conclusions can be stated.

Judgment as to the severity of a perceived aspect of the environment varies greatly from person to person. Two people in the same metropolitan area may see air pollution as high or low, while agreeing that it constitutes an impairment of the habitat. Two dwellers on the same flood plain may regard flooding as frequent or infrequent, severe or benign.

So also may the city dwellers' concern with environmental quality differ. Even when the degree of severity is seen similarly, their expression of anxiety over its occurrence may vary widely. Thus, their ability to perceive niceties and complexities of the same phenomena of clouded stream or disfigured mesa-top is diverse.

Closely linked with concern is the sense of capacity to change or adjust to the environment. This ranges from the fatalistic acceptance of any feature—pleasurable or obnoxious—to confidence in individual or collective competence to correct the perceived faults. The view of capacity to deal with environment may be expressed in relation to particular aspects of land, water, plants, and air, or it may show in a general attitude toward nature

The broad value orientations found by Kluckhohn and Strodtbeck in their study of five communities—Mormon, Texan, Spanish–American, Zuni, and Navaho—in the U.S. Southwest seem to apply more widely.[37] Their man–nature classes conform to the commonly held theory that people in their orientation toward nature may be grouped as seeing man in a position of: (1) mastery over nature, (2) subjugation to nature, and (3) harmony with nature. These orientations are seen as related on the one hand to other cultural behavior, motives, and perception of reality, and on the other hand to the social structure and process of groups.

But why are there these great and persistent variations? The circumstances in which attitudes may change or be open to change may offer some clues, although it is unlikely that the variations can ever be wholly accounted for. Ingrained in the mythology of resources management are a number of explanations that apparently do not hold water in contemporary American society. For example, no close relation has been shown between physical setting and attitudes. In the semiarid landscape of the Southwest, the value orientations toward man in relation to nature do not reveal homogeneity with regard to the same landscape: Subcultures have different orientations toward the same physical phenomena but there are not absolute differences between distinct cultures; the same components appear in different rank orders.[33] In the recent Chicago studies of attitudes toward water, American young adults do not appear to vary accordingly to the aridity or humidity of the environment in which they spent their earlier years. Neither do their attitudes seem to differ with religious training and membership. If these negative findings are correct, much of the belief popular among government officers that people raised in dry areas have distinctive attitudes toward water in contrast to those raised in the humid East is challenged. The public expression of concern about water may be different in Nevada than northern Maine, but explanation must be sought beyond the physical aspects of childhood environment.

Four sets of factors do appear to play some kind of part in attitude formation: the decision situation, the individual's experience with the environment, his perception of his role, and his competence in dealing with its complexity. A different classification of the factors no doubt could be more systematic but these groupings are convenient.

Perhaps the most careful studies of the circumstances of public choice of environmental quality have centered upon the issue of whether or not public water supplies should be fluoridated and on the social situations in which public action is taken. The decision to fluoridate as a measure against tooth decay often appears as a single question for popular or council vote. Studies made of a few of the communities in which it has been proposed and adopted or rejected since 1944 throw light on the generality of knowledge as to attitude formation.[39] Paul, Gamson, and Kegeles, in reviewing what is now a large literature of social studies, point out that people who feel deprived or alienated by society tend to express resentment by voting against fluoridation, and that the local leaders of opposition are moved by feelings of the "remoteness and impersonality of the sources of power and influence affecting the daily life of the individual." When the histories of fluoridation campaigns are examined, it is observed that the same action which would be advantageous at one stage may set back the effort at another stage, and that often the leaders of campaigns, some of them professionals, may work against their own purposes because of their inability to recognize the roles expected of them. Although there has been considerable analysis of demographic, educational, and economic characteristics of voters and leaders, the more critical points for further investigation seem to center on personality traits and on the local social and political situation in which the decision is made.

Few issues offering choice of environmental quality have been investigated in as much detail as the fluoridation disputes. The aims are less clear and the range of possible means is much wider when an ordinance to ban billboards is up for a vote, or when the farmers' use of pesticides is at stake. Less is known about effects which the circumstances of social organization and personal interaction may have. In an interesting review of studies of why American farmers have been slow to accept recommended soil conservation practices, Held and Clawson examine the scattered evidence on farmers' attitudes toward erosion control measures and find that while certain factors, such as reluctance to change old methods and age of operator, may be significant they should be examined in the contest of the tenure, farm management, and cost–price relations in which the farmer acts.[40] The parts played by perception of soil conditions and by personality have received only passing attention.

Probably the greater part of studies to date have dealt with the intricate set of relations involved in human response to environmental stimuli. An excellent sampling of representative work is given by Kates and Wohlwill in a recent issue of the *Journal of Social Issues*.[41] They note the paucity of psychological study of the effects of physical environment on man's behavior, and call attention especially to its significance for the professions that design new rural or urban environments.

At the most elementary level, it was shown that in the two Georgia towns noted above the town which found its water taste unsatisfactory received water from time to time from an alternate source having less pronounced taste, whereas the town regarding the taste as satisfactory drew only on what the other branded an obnoxious source. Experience counts, but does not have a simple linear relation to either perception of the environment or willingness to deal with it. Thus, Kates finds, flood plain dwellers with direct exposure to floods have different perceptions of the hazard and a greater propensity to cope with it. Lucas shows that the canoeist views the same wilderness differently than does the motorboater, and that the responsible government officials have perceptions conforming to neither. Saarinen demonstrates that wheat farmers on the Central Great Plains become more sensitive to drought hazard up to late middle age, and that then their awareness declines sharply. People who are more annoyed by noisy aircraft tend to be those who fear air crashes, who are less convinced of the importance of the air base to the area's welfare, and who are also annoyed by automobile noise. Only a few cross-cultural comparisons have been made. Each such finding throws light on the wisdom of public measures to manage an aspect of environment by sharpening the understanding of how individual citizens and officials view the same physical landscape.

If a major aspect of the individual's perception of the world around him is related to his sense of his own role in that world, then it becomes important to seek out his identification of himself. Oftentimes students of environmental problems like to categorize themselves and others as behaving according to a professional stereotype. The economist optimizes net returns, the engineer gets the right things built, and the conservationist stops the *wrong* things from being built. There are niceties and colorful elaborations that need not be repeated. Just how much the individual's identification by training, professional status, and interaction with his peers leads him to behave in particular ways toward his environment has not been demonstrated. By analogy with other professions, such as medicine,[42] it might be expected that the sense of vocational role would be strong and that it would be reinforced by a high degree of self selection among students who, sharing certain stereotypes, choose a profession that they hope will be congenial.

A fundamental line of inquiry is followed by Strodtbeck and his associates in examining sex identification. Because it has relevance both to the individual's view of the world around him and to his sense of role in interaction with other people, sex identity may be a powerful means of recognizing personality traits that are significant in formation of attitudes toward environment. In the study of attitudes toward water, it was found that young American men when confronted with situations in which water problems were presented as either severe or not severe, and in which the possibility of taking positive action was seen as either promising or not promising, responded very differently according to the sex role with which they consciously and unconsciously identified themselves. Thus, the man who was both consciously and unconsciously strong in male characteristics was more likely to take action if he was told the problem was capable of solution, whereas the one with strong identification of himself as having female characteristics had the greater propensity to act when the problem was not likely of solution. Other findings are given in the report already noted. The point here is that role identification may turn out to be a highly significant factor in attitude formation.

The fourth set of factors may be grouped under the heading of what Henry and Schlein call "affective complexity."[43] This refers to the personality attributes that permit an individual to be aware of complexity in the world around him, and to respond to them without being entirely defensive or threatened. It implies openness to impressions from the outside and ability to confidently incorporate them in guiding his own behavior.

Although no studies have been made of this set of attributes as they relate to natural resource uses, the approach seems worth noting as aiming at situations that often attach to management of the environment. Quality decisions always refer to environmental change, to individual preferences for change, to a complex environment, and to programs with ambiguous aims. Much of the effort to change the urban scene presumes the response of persons who, finding the new city in conflict with the value orientation of their culture and the preferences cultivated by past experience, have the personality attributes to be able to explore modifications of both the city and their own behavior without merely launching war upon the city.

The scholar who predicts what future preferences the public will express for the quality of water or air, and the administrator who wonders how far a later constituency may tolerate a current decision as to standards, may ask how likely are the underlying attitudes, once tagged, to change. Also, judging from the number of students of re-source management who appear to feel that what the people should prefer coincides with what they themselves prefer, there are some who brood over how they can manipulate public attitudes in what they regard as the right direction. Indeed, a considerable part of the public informa-tion expenditures of the federal and state departments dealing with natural resources is based on conviction that a flow of facts about re-sources and their use will influence public action either by changing attitudes or by providing information on which people can act more intelligently. The Chicago study on attitudes toward water finds pro-nounced differences among managerial groups in their belief in the degree to which their actions can modify public attitudes.

Insofar as the attitudes are related to role identification and affective complexity they may be regarded as largely inflexible. The decision situation—the time of the vote, the leaders who force the decision, the way they phrase the question—is much more subject to alteration. Among the numerous aspects of environmental stimulation, probably the one most susceptible to change is the information about environ-mental conditions and ways of managing them. Although certain findings suggest that the information alone, as in the case of a flood hazard map or a government pamphlet about wind erosion, may have little effect upon attitudes toward those phenomena, other studies indicate that if the situation in which choice is exercised is modified or if the individual's sense of efficacy in dealing with the confusion of the world is changed suitably, the information takes on different significance. Given favorable circumstances (and this qualification may be crucial) there is no reason to think that some amount of shift in attitude would not follow the receipt of new information about the environment.[44] Just how far the shift will go, and just how much personality traits, such as role identification, will have to do with it, is far from clear.

The most difficult question remaining is whether a shift in attitude would have any perceptible effect upon the decisions reached about environmental quality. Experimental evidence seems wholly lacking, and most of the observations of a curbstone character are made without a rigorous scheme of analysis. Generalizations must come from definition or from casual reflection on a few past decisions.

One striking fact is that a large number of environmental quality decisions are made by people who feel a strong professional identification. Their view of themselves as conservationists, economists, sanitary engineers, foresters, etc., may be expected to shape their perception of the environment and their competence to handle it. In these roles they not only inherit customary ways of defining significant parts of the environment but they are disposed to distort or ignore phenomena that they regard as beyond their professional responsibility or competence. (If you can't measure a diseconomy, sweep it under the rug.) Their perceptions and preferences become the implicit and usually unchallenged determinants of plans presented for public choice.

A second fact is that these professional judgments often involve assessment of public preferences that go largely unchecked. An engineer's view of public valuation of a polluted stream or a soot-ridden sky rarely is tested by investigation and commonly enters into public decision in situations in which individual citizens can express a disapproval of the plan but not of its assumptions as to their preferences. When the New York Board of Water Supply decided against using Hudson River sources it had no generalized scientific evidence on the way in which citizens of those cultural groups regard water sources, it lacked any findings on New York preferences, and it passed on its judgment in a form which eliminated any public expression of those preferences: Since it was concluded without verification that the people wanted upland sources, they were asked to vote for upland sources as the best solution. Their favorable vote could neither confirm nor deny the conclusion.

In the absence of a more adequate model of decision-making, the testing of the influence of attitudes on both officials and the related citizen groups remains largely conjectural. It may be useful, nevertheless, to outline two hypotheses that grow out of experience with water resource management debates and that do not appear to be inconsistent with observed relationships. These indicate the kind of question calling for systematic examination, and are selected from more than twenty appearing in the report of the Chicago study:

(1) Because of the complexity of systems of water management, the ambiguity of their ownership, and ignorance of the natural processes

explaining their behavior, there is a strong tendency to rely upon exterior authority for judgment as to management of water quality. In simple decision networks, where individual control of environment is large, the unknown is explained by myth: In complex networks the judgment is referred to professional experts.

(2) Perception of the effects of water management upon others is a function of the degree to which the individual regards man as a master of nature and to which he resents manipulation of himself by others.

In each case the disposition to take public action is seen as related to the personality traits of the individuals involved. How much these are confined or magnified by the social setting in which the decision is reached is difficult to say.

Until recent years a high proportion of public decisions on resource management in the United States were taken following great natural disasters or in anticipation of serious human deprivation. Flood control legislation often followed in the muddy wake of major floods, and soil conservation measures sprang up in the lengthened shadow of dust clouds. Timber management was promoted in part by the anticipation of a future timber shortage. Much of the rhetoric hinged on the fear of a reported crisis or of a new one looming in the years ahead. Such appeals are still strong, as with the brooding concern for the human effects of pesticides and fungicides and with the dark prediction of national water shortage. However, the rising level of per capita production and the accelerating pace of technologic change enlarges the conditions of choice in the direction of greater freedom. As shown by a recent report by the Committee on Water of the National Academy of Sciences,[45] the unfolding opportunities for water management are in exploring the whole range of possible alternatives in transactions with the environment, and in weighing their relative social impacts.

This is a turn away from the customary promotion of single solutions in an atmosphere of present or impending crisis. Consideration of alternatives for changing the environment implies less reliance on choices by a technical elite and more confidence in a base of citizens who have the maturity to deal with complex and probabilistic conditions. To the extent such a shift occurs, sensitivity to the direction of public attitudes, as well as to their limitations, may be expected to take on greater importance.

Faced with trying to understand public decisions on a stinking stream and a scarred landscape such as those presented to Boulder's voters, social science can offer a few sturdy methods and a larger set of questions that remain unanswered. By content analysis it is possible to define the issues and the attitudes toward them as articulated in the public argument. By opinion survey of a representative sample of the population, the expressed attitudes of sectors of the electorate can be assessed, and a prediction of voters' behavior can be checked against the vote itself. By analysis of the voting situation a rough judgment can be reached on the extent to which conflicts or compacts among public officials and political groups in the community may so operate as to obscure any voter preference as to the kind of environment the people prefer. There are slight but provocative grounds for expecting that the stated attitudes would vary in some degree with length and type of the respondents' experience with stream and mesa, that perception of severity would vary with social status, and that propensity to act would be related to role identification and affective complexity. These and other data provide an initial base from which to speculate on the situations in which various types of information might promote changes in attitudes if given to the public at the appropriate time.

Because there are no satisfactory models of the decision process or of the interaction of factors affecting attitude formation, the speculation for Boulder or any other community could, at best, only explore pragmatic relations or tentative theory. Basic research is needed on decision processes and attitude formation, particularly in settings where resource management produces nonvendible benefits. The network of decisions should be described in sufficient detail to permit recognition of power relations among individuals and groups. The typology of attitudes toward environment invites much more precise analysis. These attitudes deserve searching examination in experimental conditions where the personality traits of the subjects are known and where the inputs of information and the decision situation are partly controlled. From those investigations may be expected increased understanding of human response which would permit a more incisive wording of questions for opinion surveys and, in turn, more intelligent interpretation of their results. An auxiliary step would be thoughtful appraisal of environmental quality features of opinion surveys of the past 25 years in order to recover data that has been lost from sight.

As these studies proceed they will throw light on how decisions in truth are made, on how the professional's own preferences figure in the proposed solutions, on what he thinks the citizen prefers, on what the citizen, given a genuine choice, does prefer, and on how all of these may shift with the circumstances and experience surrounding the choice. In a time when many types of environmental changes are little suited to precise definition or quantitative expression, when there are few market checks of value judgments, and when professional judgment obscures assumptions as to preferences, the future public management of the environment's human satisfactions has growing need for discovery of the delicate process by which individual preferences find their way into public choices of vista, taste, odor, and sound.

T. F. Saarinen

Attitudes Toward Weather Modification: A Study of Great Plains Farmers*

Some of the earliest commercial attempts at weather modification were those supported by farmers for the purpose of increasing precipitation. As weather modification techniques become more highly developed, it seems likely that there will be increasing interest in further experiments of this nature. Whether future experiments along this line meet with public protest or support may to some degree be conditioned by the views of the farmers since they are more directly affected than most other groups. Therefore, it is of some interest to investigate farmers' attitudes toward weather modification. What do they think of the attempts at weather modification? What kind of ideas do they have about weather modification?

These questions were included in a study of Great Plains farmers undertaken by the author in 1964. A sample of 96 farmers was drawn from six counties in the central Great Plains states. These study areas ranged from the most arid to the most humid margins of the central Great Plains. The counties selected, the numbers of farmers interviewed,

Table 20-1—Study Areas and Size of Sample

County	State	County Seat	No. Interviewed	Degree of Aridity
Adams	Nebraska	Hastings	17	— 9.24
Barber	Kansas	Medicine Lodge	16	—16.20
Frontier	Nebraska	Curtis	15	—19.16
Finney	Kansas	Garden City	17	—24.44
Cimarron	Oklahoma	Boise City	14	—27.25
Kiowa	Colorado	Eads	17	—31.39
			96	

*From *Human Dimensions of Weather Modification*, W. R. Derrick Sewell, ed. (University of Chicago, 1966), 323–328. [Department of Geography Research Paper No. 105.] © W. R. Derrick Sewell.
(Notes to this selection will be found on p. 425.)

and the degree of aridity of the various areas are noted in Table 20–1. The degree of aridity was measured by the Thornthwaite moisture index.[1]

Weather is an important variable in agriculture. Nowhere, however, are small differences in rainfall more crucial than on the driest margins of crop production as along the western edge of the wheat belt of the Great Plains. A question arises as to whether this in any way affects the attitudes toward weather modification. If so, there should be differences between the areas studied. Each of the farmers was asked "What do you think of attempts at weather modification? Are they effective?" Their replies were tabulated according to degree of belief as: belief, maybe, doubt, or don't know, as illustrated in Table 20-2.

Table 20-2—Attitudes of Great Plains Farmers Toward Effectiveness of Weather Modification Attempts

		ADAMS	BARBER	Area County FRONTIER	FINNEY	CIMARRON	KIOWA	Total All areas
Belief	No.	3	1	1	2	5	9	21
	%	18	6	7	12	36	53	22
Maybe	No.	5	1	5	2	1	2	16
	%	29	6	33	12	7	12	17
Doubt	No.	9	14	9	11	7	6	56
	%	53	88	60	64	50	35	58
Don't Know	No.	—	—	—	2	1	—	3
	%	—	—	—	12	7	—	3
Totals	No.	17	16	15	17	14	17	96
	%	100	100	100	100	100	100	100

First of all, one should note that less than a quarter of all Great Plains wheat farmers interviewed thought that attempts at weather modification were effective, while over half doubt it. A second observation is that belief in the effectiveness of weather modification attempts appears to be more common in drier areas. Over two thirds of all those who believed weather modification attempts to be effective were from the two driest areas and 40 per cent from the very driest county. It seems likely that as moisture deficiencies become greater the farmers are forced to search more diligently for solutions. This probably leaves them more open to the possibility of weather modification and accounts for the greater frequency of belief in those areas.

In each of the Great Plains counties included in the sample, there were one or more farmers who definitely believed attempts at weather modification to be effective and others who thought they might be. One might ask whether there are any consistent differences between those who believe such attempts to be effective, those who think maybe, and those who doubt it. Table 20-3 shows how certain characteristics vary with attitudes of Great Plains farmers toward the effectiveness of weather modification attempts. There appears to be a separation between the traditional and modern farmers. The more modern, that is, the younger, better-educated, and the more innovative of the farmers appear more likely to have a favorable attitude toward the present attempts at weather modification, whereas the traditional types, that is the older, less well-educated, and less innovative seem more likely to be doubtful. The three who answered "don't know" are extreme in each of these characteristics, being older, having fewer years of schooling, and slow to adopt new practices.

Table 20-3—Degree of Belief in Weather Modification Attempts and Selected Characteristics of Great Plains Farmers

Variables	BELIEF		MAYBE		DOUBT		DON'T KNOW	
	n	$\bar{x}$	n	$\bar{x}$	n	$\bar{x}$	n	$\bar{x}$
Age (in years)	21	46.0	16	46.4	56	48.0	3	52.7
Education (no. of years completed)	21	11.5	16	11.0	56	10.8	3	7.0
Innovativeness*	21	3.1	16	3.3	56	3.4	3	4.3

* Each farmer was classified according to adopted categories with a number assigned according to the speed with which new practices were adopted as follows: among the first (1), a little faster than most (2), about average (3), a little slower than most (4), among the last (5). The figures in the table represent the average for each of the groups. The final rating in the case of the Great Plains farmers depended on a combination of self-rating by the farmers, ratings of county agents, time of adoption of certain practices and interview impressions.

The Great Plains farmers made many spontaneous comments in relation to the question on weather modification. The frequency with which various types of comments were made is illustrated by Table 20-4. Most

Table 20-4—Great Plains Farmers' Spontaneous Comments About Weather Modification

Type of Comment	No. of Times Mentioned
1. Faith in future effectiveness of W.M.	15
2. Hard to control	6
3. Distrust of fly-by-night operators	6
4. Limitations in terms of conditions	5
5. How can you prove W.M. caused the precipitation?	4
6. Conflicts within areas	2
7. Conflicts between areas	2
8. Only local effects possible	2

common was the expression of a belief that in the future weather modification would be possible and often associated with this the need for more research. Two other themes often expressed in spontaneous comments were the kind of responses which indicated a certain distrust in some of the fly-by-night commercial operators and their efforts in the past; and a series labeled as hard to control. This latter group of comments included those doubting man's ability to control the type of shower, to pinpoint the rain areally, or those suggesting the possibility of triggering some unanticipated disastrous results, such as droughts or floods. Another group of comments centered on limitations in terms of conditions as they emphasized the necessity of the right kinds of clouds in order to have any successful results. Several doubtful types insisted that it would be very difficult to prove whether the precipitation resulted from man's actions and would not have occurred anyway. Somewhat less frequent were the following types of comments; conflicts within areas would be inevitable since not all would want rain at the same time, conflicts between areas might result because inducing rain in one area would in effect involve robbing some other area for which the moisture was destined, and the idea that only local effects would be possible and broader, large-scale weather patterns would not be affected.

CONCLUSIONS

The results of the survey of farmers in the Great Plains indicate that there is considerable variation in attitudes to weather modification, both among farmers in any one area and from one part of the region to another. Those who lived on the more arid portions of the region tended to be more convinced as to the feasibility of modifying the weather than those living in the more humid portions of the region. Those with a greater number of years of formal education, and those who tend to be the earliest to adopt new techniques also tend to be those who are more favorably disposed toward weather modification. The least innovative and those with the fewest years of formal education also tend to be the most skeptical about the possibilities of modifying the weather.

These findings may have some significance in the attempt to determine the extent to which weather modification programs are likely to be supported or opposed. For example, it seems very likely that such programs would obtain more local support in more arid regions. Caution should be exercised in the interpretation of the results, however, since the study was only a preliminary investigation. Studies in greater depth, designed to determine factors underlying attitudes to weather modification and to determine whether there are regional variations in attitudes, are required to test the broader applicability of the conclusions in this study.

H. George Frederickson and Howard Magnas

Comparing Attitudes Toward Water Pollution in Syracuse*

INTRODUCTION

How important is water pollution control to the general public? Is water quality a first-order public priority, high on the list of virtually every segment of the public? Or is pollution control just one of those middle- or low-level priorities that people feel should be emphasized only after more fundamental problems are solved? Is it possible that there are widely varying feelings about the importance of water purity, based on variations in individual socioeconomic and political circumstances?

For a variety of reasons it is critical that social scientists wrestle with these questions. Government operates under conditions of fiscal scarcity and keen competition for financial resources. It is vital that those who make public spending decisions have a sense of the preferences of their constituents, not only on water pollution control but on all public responsibilities. A representative democracy requires a consideration of these preferences.

There is good evidence that public policy-makers do not have very accurate perceptions of the policy preferences of their constituencies.[1] There is also strong evidence indicating that community political elites are not proportionally representative of all groups and interests in the community and that they may be selectively attentive or inattentive to demands in accord with their preconceptions.[2] Under these conditions, empirical evidence revealing "real" public policy preferences would be most useful both to policy-makers and to students of the public policy process.

The abatement of water pollution, or the improvement of water quality, is considered a public good. It is clear, however, that the distribution of benefits to be received by improving water quality is greater for some than for others.[3] The purpose of our research has been to

*Reprinted by permission from *Water Resources Research*, IV (Oct., 1968), 877–889.
(Notes to this selection will be found on p. 425.)

determine what groups or sets of individuals consider water pollution and its control more important and what groups regard it as less important than other governmental responsibilities. In this way, we can determine how attitudes vary toward the personal benefits from this public good. Then we can determine what categories of residents regard themselves as benefited more and what categories regard themselves as benefited less by water pollution control.

First, however, we must define our terms and demonstrate the importance of the subject. Public opinion here is defined as the expression of attitudes on a social issue. Not all public opinion has to do with government. Personal views of the ecumenical movement, for instance, are public opinion if they are expressed, but they have little to do with government.[4]

Why is public opinion important in American government? First, the general bounds of public policy are set by latent public attitudes. For instance, in the United States, the nationalization of industry or government control of the press are precluded by underlying public attitudes. These kinds of limitations are also seen in the operation of nondemocratic systems. The government of the Soviet Union, for instance, embarked on a campaign against religion which later had to be modified because it proved difficult to enforce and destructive to morale. Today the Soviet government has elaborate and expensive procedures for keeping in touch with public opinion to prevent similar debacles.[5] Elected officials in a democratic system acquire some of this knowledge through periodic elections and a free press, which brings us to a second reason for the importance of public opinion. On election day the broad preferences and goals of public policy are expressed by the public. Although election results carry no clear mandate for those elected with respect to some specific policy area, it is not uncommon for elected officials to act as if they had a mandate. In this way elections are considered to be very general expressions of public opinion, at least the opinion of that segment of the population that votes. Third, public opinion can play a supportive or legitimizing role for specific public policy areas. For instance, the Social Security Act of 1935 was bitterly opposed by Republicans, but public opinion has so consistently endorsed the program that Barry Goldwater recommended an extension of the system in his 1964 campaign for the Presidency. In short, the building of favorable public opinion over time can give a program the image of agreement or substantial support and thereby legitimize the acts of the original decision-makers. Finally, public opinion serves a demand function. Woman's suffrage, medical care for the aged, voting rights for Negroes, assistance for the poor, are all examples of the public expression of demands and their ultimate reflection in policy.

To determine how various categories of people view the relative importance of water pollution control as a public good, we surveyed the attitudes of the residents of Onondaga County (Syracuse Standard Metropolitan Statistical Area), New York. The survey results include a description of (1) how the research was conducted; (2) the nature of the water pollution problem in Onondaga County; (3) the attitudes of county residents toward water pollution and other public problems; (4) the relationship between an individual's age, family income, education, and place of residence, and his views on water pollution.

To discover the nature of public opinion regarding water pollution in Onondaga County, a sample was taken of the voting-age population. In Syracuse and its contiguous suburbs a grid technique was used to divide the area into numbered sections. Grid numbers were then selected randomly, as were ten residences within each section. If possible, a voting-age person was interviewed at each selected residence. Certain grid sections (about 10 per cent) in the rural parts of the county, had so few residences (less than 30) that they were eliminated from consideration before the random selections. As a consequence, there may be a slight bias in the sample away from potential respondents in very low-density areas and towards respondents in slightly higher-density areas.

In all, 1036 persons were interviewed, using a highly structured one-page interview schedule. The interviews were conducted by advanced college students (either seniors or graduate students) who were trained to read the questions and alternative answers to the respondents exactly as they were written and to register their responses. Fifty-seven per cent of the respondents were female, which builds into the sample a slight female bias. Forty-six per cent of the sample live in the central city, and the remainder live in the suburbs and rural areas, a close approximation of the urban–rural ratio for Onondaga County, 47 per cent in Syracuse City, as set out in a special 1966 New York State Census of Population.[6] The sample is regarded as representative of the universe at the 95 per cent confidence level, using the standard error of mean test.

The context of these findings is important. The water pollution situation in Onondaga County is unique and deserves consideration, for it may influence the character of public opinion.

Onondaga County is located in north central New York, just to the east of the Finger Lakes region. Of the 792 square miles in the county, 241 square miles are in the Onondaga drainage basin, which is roughly in the center of the county, as Figure 21-1 shows. The bulk of the county population (80 per cent) and most of its industry are concentrated in the drainage basin, which includes the city of Syracuse, its suburbs, and Onondaga Lake. Most of the county's water pollution problems stem from Onondaga Lake and its feeder streams. The lake, roughly rectangular in shape, is $4\frac{1}{2}$ miles long, with an average width of one mile and contains approximately 40 billion gallons of water, with a residence time of from 200 to 250 days. Four streams feed the lake, and there is one outlet.

Onondaga Lake has an average depth of 42 feet with generally low and flat shores.

Unlike the other lakes in the region, Onondaga Lake is naturally saline, although less so than other saline bodies such as the Salton Sea in California; Soap Lake, Hot Lake and Lower Grand Coulee Lenore Lake, all in Washington; Big Soda Lake in Nevada; and the oceans. Because of its salinity, Onondaga Lake was never a source of drinking water but was the center of a thriving salt industry until the early years of the twentieth century. The lake was once a popular resort and vacation spot for fishing (trout, salmon, and the Onondaga whitefish, a unique species now extinct), boating, and picnicking.

FIGURE   21-1

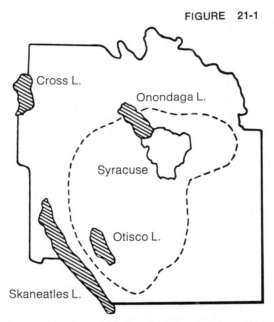

Onondaga County, Onondaga Drainage Basin, and Lake

As early as 1870 raw sewage entered Onondaga Lake from two of its feeder streams. As the area became increasingly urbanized, greater amounts of untreated waste were dumped into the lake, primarily by the area's local governments and by the New York State Fairground. Major sections of the sewer systems in the county are old and inadequate. Street drainage flows into the main system, except in a few places. A new metropolitan treatment plant (intermediate treatment) opened in 1960 substantially reduced the coliform count and increased dissolved oxygen values in the lake. Because the treatment plant operates at full capacity rain, snow, or thaw produces an untreated sewage bypass to the lake. The years of raw or partially treated sewage deposit have produced a thick layer of organic sludge at the bottom of the lake. Today the lake has a strong odor and a serious algae problem.

Since Onondaga County is a major industrial complex, the lake also receives large amounts of industrial waste, including tars, oils, cyanides, metal plating acids, calcium chloride, calcium hydroxide, sodium chloride, calcium sulfate, calcium carbonate, and chlorine. There is considerable evidence that the chemical composition of the lake has increased substantially in the 'past decade.[7]

This high level of both public and industrial-pollutant discharge into the lake has resulted in severe limitations in its use. There is an annual regatta at Onondaga Lake and some pleasure boating and sailing, but there is no longer fishing and swimming. The lake is aesthetically displeasing, and because it is situated in the center of the urban area, its polluted state is easily seen. Several scientific studies have focused on the lake's pollution, and the subject is a regular theme in the two major newspapers in the county. Candidates for major offices in the various governments in the county invariably promise a clean lake if elected. When our survey was conducted in August, 1967, no political campaign was under way, nor was there an unusual antipollution campaign being conducted. There were occasional articles on the problem in the local press during the summer of 1967, but neither more nor less than was the case in the six months before or after the survey.

In view of these conditions, what are the attitudes of county residents toward local water pollution?

ATTITUDES TOWARD WATER POLLUTION

Two means were used to specify the opinions of county residents regarding water pollution. The first means utilized a free selection among respondents, who considered water pollution a "most important," "somewhat less important," or a "least important" problem. They were not required to rank only one problem as "most important" and one as "least important" and then to place the remaining problems in order. This technique was used because it is doubtful that respondents have an ordered set of priorities in their minds. The respondents have, rather, a general feeling or sense of what they regard as more or less important, and this is what we were interested in determining. The question was asked in this way:

There are many problems which we face locally in this city and county. Of those listed below, which do you believe are the most important? Which do you believe are somewhat less important? Which do you believe are least important?

When using this technique, 56 per cent of the respondents considered water pollution a "most important" problem, 32 per cent a "somewhat less important" problem, and 12 per cent a "least important" problem. By the free selection technique, as Question 1 in Table 21-1 indicates, greater importance was attached to education and law enforcement than to water pollution as a problem. However, water pollution received more "important" votes than did employment, adequate water, welfare, maintenance of streets and roads, housing, traffic, and parks and recreation.

These results clearly indicate that many respondents considered most of these problems to be of the first order. Only three functions—maintenance of streets and roads, traffic, and parks and recreation—received more "somewhat less important" and "least important" categorizations than "most important" categorizations; the other seven functions had more "mosts" than "somewhat less" and "leasts." Although the residents of Onondaga County regard all seven of these problems as important, they make relatively clear distinctions between degrees of importance. In these degrees of importance, water pollution had a middle-to-upper-middle level of salience, compared to that attached to other local problems.

The second means of determining the attitudes of county residents toward water pollution was a more strict ordering in which each respondent was asked to rank five local problems. He was also asked to consider his priorities in light of the scarcity of fiscal resources. Question 2 was:

Since the governments in the County have only a limited amount of money to spend each year, some community problems must be taken care of before others. Of the possible problems listed below which would you like to see money spent on first? Second? Third? Fourth? Last? Parks and roads, welfare, water pollution, education, police protection.

Using this method, 12 per cent considered water pollution the "most important" of the five problems, 17 per cent the "second most important," 33 per cent the third, 22 per cent the fourth, and 12 per cent the "least important" (5 per cent did not respond). As Question 2 on Table 21–1 indicates, education and police protection were regarded as more important priorities than water pollution, whereas welfare and parks and roads were considered less salient.

Measured by either means, then, it appears that water pollution is generally recorded by the residents of Onondaga County as a social problem less pressing than education and law enforcement but more pressing than most other local issues. The finding is most revealing because water pollution in the county is obvious and relatively well

Table 21-1—The Relative Importance Associated with Alternative Areas of Public Policy
(In per cent, *N = 1036)

	Question 1 (By free selection)		
	MOST IMPORTANT	SOMEWHAT LESS IMPORTANT	LEAST IMPORTANT
Education	82	12	6
Police protection	70	20	10
Water pollution	56	32	12
Employment	52	32	16
Adequate water	43	32	27
Welfare	42	34	24
Maintenance of streets	40	42	18
Housing	38	35	27
Traffic tie-ups	27	34	39
Parks and recreational facilities	24	42	33

	Question 2 (By ordered selection under conditions of scarcity)				
	MOST IMPORTANT (1)	(2)	(3)	(4)	LEAST IMPORTANT (5)
Education	56	22	11	7	4
Police protection	18	38	23	13	8
Water pollution	13	19	34	22	12
Welfare	10	13	17	23	35
Parks and roads	6	8	13	32	40

* N indicates numbers of respondents in all tables.

understood, but it is still not regarded as the most urgent of public questions. It is unusual that water pollution is considered a middle-level priority, whereas parks and recreational facilities receive the lowest order of preference in both measures. Why should county residents be less concerned with parks and recreational facilities than they are with water pollution when it seems that the polluted waters are, or at least would be, used primarily for recreational purposes? Three reasons might account for this apparent paradox. First, water pollution is probably being interpreted as a potential threat to the well-being of residents rather than an inhibition to recreation primarily. Second, water pollution is present and obvious and may offend the aesthetic senses of residents without their being interested in the lake and its feeding streams for recreational purposes. Water pollution may have received so much attention in the local media that residents are concerned about it without necessarily connecting it with aesthetics or recreational facilities. Finally, it may simply be that large numbers of local residents are against water pollution because it seems a simple, understandable, and noncontroversial thing to be against. To attempt to answer some of these questions and to measure attitudes toward water pollution in a more precise way, some additional questions were asked.

Interest in the lake as a recreational resource was measured by two questions. The first question, as Table 21–2 indicates, concerned using the lake for swimming and boating. The second question was concerned with the fish and other animal life, such as water fowl, supported by the lake. In both instances, our sample responded strongly for action on the part of county governments to improve the lake. Slightly more than 85 per cent of the residents either "agree" or "strongly agree" that county governments should clean the lake for swimming and boating; 88 per cent "agreed" or "strongly agreed" for the supporting of fish and animal life. It appears that the lake is regarded as a recreation source, although this generalization should be made cautiously, because the questions were worded in a way that suggested this use. A much safer generalization from the responses to these questions is that county residents strongly feel that government should make the lake clean and safe for recreation.

No only do residents connect the lake with recreation, and feel that the governments of the county should make it usable for recreational purposes, but they also feel that water pollution affects them directly. In response to the proposition, "Pollution is a problem that doesn't affect me at all," 80 per cent either "disagreed" or strongly "disagreed." Without being precise about how much they are affected by water pollution, the respondents indicate that they do feel affected.

Two propositions were presented on financing the elimination of water pollution in the Onondaga watershed. The first was, "ending pollution of Onondaga Lake would be too expensive to be worthwhile."

As Table 21-2 indicates, 59 per cent of the respondents "disagreed" or "strongly disagreed." However, almost one-third of the respondents, or 31 per cent, were unable to determine whether the costs of ending pollution would be commensurate with the benefits.

Table 21-2—Five-Part Responses to Four Questions Measuring Attitudes toward Water Pollution
(In per cent, N = 1036)

	If Onondaga Lake is unhealthful for swimming and boating, the county should do whatever is necessary to make it safe for recreation.	If Onondaga Lake is not clean enough for fish and animals to live in, the county should clean it up.	Ending pollution of Onondaga Lake would be too expensive to be worthwhile.	Pollution is a problem which doesn't affect me at all.
Strongly agree	44	43	3	3
Agree	43	45	6	10
Don't know	6	5	31	7
Disagree	5	2	41	52
Strongly disagree	1	1	18	28

Each person in the sample was asked to indicate the amount of money he would be willing to pay in extra taxes each year for the next ten years to end water pollution in the county totally. In reply, 22 per cent stated that they were willing to spend three dollars, 16 per cent would give five dollars, 25 per cent would spend ten dollars, 6 per cent would pay 15 dollars, and 14 per cent would pay 20 dollars. From the responses to these questions there appears to be: first, a general feeling that it would not be too costly to end water pollution; second, a willingness to spend for such activities, and third, a wide variation in the amount each resident is prepared to pay to stop pollution.

Altogether, the responses to these questions seem to represent the following *general* attitudes toward water pollution in Onondaga County. It is felt to be a middle-level public problem which people regard as affecting them directly. The public feels that governments in the county should do what is necessary to solve this problem, and they are willing to pay for it, although in varying amounts.

CORRELATES OF ATTITUDES TOWARD WATER POLLUTION

Several additional factors were considered for each respondent in an attempt to account for some of the variation in attitudes toward water pollution and its control. Notations were made as to whether the respondent was male or female, and whether he or she lived in the city of Syracuse or the suburbs. In addition each respondent was asked his age (in some instances estimates were made), the education level of the head of the household, and the approximate annual family income (in categories of $3,000 to $7,000, $7,000 to $10,000, $10,000 to $15,000, and $15,000 and above). These data were an attempt to answer such questions as: How does education influence attitudes toward water pollution? What power does income have over the willingness to spend for pollution control? Does living inside the central city give a different perspective of the problem? Is age a salient determinant of views of pollution?

Do persons living inside the central city have a different view than their suburban counterparts of the priority of water pollution control *vis-à-vis* the other social problems with which governments deal? When using the free selection technique, differences do appear, as Table 21-3 shows. On the basis of simple ranking of importance associated with these problems, city and suburban respondents agreed that education was the most pressing. This was followed by police protection. For the third-order priority, however, city residents selected employment, whereas suburbanites chose water pollution. It is not surprising that city residents placed employment third and housing fourth before water pollution control, which is fifth, because they experience aggravated conditions of deteriorated housing and segregation and are most likely to regard work and its availability as a pressing question. It seems most unusual, however, that city residents relegated the welfare category to seventh in the group of ten, whereas suburban respondents ranked it sixth! Suburbanites, by contrast, placed housing low (eighth), whereas residents of the central city placed it fourth.

City and suburban respondents differed on the relative importance of housing, water pollution, street maintenance, welfare, water adequacy, and park and recreational facilities. City residents attached greater importance to housing, street maintenance, welfare, and park and recreational facilities than did suburbanites. Conversely, suburban respondents regarded water pollution and adequacy as more important. Some probable sources of this difference can be suggested. More suburban residents are secure in their housing and employment than are their urban equivalents. In this state of need satisfaction the importance of pure water for drinking, aesthetic satisfaction, and recreation is increased, whereas more city residents must still be seeking housing and employment goals. Once housing and employment requirements are satisfied, city residents would probably focus on the greater need for water for recreation and beauty.

The influence of age, education, and income on the free selection of water pollution priorities gives us further insights. As Table 21-4 shows, there is no statistically significant difference between those above and below 40 years of age, and between those with a high school education or less and those with some college. Income, however, does influence the salience attached to water pollution as a problem, those with higher

Table 21-3—Contrasting Measures of the Relative Importance City and Suburban Residents Assign to Alternative Areas of Public Policy
(In per cent, N = 1036)

Question 1

PRIORITY ASSIGNED BY URBAN RESIDENTS	PRIORITY ASSIGNED BY SUBURBAN RESIDENTS
Education	Education
Police Protection	Police Protection
Employment	Water Pollution
Housing	Employment
Water Pollution	Adequate Water
Maintenance of Streets	Welfare
Welfare	Maintenance of Streets
Adequate Water	Housing
Parks and Recreational Facilities	Traffic Tie-ups
Traffic Tie-ups	Parks and Recreational Facilities

	MOST IMPORTANT	SOMEWHAT LESS IMPORTANT	LEAST IMPORTANT
Education			
city (N = 478)	80	13	7
suburb (N = 558)	83	13	4
Police Protection			
city	70	16	14
suburb	71	20	9
Employment			
city	57	31	12
suburb	51	32	17
Housing			
city	54†	33	13
suburb	27	41	32
Water Pollution			
city	50†	28	12
suburb	63	23	14
Maintenance of Streets			
city	48†	36	16
suburb	34	44	22
Welfare			
city	45*	34	21
suburb	37	34	28
Adequate Water			
city	34†	29	27
suburb	51	24	24
Parks and Rec. Facil.			
city	28†	48	24
suburb	24	39	33
Traffic Tie-ups			
city	29	33	38
suburb	26	33	41

* Statistically significant at the .01 level of confidence.
† Statistically significant at the .001 level of confidence.

Table 21-4—The Influence of Age, Education, and Income on the Importance Associated with Water Pollution as a Public Problem
(*In per cent, N = 1036*)

		Age		Education		Income	
		UNDER 39 N = 504	OVER 40 N = 532	HIGH SCHOOL AND LESS N = 626	SOME COLLEGE N = 410	UNDER $7000 N = 424	OVER $7000 N = 612
Most important	N = 586	52	58	53	56	53	60*
Somewhat less important	N = 327	34	29	30	31	34	28
Least important	N = 123	12	11	13	12	11	11

* Statistically significant at the .05 level of confidence.

incomes tending to regard it as more important than those with lower incomes. It appears, then, that locational and economic factors are more likely to influence the public on water policy issues than are age and educational factors. It also appears that public policies requesting pollution abatement are likely to receive greater support among those of higher incomes who live in the suburbs.

As described earlier, the general response to the statement: "If Onondaga Lake is unhealthful for swimming and boating, the county should do whatever is necessary to make it safe for recreation" was "heavily in agreement" or in "strong agreement." When broken down by age, urban or suburban residence, education, and income, the responses differ only slightly, as Table 21-5 shows. Younger persons, persons with some college, and members of families with annual incomes of more than $7,000 indicate moderately stronger feelings than older persons, less-educated persons, or those from lower-income families on the necessity for the county to make the lake safe for recreation. These variances are not statistically significant; however, they do suggest that there is such a general level of agreement with this question that moderate variations on the basis of age, education, or income are not particularly meaningful.

As described above, both industry and government contribute to the pollution of water in the Onondaga drainage basin. Because both are so involved, it would be difficult to demonstrate that one is more guilty than the other. Nevertheless, it is interesting to probe the attitudes of the residents of the county on what they regard as the relative amounts of water pollution resulting from sewerage or industrial waste. The statement was proposed: "Industries pollute Onondaga Lake much more than does public sewerage." As might be anticipated, a large percentage of the respondents (42 per cent) stated they did not know. Still, 42 per cent either "agreed" or "strongly agreed" that industry was more at fault than governments, whereas only 15 per cent "disagreed" or

Table 21-5—The Influence of Age, Residence, Education, and Income on Agreement with Three Propositions on Water Pollution
(In per cent, N = 1036)

Proposition	Age		Residence		Education		Income			
	UNDER 40 N = 504	OVER 40 N = 532	CITY N = 473	SUBURB N = 558	0-12 YRS. N = 626	SOME COLLEGE N = 410	UNDER $3700 N = 424	OVER $7000 N = 612	N=	
If Onondaga Lake is unhealthful for swimming and boating, the county should do whatever is necessary to make it safe for recreation.	48	41	46	43	44	48	39	47	N = 457	Strongly agree
	42	44	43	43	40	41	47	41	N = 445	Agree
	5	6	6	6	7	5	7	5	N = 64	Don't know
	4	5	4	5	5	3	5	5	N = 54	Disagree
	0.4	2	0.8	1	2	0.7	0.9	1	N = 16	Strongly disagree
Chemical industries pollute Onondaga Lake much more than does public sewage.	17	20	17*	20	25	16	20	18	N = 197	Strongly agree
	27	23	25	24	25	24	19	26	N = 260	Agree
	41	40	37	44	36	44	42	40	N = 423	Don't know
	11	11	14	9	11	12	15	12	N = 120	Disagree
	3	4	5	2	2	4	3	3	N = 36	Strongly disagree
Pollution on Onondaga Lake is a problem which doesn't affect me at all.	1	4†	2	3	5	2†	5	1†	N = 33	Strongly agree
	6	15	9	11	16	7	15	6	N = 108	Agree
	4	10	7	6	12	4	13	4	N = 72	Don't know
	59	44	52	51	47	49	48	51	N = 534	Disagree
	29	25	28	27	18	36	19	36	N = 289	Strongly disagree

* Statistically significant at the .01 level of confidence.
† Statistically significant at the .001 level of confidence.

"strongly disagreed" with the statement. It appears, then, that industry is seen as the culprit more often than the government. It should be noted here, however, that the wording of the question might have resulted in a "response set" in the direction of agreeing that industries are more at fault.

When the reponses to this question are broken down by age, urban or suburban residence, education, and income, some variation was found, as Table 21-5 indicates. For instance, those living in the city and those with less education were more inclined to take a position on the question than to state that they did not know. Neither age nor residence noticeably influenced attitudes toward the source of pollution (cities and towns or industries), except for the greater reluctance of suburbanites to take a position on the question and their tendency to disagree with the statement that industry is most at fault. Suburbanites with a high school education or less were considerably more inclined both to take a stand on the question and to regard industry as being "more guilty" than were those with some college, but the difference is not significant. On the other hand, those who were from families making more than $7,000 yearly were slightly more inclined to consider industry as a greater source of pollution than were those from families making less, but again there is no significant difference.

As was seen in Table 21-2, 78 per cent of the respondents felt that water pollution in the county was a problem that affected them. Table 21-5 shows that there is some variation in this point of view on the basis of differences in age, education, and income. Persons above forty felt considerably less affected by pollution than did their younger counterparts. (In the free-selection priority preferences, respondents over forty regarded water pollution as more important than those below forty. In Table 21-5, those above forty state that they feel less affected by pollution. This is not necessarily a contradiction). The same is true for those with a high-school education or less and those whose family incomes are lower than $7,000 annually. Although there is a tendency for the respondents to feel affected by water pollution, those who are older, less educated, and less well-off do not feel as strongly or directly affected. These findings suggest the possibility that older persons may be less interested than younger persons in the water of the county for recreational purposes. Therefore older persons may not feel so directly affected by water pollution, although they regard it as an important public priority. Those with less education and income may be more likely to regard water pollution as a less direct concern of theirs, because they are not in a financial position to utilize the waters for recreational purposes or to appreciate its aesthetic qualities.

We noted earlier that respondents generally feel that governments in the county should do what is necessary to solve water pollution problems

Table 21-6—Education, Residence, Age, and Income as an Influence on Willingness to be Taxed Annually for Ten Years to Support Water Pollution Control
(In per cent, N = 984)

Willing to be taxed	Education				Residence		Age			Income				
	7 YRS OR LESS N = 38	7-9 YRS N = 61	10-12 YRS N = 493	SOME COLLEGE N = 392	CITY N = 458	SUBURB N = 526	UNDER 40 N = 482	OVER 40 N = 502	UN-KNOWN N = 46	LESS THAN $2000 N = 88	3-7* N = 262	7-10* N = 301	10-15* N = 209	OVER 15* N = 78
$ 0 N = 202	38†	36	23	11	17	24	12†	26	53	38†	24	14	13	16
3 N = 143	12	25	15	13	14	15	14	15	11	23	19	16	8	3
5 N = 165	12	14	22	15	17	15	19	15	11	8	22	21	14	10
10 N = 249	2	8	23	28	26	25	29	23	13	17	24	28	28	28
15 N = 71	0	4	5	9	8	8	7	8	3	2	3	7	15	13
20 N = 154	6	13	12	24	18	13	19	13	7	12	8	14	22	30

* In thousands.
† Statistically significant at the .001 level of confidence.

and that they were willing to pay for it, although in varying amounts. Table 21-6 indicates what percentage of respondents were willing to be taxed at particular levels to solve the problem. To what extent, then, does age, income, education, and city or suburban residence influence willingness to spend for the elimination of water pollution?

From an examination of Table 21-6, the following generalizations are valid. First, increases in education are associated with a greater willingness to be taxed at higher amounts for attempts to control water pollution. Second, no clear picture emerges from the contrast between the willingness of city and suburban residents to be taxed to pay for the elimination of pollution. In the middle categories (from three to 15 dollars), responses are very similar, but at the extremes (nothing or 20 dollars), city residents were considerably more willing to be taxed to support pollution control than were their suburban brothers. Third, those over forty seem notably less willing to pay for improved water quality than those under forty. Finally, higher levels of income are clearly associated with a greater predisposition to regard favorably increased taxation for water pollution control.

DISCUSSION

What conclusions can be drawn from the findings of this research? A basic conclusion is that water pollution is generally regarded as a serious public problem and that public officials and institutions are seen as responsible for its control and elimination. Probably our most *important* finding is that persons regard water problems differently, on the basis of differing personal characteristics.

With respect to the relative importance attached to water pollution in comparison with other local problems, it is clear that persons of lower socioeconomic status who are likely to live in the center city attach less salience to this problem. The more affluent, the better-educated, and the younger respondents feel more directly affected by water pollution and place it higher in their set of policy preferences. In addition, they are more willing to be taxed for water pollution control purposes than are the less educated, the less affluent, and the older.

Water pollution control emerges, then, as a middle-class issue. Costly public programs to abate pollution, such as the Pure Waters Program (a one billion dollar bond and spending effort) in New York State, can be seen as most directly serving the preferences of those who attach high importance to water pollution as against other public programs, or they can be seen as serving the better-educated, higher-income persons who tend to be suburbanites. From this evidence it is clear that those in lower socioeconomic categories, chiefly in the cities, regard other problems as more pressing. It is not their priority preferences that are determining responses, for it is the middle-class majorities and the relatively well-educated and well-off influentials in the state and county who have a greater impact on public policy.[8]

Still another factor is involved. Not only do respondents in middle and upper socioeconomic categories regard water pollution as a more pressing problem. They probably also regard it as a solvable problem. If enough money and skills were made available, a technological victory over water pollution could be achieved. The solutions to many other kinds of public problems do not seem so readily accessible. If the most effective methods for solving housing or employment problems could be decided upon, funds and problem-solving skills could be directed to the benefit of lower-status individuals, But the solutions of housing and employment problems are more controversial and considerably less certain in their results. This suggests that there is a tendency to direct skills and resources to those public problems which are less controversial and amenable to technical victory. However, the findings of this research provide no evidence for this hypothesis; they merely suggest it.

As circumstances change, public opinion changes. The measurement and understanding of public orientations is a means by which governments can gauge responses to changing conditions. It is certain that water pollution is a characteristic of an urbanized, industrialized, and growing society. As Onondaga County has grown and has become more urban and industrial, the quality of its water has noticeably decreased. This research indicates that the majority of county residents are concerned about pollution and feel that government is responsible for a remedy. They also seem to feel that they can afford that remedy. The New York State Pure Waters Act and the bond issue, coupled with money from the federal government and county sources, will enable the county ultimately to respond to prevailing public opinion.[9]

Part Six

Policy Conflict

It is self-evident that there is conflict in politics. For every policy issue, there are various viewpoints among the various participants, with some finding one issue of greater urgency than all other problems. Disagreement also often arises over the meaning of the information available. Opposing demands are voiced and different priorities are set by those involved. In addition, there are often externalities which have great bearing on any resulting decision. And even when an agreement is reached on all of the input factors, there is seldom a consensus on which alternative policy should be pursued.

The problems of pollution control are illustrative of the general conflicts in natural resource policy. Plato once said:

> You cannot poison the soil, or the sun, or the air, which are . . .
> elements of nutrition in plants, or divert them or steal them.
> But all these things may very likely happen in regard to water,
> which must therefore be protected by law.*

Little did he know that we *could* pollute such other substances—and would. Plato proposed rules and penalties for polluting water, but we did not generally respond to this need for regulation until relatively recently. Thus, we have allowed resources to be inadequately protected and pollution has resulted. Pollution is now a new battle-cry—but it should have been an old one.

Pollution is the result of misuse of our environment. We can defile air, earth, water, forests, and even the atmosphere (with sound). As "pollution" is a heavily value-laden term to describe this misuse of our natural resources, it also tends to be descriptive of a relative judgement. What is considered to be pollution by one may not be by another.

For example, for many purposes water may not be considered polluted if it is tested and found fit to drink. That same water, however, could still be discolored, malodorous, and bad tasting. It could lack these undesirable properties but have too high a nitrogen content, which would promote algal

*Plato, *Dialogues*, II, trans. Benjamin Jowett (New York: Random House, 1937), p. 594.

growth (as at Lake Tahoe where water fit to drink is not fit to dump into the lake). Thus, the nature of pollution problems is value oriented. Everyone agrees that pollution is "bad," but individuals seldom agree on what constitutes unacceptable pollution.

This section presents four different resource areas where there are broad choices of policy. The first article, by M. M. Kelso, deals with the varied conflict-producing factors in American land policy. Robert Rienow examines the problems of ocean resources. Conflict over a wilderness area is described by Robert C. Lucas, and George Hagevik writes on the difficulties of setting standards for air quality.

Some sort of conflict surrounds each of our natural resources. It is not productive to ignore it or even to try to eliminate it; but it is necessary to work with conflict by responding to it. Eventually decisions must be made.

M. M. Kelso

Resolving Land Use Conflicts*

When the first nomadic hunter drove another from the water hole about which he found his quarry, a land use conflict took place. When the early American frontiersman pushed into the wilderness with his gun, powder horn, shot pouch, and hand axe to protect himself from the prior claims of the aborigines, a land use conflict took place. So did one occur, too, when the later settler in the same community intimidated the federal government's land agents who were attempting to expel the earlier settlers from lands they had never legally acquired from the sovereign power that own them. And again one occurred when the western cattleman "shot up" the sheepherder's flock and, in solemn assembly with his peers, voted favorably for "law and order" by approving a resolution to his state's legislature asking that it declare the killing of a sheepherder to be a misdemeanor. Again did land use conflict arise when the increasing demands of California placer miners for water for their sluice boxes led earlier users to declare the doctrines that ripened into the American common law of "first in time, first in right" embodied in water law.

And so we could go on—Germany's "Lebensraum" of World War II, the Japanese in Manchuria in the 1930's, the distaste felt in any urban neighborhood for a saloon close to a school or for the abattoir on the next street, the concern felt by the citizenry for the unnecessary loss of the top six inches of soil on which life depends or over the ejection by some of effluvium, flotsam, and jetsam into the water we use and play in, or into the air we breathe. So could we point to the exploding city, the "encroachment" of surburban dwellers onto the rural countryside and the resultant conflicts over schools and sewage disposal and taxes, and over trespass on the farmer's fields and harassment of his livestock and himself.

This seemingly unnecessarily long repetition of homely and familiar conflicts serves a purpose. Land use conflicts run like a thread—or like a number of threads—through the fabric of all cultural history and are

*Reprinted from *Land Use Policy and Problems*, Howard W. Ottoson, ed. (University of Nebraska Press, 1963), 282–303. © 1963 by the University of Nebraska Press.

(Notes to this selection will be found on pp. 425–426.)

weaving forward in the fabric of contemporary life no less, perhaps more vigorously and pervasively than ever before. To discuss land use conflicts and their resolution, then, is, in a sense, to discuss a prevalent divisive force in social living and a main element in the conflict pattern that constitutes social organization and process.

WHY DO LAND USE CONFLICTS ARISE?

Land resources are limited, wants are limitless. In this basic premise of economic and political theory lies the basic cause of land use conflicts.

Wants not only are limitless but are diverse. Different persons have different wants and different value-structures for the ranking of those wants.

Persons are the bearers and expressers of wants. Different persons are transient in different degrees; the want-structures each has likewise differ in their fluidity. Hence, the structure of wants in a community changes as time passes and as people move about.

Land, in contrast, is far more rigid in its fundamental attributes of spaciousness, location, and elemental content. Spaciousness and location, as fundamental physical attributes of land, are absolutely inflexible; land's elemental content is relatively inflexible, though some of its elements may be depreciable under appropriate circumstances.[1]

It is a reasonable generalization, then, that land use conflicts arise because people and their want-structures are transient and transitory whereas land is fixed in space and content.

Land use conflicts arise as different people having different and changing want-structures contend for the control and use of inflexible units of land resource. The "persons" among whom such conflicts occur may be individuals, groups, or institutions. But whatever they are, their want-structures differ among them in space and time.

Superficially, this conflict appears no different than the identical conflict that appears between people over any scarce property object. What gives peculiar dimensions to land use conflicts are (1) Land is completely passive in the conflict. A land unit is what it is; its fundamental supply of location, space, and elemental content cannot be increased through entrepreneurial choice and the dynamic process of creation, use, depreciation, and replacement.[2] (2) The land unit cannot move to or away from situations of scarcity or surplus. (3) The only way by which one use of land can expand is by displacing another use, not by "creating" an enlarged "supply." (4) Because land and its attendant uses are peculiarly tied to locations, it frequently happens that the use made of one land unit affects the uses made of other land units, and no one of the units can move into a more favorable or away from a less favorable situation. The user of the land can move but only by disinvesting one use on one tract and reinvesting it on another tract elsewhere. "Sunk" investments in land take on the immovable characteristic of land but not of fixity of content—sunk investments are depreciable in a sense and to a degree that land is not. (5) Man may, to a degree, affect the elemental content of land, particularly in a way which may cause diminution of the elements it contains. Some of this diminution may be reversed only with great difficulty. In consequence, intertemporal conflict between different land users at different times is ever-present. (6) Land is, in a peculiar sense, the "reality" on which societies stand and live. The use of all land units will always be endowed with values to the society as an aggregate of members that transcend and may conflict with those of the transient human occupants of each unit. The user of land today will always be in conflict with the shadowy user of the future and with his present self-appointed spokesman.[3]

Conflicts over land use arise for all these reasons between and in all combinations of single individuals, private groups, institutions, uses, and time periods. To say that land use conflicts involve all single individuals, private groups and institutions, and all land uses in all time periods is but to reemphasize that land use conflicts are diffused throughout the fabric of all cultural history and are a main element in the conflict pattern of social organization and process.

SOURCES OF LAND USE CONFLICTS

Among what persons and in what situations do land use conflicts arise, and over what issues? It will be most useful to consider such sources of land use conflicts in the context of the pairings of persons and their institutions between which the conflicts occur. These "pairings" for the study of conflict are (1) between and among private users; (2) between private and public users; (3) between and among different public users; (4) between current and future users; and (5) among uses.

Conflict Between and Among Private Users

Control over a land unit is sought by a private person or group in order to practice a use or combination of uses on it. Conflict between private individuals or groups, then, really turns out to be a conflict between *uses* or between *ways* in which a given use can be practiced on the unit. Uses, or ways of use, are outcomes of management and decision-making; therefore, conflicts between individuals further turn out to be conflicts over management decision-making relative to uses or ways of carrying out a use on a land unit. One individual says a certain unit of land should be used for cotton farming; another says it should be used for urban subdivision. This is conflict over use between private individuals. Or, one individual says that the best he can get out of a tract of land is $75 an acre farming it to cotton whereas another individual says that he can get $150 an acre out of that same tract of land farming it to cotton, and "takes" it away from the first, or tries to do so, through the conflict process of "bargaining." This is a conflict over management decisions relative to the use of a given unit of land.

The individuals among whom these conflicts take place will be flesh-and-blood persons acting in their own interests or as representatives of institutions such as corporations, cooperatives, clubs, etc.

One source of conflict over land uses then, is a conflict between private parties over how "best" to use a given land site. Such conflict may involve "on site" conflicts, "off site" or "between site" conflicts, and even conflicts between years of use. *On*-site conflicts are those such as the cotton farming versus urban development illustration used above. *Off*-site conflicts are those in which the use of one site has repercussions on another site, such as exploitive use of a watershed creating flood and silt damage to other sites downstream. Interyear conflicts are those between users of a land site today and those who will or expect to be users of the site tomorrow. This conflict is more fully discussed here later.

Conflicts Between Private and Public Users

A line is hard to define between private groups and institutions and that sovereign group we call "the public." For our purpose, the crucial line of distinction turns on the source of power over land. The public, relative to land use, is that group to which power over land attaches solely because the land unit lies within the area of political sovereignty of that group; private groups and institutions are those to which power over a land unit attaches by virtue of a relinquishment of power to the private group or institution by the public sovereign.

The structure of wants of the public group embraces many high utility wants, the satisfaction of which is not attainable by private individuals or groups; hence, they do not enter into the determination of "market value." Market values will not, therefore, reflect all values included by the public within its calculus. Conflict arises because private individuals and groups approach the use of a particular land unit with a different structure of wants and ordering of values than do public groups possibly composed of the same individuals. These differing structures of wants and ordering of values relative to land use arise from differences in: (1) the wider array of utilities included in the public's (in contrast to the private person's) want-structure at a single point in time, and (2) in the time structure of utilities of private individuals and groups in contrast to that of public groups.

Breadth of Utility Inclusion and Land Use Conflict—The public stands for the widest possible grouping of parties of interest in the use of a particular land unit. The structure of wants and ordering of values of this most inclusive of all possible social entities will necessarily and always be different from the structure of wants and ordering of values of private groups and private individuals. Because the structure of wants and ordering of values as between the private and public users of a land site inevitably will be different, judgment by each as to what constitutes "best" use of that site will necessarily also differ and be in conflict.

Any decision-making unit experiences economies and diseconomies that are external to its sphere of control. External economies and diseconomies have the peculiar economic significance that their impingement on the user of a given land site causes his management decisions about the use of that site to be different than they would be were he to bear or enjoy a proportionate share of the offsetting costs or benefits that apply; in other words, his management decisions are different than they would be if the benefits and costs were *internal* economies and diseconomies. As between the public and private interests in the use of a particular tract, economies and diseconomies that are external to the private user are virtually certain to be internal to the public user. Being external the one and internal to the other causes such economies and diseconomies to have differing significance in decision-making as to what is "best" use for that site. Even in those not uncommon cases wherein a public group also experiences external economies and diseconomies in the use of a given site due to the fact that some of the consequences of its use lie outside the political boundaries of the public concerned, even in such cases the structure of economies and diseconomies as seen by the public group will be different from those experienced by the private users of interest. Being different, they will be in conflict.

Time Structure of Utilities and Land Use Conflict—In addition to land use conflicts growing out of differences in the breadth of utility inclusion by the public in contrast to private persons over land use are those land use conflicts growing out of differences in the time structure of utilities as between the private and public users. The public interest usually expresses more concern about "generations yet unborn" than do private individuals and groups. Why this difference should exist is not our purpose to go into here. It may be simply that the elected representatives of private individuals, once in the legislature, are no longer closely associated with private interest in land use and hence can be more "social" minded and "impersonal" about it; or it may be that the institutional pressures for perpetuation of the political institutions and culture of the group cause public policy-makers to be more concerned about the welfare of the future than is true of individual decision-makers acting as individuals. But whatever the reason, difference in concern between private and public decision-makers over the welfare of those vague and shadowy individuals who will compose the future results in a further difference in the structure of wants and ordering of values as between public and private groups and a consequent difference in judgments as to what constitutes best land use for a particular site.

Conflict Between Different Publics

In the United States, a hierarchy of public exists with sharpest cleavage between state and federal sectors. Also in the United States, different bureaus within a single governmental sector have responsibility or concern over land use. Consequently, conflict over land use in the United States may arise between these different public units as well as between different individual users and between public sectors and the private sectors generally. Each of the "political publics" that constitute the United States from municipality to federal, and each of the governmental bureaus of all these "publics" that has some responsibility or concern over land use will have a different hierarchy of wants and ordering of values and hence will express conflicting judgments as to which uses of particular land sites will maximize attainment of its goal. In this respect, conflict between public sectors concerning land use arises from the same basic cause and expresses itself in an essentially similar manner to conflicts among private individuals and groups. The differing "publics" have different value structures because they represent different combinations of individuals and serve different legislatively established ends. Not only will their value-structure differ, but the qualities and magnitudes of the external economies and diseconomies peculiar to each also will differ. Consequently, it is no more strange for the federal government and a state government to be in conflict over the "best use" of the waters of the Missouri River or over the ownership of the public grazing lands, or for the Forest Service of the Department of Agriculture to be in conflict with the Bureau of Land Management of the Department of Interior over best use of their intermingled holdings than it is for private individuals to come into conflict over similar questions.

Conflict Between Current and Future Wants

Whether a conflict over land use is interprivate, private versus public, or interpublic, differing values attaching to time will influence the structure of wants and the ordering of values of each contender in the conflict and hence will color the judgment of each party as to "best use" of the land site in question. Present satisfactions from the use of a land site, in contrast to alternative identical future satisfactions, will have different values due to differences in time preference and in the marginal productivity of capital to the different individuals and groups. Time preference reflects the psychology of decision-makers relative to waiting for satisfactions in place of enjoying them now and is a composite of the psychology of self-denial and an appraisal of the risks and uncertainties entailed. The marginal productivity of capital is a measure of the net addition to want-satisfying production generated by additional units of capital investment. The propensity for saving versus spending, together with the marginal value product of additional capital investment, determines the marginal discount for time in the value-structure of each individual group or public. The marginal rate of time discount sets the limit of profitable deferral of consumption and of investment and hence determines the time cost of investment for that decision-maker. When this time cost is low, land uses that exhibit long continuing output streams, albeit at lower current levels of output, will be favored, over uses whose output stream is larger at present but of shorter duration. When this time cost is high, the reverse will be the preferred choice. As a result, differing valuations by different people, different private groups, and different publics concerning time preference, together with different managerial decisions concerning the marginal value product of capital in different uses will affect decisions by these different parties as to what is "best" use for any land site at any given time. Conflicts arise because of differences in the way individuals and groups, both private and public, appraise and evalue the future.

Conflicts Among Uses

It turns out that whether the land use conflict is between private parties, between the private and public sectors of the economy, between public groups, or between current and future wants, it is really a conflict between land uses. Land uses are a product of decision-making; decision-making is an outcome of value structures and the niggardliness of nature as it is expressed in diminishing returns. It is because the structure of wants and value orderings differ as between individuals, private groups, and public bodies, and because for each the structure of wants and values varies as between the present and the future that conflict over land use occurs. Land *use* conflict is broader even than conflict among different individuals, for conflict between *uses* can impinge on even a single individual. An individual may be "in conflict" with himself. Decisions must be made by him as to "best" use of the site on which his interest is centered; if a decision problem for him exists, alternative uses exist; if alternative uses exist, they are in conflict "for" the site. When such different alternative uses represent different "individuals," the conflict is interindividual as well as interuse; when they impinge on but a single individual, they are intraindividual but interuse.

It turns out that land use conflicts arise because of differences in the structure of wants and orderings of values among different individuals and groups and differences in the judgments of individuals over the productivity of given sites in different uses in different time periods.

DISSOCIATION OF THE INCIDENCE OF BENEFITS
AND COSTS

The incidence of external economies and diseconomies has been given prominence in the foregoing discussion as a source of land use conflicts. External economies and diseconomies are synonymous with dissociation of the incidence of benefits and costs. External economies and diseconomies are simply benefits and costs that impinge upon the decision-maker but over which his powers of decision contains no power. He bears costs dissociated from attendant benefits or he enjoys benefits dissociated from attendant costs. If all parties of interest in the use of any land site shared in costs incident to use of the site and proportional to their expected benefits, and if all shared in benefits proportional to their incurred costs, then the market process of "bargaining," and the purchase and sale of privileges and burdens associated with land uses could be relied upon to resolve all land use conflicts.

But it is just because this Elysian perfection seldom, if ever, obtains and because individuals, private groups, and publics are trying continuously to gain benefits and repel costs incident to land use that something more than pure market process must be relied upon for the resolution of land use conflicts. Conflicts growing out of the dissociation of benefits and costs are always interpersonal conflicts, but they have their intertemporal and interspatial dimensions as well.

It frequently occurs that use of one space unit endows another space unit with costs (but no benefits) or with benefits (and no offsetting costs). The recipient of such windfall *benefits* usually resists attempts to assess charges against him for the benefits, whereas the recipients of windfall *costs* usually push upon their source for remedy. Sometimes, when the recipient of the windfall *costs* is the intangible, faceless, formless "general public," push on the source of the costs for remedy is slow and halting. Under other circumstances, when the recipient of the windfall costs is one, or one of a few, private persons and such costs stem from public action to general public benefit, the burdened private persons are ineffectual in their push for remedy because of disparity in political and economic strength.

Such conflicts growing, as they do, out of dissociation of benefits and costs cannot be resolved within the framework of the market economy so long as there exists no way in the institutional structure to assess costs proportional to benefits or to claim benefits proportional to costs.

Dissociation of benefits and costs has its intertemporal dimension also. When a land site is committed to a present use at the expense of an alternative future use, or vice versa, it frequently occurs that the future benefits or burdens will accrue to individuals not yet on the scene, hence truly voiceless at the moment when the crucial decisions must be taken.

Conflict then arises between those who admittedly favor the present (or short-run) uses against those individuals existent at the same point in time who have a more highly valued future benefit or who have an emotional attachment to those shadowy future persons whose spokesmen these present individuals elect themslves to be. Upon occasion, the conflict may run the other way. It sometimes happens that those who hold a long-run beneficial interest are in the position to control, over against those who see a more valuable (to themselves or to society) short-run value from larger current outputs at the expense of future outputs. In either event, the conflict grows out of differing dissociation of benefits and costs as between present and future users.

Both of these types of conflict, whether interspatial or intertemporal, are apt to reduce the level of want satisfaction of which a land site is capable. If benefits and costs are dissociated, the production of benefits unconnected with costs will be pushed to marginal products of zero value, whereas unavoidable costs incurred without offsetting benefits cannot be curtailed to equilibrate with resultant marginal value product. Hence, "too many" inputs will be committed to the production of "un-costed" benefits or to the imposition of "unbenefited costs." Dissociation conflicts result in distorted land use and development.

ARE LAND USE CONFLICTS GROWING IN NUMBER AND INTENSITY?

Though there is no ready way to measure their intensity, it would seem quite obvious that land use conflicts are growing in number. It would seem quite logical, too, that they are growing in intensity. Primarily this rise in number and intensity of land use conflicts would seem to result from increasing population, an increasingly complex society, and rising levels of want satisfaction in the society.

An Increasing Population and Land Use Conflicts

An increasing population means simply that an increasing weight of people puts more pressure on the resource base, more pressure on space, more crowding, more jostling, more stepping on toes. Interpersonal, private versus public, present versus future conflicts relative to land use will increase. Public versus private conflicts will grow as the public groups become more aware of their collective needs and more vigorous in curbing individual land uses than run counter to the public's welfare; the greater pressure of population on resources will increase the concern that many have for the future resource base, space for future men to live in, and will lead to more vigorous action to curb present uses in favor of the future.

An Increasingly Complex Society and Land Use Conflict

Our contemporary society is marked by a growing population, a more intricately structured economy, and a more richly developed governmental system. The social machine is more complex, more efficient, and more productive but more sensitive and more temperamental. All this brings increasing possibility of conflict between individuals, groups, and publics in all areas of life. Conflicts over land use are no exception.

Rising Standards of Living and Land Use Conflicts

One outstanding characteristic of our contemporary society is its ability to satisfy rising levels of want satisfaction because of rising technological ability for resource exploitation. Because we can satisfy our wants increasingly far down the utility scale, increasingly far-removed from the basic animal want of pure survival, an increasing number of individuals in our society reach, in their utility systems, articulate levels of concern for the yet inarticulate future generations. Simultaneously and in a contrary direction, other individuals are able to reach farther down their personal utility scale for present want satisfaction in preference to future satisfaction because technology has lifted (for them) the specter of future resource shortage. Conflict over land use decisions increases between the group that asserts we can afford now more than ever to protect the future against land shortage and the other group that says we can afford now more than ever "to live high on the hog" because technology will take care of the future.

LAND USE CONFLICTS AND RESOURCE DEVELOPMENT

Superficially viewed, conflict over land use may appear to be a deterrent to efficient land use and resource development. But a more thoughtful analysis reveals that maximum efficiency of use and maximum development can occur *only* in the context of conflict over land use. An absence of conflict implies a static society; a static society is a nondeveloping society.

Development is dynamic; it implies the existence of a dynamic society. Dynamics *are* change; change *is* alteration in land uses within and over time. Hence, necessarily and implicitly, dynamics are conflicts between proponents of divergent and alternative land uses. Development can only occur within a context of change and change only occurs within a context of conflict.

It is not conflict that is the deterrent to efficient resource use and development. The deterrent is failure to resolve the conflicts that necessarily must arise so that the changes that imply development can proceed in an effective and orderly manner. An enhanced efficiency of resource use and development does not rest on the elimination of conflict but upon its timely and orderly resolution. The few remaining pages of this paper will be devoted to an examination of where attention must center for the attainment of timely and orderly resolution of land use conflicts.[4]

RESOLVING LAND USE CONFLICTS

Resolving land use conflicts involves much more than prescribing goals such as maximum land use efficiency, or maximum area income or aggregate benefit; nor is it a problem of technology or of cost miminization; nor is it a matter of engineering, nor of production economics. Resolving land use conflicts consists in the attainment of workable relations between people—people as individuals, as private groups, and as publics—through the volitional and institutional devices that have been called *bargaining* and *rationing* transactions.

Collective Action and the Control of Individual Action

Resolving interpersonal conflicts outside the pale of organized society is a matter of pure physical powers, of the law of tooth and claw. Exactly similar conflicts are resolved within the *framework* of organized society because there is also a recognized and realized mutuality of dependent interests—interdependence as well as conflict. Within organized society, collective power prescribes working rules under which interpersonal conflicts, in the interest of attaining mutuality, may be or must be resolved. The establishment and enforcement of such working rules by the collective superior against the citizen inferiors are *rationing* transactions. Conflicts resolved between citizens as equals within prescriptions laid down by these "superior" working rules are *bargaining* transactions. In either case, conflicts are resolved through collective action in control, liberation, and expansion of individual action.[5]

Wherein lies the collective power that is the source of collective action in an organized democratic society? It lies in group or public sovereignty which is "collective action in control of violence"[6] or in the democratic monopoly of physical power. Public sovereignty is epitomized by physical power as distinguished from private sovereignty which rests in economic and moral power. It is public sovereignty that makes things lawfully useful for it bestows ownership without which use is illegal and with which specific uses are prohibited or required or classed as permissive. Public sovereignty, which is collective action, is inseparable from property and vice versa. The public sovereign in an organized democracy is composed, collectively, of the politicians, the legislators, the executive, and the judiciary. It is the policy-making power of the sovereign, i.e., of the electorate or the legislature, that lays down the rights, duties, liberties, and exposures of its constituent "citizens" relative to their interpersonal relations over land sites and the uses thereof. A republican democracy, such as that of the United States, is a complex, interrelated structure of such prescriptions laid down by the whole body politic, by the elected representatives of the whole, by the executive enforcing the legislative rules as he interprets them, and by the judiciary interpreting the meanings of words and the limits to the sovereign power. Such land policy prescriptions by the democratic sovereign define the limits to, and the content of, property which turn out to be working-rules that define the interpersonal rights, duties, liberties, and exposures of citizens relative to some common land site and its use. Those working-rules govern individual actions toward one another as they are jointly involved in the same land site. The processes by which these working-rules are specified and enforced are rationing transactions; their consequence is the rationing of freedoms and restraints among persons toward one another and toward land.

Rationing Transactions and Land Use Conflicts

Rationing transactions "apportion access to the benefits and burdens"[7] of land use among persons, and they specify the limits within which land use decision-making will be left to bargaining between legal equals. Rationing transactions apportion the rights, duties, liberties, and exposures of affected persons toward one another to the extent that each has or may have common interest in a unit of land and its use. Rationing transactions define the limits to and the content of rights over land use held by each person who falls into some defined relation to that land; it defines simultaneously the correlative duties of all other persons to respect those rights; further, it defines the limits to and the content of the liberty, which is the freedom, of the right-holder to act as he pleases relative to the use of that land subject to his correlative exposure to the liberties, that is the freedoms, of all other persons to act as they please toward the use of that same land.

Thus, rationing transactions serve as resolvers of land use conflicts. Such conflicts are resolved in a democracy by that "bargaining" process called "rationing" which lays down the working-rules which specify who can or who may do what with what land. Some of these rules will define limits of use and of benefit available to specified persons relative to any land whatever; others of the rules will define such limits of use and benefit available to any person whatever relative to some specified class of land. Zoning, for example, directs that no person whatever can apply a specified use to a specified site; on the other hand, restrictions on transfer of title to land, for example, may direct that no person of the class "owner," relative to any land whatever, can specify in his bequest of that land to his heir that it must henceforth and forever be transferred only to the eldest son. Another example: restrictions on transfer of title may specify that no person of the class "oriental", may hold fee simple title to any land whatever. The working-rules laid down as a result of rationing transactions turn out to be outright statements of what any person or specified classes of persons "must" and "cannot," "may" and "need not," do with land in general or with some defined class of land.

The working-rules laid down by rationing transactions are best represented in the United States by the following familiar property and property regulating institutions: urban, metropolitan, and rural zoning; real estate taxation; tespass and right-of-way regulation; rights to access and use of surface and ground waters; laws and regulations pertaining to the disposal of the public lands, and to mining, grazing, and logging thereon; crop acreage allotments; land use regulations for erosion control; weed control laws; legal provisions for the organization and operation of land and water districts of many sorts; provisions of law requiring the "unitizing" and otherwise regulating extraction of oil from the ground, and many more.

What is it that all of these rationing rules have in common? Each is an expression of sovereign power, rationing among specified persons or persons in general rights to use of and control over specified classes of land or over land in general together with specification of the correlative duties imposed upon all other persons not to interfere; further, each specifies the limits to the liberty of the right-holder to bargain with and propagandize others over the use and control of that land together with his correlative exposure to the bargaining and propaganda powers of others.

When land use conflicts arise, they may be resolved by alteration of the existing rationing rules; for example, when scattered settlement in the cut-over areas of Wisconsin led to conflicts between such settlers and the residents of the more thickly settled portions of the counties, "rural zoning" as a new "working-rule" was developed. Resolving land use conflicts under rationing rules results, in other cases, *not* in alteration of the existing rules, but in the application and enforcement of the existing rules to a particular conflict situation. When the rationing rule specifies that no farmer shall produce more than a specified acreage of cotton, it simultaneously specifies the limits to his duty to obey the orders of the federal enforcing officer, and the limits to his rights to appeal the order to higher authority and to the courts. The rationing rule, by specifying the content and the limits of the farmer's and the officer's rights and duties, may resolve the conflict, but, if not, it will be resolved by the judiciary determining the facts of the case and the meanings of the words that compose the rule. The process is the same, only its content changes, when the conflict is over the establishment of a disagreeable business within a community, or over the size of lots on which a builder may build homes, or over the time and volume of diversion of water from a common supply. In all such cases, the working-rules have been laid down by rationing transactions embedded in the political and legislative process. They are then applied in practice by agents of the sovereign who, in the eyes of the court, are equal but not superior to the citizens, or, if the conflict is between two citizens, each as an equal before the court.[8]

Rationing transactions resolve land use conflicts, then, by specifying the rights, duties, liberties, and exposures of parties in conflict concerning access to and control over the use of land. Resolving the conflict may be the result of new rules laid down by the rule-making (i.e., the legislative) arm of the sovereign, or through the interpretation and enforcement of existing rules through the executive and judicial arms of the sovereign.

Bargaining Transactions and Land Use Conflicts

The working-rules that result from rationing transactions specify what must and what need not, but may be done, by and between persons relative to land. By their very nature, i.e., setting up the "must" and "need not" limits of one party and the correlative "must not" and "may" limits of all other parties, these rules specify the uses and benefits of land that are left open to free and equal bargaining between persons. This is the area of permissiveness—where persons may do or may refrain from doing whatever they can get away with through negotiation with and persuasion on their rivals. This is the area of the bargaining transaction. Within this area, the limits to and content of which are defined by the rationing transaction, each party is subject to the negotiational power of each other party, and land use conflicts are resolvable through bargaining; that is, by buying and selling among legal equals, rather than by order from legal superiors, the benefits and burdens that go with land control and use. This is the area of negotiation between equals under law, of freedom of choice from among alternatives by contenders in conflict. Within the limits of the bargaining transaction, the conflicting parties are free to discuss, dicker, cajole, persuade, propagandize others relative to any land site and its use in which they have mutual interest. It is the area within which one has the liberty to use any tactic designated by the working rules as persuasive (but not coercive) and in which, at the same time, one is exposed to actions growing out of an equal degree of liberty on the part of others. Herein, one is restrained from using—that is, has the duty not to use—any tactic defined as coercive, subject to the right of the sovereign's agent to restrain him with force, if necessary.

This area of conflict resolution has been deeply tilled by economists, for this is the area of "utility maximization" through market exchange of land use privileges and through maximization of efficiency through management. There is no need for me to repeat here the elaborate structure of economic principles that has been erected to explain, rationalize, and prescribe the behavior of people in resolving conflicts within the limits of their liberty to bargain and to manage.

Working-rules pertaining to land use may prescribe that title to, control over, or use of specified tracts or classes of land for specified use may be taken by the sovereign for public use with compensation to the private claimant. But working-rules may, on the other hand, prescribe that in the case of certain public conflicts with private owners over land use and control, the public cannot, through the superior–inferior relation of rationing, take the land use privilege from the private individual. The rules may specify, in such cases, that the public can act only through its agent behaving as an equal to the citizen–owner and can acquire access to control over or use of the land in question only through the mechanism of the bargaining transaction. In other words, the working-rules relative to land and its use may specify that the public and the citizen are equals and must resolve their conflicts toward specified uses of specified lands through the process of negotiation, persuasion, and voluntary sale. Thus, bargaining transactions not only resolve land use and control conflicts between private citizens, but also between private citizens and the publics within spheres specified by the working rules of the society as worked out through rationing transactions.

ARE LAND USE CONFLICTS RESOLVED—AND HOW?

If, in the context of these questions, one means by "resolved" that inner and outer tensions have been relaxed, one must admit that conflicts are not resolved in this sense. Conflicts are not "resolved" in the sense that the sources of irritation—like a stone in the shoe—have been removed, but only in the sense that a workable degree of social order and interpersonal mutuality have been maintained by (1) collective rationing of rights of access to land use privileges among private individuals and groups and the collective itself, together with (2) the rationing of liberties to bargain among legal equals in the resolution of those of their interpersonal conflicts not covered by their assigned rights. In this manner, practical order and working mutuality have been maintained in the course of the history of land policy in the United States. Conflicts have not always been resolved easily or quickly, or even rightly, but social order has been generally maintained. Neither have land use conflicts always been resolved equitably—that is, with an abstract, ideal degree of mutuality. The big step forward taken by the United States during the last 150 years in the age-long struggle of man towards the ideals of mutuality and equity has been the working out of a system wherein the sovereign superior who prescribes the working-rules for land use and decision-making has become, himself, a collective of the citizenry. The outcome of importance that transcends all else, has been that the working-rules laid down in the United States governing relations among people regarding land use and control are a consequence of rationing transactions wherein the policy-making representatives of the citizenry "bargain" among themslves to apportion the benefits and burdens, the privileges and penalties, the liberties and exposures attendant upon land use. The advent and slow perfection of the rationing transaction in western democracy over the past several hundred years has resulted, finally, in the elimination of the previously dominant master–servant relation from the area of policy-making and has made policy-making, in land use and control as in all else, the prerogative of the citizen-collective prescribing working-rules arrived at through rationing transactions. In this way, the citizen–collective governs itself by maintaining workable order and practicable mutuality *among* its citizen-members and *between* its citizen-members and itself. By perfecting the rationing transaction, the resolution of land use conflicts in the United States has been made democratic and capitalistic rather than monarchic, feudal, and dictatorial. It is the rationing trans-action, as it evolves and develops, that will in the future resolve the problems of the public interest in private land, of the private interest in public land, and of interpersonal conflicts with respect to land use in space and time. As we pursue our research and planning for political and economic growth in the area of land use and control, our attention must center, increasingly, on the content and process of the rationing trans-action in our politicoeconomic system for it is here that more orderly and more equitable resolutions of many current and prospective land use conflicts will be found.

Robert Rienow

Manifesto for the Sea[*]

Jeremiah, as he wailed "There is sorrow on the sea; it cannot be quiet," was seemingly but drawing a literary backdrop for his lamentations. Even he could not have anticipated that one day the mighty oceans would be literally the subject of despair.

The myth of great and unfathomable seas—a limitless frontier of exploitation—lies at the base of the legal and political regime that marks man's historic relationship to those seas. We still intone with Byron:

> Roll on, thou deep and dark blue ocean, roll!
> Ten thousand fleets sweep over thee in vain;
> Man marks the earth with ruin—his control
> Stops with the shore.
>
> ——*Childe Harold*

And because we are mesmerized by the endless beating of the eternal waves into agreeing with the poet that the seas are invincible, we admit, long after it is thoroughly outmoded, the doctrine of *res nullius*. Even as we maul and poison the oceans, destroying the delicate chains of life so intricately assembled, we stubbornly cling to the doctrine that the sea is big enough to absorb the assorted blows of man, individually and collectively.

We have not yet adjusted our thinking to the mastery of technology. Because the seas could gulp a schooner and all hands aboard without a belch. we forget that a loaded 200,000-ton oil tanker is an indigestible item. Because a liner or two could spew their slops overboard with impunity, we have come to believe that we need put no limits on the filth that we pipe to the depths. Because the once-pure oceans are seemingly illimitable, we make them the dumping grounds for the hottest by-products of our atomic age, a deadly assortment of long-lasting radioactive wastes.

Yet because these premises are false, a critical urgency has arisen. Hundreds of conglomerate nations, pressed by burgeoning, hungry

*Reprinted from *American Behavioral Scientist*, II, No. 6 (July–Aug., 1968), 34–37. By permission of Sage Publications, Inc.
(Notes to this selection will be found on p. 427.)

populations, are now attacking the seas with the full vigor of unrestrained technological prowess. If we would save them and their resources from death, we must soon cease the abuse and establish a new protective regime of law not yet imagined by man—a law able to combat the massive destructive powers which humanity has come to possess.

Our entire philosophy is contrary to our need. It is the ancient, worn-out credo of "inexhaustible" resources, the myth which has so grossly impoverished our once rich resource base. But in the case of the seas, the myth has been multiplied a thousand times.

Indeed, we use the seas not only as a soporific against the reckoning that our fecundity and industrial productivity must surely impose upon us, but as a glittering promise beyond anything we have yet known. Predicts Dr. William A. Nierenberg, Director of Scripps Institution of Oceanography, in an outburst of optimism: "We're learning more and more about food chains and we know the oceans could yield enough protein on a sustained basis to feed 30 *billion* people."[1]

Not only unlimited food, such as it may be, will be seined from the ocean's depths, but minerals will be mined, oil tapped on its floor, and great underseas cities glimmer through its watery aisles, cloistered havens for our unwanted millions. Dr. Donald F. Hornig, Science Adviser to the President, summarized these bullish prophecies by concluding that"The ocean is big business right now, and the rate it's going, it's reasonable to expect it will become an even bigger business in the years ahead."

This frontier legend of the seas paints a pristine, limitless, and romantic cornucopia of the deep. With oceanographers chafing in the lead to generate the enthusiasm, we are regaled with fabulous statistics. There are 1.5 trillion tons of manganese nodules pimpling the ocean floor, enough minable phosphate material off the coast of Mexico to last, at present rates of consumption for 4,000 years, and enough oil to fill 25 per cent of the entire oil production of the world.

This, then, is our image of the sea—a prodigally bounteous, untamed frontier bursting with potential riches for all. The myth is founded on public ignorance of a type foreboding of tragedy. It is abetted by a less than honest assessment by the sea's fervent exploiters. Minerals and oil may be there in untold quantities, but the dangers to men, and the pollutive destruction of the waters in obtaining them, are never stressed. As for the sea harvest of food which is depended upon to stave off the famines to come, the fatuity of such predictions is that they ignore completely the nature and delicacy of the sea's life chains. And there is no note taken of the fact that the productive part of the sea is largely on its fringes—the continental shelves, the bays and estuaries. The wide expanse of the sea is ecologically a watery desert.

"Preserving habitat for salt-water fish requires controlling the development of tidelands, tidal bottoms, and all the fringing brackish water habitat. This is the part of the sea called the *estuarine zone*. The word estuary as used here describes any of the protected coastal areas where there is a mixing of salt and fresh waters, including all the tidal rivers, marshes, tideflats, lagoons, bays, and shallow sounds," explains John Clark, writing for the American Littoral Society.[2] "Two out of every three species of useful Atlantic fish," he adds, "depend in some way upon tidal lands and the shallowest of our bays for their survival. Even oceanic fish often have complex life cycles which bring them into coastal bays, lagoons, and tidal rivers at tiny young stages of their lives."

It has been estimated that 90 per cent of the salt-water fish are taken in shallow coastal waters. More importantly, the parts of the ocean bordering the land are the fertile environment in which flourishes the plant growth on which bait fish, shellfish, shrimp, and plankton all thrive. The richest coastal marshes produce ten tons of plant stuff per acre per year—more than six times the amount (one-and-one-half tons) of wheat produced per acre, on a world average.

Even the undersea farming that excites the imagination of some scientists is planned to take place in the estuaries, coastal swamps, and shoreline areas. Dr. John H. Ryther of Woods Hole Oceanographic Institution points out that the productivity of the $1\frac{1}{4}$ million acres of mangrove swamps in the Philippines, if applied to the raising of milkfish in ponds, would in itself produce a tonnage of protein food equal to the present fish harvest of the entire United States. Aquaculture is designed to be practiced near the shores.

Yet is has been made evident that the seas are most shockingly vulnerable to the insults that stem from the activities of man in the very place where man and ocean meet. The traditional "accepted" use of coastal waters for the outfalls of municipal and industrial sewage systems is now seriously questioned, as the wastes mount geometrically. "In recent years," says a team of scholars, "many have realized that, although the oceans contain an almost limitless supply of diluting water, other beneficial and economically important uses of the near-shore ocean waters must be considered when an ocean outfall is designed for the disposal of sewage."[3]

Up to now the pollution of harbors, bays, and estuaries has been carried to the point of hazard or nuisance on the basic assumption that the tidal scrubbing would be effective. We are, indeed, with our overburden of wastes and our identification of coastal waters with the vast expanse of the oceans, destroying an environment which is at the same time both separate from the seas and yet highly interdependent. The multiplication of people and their industries is fast rendering barren the most fruitful part of the seas. "Coastal and estuarine regions of the sea which receive large amounts of organic wastes often produce sulfides from the bottom sediments in concentrations so high that animals and plants inhabiting these environments are damaged seriously."[4]

Direct outfalls may make of a bay or harbour a disease-ridden and noisome thing, as in the town of Winthrop Harbor in the Boston vicinity. There, the fascinating and profitable array of life forms that marks a seacoast was suffocated by an overwhelming growth of sea lettuce, feeding on the ingredients of the raw sewage that was being dumped in ever greater quantities from the North Metropolitan Sewer near Deer Island.

As we continue to pollute each of our 22 watersheds, all the vast quantities of inland wastes are added to the coastal burden of pollution. All up and down the coasts, each river spills its accumulated filth and contaminants at its mouth, in volumes that even the indefatigable tide cannot overcome. With river valleys the choice habitation of man, follows that the rivers provide the plumbing system for most of mankind, and the coastal waters of the seas become an elongated septic tank. The Thames estuary is today a notorious sewer. The domestic industrial effluents of a million people pour down the estuary of the once-lovely River Tyne. Should you consult the engineering manuals rather than the travel folders, you will find, instead of a lyric description of the sunrise over Hawaii's famed Kailua Bay, the less savory discussion of the sewage daily discharged·into it. You will be enlightened by the figures of sewage burden from Nanaimo and the sulfate discharge of the 700-ton-a-day mill into the Northumberland Channel of the North Pacific.[5] Yet the time is close at hand when the very odor alone of such waters will force the tourist agencies (albeit for a different reason) to join the ecologists and engineers in their mounting concern for the debauchment of the world's bays.

Added to the befoulment by sewage and industrial effluents, we now face the swelling floods of thousands of concoctions of pesticides and herbicides which drain constantly down into the rivers' mouths. It was the late Lloyd Berkner, eminent scientist and dean of the Dallas Graduate Research Center, who first called attention to the lethal effects of these pesticidal compounds on the floating diatoms of the sea, manufacturers of 70 per cent of the oxygen in the air we daily breathe.[6]

Long-lasting DDT is particularly deadly to fish life. The Interior Department reveals that "one part of DDT in one billion parts of water kills blue carp in eight days."[7] Yet this vicious and discredited pesticide, which has proved to be all but eternal in its toxicity and is peculiarly lethal to aquatic life is flushed off the watersheds of every major farming country without restraint into the most productive areas of the world's oceans. Pomeroy *et al.* mention the depredation visited upon mullet (*mugil cephalus*), menhaden (*brevoortia tyrannus*), and the commercial shrimps (*penaeus spp*) which enter the marsh creeks in spring and spend most of the summer feeding there.[8]

Many of the pesticides, indeed, were particularly "formulated to combat terrestrial arthropods—spiders, insects, etc., distinguished by their jointed feet and limbs, segmented bodies, and horny skeletons. In other words, what selective toxicity is built into these pesticides is directed to the arthropods. Unfortunately, it happens that a number of our most valuable marine food species, including lobsters, crabs, and shrimp, are also hapless arthropods."[9] It has also been found that some varieties of plankton important in the diet of oysters and clams are especially vulnerable to minute concentrations of herbicides, much smaller concentrations than are employed for the extensive weed control programs upstream.

As if sewage, industrial effluents, and pesticidal–herbicidal compounds were not enough, our civilization makes still another death-dealing assault upon the nurseries of the seas. The fallout from nuclear explosions that spreads itself about the earth in the falling rain also gathers in the watersheds' drainage, collecting finally in the estuaries along with the wastes that spill out of uranium mills,[10] dribble from atomic installations, and find their way from industrial and medical applications to the outfalls on the banks. Thus, the Severn, the Blackwater, Britain's Solway Firth,[11] as well as the seas off the Irish and Netherland coast, are causing increasing concern because of their growing concentrations of radioactive wastes. Over the short period of six years there has been a progressive and measurable increase of Strontium 90 and Cesium 137 in the coastal water, fish, mussels, and shrimps in the North Sea.[12]

These are but examples; the threat is universal. A careful evaluation by a team of scientists repeats that "Future additions of *significant amounts* of radionuclides to the estuarine and marine environment, whether accidental or intentional, will almost certainly occur in a variety of climatic, geographic, and geologic areas."[13]

As if this steadily advancing radiation of our seafood nurseries were not fast enough, we are still (after more than 20 years of waste disposal research) directly dumping our radioactive poisons into our coastal seas. "A Canadian report states that more than 16,000 drums, each containing 55 gallons of low-level waste, were dumped off the coast of California from 1946 to 1957. At Harwell (U.K.) contaminated solid waste, consisting of building material, protective clothing, laboratory equipment, animal remains, etc., is first reduced in volume as much as possible, and subsequently either stored or discharged into the sea. The total volume of this waste amounts to approximately 3200 cubic feet per week, weighing about 29 tons."[14]

The pressure for this kind of sea disposal of radioactive wastes becomes intense as one ponders the fantastic estimates for the future. "In the United States, it is estimated that the nuclear power industry will have produced three thousand million curies of radioactivity in 27 million litres of solution by 1970, and 60 thousand million curies in 1.1

billion litres of solution by the year 2000."[15] The safety of these disposal arrangements, which has the support of a body of scientists, has been founded on a pair of assumptions: that there are "deeps" where the lethal debris will remain isolated, and that what escapes will be greatly diluted.

Both assumptions are currently challenged. Many experts hotly argue that our research as to the circulation, mixing, and sedimentation in the deep sea is pitifully inadequate. Russian scholars are most doubtful about the current practices. Nicolas Gorsky, a member of the U.S.S.R. Geographical Society, notes the vertical mixing or circulation described by Professor Zubov which "ventilates the deep layers of the ocean and also raises to the surface a layer rich in nutrient phosphates and nitrates, forming a basis for abundant life. But this process will bring death if pernicious radioactive solutions from the waste products of the atomic industry accumulate in the ocean depths."[16]

More important, Professor Gorsky describes another similar phenomenon known as "upwelling." Because of winds, currents, or the relief of the ocean bed, deep, cold layers of water, laden with nutrients, come to the surface and lap the continental slope or the submerged banks. This phenomenon is especially marked on the Atlantic coast of North America, the California coast, and the western coast of both South America and Africa.

"The regions where upwelling occurs are exceptionally rich in plant and animal life, including fish. If the water rising to the surface should be contaminated with substances dissolved out of radioactive wastes it will mean the end of the highly productive fisheries in these regions."[17]

Indeed the Russian conclusion is that it is impossible to isolate or localize the poisoning of the seas. Even if the currents and movement of the water did not focus on the shores, the concentrating factor in the oceanic food chains is itself a competent countervail to dilution. Thus, in the central Pacific Ocean, "plankton were found to contain on the average nearly 500 times the general water concentration of fallout activity. An examination of the fish of the German bight coastal area shows that the radioactivity level remains constant even when nuclear tests decrease."[18]

We cannot register all the land-based insults to the ecosystems of the seas. But there is one more we must note: the threat from off-shore and shore-based oil drilling operations as well as by the still very inadequately policed regulation of oil spillages, accidental and deliberate, from ocean-going vessels.[19] Thus there exists an insensate and unremitting strangulation of the world's bays and estuaries wherever demographic and economic growth press the shores. Against all this assorted mindless aggressiveness of man, smugly ensconced behind the legal embattlements of the nation-state, the seas are wholly defenseless, open to their ultimate death. The sole item of concern over Earth's oceans has, to date, centered on the traditional, barnacle-encrusted, primitive doctrine of the freedom of the high seas. This outworn manifesto is comprised of: "(1) freedom of navigation; (2) freedom of fishing; (3) freedom to lay submarine cables and pipelines; and (4) freedom to fly over the high seas."[20]

All of these are exploitive rights; they do not pretend to tackle the preservation of the common seas or the ecological realities concerning their survival as living elements in a world suddenly drenched in an out-pouring of pollution, poisons, and petroleum. At our breakneck and improvident pace, we now face the eventual destruction of our most productive asset of the future for lack of laws to protect it. "The catchy phrase 'Freedom of the Sea'" remarks Edward W. Allen, "bespeaks a noble concept, that is, if applied with noble aspirations, but it can be a deceptive cliché if utilized to conceal ignoble motivations."[21] The day when a tide could scrub the estuaries clean and there still existed inter-minable miles of lonesome beaches, when the seas could absorb our ecological insults, is long past.

When will we come to grips with the exploding issue of marine pollution? We have grappled tentatively with the question of the rights of co-riparians in an international drainage basin to a proper share of whatever water is of acceptable quality. It is asserted that "there are principles limiting the power of states to use such waters without regard to injurious effects on co-riparians."[22]

Hopefully, there are few defenders today of the Schooner Exchange doctrine—the principle invoked by Attorney General Harmon in the Rio Grande dispute of 1895—that the jurisdiction of a state within its territory is exclusive and absolute and susceptible only of self-imposed limitations. In contradiction, what a nation does with its rivers, states Griffin, is subject to the legal rights of each co-riparian state in the drain-age basin. "No international decision supporting any purported principle of absolute sovereignty has been found."[23]

It is some advance to formally recognize that the seas are an inter-national drainage basin of which all littoral states are "co-riparians." For on ecological principle alone (however the legal precedents direct) the well-being of the seas as a living, productive ecosystem for the benefit of the community of nations is wholly dependent on what happens to the margins and the land masses.

However, at present we concede jurisdiction over marginal seas on grounds of defense to littoral states because we still assume their stake is superior to that of the community of nations. The international approval of the continental shelf doctrine and the adoption of the conven-tion of Fishing and Conservation of the Living Resources of the Sea give an authority to coastal states also on the basis that they have a primary interest.

Thus the primary legal interest continues to be exploitive; it is a matter of staking out national claims under the misleading guise of "conservation." The direction of American concern is evident from this budget extract: Out of an annutal total of $462.3 million for United States federal marine science spending, $191.6 is for national security, $49.2 for fisheries development and seafood technology, and but $9.4 million for pollution abatement and control.[24]

The present flabby attitude of the nation-states, that condones the destruction of coastal waters by the drainage of poisons and pollutants, is a malignant threat to the welfare of the seas and therefore to the welfare of mankind. It is imperative that we develop a modernized legal regime that affords protection to the maritime interests of the community of states as a whole. This objective calls for the international regulation of watersheds with the family of nations viewed as co-riparians.

A. P. Lester, British barrister, while assessing the rights of riparians to clean water, noted that "state responsibility for extraterritorial damage to the territory of another state has been based upon the concepts of neighborhood, abuse of rights, and international servitudes."[25] None of these principles in its traditional garb is adequate to the preservation of the physical integrity of the sea against the destructive forces and wastes of twentieth-century industrialism.

If Grotius in his day could find a common stake of all the riparians to the water of a river, certainly we today must recognize the valid claim of the family of nations to productive coastal waters and estuaries. Having identified the fringes of the seas as the vital element in the seas' well-being, and the growing dependency of all of mankind on the future harvest of the oceans, one must readily conclude the superior claim of the international community to the ecological health of coastal waters.

Unless we want to be faced with the globe-enveloping spectre of a dead and stinking ocean, we are faced with the task of somehow evolving an international regime of oceanic stewardship. Besides international controls of pollutants and of the use of rivers and estuaries, such a regime would embody a creative application of the legal principle of servitudes, under which sovereign jurisdiction over rivers would yield to the prescriptive rights of the family of nations to a viable system of seas.

There is little time left to debate the juridical niceties. Already the chlorinated hydrocarbons (DDT, its cousins and derivatives) have traveled the biological waterways and concentrated in the complex oceanic food chains, so that not only is every species of fish used by man contaminated, but the carnivorous birds who feed on seafood are in real trouble. Biologists report that the last twenty remaining pairs of Bermuda petrels are dying out for want of fertility of eggs because of DDT; their extinction is forecast within ten years. The peregrine falcon is now extinct as a breeding bird along the east coast of the United States. Ducks, geese and gulls are often so loaded that their eggs are "hot."

The irony is that man, who is the source of all this poisoning, is himself the end of these many varied food chains; he eats the choice large fish who have concentrated the poisons from algae all the way up, and he thus becomes the final residuary of the very lethal concoctions he has created to use on other life. Indeed, it should be evident that he cannot long continue in such folly without jeopardizing his own existence.

What we need now is an entirely new manifesto of the sea built not, as in the past, on legal limitations alone, but constructed primarily on the ecological realities of a sick sea in what may be fatal crisis.

Robert C. Lucas

Wilderness Perception and Use: The Example of the Boundary Waters Canoe Area*

A. Wilderness as a Resource

For centuries North American wilderness was viewed only as a land to be developed—cleared and farmed, mined, or logged. The wilderness was a challenge. If the challenge was met, material benefits could be drawn from the former wilderness. Now, however, many people in the United States and Canada see wilderness as a resource in its own right. These people oppose conventional development of the remaining wilderness and argue that such areas have greater utility in their wilderness state. Groups such as the Sierra Club, the Wilderness Society, and the Quetico Foundation present this argument forcefully and seek to influence resource management in the direction of wilderness preservation.

Changing ideas provided the impetus for the re-evaluation of wilderness, and economic conditions made the shift possible. The late eighteenth and the nineteenth centuries constituted a period of major reinterpretation of the resources of scenic wildlands. Before that time, Americans seldom wrote of nature or scenery with aesthetic appreciation.[1] For example, William Bradford described the New England wilderness as hideous and desolate.[2] European ideas, particularly Romanticism and a growing scientific interest in nature, influenced American writers such as Bryant, Emerson, Thoreau, Irving, and Muir and they along with painters began to portray scenery as an object of beauty.[3]

Besides the new attitude towards the natural scene, the almost complete conquest of the wilderness gave a certain scarcity value to the remnant.[4] The status of the frontier movement, as a national epic, encouraged keeping some wilderness as a symbol of the frontier and as a setting for re-experiencing its challenge.[5] Finally, the general mastery of

*Reprinted by permission from *Natural Resources Journal*, School of Law, University of New Mexico, III (Jan., 1964), 394–411.
(Notes to this selection will be found on pp. 428–429.)

the more productive portion of the original wilderness reduced the incentive to develop the remainder. The agricultural frontier, in fact, has retreated as production of the agricultural crops has risen, although mining, logging, and highways continue to spread.

B. The Wilderness Resource

"Wilderness" is difficult to define precisely.[6] The Wilderness Bill states: "A wilderness, in contrast with those areas where man and his own works dominate the landscape, is hereby recognized as an area where the earth and its community of life are untrammeled by man, where man himself is a visitor who does not remain."[7]

The most easily defined wilderness is that area officially established by law or administrative declaration. The largest acreage of such established wilderness is located in the national forests of the United States. In 1961 this consisted of 83 areas and over 14 million acres, which is about eight per cent of the National Forest System.[8] This acreage has been stable since the late 1930's.[9] The areas are roadless and closed to timber cutting. Other uses, such as grazing or water impoundments, are more restricted than on other national forest areas.

The National Park Service in the United States has no specific wilderness areas. All land under its jurisdiction which is located away from roads or other developments is considered wilderness and is closed to logging, grazing, and usually to hunting.[10] The National Park Service recently classified 66 of its areas as scenic-scientific parks and monuments, in contrast to more purely historical sites.[11] These 66 locations included over 22 million acres. About 7 million acres were considered wilderness in the study conducted by the Wildland Research Center under a strict definition[12] (a definition that excluded 2 million acres of established national forest wilderness). Like the national forest wilderness, national park wilderness appears to be holding its own in acreage.

A few state areas are established as wilderness. The largest is the Adirondack Forest Preserve in New York; however, it includes a good deal of intermixed private land.[13]

Informal or unreserved wilderness is also important but more difficult to define or measure. The Wildland Research Center considered that almost 9 million acres of unreserved land met wilderness standards, compared with over 19 million acres of established wilderness.[14] This area is probably declining because of lack of formal designation, and because it often surrounds established areas and thus is more accessible.

These wilderness areas have two main attributes. First, they are closed to recreationists using mechanized transportation including jeeps, motor scooters, airplanes (with a few exceptions), and motorboats (with more exceptions). Second, ecological conditions are relatively undisturbed although probably quite different from pre-white entry characteristics because of fire protection, exotic plants, diseases, animals, and recreation use, to name but a few influences.[15]

There is, however, another type of area, semi-wilderness, which provides a refuge from mechanized recreation but permits some logging and other uses. Established semi-wilderness is rare. The Boundary Waters Canoe Area of the Superior National Forest in northeastern Minnesota is the only example found in the United States. Its name prior to 1958, the Superior Roadless Area, suggested its character as a refuge for rugged recreation, but it was inaccurate because temporary logging roads, closed to the public, do exist there. Canada has several semi-wilderness areas. Both the Quetico and Algonquin Provincial Parks in Ontario are managed in this way. The Boundary Waters Canoe Area, which is the focus of this article, adjoins Quetico Provincial Park to the north; the two combined (often also including some of the surrounding land) are called the Quetico–Superior Area. These two semi-wilderness areas cover about 2 million acres (Figure 24–1).

This rarity of established semi-wilderness is surprising. Robert Marshall, who contributed greatly to the development of the national forest wilderness areas and founded the Wilderness Society, called for semi-wilderness in 1933.[16] The Outdoor Recreation Resources Review Commission,[17] the Wildland Research Center,[18] and a recent recreational planning monograph[19] have repeated Marshall's plea. Informal semi-wilderness is probably shrinking fast. As recreation booms, improved public roads, public recreational facilities, resorts and especially summer homes are spreading into many unreserved semi-wild areas.

C. Resource Use

A wilderness area serves a number of uses. It can be a setting for education and research, a protected watershed, and, simply by existing, a source of psychological satisfaction as a symbol in some natural philosophy. The main use, however, is for high-quality recreation, frequently with inspirational overtones. The Forest Service estimates there were 757,000 visits to established wilderness-type areas in 1961, out of a total of 102 million visits to the national forests.[20] In 1960, 1,100,000 visits were estimated for national park wilderness[21] compared to 65 million for the entire National Park System, omitting the National Capital Parks.[22] The Boundary Waters Canoe Area tallied 217,000 visits in 1961,[23] which is a very substantial proportion of all wilderness visits.[24]

Use has generally been increasing somewhat faster for wilderness areas than for conventional recreation areas.[25] Visits to the Boundary Waters Canoe Area rose 12 per cent a year from 1946 to 1960 (before a change in estimation procedures sharply increased use figures); this is close to the national figure for wilderness visits. A tenfold increase in wilderness man-days has been projected for the year 2000, and an eightfold growth

The Regional Setting of the Quetico-Superior Area

FIGURE 24-1

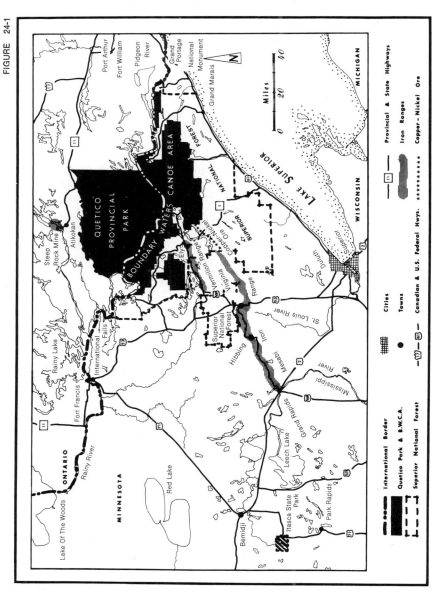

for the Boundary Waters Canoe Area.[26] This compares to a threefold increase projected to the same year for all outdoor recreation, and a fourfold projected expansion in general camping.[27]

I

PERCEPTION OF THE WILDERNESS RESOURCE IN THE BOUNDARY WATERS CANOE AREA

For both public agencies and the visitors, three elements of environmental perception in the Boundary Waters Canoe Area will be considered: (1) the importance of the wilderness qualities relative to other potential uses, (2) the area considered to be wilderness, and (3) the essential characteristics of the wilderness—particularly the types of uses accepted.

The recreational visitors to the Canoe Area were studied in 1960 and 1961. A random sample distributed with equal probability over the entire area during the summer season was interviewed.[28] Almost 300 groups were questioned, and data were recorded on a formal questionnaire. A major part of the data collected dealt with wilderness resource perception.

The resource managers include the staff of the Superior National Forest, regional and national Forest Service officers, and to a limited extent state and county officials. Although this group was not studied directly, the development of the policy of management for the area was studied. Based on this information and considerable informal contact with the national forest staff, some inferences about resource managers' perception were drawn and are presented here.

A. The Resource Managers' Perception

The Superior National Forest was established in 1909 (the same year as Quetico Park). The area was viewed as conventional forest land, in need of roads and development, although there had been some earlier proposals for an international park.[29] After World War I an extensive road system was proposed, but a different picture of the resources of the area and its potential was presented by a young landscape architect in 1921. Arthur Carhart, employed by the Forest Service regional office, visited the area and stressed the value of the now unique forested land and undeveloped lakes and streams in a plan prospectus.[30] Basically he proposed the semi-wilderness management now practiced, combining logging with "the presentation of natural scenic beauties" along the waterways, and the exclusion of auto recreation.

The ideas in the Carhart proposal were taken up by private groups and gradually adopted by the Forest Service. The importance of the wilderness aspects of the area grew in the managers' view from minimal, or even negative, to dominance.

The area considered to be wilderness by the Forest Service has generally corresponded closely to the changing official boundary (Figure 24–1). This official area grew until 1939, contracted slightly in 1946, and has been stable since then. The map shown in Figure 24–1 is in front of the National Forest staff almost daily, and the boundary strongly affects their daily plans and activities.

The resource managers' view of appropriate uses in the Canoe country has also changed. The decision to exclude public roads was made, unmade, and remade by the Forest Service and the Secretary of Agriculture in the 1920's. After 1926, the decision was firm.

Water impoundments were proposed on a large scale in 1925, weighed at the international level, and rejected in 1934. The International Joint Commission announced:

The boundary waters referred to in the Reference . . . are of matchless scenic beauty and of inestimable value from the recreational and tourist viewpoints. The Commission fully sympathizes with the objects and desires of the State of Minnesota and the Quetico–Superior Council . . . that nothing should be done that might mar the beauty or disturb the wildlife of this last great wilderness of the United States.[31]

The commission did state that under different conditions in the future some carefully controlled dams might be considered, but approval by each country would be a prerequisite. This appears to have been a meaningless concession to the development interests, because the Shipstead–Nolan Act prohibited water level alterations in the Minnesota portion of the Quetico–Superior.[32] The area covered by this act included almost all of the Canoe Area, plus a considerable amount of land outside the area.

Another provision of the Shipstead–Nolan Act withdrew federally owned land from private entry (except for agriculture, which was virtually nonexistent), recognizing that more cabins and resorts were inappropriate in a wilderness environment.[33]

A third provision of this 1930 law was specific protection of forests for 400 feet from the shores of navigable lakes and streams.[34] The Forest Service has also applied these restrictions to the small part of the Boundary Waters Canoe Area outside the area defined by the Shipstead–Nolan Act, supporting the statement that the map boundary defines "the wilderness" for the resource managers. In 1941 the service established a zone closed to *all* logging covering the northern third of the area, and in 1948 the Service prohibited logging in even wider waterfront strips where topography would expose cutting to canoeists or boaters.[35]

Air traffic to cabins and resorts and for fishing trips mounted after World War II, and after a prolonged and sharp controversy, airplanes (except for administration) were banned below 4,000 feet above sea level by order of President Truman in 1949.[36] The courts upheld the order.[37]

In 1948 about 14 per cent of the Boundary Waters Canoe Area was privately owned, and about 45 resorts and 100 cabins were located in the supposed wilderness.[38] The incongruity of this situation was recognized early. In 1926 it was decided that in the future no leases for resort or summer home sites would be granted on at least 1,000 squares miles of national forest land containing the best of the lakes and waterways.[39] The means to eliminate developments were limited, however, until 1948 when the Thye–Blatnik Act[40] was passed. This law authorized acquisition of developed property and appropriated money for purchases. The funds for acquisition have been increased several times and now total $4,500,000. Only a few private properties now remain, and within the past year the federal government has resorted to condemnation, which will probably result in completing acquisition soon.

Motorboats in a wilderness canoe country have also been recognized by the managers of the resource as being inconsistent. The Forest Service has moved cautiously on this problem, perhaps because of the large number of boaters using the area but also because of uncertainty as to the extent of their legal jurisdiction over navigation, which is generally within Minnesota's authority.[41] The policy is that motorboats "will be prohibited except where well established."[42] No map of prohibited areas has ever been issued, so the restriction is toothless. Motorboats are being restricted somewhat, however, starting in 1963, under the Secretary of Agriculture's regulation number T–15, which prohibits leaving unattended trailers, boats, and other equipment on National Forest land. In the Boundary Waters Canoe Area this will stop the storage of boats over portages on many interior lakes and reduce the amount and area of boat use.

Quetico Provincial Park has generally similar policies, except that a lack of private land has eliminated the acquisition problem, and a small local population and an abundance of informal wilderness has reduced the controversy over the air ban and other restrictions in the park.

In summary, the resource managers have increased their evaluation of the relative importance of the wilderness qualities of the Canoe country. The area considered wilderness was first vague, then was defined, gradually grew, and has been stable for 25 years. The standards of how a wilderness should be used if it is to be a wilderness have been defined more sharply, restricting more and more commodity and recreational uses other than canoeing in an undeveloped setting. These changes in evaluation were largely a reflection of national trends in thinking within forestry, the United States Forest Service, and the conservation organizations, some of whom took a particular interest in the Quetico–

Superior. All of the administrators' attention so far has been on eliminating *inappropriate* uses; no policy prevents *excessive* use of a resource which has solitude and relatively unmodified physical conditions as major components, although the managers are aware of this problem and concerned about it.

B. The Recreationists' Perception

The visitors to the Canoe country in 1960 differed markedly in their view of the resource, both among themselves and with the resource managers. They differed on all three counts: importance of wilderness, area of wilderness, and essential qualities of wilderness.[43] There was order, however, in the variation related to the type of recreational activity being pursued.

Wilderness was a major attraction for canoeists, important for roadside campers, but secondary for all other visitor types. Table 24–1 presents

Table 24-1—Per Cent of Parties Citing Certain Qualities as a Basis for Choice of the Area (Summer, 1960)

Type of recreationist (and number)		NON, VAGUE, TAUTOLOGICAL	WILDERNESS*	FISHING	SCENERY	FACILITIES
Canoeists	(85)	6	71	29	28	6
Paddlers	(64)	6	73	16	28	8
Motorized	(21)	5	62	67	24	0
Day-use	(9)	33	33	33	11	0
Auto campers	(83)	8	51	30	31	13
Boat campers	(23)	17	35	48	26	13
Resort guests	(57)	12	39	42	42	9
Private cabin users	(21)	38	10	14	33	0
Total	(278)	12	49	33	32	9

Attractive qualities cited

* The six major types of recreationists (ignoring the subdivision of canoeists) differed significantly in the frequency of mention of wilderness attributes at the .995 level when tested by chi-square. The other qualities were not tested.
Note: All responses, sometimes three or four per party, were tabulated; therefore, the totals exceed 100 per cent.

responses to the question: "Does this area have some characteristics that caused you to come here rather than some other vacation region in the United States or Canada? If yes, what characteristics?" ("This area" was defined for the respondents and included the Boundary Waters Canoe Area and its immediate periphery.)

It is interesting to note that the two classes of canoeists differed markedly in their view of the area's distinctive attractions. The paddlers

The Area Considered "Wilderness" by the Paddling Canoeists

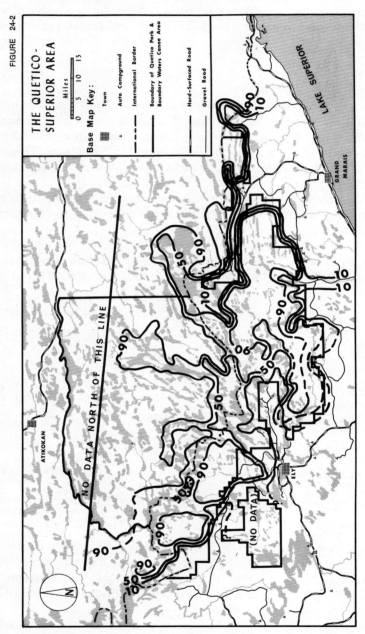

The isoline values are the per cent of parties visiting each area which described that area as being "in the wilderness." The broken portions of the isolines indicate that data were lacking and subjective estimates were made. The map is based on 1960 data.

viewed the area as a wilderness in which to travel and camp. The canoeists using outboard motors saw the area as a place to enjoy wilderness fishing. Similarly, the boat campers differed from the car campers. Previous research has contrasted the wilderness images of canoeists and campers, grouping these quite different subtypes of canoeists, and perhaps campers as well (the definition of a camper is unclear).[44]

The area considered wilderness was estimated by asking each sample group, "Do you feel that you are in 'the wilderness' now? Where did the members of your group feel 'the wilderness' began?" "Wilderness" was not defined. Each group's route was also obtained and mapped. This made it possible to classify each lake or section of road visited by the group as wilderness or not-wilderness, in their terms. The aggregation of these classifications produced wilderness-perception maps for each user type, with isolines indicating the proportion of visitors considering that place as wilderness. Figure 24–2 is this map for paddling canoeists. This was the most demanding group (and produced the most complex map). The paddlers' wilderness is smaller than the officially defined area, even if the 10-per cent isoline is taken as the limit. Only one significant area, directly north of the town of Ely, was outside the official boundaries but inside the paddlers' wilderness. It should be pointed out that the location of the official boundary was not well known among the public.

A summary map was drawn (Figure 24–3) from the series of maps for each user type, taking only the 50-per cent isoline from each. All the groups except canoeists were quite similar in their areal perception of the wilderness. Whether people slept in beds in a resort, camped by their cars, often in a trailer, or bedded down on the ground on a rocky islet reached by a cruiser, they all entered their wilderness at about the same places. What all of these groups had in common was the use of boats rather than canoes. All of these boating groups saw the wilderness as much larger than the established area. The three separate official areas fused into one large wilderness. The 90-per cent isolines were also very similar for these boating classes, and approached the official boundary fairly closely.

The motor canoeist sample was too small for a satisfactory map, but the data suggest that such a map would be intermediate between the paddling canoeist and the motorboaters.

The views of the essential characteristics of these differing wildernesses can be inferred in part from the maps, and were also directly investigated in the interviews. Again, the type of water transportation seems to account for a large part of the variation.

The paddlers' map shows that roads are almost never in "the wilderness." The effect of buildings was not directly tested, and since buildings

The Area Considered "Wilderness" by at Least 50 Per Cent of the Visitors in Each of the Four Major User Types

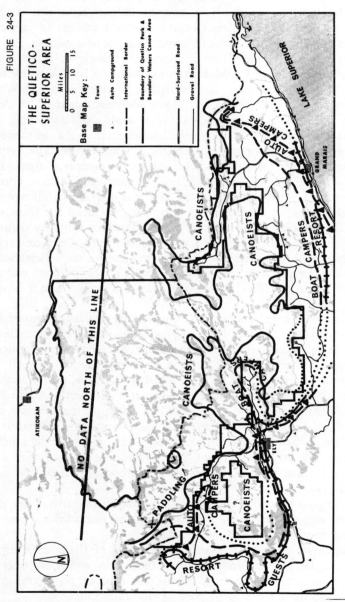

The area in the interior—that is, away from the roads and generally to the north of the line for each user type—was rated as "wilderness" by 50 to 100 per cent of the visitors of that type reaching the area. The dotted portions of the lines indicate data were lacking, and subjective estimates have been made, based on 1960 data.

and motorboats go together the two effects cannot be completely separated in interpreting the maps.

However, recreational use seems to affect the paddling canoeists' wilderness perception importantly. Heavily used areas were much less often considered wilderness. Moose Lake, located east of Ely and the most heavily used point, was considered nonwilderness by all 23 paddling canoeist groups that were sampled there. Total seasonal visitors for each location were estimated and the places were ranked accordingly. The locations were also ranked on the basis of the per cent of the paddling groups classing each location as wilderness. The Spearman rank correlation coefficient for the visitor and the wilderness ratings was —.42. This correlation seems fairly strong when it is considered that season-visitor totals are only a rough index of the number of other visitors observed by the sample parties on a given lake, particularly because of the variation in lake size. The absence of buildings where use was heavy did not raise the level of perceived wilderness.

The type of use encountered seemed even more important to paddlers. Comparable levels of use produced a higher level of perceived wilderness where boats were absent (about three times as high, generally). This antipathy for boats was also brought out in questions about the groups' reaction to meeting other types of groups. Of the paddling canoeists, 61 per cent disliked meeting motorboats, 37 per cent were neutral, and only 2 per cent (one party) enjoyed meeting other boats. In contrast, only one group disliked meeting fellow paddlers.

Remoteness, surprisingly, did not have an identifiable relation to the paddlers' wilderness. Where use was comparable, lakes near access points were perceived as wilderness as often as those four or five portages away. This findings needs further substantiation, but it may have interesting implications for a policy establishing more small wild areas.

Logging appeared much less incompatible with wilderness recreation than crowding and conflicting types of recreation.[45] The area northeast of Ely was not generally considered wilderness by canoeists. This area is in the no-cut zone, but it is heavily used by canoeists and boaters. Lightly used, boat-free areas in the west and south-central portions of the Boundary Waters Canoe Area were being logged, but they were considered wilderness by almost all of the sample parties there. These samples were small, of course, because of light use.

The hypothesis that use was light because people were avoiding the logging areas cannot be definitely rejected at this point, but it appears unlikely. Only 30 per cent of the sample even knew logging was permitted. This compares to 28 per cent of the Wildland Research Center's smaller sample.[46] Only 8 per cent of the canoeist sample reported noticing any signs of logging, and only half of these objected to what they observed. Low local relief and lack of travel off water routes appear to make the restricted timber harvest policy quite effective. However, public opinion appears strongly opposed to the idea of logging. The Wildland Research Center found 75 per cent of their sample (91 per cent of the sample were canoeists) opposed to timber cutting.[47]

The motorboaters were not as demanding in wilderness standards as canoeists. Roads were accepted in their wilderness. Over half of the groups in each boating type entered their wilderness after passing the last town on the forest roads. Some of these roads are asphalt-paved, but they are relatively free of signs and buildings. Lakes with buildings were still considered wilderness by almost all motorboaters.

Motorboaters tolerated recreational use at high levels. Even on the most heavily used wilderness lake—Moose Lake easy of Ely—58 per cent were in their wilderness and 79 per cent of the boaters reported they were not bothered by crowding at all. Only 7 percent were "bothered quite a bit" by crowding. In contrast, at the same location, only 45 per cent of the paddling canoeists made no complaints about crowding, 29 per cent were "bothered quite a bit," and none considered Moose Lake to be wilderness.

The visitors using powerboats did not distinguish between the types of recreationists encountered. Boats and canoes were perceived essentially as one class, except that somewhat more motorboaters reported enjoying meeting paddlers, apparently as a touch of local color. Only 3 per cent of the boaters disliked meeting other boaters or motor canoeists. None objected to paddlers. Neutrality towards boats and motor canoes marked 73 per cent of the sample, and 55 per cent were neutral towards paddlers. One fourth enjoyed meeting boats or canoes with motors, and 45 per cent enjoyed meeting the purists doing it the hard way—the paddlers.

Logging was observed by a slightly higher proportion of boaters than canoeists. This is probably because the question included a broader area than the Boundary Waters Canoe Area, and these groups tended to see and report logging trucks and other activities associated with logging outside the established area more often than canoeists. Of the boaters, 21 per cent observed logging but only 8 per cent were bothered by what they saw.

Resource perception has been differentiated on the basis of the type of recreation, particularly the type of transportation used. This, in effect, says that the choice of a boat or canoe reflects a cluster of present values and ideas. The stability of this relation over time is unknown; the effect of future technology is unforeseeable. The clusters of values are also unlikely to remain constant. Many questions remain to be answered—and some yet to be asked—about the development and meaning of outdoor recreational resources and the wilderness.[48]

II
RESOURCE USE AS INFLUENCED BY PERCEPTION

Three rather different perceptions of the wilderness resource of the border lakes held by three groups (managers, canoeists, and boaters) have been presented in this article. To what extent do these perceptions influence the use of the resource by these three groups?

A. Resource Managers

Much of the influence of the land managers' view of the resource was reflected in the policies developed, and this has already been discussed. However, there are a few other indications of the effect of their resource perception. The examples which come to mind all hinge on the perception of the boundary of the wilderness. I have suggested that the Forest Service thinks of the line on the map as the boundary. Indeed, the law requires them to do so in many ways, such as road building, logging, and private airplane travel. One result of this view is that the Forest Service has favored improving access roads to make it easier and pleasanter for people to reach the wilderness, which the Forest Service has assumed is the attraction and has considered to begin at the official boundary. But to many visitors these roads are located in their "wilderness": only 38 per cent of the sample groups thought that "straightening and blacktopping more roads" was "a good idea."

The same resource image may have contributed to the location of many boat accesses and campgrounds at the ends of the roads, as close to the wilderness as possible, while some large, attractive lakes outside the official wilderness area have no developments.

In a few cases in the past, this view of the resource may have contributed to decisions to bring access roads directly to lakes partially within the Boundary Waters, building past other lakes which are on canoe routes to the peripheral lakes, and thus reducing the effective size of the roadless area. This may have had some role in the construction of the last section of the Gunflint Trail many years ago, or of the road to the shores of Brule Lake after World War II. There seems to have been some reappraisal on this point, and plans to extend a road and make access easier on the Moose River have been set aside.

B. Recreationists

The canoeists used almost all of the area, penetrating to the core. This was most true of the paddling canoeists and appears consistent with the high value they place on the wilderness attraction, their perception of a small wilderness located in the core, and their objection to crowding at a low level of use.

However, canoeists were heavily concentrated at one access point. Over half used Moose Lake, although there were more than fifty other possible starting points, at least twenty of them seemingly very attractive. This is not consistent with the objection to crowding. The basis for the popularity of Moose Lake appeared to be its location deep within the interior (the road to the lake is surrounded by the Boundary Waters Canoe Area) and its closeness to the main, central entry to Canada's Quetico Park. These aspects of the situation are all evident on the map, but new visitors learn of the heavy use only after the choice of route is made. Knowledge of alternative locations may be limited, but this was not studied.

Another element in the wilderness perception of many people apparently affects the distribution of use. That is the lure of the North and Canada. Thus, the separate portion of the Boundary Waters Canoe Area south of the road running north and west from Ely was almost unused.

The motor canoeists did not go as far as the paddlers. In most cases they apparently went just far enough to find their wilderness fishing.

The motorboaters, on the other hand, were concentrated around the periphery and on several large international border lakes with truck or tramway portages leading to them. Most of the core was unused. The attraction of the North was weak. This is consistent with boaters' greater interest in fishing and scenery than wilderness, their large wilderness, and their lack of concern with crowding.

CONCLUSION

All resources are defined by human perception. This has been said more often than used as an organizing concept in research. The importance of resource perception is particularly obvious for recreational, scenic, and amenity resources because of the internal, personal, and subjective way such resources are used. Within the general class of amenity resources, the perception of wilderness resources is even more obviously necessary to understanding or action because of the prominence of the subjective aspect.

Despite the complete subjectivity of wilderness and the variation in its perception, neither the social scientist nor the land manager need throw up his hands in bewilderment. Empirical research in one wilderness-type area, the Boundary Waters Canoe Area, suggests that considerable order can be imposed even upon subjects as elusive as solitude and beauty.

This order in perception of the wilderness resource has implications for the management of the resource. The implications all suggest a more flexible concept of "the wilderness" by the resource managers, both in area and in content. There are two main wildernesses—the paddling canoeists', and the motorboaters'—with a smaller group of motor canoeists defining an intermediate wilderness. None corresponds closely to the official wilderness.

The differences between these wildernesses may provide a key to increasing the capacity of the area in order to provide high-quality recreation. The highest priority use by established policy is wilderness canoeing. The canoeists' wilderness is easily destroyed by heavy use, especially boat use. The boaters value wilderness much less highly and fishing more highly, accept heavy use, and are usually in their wilderness before they reach the areas used by the canoeists, or the canoeists' wilderness. It would seem that the canoeists' satisfaction could be raised, or kept high as visitors increase, without reducing the motorboaters' satisfaction by concentrating new access points, campgrounds, and resort or cabin site leases, and managing the fishing intensively in the band of forests and lakes away from the Boundary Waters Canoe Area but inside the wilderness for most boaters.[49]

The study also implies that a decision must be made between limiting the numbers using a wilderness and letting the wilderness as defined by the visitors vanish from overuse. This disappearance has already taken place in part of the Canoe country for the more sensitive types of users, and use trends suggest that the wilderness will retreat farther in the future for all types of visitors if use is unlimited.

The same zoning approach might have value in western mountain wilderness-type areas. The paddling purist may have his counterpart in the "backpacker." The jeep or motorscooter may play the motorboat's role.

The wilderness perception framework for research may be useful in developing the semi-wilderness concept and applying it to different settings. Despite the apparent objection to the idea of semi-wilderness in the abstract in the Canoe country, pragmatically the system seems quite successful. There may be critical points in all competing uses which correspond to breakpoints in wilderness perception by certain classes of recreationists. Empirical research within this theoretical system may identify these thresholds. Perhaps some wilderness should have pre-Columbian ecological conditions restored insofar as possible and use limited to a few backpackers, while other "wilderness" may only need to be a place where a family can pitch a tent by their car isolated from trailers, portable electric generators, and transistor radios. If research on wilderness perception can identify segments within this range which are characteristic of certain types of recreationists, it should be possible to increase both the amount and quality of wilderness recreation. Greater diversity in wilderness management will probably increase the complexity of administration, but growing use and changing perceptions may make more flexibility essential in the future. Guidelines will be needed.

George Hagevik

Legislating for Air Quality Management: Reducing Theory to Practice*

INTRODUCTION

Air pollution is more or less representative of the nation's increasing environmental problems in that while it has been with us for some time, it has only recently grown to a scale where differences in degree have begun to become differences in kind. Up to some level of concentration, disposal of wastes is for the most part a local irritation. But, at a certain threshold, costs to society start to increase significantly. This phenomenon has resulted in a considerable redefinition of air pollution problems. For example, the concern is no longer so much with smoke damage as with harm from photochemical smog and other synergistic effects. Also, a higher aspiration level on the part of the population of metropolitan areas has resulted in a reduced tolerance for anything impairing the quality of the environment. These and other changes in the nature of the air pollution problem suggest a new or at least a broader view of planning for air quality management.

The regulatory machinery for dealing with the air pollution problem is still for the most part of a primitive variety. The Air Quality Act of 1967 assigns primary responsibility for devising the regulatory mechanism to state governments, subject to review by the Department of Health, Education, and Welfare (HEW),[1] and appears to contemplate that new legislation or regulatory action will appear at the state and local level as soon as HEW provides the data and criteria for which it is responsible under the act.[2] The resultant need for review of laws and standards, coupled with changing perceptions of the problem, suggest that a new generation of legislative responses at the state and local level is to be both

*Reprinted with permission from a symposium, "Air Pollution Control," appearing in *Law and Contemporary Problems* (Duke University: Durham, N.C.), XXXIII, No. 2 (Spring, 1968). Copyright, 1968, by Duke University.
(Notes to this selection will be found on pp. 429–433.)

hoped and looked for. In the formulation of this new response, greater sophistication will be needed if the considerable costs involved in air pollution abatement are to be minimized, and it is not clear that existing air quality management efforts are yielding the experience necessary to guide the legislatures in this direction. Perhaps greater assistance will come from economists and other experts who can recognize that the legal attack on air pollution requires a new strategy, not just further adaptations of old approaches originally designed to deal with zoning and nuisances.

This paper first attempts to set down some basic social science theory about the economics of air pollution and about decision-making in general. It then seeks to apply this understanding in the development of a hypothetical regulatory program for dealing with stationary sources of pollution. This hypothetical program owes little to existing control efforts and is conceived in the understanding that regulatory officials must be enabled to operate effectively even in the dim light of partial knowledge defining and relating the social and technological aspects of air pollution. Since the program is merely sketched, it will not serve as a blueprint but only as a stimulus to new thinking about air quality management and the organization for carrying it out.

I

THE ECONOMIST'S VIEW—EFFLUENT FEES

Readings in welfare economics published during the last 30 years are replete with references to smoke damage as a classic instance of what are called negative externalities.[3] Such discussions, however, have been of more value to economists interested in the further theoretical development of welfare economics than to the air pollution control officer concerned with actual abatement and control activities. Unfortunately, in this instance the spillover from theory to practice has been minimal. Why is this the case? For one thing, the economic theory requires limiting conditions and large assumptions about the data available, neither of which can be fulfilled in practice. The problems of collecting data on such subjects as air pollution damage and the contribution of each emitter to existing concentrations are staggering, to say the least, and economists have not had the fortitude or the means to tackle the measurements necessary to make concrete control proposals. Sheer complexity has discouraged interest, and, until very recently, there was apparently less investment by government and private funding agencies in this field of economic research than the need seems in retrospect to have warranted. In any event, the theory has proved not too difficult to master, but attention is only beginning to focus on the need for data and practical means of developing these data or compensating for the lack thereof. The 1966 volume, *The Economics of Air Pollution*, edited by Professor Harold Wolozin, is probably the best single indicator both of economists' increased interest in the problem and of the gulf remaining between theory and practice.

The practitioner looking for practical answers in the Wolozin volume will be disappointed for it is little more than a summary—albeit an excellent one—of the state of the art. The primary contribution of the book is that it brings relevant economic theory to bear on the problem, explicitly or implicitly reveals the advantages and weaknesses of the economist's approach, and suggests data deficiencies and research needs. The consensus of the participants in the forum from which the book was drawn seems to be that the problem has been defined and that the task for the next few years is to gather data and do research that might lead to estimates of the necessary answers. If an analogy to water quality management holds, the estimate of a few years seems optimistic. For, even though economists have been concerned with water resource development for some time, Allan Kneese's seminal work on water quality, *The Economics of Regional Water Quality Management*, did not appear until 1964.

The economist's views on air quality management can be usefully reviewed in a brief manner. Most economists would state the problem in this way: The discharge of pollutants into the air imposes on some people costs which are not adequately borne by the sources of the pollution due to the failure of the market mechanism, resulting in more air pollution than would be desirable from the point of view of society as a whole. The "classical" economic theorist's distinctive approach to the problem is manifested in his belief that the objective of pollution abatement programs should be to minimize the total of (*a*) air pollution damage costs and (*b*) the costs incurred in any program to alleviate that damage. Any given level of pollution abatement should be reached by the least costly combination of means available, and the costs of any decrement of pollution should not exceed the benefits obtained by the reduction. Thus, the standard theoretical approach would be to calculate the damage to each receptor from polluted air containing various amounts and kinds of effluents. Such a calculation would permit measurement of the benefits to be expected from proposed abatement projects. Next, one would calculate the cost to each pollutant source of abating its emissions in varying degrees. The optimal allocation of the air resource would then require that pollutants be prevented from entering the atmosphere at levels which would inflict more marginal damage on receptors than the marginal cost to the source of preventing the pollution.[4]

The operational procedure which economists would recommend for achieving this optimal condition would include an evaluation of the damage done by the emission of incremental amounts of pollutant into the air at any given location and time and an assessment of a corresponding charge against the emitters. The charge would thus reflect the marginal costs that the sources impose on others. It would be determined by relating ambient air quality to rates of emission, using air monitoring networks and relatively simple atmospheric diffusion models.

The principal advantage from the economist's point of view of "internalizing" the cost by means of a government-levied charge on the source is that the economic units involved can decide on the best adjustment to be made in light of the costs and benefits they perceive. Those firms which can reduce emission at a cost that would be less than the charge will do so to avoid being assessed the charge. Those firms which *cannot* reduce emissons at a cost that would be less than the charge would elect to pay the fee but would nevertheless have a continuing incentive to reduce emissions. Thus, the optimal level of pollution abatement will be approached by the method that is least costly to society as a whole.

Under this system, management rather than government officials would bear much of the burden of investigation and decision-making, and management is said to be better able to evaluate the advantages and disadvantages of the various ways of dealing with the effluent problem and to choose the best mix. This is held to be preferable to being restricted to any one abatement technique. Implicit in the economist's view is recognition that the optimal level of air pollution abatement is closely tied to the technological processes involved, with the least-cost solution being in many cases a complex combination of process changes and treatment of effluent; in some cases, moreover, the least-cost solution might involve partial abatement and payment of the lower effluent fees associated with the remaining emissions. The continuing incentive provided by the effluent fee to search for additional or alternative ways of abating discharges involves a much different response than that compelled in a straight enforcement action. Enforcement by criminal proceeding or by injunction or cease and desist order, for example, would provide no real alternative to incurring the abatement costs, whatever they might be. Moreover, enforcement programs that would compel the adoption of specific technology would altogether destroy the incentive to explore alternative abatement techniques or to combine approaches to achieve the maximum efficiency in pollution reduction.

A system of effluent fees has additional theoretical appeal because of its adaptability to changing or variable circumstances. Fees can be varied up or down in accordance with weather conditions, the time of day, the season of the year, and other factors in order to correlate emitters' costs even more closely with the damage caused. The theoretical advantage of this flexibility may be difficult to realize in practice, however, and indeed may even prove a liability. Given the vast inadequacy of data and the probabilistic character of the factors that might be reflected in variable fees, the schedule would take on an appearance of arbitrariness that might be difficult to dispel. We have here one key to the unlikelihood that effluent fees will soon play a major role in air quality control.

The primary problems with effluent fees are simply the shortage of data and the lack of agreement on many of the theoretical problems that are presented. The major information deficiency is in the measurement of damages attributable to particular pollutants, and myriad conceptual and informational problems in here in the allocation to individual polluters of the share of the total damages for which they are "responsible." Perhaps most difficult of all is the theoretical problem of allocating damages to specific polluters when synergistic effects occur—that is, where the combination of two or more pollutants, such as sulfur oxides and particulates, causes greater damage than either pollutant could cause alone. Problems of equity are also presented by the need to allocate damage costs between new and existing industries. Finally, there are also doubts that monitoring technology is adequate to permit effective enforcement of an effluent fee system. Especially where there are numerous small polluters to be monitored, such a system would be costly to administer.

Another problem, which must be faced in any regulatory system, with or without effluent fees, has to do with the determination of who should benefit from the use of the air resource. If air is to be treated as a free good for the receptors, including humans, plants, and animals, certain costs are thus imposed on others who may wish to use the air for waste disposal. Theoretical discussions seldom deal with why these costs should not be allocated according to "practical" considerations such as the supposed ability of industry to pass on added costs to consumers and the apparently greater ability of industrial firms to select and apply the least-cost solution (including the possibility of paying adjoining landowners to move or take protective measures). An effluent fee program might be designed to encourage such flexibility, but administrative problems would again seem to be overwhelming in the short run.

While these many problems and data shortages will handicap any program of enforced abatement which purports to compare abatement costs and the benefits derived therefrom, an effluent fee program would also have to survive legal attacks based on arguments of apparent discrimination and abuse of the taxing power. As understanding of the nature of air pollution and pollution damage costs increases, effluent fees may become more feasible and may ultimately fill an important role in air pollution control. But today, while the assignment or sale of emission or receptor rights has theoretical appeal, the pricing of such rights still requires some sort of centralized decision-making system. Such a system, as it might now be constituted in our political and institutional environment, would yield only a few of the advantages that a fully market-oriented system, from which it is conceptually derived, would produce.

Finally, a basic complaint against the theoretical underpinnings of the effluent fee approach has been raised by Wolozin, who states:

My skepticism is based on the unfortunate fact that we do not know enough in an empirical way about the effects of taxation on business policies and human behavior to be at all certain about the outcome of any scheme of tax like effluent fees. Even the underlying theory can be questioned.[5]

This questioned theory is, of course, the conventional neoclassical micro-economic model, which depends upon the postulate of rationality and the concept of the firm as a profit maximizer. Since these assumptions have often been criticized as unrealistic, Wolozin suggests that a more useful approach might be to view the goals of the firm in relation to its position as an organization in a political and social system.[6] Wolozin's point is not well taken, however, for it seemingly ignores three fundamental con-siderations. First, many significant polluters will in fact be entrepreneurs in the traditional sense rather than firms in which management has become independent of ownership, the condition usually cited as having under-mined the profit maximization postulate. Second, the proposition that management generally prefers lower costs to higher is a principle which has never been directly criticized, and it holds largely true even in regulated public utilities where "regulatory lag" permits realization of profits wherever unanticipated cost savings can be accomplished.[7] Finally, Wolozin misses the notable fact that management's presumed social responsibilities, which are so strongly emphasized by those who would contest the profit maximization postulate, are also at work in this field, assisting in the achievement of the social goal of a cleaner environment. One might predict, therefore, that effluent fees, by raising the cost of *not* fulfilling a perceived social responsibility to abate, will yield dividends *greater* than traditional theory would anticipate.

In sum, effluent fees have a solid theoretical foundation, but the practical problems associated with establishing and enforcing a fee schedule appear so great that immediate adoption of this approach seems unlikely. Understanding of the air pollution problem and the regulatory challenge it poses nevertheless requires a grasp of effluent fees' potentiality, since a system of fees may be the ultimate goal toward which regulation should evolve. Vickrey's advocacy of an effluent fee program rests in part on the consideration that it would force the regulator "to bring the problem into perspective, and tends to put something of a restraint on the pure air enthusiast who might at times be inclined to impose standards that would entail too high a cost relative to benefits."[8] One premise of the hypothetical regulatory program developed below is that the cost–

benefit principle can also be implemented in a program of direct regulation and that the lesson Vickrey wants taught can be learned without opting for effluent fees as the dominant regulatory approach.

II
CHOICE OF A CONTROL PHILOSOPHY

A. Alternative Approaches to Control

In addition to the effluent fee approach, payments and direct regulation are other approaches to environmental quality management problems.[9] Direct regulation is somewhat different from the other two in that it is nonfiscal. The payments approach includes not only subsidies but also reductions in taxes that otherwise would be collected. Common examples include the subsidization of particular control equipment, accelerated depreciation, and tax credits for investment in control equipment. Direct regulation includes a mixed bag of licenses, permits, registration, zoning, air quality and effluent standards, and the enforcement of standards through regulatory bodies and the courts.

1. *Payments*—One possible payment system might rely on selective payments to waste contributors for the purpose of motivating them to restrict emission to an optimal degree. These payments would in principle be equivalent to the off-site costs imposed by increments of waste discharged and would vary with atmospheric conditions and effluent location, as well as with the quantity and quality of effluent. Since this sort of payment would be similar in theory but opposite in approach to the effluent fee scheme, the criticisms and difficulties mentioned above would apply here also.

The more typical proposed under the payments heading, however, relates to tax relief or subsidies. Such proposals are a popular topic these days, particularly among industry representatives and members of Congress, but they have only one substantial argument in their favor—there is less resistance to a program of subsidies than to programs of regulation. There are, however, a number of problems with the payments approach. As Mills states:

[T]here is a strong practical argument against most of the policies under the payments heading. They are simply payments for the wrong thing. The investment credit proposal will illustrate the deficiency that is common to others. An investment credit on air pollution abatement equipment reduces the cost of such equipment. But most such equipment is inherently unprofitable in that it adds nothing to revenues and does not reduce costs. To reduce the cost of such an item cannot possibly induce a firm to install it. The most it can do is to reduce the resistance to public pressure for installation. Common sense and scattered bits of evidence suggest that these payments policies are costly and inefficient ways to achieve abatement.[10]

More specifically, it would be difficult to decide how much to pay to whom for any level of pollution abatement since there is no commonly accepted level of air quality from which payments could be computed. The taxpayer's feelings of equity might also be violated since the industrial firm, in not having to consider pollution abatement as a cost of production in the same sense that labor and capital are, would rely on payments raised at least partially by higher taxes on other taxpayers.[11]

Payment schemes, tax credits, or accelerated depreciation may also bias the technique used for control in an uneconomical direction because they tend to promote construction of treatment facilities when adjustments in production processes, products, or inputs might achieve the same result at lower cost and might even increase productivity. Tax writeoffs of capital cost are also at a disadvantage because they are not capable of reducing all abatement costs. It has been estimated that capital cost accounts for only about one eighth of the air pollution abatement costs for a typical firm.[12] Indeed, fuel substitution alone is estimated to be the least-cost alternative in over 60 per cent of the cases involved in air pollution abatement.[13]

Grants and loans have the same objectives as tax writeoffs in that they lower the cost of capital expenditures. Thus the criticisms suggested above apply. However, it has been suggested that if grants were made for both capital and operating costs and administered through air quality management organizations this particular criticism would lose much of its bite. But it must be remembered that extensive reliance on grants and loans suffers from the uncertainty of fluctuations in legislative appropriations.

2. Direct Regulation—Although the ideal method for dealing with the effects of the unidirectional external diseconomies associated with air pollution would be a system of effluent charges, it is often suggested that the best operational method for dealing with practical problems is direct regulation. Existing federal policies on air pollution abatement mostly fall in the category of regulation and enforcement activities.[14] The advantage of this approach is that it permits the government to take interim steps even though it has almost no idea of relevant measurements. For example, if people's eyes were burning because of obvious emissions from an industrial plant, it would be logical to require filtration of these emissions even if one had no way of measuring the amounts of the emissions. Such regulation can be justified since, as a report of the staff of the Senate Committee on Public Works states, "Whatever yardsticks are employed, it is clearly evident that the cost of property damages alone from air pollution is great—far greater than the amounts devoted to its abatement by industry and all levels of government."[15] The implication seems to be that there is little chance of the costs of such a program exceeding the benefits.

Not all economists view direct regulation with complete suspicion. Crocker states:

Given the uncertain quality of available physical, biological, and economic information, and the potentially high costs associated with the gathering of additional information about atmospheric pollution problems, the control authority, in order to impress receptors and emitters with the necessity of regarding the air's two value dimensions as scarce economic resources, appears to be justified in setting minimal standards.[16]

A greater commitment to standards is evident in the writings of Paul Gerhardt, an economist with the National Center for Air Pollution Control. He states:

A polluter faced with the necessity to comply with a law or suffer punishment will generally find the least cost set of control or have no one to blame but himself. He will pass cost increases along to customers in the form of price increases or to equity holders in the form of reduced profit shares. Optimum allocation will be preserved as the public makes new choices about their spending and investing patterns. Administrative costs could be less than for some alternatives as there would be no complicated tax revenue emission charge or payment system to operate.[17]

But, as expected, relative simplicity is not achieved without certain costs. One objection to direct regulation is its allegedly extreme inflexibility which results in considerably higher costs than would more selective abatement. To use an example from water pollution, the Federal Water Pollution Control Administration found in the Delaware River Basin that simple equal-proportional reduction of all waste loads would cost 50 per cent more than achieving the same quality standard by requiring firms to reduce their waste loads in proportion to their harmful effects.[18] In the case of air quality management, the Federal Coordinating Committee on the Economic Impact of Pollution Abatement suggests that the cost of achieving a specific air quality standard could increase by 200 to 400 per cent if equal–proportional reduction on a year-round basis were attempted.[19]

The argument over the desirability of direct regulation cannot be resolved on the merits here. It is perhaps more important, however, to note that government already appears to be committed to direct regulation as the preferred means of dealing with the air pollution problem, although subsidies and tax concessions will continue to appear. While Congress did not see fit in the Air Quality Act to enact the President's proposal for a program of national emission standards for all polluting industries, such standards are still under consideration.[20] Moreover, most state and local abatement programs are based on strict prohibitions of the emission of specified concentrations of pollutants. Against this background, the final section of this article, in developing a hypothetical program of direct regulation, is premised on these judgments, among others: (1) that government has already opted for a direct regulation approach, (2) that such an approach holds fewer dangers of resource misallocation and inequity than would a payments or subsidy program, (3) that direct regulation would be more likely to operate effectively with necessarily imperfect data than would an effluent fee approach, and (4) that its legal status might be somewhat less open to question than an effluent fee program simply because it is somewhat less of a novelty in the spectrum of public policies. Finally, while it is believed that there is already a commitment to regulation, the shape of the regulatory machinery, the details of the policies to be implemented, and the decision-making methodology to be employed do not seem to be finally determined. The hypothetical program is thus framed to encourage maximum flexibility in pursuit of least-cost solution, which economic theory tells us are important and can help us to find.

B. A Larger View of Decision-Making

To this point the review has been over what should be familiar ground. Unfortunately for many practitioners in the field of air quality management, knowledge relating to benefit-cost ratios, marginal cost pricing, and optimal taxing schemes has been secondary to the necessary concern with temperature inversions, wet scrubbers, filters, and the like. This is the case even though air pollution is in a fundamental sense a social and economic problem the solutions to which have to be worked out within a complex political and institutional framework. Technological means are currently available to purify the air to any desired degree, but costs increase significantly as more control is desired.[21] The economist's view of air quality management is important because we are finally perceiving a condition of scarcity so central to his thinking. Air is now viewed as a congested facility, and without the attempt at evaluation he provides, the desirable objective of reducing the level of pollution in the atmosphere by the least costly means possible would be difficult to achieve.

Since pollution abatement is primarily a matter of avoiding costs, programs need to be initially evaluated from an economic point of view for, as Turvey has noted, "even though an economic calculation of gains or losses is often not sufficient to reach a well based decision, it is nearly always an essential preliminary."[22] This determination of sound economic policy in air quality management requires an accurate and continuing evaluation of the costs of abatement relative to air pollution damages.

Viewing costs avoided as benefits, decisions need to be sought that maximize the present value of net benefits.[23] Ideally, this analysis would be directed toward finding abatement efforts that equate incremental abatement costs and the value of incremental damage costs reduced.[24] But even a less sophisticated approach could measure abatement costs so that they include both administrative costs of control and capital and process change costs associated with abatement. Tools of evaluation, whether in sophisticated or crude form, need to be applied not only to the theoretical ideal of effluent fees and charges but also to the actual or potential use of payments and continuous and noncontinuous emission standards under a program of direct regulation.

While direct regulation seems to be emerging as the dominant control philosophy, the regulation to be undertaken may nevertheless comprise subsidies, licenses, permits, effluent charges, emission standards and variances therefrom, emergency powers, and some reliance on market forces. Experimentation with regulatory approaches to determine the best mix of such control techniques is desirable, and this need should be recognized by HEW in its review of state enforcement plans under the Air Quality Act. Such experimentation can be accomplished most readily by a control agency that is given broad powers with discretion to choose the tools needed for particular purposes. The hypothetical regulatory program described below contemplates such experimentation.

The overriding decision-making issue in this field is simply the difficulty of regulating an activity requiring prompt and decisive regulatory attention under conditions of imperfect knowledge, information, and understanding. The need for experimentation stems from these uncertainties. Ridker, commenting favorably on the need to get on with the job of regulating and the desirability of regulatory experimentation, quotes a British air pollution control official as follows:

You Americans behave as if you have sufficient time and money to investigate a problem to death before you decide to act. In Britain we take note of a problem we do not like, take some action to correct the problem, and then do research after the fact to determine whether we were right.[25]

Such a purely seat-of-the-pants approach might not be politically feasible in this country and might be open to legal attack. Nevertheless, regulation must proceed with only partial knowledge, and if sensible and progressive regulation is to be achieved, substantial decision-making powers must be delegated to control agencies along with the discretion to experiment and innovate control approaches. The challenge becomes one of devising an effective decision-making process, with the decision-maker's discretion structured and guided by legal principles, growing technical understanding, and clearly defined legislative goals, and with opportunities for participation by affected parties in the decision-making process. Social science theory can again be turned to, this time for guidance in the shaping of such a regulatory program.

III

THE ROLE OF BARGAINING

Social scientists have developed a plethora of overlapping and competing theories and models of the decision process. The literature on the subject is vast, and any attempt at synthesis here would only result in confusion for the reader.[26] What is needed at this stage is a theoretical framework that relates social, political, and economic behavior to the institutional structures under consideration in a program of air quality management. Such a framework, concerned with the actors in the decision process, the strategies they pursue, the nature of the information available to all parties, and the environment in which decisions are made, would be of great assistance to legislators attempting to develop more rational regulatory institutions for securing pollution abatement. The following discussion may help to provide a conceptual approach to the formulation of an effectively functioning control program.

A. Theory of Conflict Resolution

Significant public policies originate in the conflict of group interests.[27] The peaceful resolution of these conflicts is generally achieved through reconciliation, compromise, or an award process in which both parties agree to accept the verdict of an outside person or agency.[28] Reconciliation relies on discussion to lessen the differences of opinion between the participants. Compromise uses the mediation and conciliation aspects of bargaining, while an award is achieved through arbitration or legal trial. In air quality management or in any other environmental management program none of the three types of resolution can be considered as an independent technique for pollution abatement, although one form might predominate. Indeed, Boulding asserts that reconciliation and compromise might occur simultaneously, that some reconciliation may be necessary before compromise is possible, that there are likely to be elements of discussion and propaganda in bargaining situations, that in arbitration cases or in court proceedings there are often elements of bargaining and reconciliation before the award is announced, and that an award might not be accepted unless it has been preceded by informal reconciliation and bargaining.[29]

Game theory has become one principal avenue for research on conflict resolution, and it is usually defined as the formal study of rational decisions in situations where "two or more individuals have choices to make, preferences regarding the outcomes, and some knowledge of the choices available to each other and of each other's preferences."[30] It is concerned with situations—games of strategy—in which the best course of action for each participant depends on what he expects the other participants to do, with the outcome a function of what choices are made by the other actors. The individual decision units have only partial control over the strategic factors affecting their environment, since the essence of the game is that it involves adversaries whose fates are intertwined. In a sense each group or individual faces a cross-optimization problem in which plans must be adjusted not only to one's own desires and abilities but also to those of others.

Bargaining, which is defined as the process by which a tolerable settlement for all participants is reached,[31] falls within the theory of games but is a species of game in which relatively little progress has been made, partly because it includes situations involving common interest as well as conflict between opponents.[32] Cooperation is useful in this type of game because within some range of possibilities both parties will be better off with a solution, i.e., bargain, than without one. Conflict is involved because within this range of solutions the participants compete for the most favorable distribution of benefits. Thus, while both parties are interested in the adoption of some solution, they have divergent interests with regard to the particular solution that is adopted.[33]

Although bargaining has been widely studied and discussed, it is not always clear, as McKean has pointed out,[34] just how bargaining works. Because of this lack of knowledge, bargaining is often viewed as a constraint in decision-making rather than as a variable that could be manipulated to achieve a least-cost solution.[35] The usual explanation for this situation is that there are no generally accepted operational criteria for determining economic efficiency, that there are many competing groups with diverse interests and values seeking to influence policy-making, and that a variety of political, social, and ethical as well as economic considerations are involved in the making of public economic policy. The policy process involves the striking of balances and the making of compromises more often than the finding of "correct" policies or the choice between "right" and "wrong" in any absolute sense. Given the suggested importance of bargaining in the decision-making process, bargaining should no longer be viewed as a constraint within which one attempts to optimize. There are obvious costs and benefits associated with shifts in bargaining behavior that can be identified. Current and anticipated research on decision-making in air quality management needs to take cognizance of the role of bargaining, and the researcher should seek to identify the costs and benefits attached to any bargaining solution.

While economists and mathematicians have developed highly sophisticated approaches to game theoretic decision-making, such methodology might be only tangentially relevant to decision-making in air quality management. For the social scientist that which is conceptual and rudimentary in game theory is the most valuable.[36] Rather than being thought of as formal "theory," it is now viewed as a framework for analysis which can be adapted and modified according to specific needs. In essence, it provides a point of reference for examining a problem and gaining needed insights without accepting the often unrealistic rules of the game. With this in mind, the following section reviews some of the insights gained in the study of the bargaining aspects of game theory that might have potential application in devising a regulatory framework for air quality management. Because it is within the legislative power to change the rules and context within a particular "game" situation, understanding of the forces at work would assist in making institutional and substantive adjustments that will contribute to more nearly optimal outcomes.

B. Some Insights from Bargaining Theory

1. Continuous Games—Research on conflict situations clearly shows that negotiation and bargaining operate best in situations where the subject in contention can be divided into parts that can be dealt with sequentially. This incrementalism, whether achieved by changes in moves or in value systems, is of considerable importance.[37] To draw the analogy of chess, players move in turn, each moving a piece at a time; the game proceeds at a slow tempo by small increments and is of an indeterminate length. The game changes character in the course of play by a succession of small changes that can be observed and appreciated, with plenty of time for mistakes of individual players or mutual mistakes which can be noticed and adapted to in later play. In an uncertain situation, a person is often saved from making a strategic error if he hesitates, so the capacity to make future decisions is not relinquished.[38]

The decomposition tactic in bargaining can be applied to either threats or to promises, and can be viewed as a necessary prerequisite for making a bargain enforceable. This is so since there is a perception on the part of the participants that future possibilities for agreement will not develop unless mutual trust is created and maintained. The participants need to be confident that each of them will not jeopardize opportunities for future agreement by destroying trust near the start of the game. [39]Such confidence is naturally not always in evidence, so decomposition serves to encourage the same expectations on the part of all participants. An aspect of building mutual expectations is that if a threat can be decomposed into a series of consecutive threats, there is an opportunity to demonstrate to an opponent during his initial reaction to a threat that you "mean business," thereby making the continuous game a learning experience.[40] Although it is possible that future opportunities for bargaining are not anticipated, a semblance of a continuing game can be created by separating the issue at stake into consecutive components. The principle is also apparent that it is poor strategy to require compliance in terms of some critical amount or degree that would be deemed mandatory, for action geared to increments has a greater chance of success than one that has to be carried out either all at once or not at all once some particular point has been reached.

This is a concern of some importance in environmental management situations since they are structurally "lumpier" than chess games. There is no continuous range of choices open to the polluter and the abatement officer. Due to the initial administrative and psychic costs and the initial and marginal capital costs, moves have a considerable impact, and it is usually difficult to project a control situation more than a move or two ahead. The pace of the game can bring things to a head before much experience has been gained or much of an understanding reached unless ways are found to increase the number of possible moves. The use of incrementalism in structuring pollution abatement progress eases the impact of each move and allows the participants to acquire both knowledge of each other and experience with the particular problem at hand. Costs are spread over a longer period of time, and the slower pace of the process and the indeterminate length of the "game" reduce the possibility of crisis. Because of these advantages gained through the use of incrementalism, one would expect that conscious attempts would be made to increase the number of "moves" and extend the life of the game. It is of interest that the Air Quality Act specifies that multiple actions must take place before final regulatory action occurs.[41] These steps make the process more incremental in nature, thus gaining for the participants the advantages described above.

Another aspect of the continuous game which must be considered is that negotiating processes develop certain rituals, and attempts to bypass or reduce these rituals may destroy the negotiating process itself.[42] For example, the parties begin the proceedings with somewhat bombastic statements that set the initial boundaries to the negotiations. There is a period of withdrawal designed to make it appear that the commitments are genuine. The parties know, however, that the commitments are not absolute; otherwise the negotiations would break down. There may follow a process of trading by which mutual concessions are made, and there may have to be a period during which, even though no visible progress occurs, the incipient settlement is in fact developing. The resolution of conflict through bargaining thus involves the difficult institutional problem of arranging these ritual elements in the proper order and proportion.[43] Because legal procedures may be too inflexible to permit the proper mix of ritual elements required by the bargaining and reconciling processes, a formal legal proceeding may often be a poor way of handling a conflict in air pollution control.

2. Focal Point Solutions—In bargains that involve quantification of solutions, such as the setting of emission and ambient air standards, there seems to be some appeal in mathematical simplicity. Outcomes tend to be expressed in even numbers since they provide good "resting places."[44] Thus a compromise at 47 per cent is much less likely than at 50 per cent. Just as the mathematical properties of a game can influence its outcome, the perception by the participants of the historical, cultural, legal, and moral properties of the game can serve to focus expectations on certain solutions. A "focal point"[45] solution has characteristics that distinguish it qualitatively from surrounding alternatives. Unlike the numerical scale, which is too continuous to provide good resting places, qualitative principles are more difficult to compromise, and focal points thus generally depend on qualitative principles. But a commitment to a principle that provides the basis for a numerical calculation which comes out at a specific number may provide the support for a stand at that point.

The outcome of any game can best be characterized by the notion of converging expectations.[46] A good example is the remarkable frequency with which long negotiations over complicated quantitative formulas or shares in some benefits and costs are ultimately influenced by a seemingly irrelevant previous negotiation. Precedent seems to exercise an influence that considerably exceeds its logical importance since both parties recognize it as a focal point. Past bargains become precedents for present situations in that they often remove from conscious consideration many agreements, decisions and commitments that might well be subject to renegotiation as conditions change.[47]

If the outcome of a game is seemingly already determined by the participants' perception of the configuration of the problem itself and where the focal point lies, it would seem that the scope of bargaining skill would be insignificant. But it can be argued that the obvious outcome depends greatly on how the problem is formulated, on what analogies or precedents the definition of the bargaining issue calls to mind, and on the kinds of data that may be available to bring to bear on the question in dispute. Thus bargaining skill in air pollution control can be seen to be important before bargaining actually begins by being able to give prominence to some particular outcomes that would be favorable.

C. Conclusions on Bargaining Theory

Several aspects of the many facets of bargaining have been reviewed. These aspects—incrementalism, ritualization, continuing negotiation, and focal point solutions—all suggest that rationality in bargaining outcomes is a function of basically psychic phenomena. At first this view may appear to run contrary to the accepted economic notion that "rationality" is evident only in the minimum-cost solution. But a broader view of decision making may suggest that the least-cost solution is most readily approximated through procedures which take full cognizance of the psychic elements in any bargaining situation and which channel these elements in the direction of a mutually sought, economically sound goal.

V

THE ON-SITE INCINERATION EXAMPLE

An example of decision-making in air quality management that helps to illustrate the discussion of bargaining is the attempt to reduce particulate emissions in New York City. During the mid–1960's the heightening concern of the public in New York City with air pollution was focused on visible suspended particulates. During this time, more than 90 per cent of the 50,000 complaints received per year by the department of air pollution control were related to visible emissions. Public attention was particularly focused on the approximately 12,000 apartment house and commercial incinerators which emitted an estimated 8,400 to 9,000 tons of particulates per year into the atmosphere. These incinerators became the first important issue in air quality management to face the city administration.

In 1966, responding to public pressure, the city council passed, in some haste, a local law dealing with the reduction of sulfur dioxide emissions from fuel burning, the use of bituminous coal, the upgrading of municipal incinerators, the upgrading of existing private on-site incinerators, and the banning of incineration in new buildings. Of particular interest is the section of the law prohibiting construction of residential and commercial on-site incinerators after May, 1968, and requiring the upgrading of all existing ones.[48] The first deadline under the law was May 20, 1967, a year after its passage. At that time the owners of an unknown number of incinerators in buildings of seven or more stories were to have completed construction of unspecified control equipment to meet criteria for levels of emissions which had at that time not yet been defined. Local Law 14, as it was called, also had a May 29, 1968, deadline for the upgrading of buildings under seven stories. The law states that the process of upgrading includes the "installation and use of an auxiliary gas burner and control apparatus as may be defined by the [commissioner of air pollution control]."[49] Basically the required procedure involved the installation of a firebox that burns the refuse efficiently and a scrubber system—a motor-driven device to force the smoke through a special water bath that will remove the heavy particulates. Only compactors would be permitted in new multiple dwellings. This fairly direct attempt at controlling particulate emissions, although not an ideal approach, might seem to some people a useful first step in the direction of cleaner air. Unfortunately it was not.

Why was this the case? The initial problem was that the department of air pollution control had relatively little time to develop specific criteria for upgrading as required under the law. As a result, the criteria were not formally adopted by the board of air pollution control until five months before the actual upgrading of the first group of apartment houses was to have been completed. A second problem was that the department of air pollution control had no enforcement powers to require compliance before the May 20, 1967, deadline. The options were to seal every non-complying incinerator on or after that date or expedite compliance later. The first deadline came and passed with few completed upgradings. At one time about 60 incinerators were under seal by the department. This state of affairs was partially due to questions that were raised as to who would *not* be required to upgrade their equipment. In an interpretation of Local Law 14 the city corporation counsel ruled that the law permitted every incinerator which had been installed before on-site incinerators became mandatory in 1951 to be closed down voluntarily rather than upgraded. Then, in August, 1967, the corporation counsel interpreted the absence of any incinerator provision in the new city housing maintenance code to mean that almost all existing incinerators were now "voluntary" and could close down rather than upgrade, which meant that the owner might convert to refuse chutes and handle raw or compacted refuse.

An additional complication was a virtual moratorium that was declared on public statements on the issue by the city administration on the ground that the commissioner of air pollution control was being sued by the New York Real Estate Board and some private real estate interests for imposing a law that was deemed to be "arbitrary and capricious." Another factor was that the department of sanitation was not prepared to collect an unknown amount of refuse that formerly was burned. Although there were other reasons why the sanitation department could not be counted on to collect the refuse, the Department cannot be blamed for viewing with alarm the prospect of picking up some unspecified amount of refuse that was previously burned in on-site incinerators.

As a result of these developments the city administration finally decided that the law in its original form was unworkable. On the basis of the experience gained, the law was amended in two ways that are more in agreement with the minimum cost approach and bargaining theory. These amendments related to the generation of alternatives to upgrading and the time of compliance dates.

Before the amendments were introduced, a cost study of the alternative ways of approaching the problem of reducing particulate emissions from on-site incinerators was carried out.[50] The study considered the varying size of buildings, operating expenses, labor costs, capital investment, and the distribution of unit costs among a number of apartments. The results of this research indicated that the larger buildings would find it most economical to upgrade and that middle-sized buildings could be left to decide for themselves whether it would be cheaper to compact or to upgrade. It was predicted that only buildings which had about 50 units or less per incinerator would find it more economical to shut down. Using these data, the department of air pollution control estimated the refuse output from the projected shutdowns and determined that the department of sanitation could handle the additional volume of a three-year period. Although the actual amendment to the law as passed by the city council did not include giving the option to every landlord to choose the method which he considered to be the cheapest, the option to shut down for buildings with forty or fewer dwelling units per incinerator was passed as a direct result of the economic analysis.

Another amendment provided a deadline for submission of compliance plans six months prior to the completion deadline. Various strategies of noncompliance that were so successful under the original law have a much lower probability of success now that the department of air pollution control can use an incremental approach to pollution abatement, which will avoid unexpected reactions and smooth out the "lumpy" features of compliance programs. In keeping with bargaining theory, the "game" is spread out over a longer period of time.

The on-site incinerator example did not, of course, involve bargaining except in a very general sense, since the behavior that was observed involved noncompliance on the one hand and frustrated attempts at enforcing an unrealistic ordinance on the other. The sample does, however, clearly convey both the relevance of decision theory to explain the way decisions are made and the importance of comprehending the least-cost principle in a program of direct regulation. Some further reflection on the role of bargaining as it is apt to evolve in air pollution control programs and other environmental management programs should suggest that the least-cost solution can and should be sought in a regulatory program, both by explicit recognition of the cost-benefit nexus and by giving bargaining a chance to function in conjunction with market forces. Indeed, it is possible to assert that regulation strategically employing cost–benefit analysis and market forces can yield solutions to particular pollution control problems that the regulators themselves are not wise enough to devise.

VI
DEVISING A HYPOTHETICAL REGULATORY SCHEME:
BARGAINING AND THE LEAST-COST SOLUTION

A. The Shape of Regulatory Programs, Present and Future

New York City's amended incinerator rules represent an across-the-board legislative attempt to control gross pollution from a very common type of emitter. While bargaining theory explains in some measure the experience with the original attempt and the evolution of the amendments, no opportunity for individual bargaining was actually observed. However, control of other types of pollution will almost necessarily involve ad hoc regulation of individual industrial polluters who cannot appropriately be dealt with by general legislation or rule-making.[51] In these circumstances face-to-face bargaining will be almost essential as a means of dealing with individual polluters.

As local air pollution control ordinances and statutes are now formulated, bargaining does not have a clear chance to operate, though practice almost inevitably opens some opportunities for give and take between polluters and the control agency in both the standard setting and compliance stages. Most of the legislation, which appears to have been modeled after zoning legislation, either establishes fixed emission standards or delegates the setting of the contemplated standards to the control agency. Because fixed standards not only conflict with the least-cost principle but may raise potential constitutional problems, the statutes generally provide for variances to be granted by the agency. A typical variance provision is this one from the Illinois statute:

The Board may grant individual variances beyond the limitations prescribed in this Act, whenever it is found, upon presentation of adequate proof, that compliance with any provision of this Act, or any rule or regulation, requirement or order of the Board, will result in an arbitrary and unreasonable taking of property or in the practical closing and elimination of any lawful business, occupation or activity, in either case without sufficient corresponding benefit or advantage to the people.[52]

The hardship required to be shown is a considerable one, though much is left to agency and court interpretation. One would have to conclude that, while the typical statutory language appears to permit variances only in extreme cases—perhaps only in those having constitutional dimension[53]—an agency might, by seizing on the requirement that there be a "corresponding benefit or advantage," indulge in as much comparison of benefits and costs as it might wish. On balance, however, existing legislation appears to give less than sufficient sanction to methods of finding least-cost solutions.

The Air Quality Act of 1967 provides that states shall give effect to federally determined air quality criteria and control techniques once they are promulgated by HEW, which is also granted power to review the standards established and the proposed plan of enforcement.[54] It was apparently contemplated by Congress that new state and local legislation would be forthcoming, and this expectation, coupled with a fairly clear congressional mandate that pollution control be undertaken selectively in light of technological and economic feasibility,[55] suggests that new thought should be given to devising machinery that will be capable of doing this job most effectively. Indeed, if the concepts of "technological and economic feasibility" are equated with cost–benefit analysis, the question arises whether many existing regulatory schemes might fail to meet the approval of HEW. The issue that is raised is whether the federal act would justify HEW disapproval of state and local legislation on the ground of heavyhandedness, or lack of willingness to discriminate among polluters on the basis of the many economic and administrative factors that are comprised in an optimal, least-cost solution. The act suggests that review is limited to assuring only that maximum effectiveness is achieved,[56] and HEW may be motivated to review only for weakness and not for potential economic hardship on polluters.

The remainder of this article, drawing on these speculations, sets forth some ideas about the shape and function of air quality management programs that can best approximate least-cost solutions. As noted earlier, the outlook is for programs of direct regulation rather than for the sort of effluent fee approach advocated by the welfare economist. While the data shortages that prevent implementation of effluent fees will also plague programs of direct regulation, the latter approach is more familiar and, as noted earlier, can probably sustain a greater amount of regulation in relative ignorance than could a more novel system. But in keeping with the "new federalism," which is often praised as lending itself to experimentation and innovation in ways of attacking particular problems, HEW should not, in exercising its supervisory powers, restrict states to traditional patterns of regulation. Indeed, the regional approach to regulation specified by the Air Quality Act would seem to anticipate and encourage new departures. Such innovation and experimentation at the regional level might produce significantly improved regulatory procedures.[57]

B. Structuring a Regulatory Program to Facilitate Bargaining

The regulatory setup we conceive of in the following discussion is the one most common in other systems of direct economic regulation. It features an independent regulatory body (the "commission") supported by a staff of legal and technical experts. Membership on the commission is for a relatively long fixed term, and, because of the nature of the issues to be encountered, the members might be required to have expertise of specified types. Thus, a three-member commission might comprise a lawyer, an economist, and a pollution control engineer. The commission would operate as an independent decision-maker, and its final rulings would be subject to judicial review. The agency staff bears the major enforcement burden and provides the evidence and expertise which guides the commission's efforts.

Any attempt to hypothesize about the outlines of an enforcement program that attempts to approach a least-cost solution through administrative means must recognize the desirability of avoiding the use of litigation before either judicial or administrative tribunals as the primary means of achieving abatement in individual cases. The limitations of both legal and technical staff resources, the importance of achieving prompt relief, the difficulty of resolving difficult and highly uncertain technical issues in an adversary proceeding, and the considerable administrative costs involved, all point to the need for minimizing the use of litigation whenever possible.[58] The approach that would be most helpful in achieving this objective would be to structure regulation to encourage the use of bargaining and settlements as the primary means of accomplishing regulatory objectives. Such a structuring would most likely include the following conditions:

(1) The control agency's regulations should provide for establishment of formal communication with both actual and potential polluters. Thus it might be required that all polluters withi the agency's jurisdiction file reports with the agency on their present emission levels and perhaps a ten-year estimate of anticipated increases or decreases in these emissions. Other continuing contact would also be desirable, and informal conferences could be called that would bring the agency staff, trade associations, and other interest groups together to discuss the local problems. The author's interviews with Los Angeles Air Pollution Control District personnel confirm that informal conferences have been a key element in successfully controlling stationary sources of pollution.

(2) The agency's potential sanctions must be substantial but flexible enough so that they could be adjusted to the nature and magnitude of each particular problem confronted. Massive fines for emitting a small amount of pollution, for example, would be a poor agency strategy since it would distort the credibility of the agency's image as an arbiter of the public interest.

(3) The sanctions must put no premium on delay. Thus, a retroactive effluent charge, perhaps accumulating from the date of the agency's complaint, might be provided as a means of compelling a polluter to engage in bargaining in good faith. Filing of a complaint would thus constitute in itself a significant sanction and would most likely lead to bargaining before a formal proceeding was initiated, much as the Federal Power Commission and the Federal Communications Commission have tended to bargain for rate reductions without starting a formal rate case.[59] With this strategy, bargaining would also be encouraged after a complaint was filed.

(4) Paradoxically, although the agency's sanctions must be strong enough to encourage polluters to bargain in good faith, they should probably not be so strong as to allow the agency to enforce its will without some recourse to bargaining. This surprising condition—that

weaker sanctions may be desirable—is dictated by the conclusion of studies of mixed conflict and cooperation situations that the "game" will not be considered in good faith unless each side has something to win and something to lose, and that both must be in a position to lose if an outcome is not achieved. The final sanction of formal proceedings can and should be costly to both the agency and the polluter. Both this and the previous condition reflect the fact that inequality or imbalance in the strength of each party's sanctions will bias the outcomes of bargaining. The proper balance may be difficult to achieve but must be sought if something approximating the optimal, least-cost solution is to be arrived at.

(5) If informed bargaining is to operate to the public's advantage, the agency must be adequately staffed so that it is known that its sanctions will not go uninvoked if agreement is not reached or if bargaining is not conducted in good faith. The abatement of 90 per cent of the emissions from stationary sources of air pollution in Los Angeles County, for example, was achieved in part through the efforts of several hundred air pollution control district employees. The New York experience recited above also illustrates the importance of credibility of sanctions.

(6) Public utility regulation points to the fact that the public's representatives at the bargaining table must be neither altogether free of nor unduly subject to political influence, in order, first, that excessive zeal or laxness can be checked and, second, that polluters may not accomplish through influence what they are unable to achieve by negotiation. Judging with respect to this one point, one might argue that the regulatory framework has been more effective in Los Angeles County than in New York City. California legislation authorizes any county to set up its air pollution control district by resolution of the county board of supervisors declaring the need for the district to function. The districts are granted the power to "make and enforce all needful orders, rules, and regulations."[60] and Los Angeles County was given considerable latitude in attacking its local problems. New York City, like Los Angeles County, has the power to adopt and enforce rules and regulations and authority to require permits and control devices on pollution-generating equipment.[61] but experience to date as was revealed by the on-site incinerator study, has been that the city council has actively intervened in the department's regulatory program. A comparative study of the two agencies shows that Los Angeles Air Pollution Control District has had much more freedom in the development of rules and regulations.[62]

(7) Experience with other types of regulation also suggests the desirability of maintaining public control of administrative discretion through openness in decision making. Thus, the data submitted by both the polluter and the agency staff, the terms of the settlement itself, the staff's reasons for accepting it, and the commission's approval should be on

public file.[63] Also useful might be annual or more frequent reports of settlements, together with underlying data, which could be used by the legislative body to which the agency is responsible.[64]

(8) A final precondition for effective bargaining is a clearly defined legal framework within which bargaining can operate. This is essential so that the bargainers—the agency staff and the individual polluter—can largely avoid differences on questions of legal principle while concentrating on the development of the technical and economic data needed to reach a judgment about potential least-cost solutions.[65] Included among the many issues that ideally need to be resolved and eliminated from dealings with individual polluters are as many of the overriding facts as possible about the air pollution problem in the particular airshed. Such questions as estimates of pollution damage in general and attribution of this damage to particular pollutants would be best resolved authoritatively after public hearings open to all interested parties. Bargaining with individual polluters could then proceed without calling these matters back into question. Further discussion below considers how certain specific issues are better resolved in general agency rule-making proceedings than in case-by-case bargaining or adversary proceedings.

If conditions such as the foregoing could be created, face-to-face bargaining could be made to serve an important function in the administration of an effective air pollution control program. It is argued that the advantages would be many, including the establishment of cooperative attitudes between regulators and industry, which would encourage a joint search for solutions to problems; a de-emphasis of fact finding through quasijudicial processes and the avoidance of "swearing contests," which are characteristic of adversary proceedings requiring expert testimony; speed, flexibility, and efficiency in the sense that appellate proceedings and time-consuming judicial review would be avoided; and a more efficient use of technical administrative, and legal staffs.

C. Toward a Least-Cost Solution

There is an axiom among engineers that one can "go slow by running too fast." Although this statement can be interpreted by control officials with some justification as a polluter's excuse for doing nothing, the establishment of the preconditions for an effective control program is a case where the axiom applies. The structuring of the process that will produce efficient resource allocation depends in large part, as we have noted, on the decisions of the legislators who create the sanctions and provide the enforcement staff and on the establishment of a clear legal and factual framework within which to operate. Since a prime objective is to keep as many issues as possible out of litigation, the agency needs the authority to negotiate concerning factual uncertainty. Given the state of the art in environmental management, the legislators need to realize that the "best guess" approach requires that some substantial degree of discretion be given to the agency and its technical staff.

The commission will begin developing the necessary legal and factual framework by holding public hearings as a prelude to authoritative findings on these factual issues:

(1) The total damages attributable to air pollution in the airshed.

(2) The allocation of these damages to each pollutant or each major group of sources. The findings on these first two points need not be sufficiently detailed to satisfy a welfare economist, and it is obvious that the goal is simply the best estimates possible.

(3) An inventory of emissions, including the total amount of each pollutant emitted at particular times and in particular areas.

(4) The relationship of emission levels to the assimilative capacity of the ambient air. This would be determined by using a relatively simple atmospheric diffusion model and air quality monitoring devices. Thus, New York City is now putting into operation an aerometric system of monitoring stations which record and transmit data on levels of sulfur dioxide, dustfall, suspended particulates, and smoke shade on a continuous basis to the department of air pollution control; New York has also developed a simple model which fairly accurately describes the complex diffusion of pollutants in the city.

(5) The objectives of the abatement program, stated in terms of air quality and the level of damages anticipated as optimal for the airshed as a whole.[65a]

Some of the foregoing factual judgments would be based in part on the air quality criteria to be issued by HEW under the Air Quality Act.[66] Additional evidence would be required, and the agency's conclusions should be buttressed by subsidiary findings and a reasoned opinion. All such findings would be subject to periodic review and revision, each time following the procedures employed in the initial formulation. Taken all together, these findings should give a sufficiently clear picture to allow our decision-making and bargaining framework to begin functioning.

An additional matter that the agency would probably find it appropriate to resolve in a rule-making proceeding is the development of a generalized technique for determining a polluter's contribution to the region's overall concentration of pollutants. Once this issue was settled in principle, the questions at issue with each polluter would be (1) his respective contribution of pollutants to concentrations in the ambient air, which would probably be fairly close to the proportion of total emissions for which he was responsible, adjusted for such factors as wind, timing of emissions, and stack height; and (2) the polluter's costs associated with varying levels of abatement.

Ideally the agency staff would be able to negotiate effectively within this framework of settled legal and economic principles and authoritative general findings of fact concerning the extent and danger of pollution. The issues at stake in the bargaining with individual polluters would be almost exclusively factual and would be susceptible to quantified solutions, thus facilitating some compromise in areas of valid doubt. Focal point bottlenecks could be largely avoided since matters of legal and economic principle would have been eliminated for the most part by rule-making; where legal questions did arise they could be set aside for separate authoritative decision by the commission. Such procedures would allow time for incrementalism to operate to narrow gradually the range of possible results, and the continuing negotiating machinery, which would be focused primarily on technical issues, would provide a hospitable climate for the resolution of these issues.[67]

The strategy of a least-cost solution within a bargaining framework suggests that the legislative body to which the control agency is responsible must clean its own house first by upgrading or abandoning any municipal incinerators it operates and reducing the emission levels from governmental heating and generating plants. This is necessary to avoid the embarrassing—and legitimate—charge that a governmental jurisdiction is forcing the private sector to clean up its pollution while continuing to pollute the air itself. This has been a continuing accusation in New York City where the municipal incinerators had not been upgraded by the time private on-site incinerators were to be upgraded.

The agency's next move would be to tackle the sources of air pollution which can have their levels of pollutant emissions reduced in fairly straightforward ways that clearly yield greater benefits than costs. This might mean that the agency should proceed against those polluters who are perceived by both the control agency and the public at large as the most significant polluters of the atmosphere in the jurisdiction, but not always. For example, it is now recognized in New York City that the formulators of Local Law 14 made a strategic error in the structuring of the legislation by requiring that initial action be taken against on-site incinerators even though they were a source of easily visible localized particulate concentrations.

Initial agency action, in addition to avoiding potential charges of being "arbitrary and capricious," must consider the impact of highly localized costs in relation to diffuse benefits and whether the technological and administrative solutions to problems are at hand. In the New York case, it can clearly be argued that a much greater reduction of air pollution could have been achieved at a lower cost to individual polluters by proceeding initially against the emissions of sulfur oxides and particulates resulting from the burning of fuel oil. A technical solution—switching to low-sulfur oil—was available which could be implemented without too much difficulty.[68] In fact, due to difficulties involved in getting thousands of on-site incinerators upgraded or shut down, the program to change to a low-sulfur fuel, which was initiated after the incinerator upgrading, yielded tangible benefits much sooner.

Selecting the initial target in this manner has considerable implications in terms of later control efforts. A demonstrated success gives the agency a good image, reflects positively on the elected officials who give the agency support, and lessens the opposition of businessmen to control efforts aimed at them. The stage is also set for conflict resolution procedures such as negotiation and bargaining rather than for the polarization of attitudes that results in litigation.

One of the more important matters that should concern a control agency operating under our system is the establishment of a method of determining the maximum abatement expenditure—or level of abatement —that could be required of an individual polluter. This complex question has practical importance because all polluters cannot be attacked at once and the marginal unit abatement costs apparently justified when pollution levels are high will seem inappropriate when more nearly tolerable concentrations have been achieved.[69] All polluters should be subject to the same maximum, however, and the derivation of this maximum is extraordinarily difficult. A very rough figure can be derived, however, if air quality standards or goals—indicators of the level of air quality desired within a given jurisdiction—have been developed from objectives and constraints specified in the legislative process and in HEW's air quality criteria. Beginning with these goals, which will necessarily include estimates of the abatement outlays required to achieve them,[70] the agency can arrive at a general estimate of the theoretical emission level at which all marginal expenditures would equal marginal benefits. No polluter should be required to abate below that emission level which he would be permitted to maintain under such optimal conditions, or, in other words, to pay more for a unit of abatement than would yield a net gain if optimal conditions prevailed.

CONCLUSION

Optimizing methods are a guide to decisions, not a philosopher's stone that substitutes for decision. With a view to achieving practical results, it has been pointed out how bargaining might contribute to finding a least-cost solution. Although bargaining is often viewed as a distributional device rather than one that promotes efficiency, it has been shown that the latter view can also be taken. Having been directed, or having found it expedient, to adopt a cost-benefit approach, the control agency would be responsive within our framework to polluters' arguments based on a comparison of marginal benefits and costs associated with alternative emission reduction techniques. The polluter would most likely be inclined to hold our for the lowest-cost remedy and to develop and advance in the negotiations alternative ways of accomplishing the objectives being sought—an advantage, it will be recalled, usually associated exclusively with effluent fees as a control mechanism. Market forces will thus aid the controllers in seeking the most efficient approach to pollution damage reduction. For these reasons the outcome of a properly structured bargaining process should not deviate too far from economic rationality.

The hypothetical regulatory program we have outlined probably represents an ideal difficult to achieve in our society today. Why it may be so is a matter for conjecture and concern, and the most pessimistic conclusions one might draw is that the law and the legal system are in many respects incompatible with the scientific pursuit of optimal conditions under constraints of uncertainty.[71] We have proposed a scientific approach to pollution control requiring gross estimates of pollution damage and abatement costs. A problem of concern in this framework is the difficulty of making damage and cost estimates having enough objective validity to withstand legal attack when viewed as the product of a hearing record which must contain "substantial evidence" to support the result reached. In many repects informed guesses will be all that the control commission can show, and honesty should compel the commission to admit the depth of human ignorance on the questions in issue and to acknowledge frankly that its findings are made for the purpose of getting on with the abatement job. Courts would then be faced clearly with the problem of allowing regulation to proceed in the dim light of partial knowledge or to cease until science can provide light enough to satisfy the judicial sense of what due process requires.

Experience with the regulatory process in general suggests, however, that agencies do not as a rule confess ignorance but rather pretend to omniscience. While often not disclosing the true basis for their decisions and allowing their opinions to be written in "judge proof" boilerplate by their legal staffs, the agencies assume an air of knowledgeability that belies more than it reveals. This attitude might work in air pollution control as well, and the temptation to adopt it will be great. Control commissions may prefer to fill their opinions with statistics and data and to conclude by solemnly declaring, "Having considered all of the evidence and the relevant legal principles. . . ." The results may be unimpeachable for the simple reason that the underlying principles relating such items as costs to benefits are not stated and thus not subject to review. The alternative may be unattractive in administrative circles because the necessary estimates are of such precariousness that they can be defended only by candor about the depth of the problem and by apparent conscientiousness in approaching it. Nevertheless, the courts should learn to insist on full disclosure in lieu of obfuscation. Once this is obtained, judicial review should then require only the exercise of the agency's expert judgment on the best information and data available, incomplete and unsatisfying as it may seem. In no event should the courts prevent effective regulatory action solely because science has not yet yielded the secrets needed to realize the regulatory ideal.

Part Seven

Resources Administration

Many policy discussions are focused on the great public institutions of democracy—like Congress, the Presidency, or the Supreme Court. But only a portion of policy is made in these high places. Policy actually gets its real substance in the lower courts and at various bureaucratic levels.

As problems and information are communicated to the formal decision-making organs of government, natural resources administrators have many opportunities to become important in the process. They often can determine which problems are to become political issues. It is also their business to collect, analyze, sort, and forward information on the problem area. The results of their study can reflect the perspective which they have of an issue, without calling into question their professional status. They are quite often the recognized "experts" on their own subject matter and have developed contacts in the public sphere who can be mobilized readily to support the agency position.

After a formal policy decision is made, it is communicated throughout the organization for implementation by the administrators. Here again they have an opportunity to exert great influence. As a general policy is put into operation, it often requires secondary decisions to spell out functional details which result from administrative decisions. Such further amplifications and policies are made following the experience of executing policy upon the public constituency.

Administrative factors—such as the competence and training of the administrative personnel and the nature of the organizational framework, whether decentralized or centralized, large or small—also come into play. Thus the substance of natural resource policy may often lie within the resource agency; and its personnel may be the most important policy-makers around. Administration is always important; in natural resources, it is vital.

Fortunately there is a rich literature in resources administration. Among those who have made significant contributions to the knowledge of the environment are researchers on public administration. Here are included the contributions of four of them: Stanley A. Cain has written on "Environmental Management and the Department of the Interior;" George R. Hall has analyzed multiple use policy; Vincent Ostrom has studied administration centered on one resource—water; and Joseph L. Fisher takes a look at "Resources Policies and Administration for the Future."

Stanley A. Cain

Environmental Management and the Department of the Interior*

No organism can exist except in relation with its environment. Life itself is a constant interaction of the living body and its environment. Energy flow and cycling of substances are constant phenomena within a living organism as well as between it and its environment. While the environment sustains life, living processes change the environment, and while the conservation of energy and matter has ultimate pertinence, many things can go wrong for an organism, a species, or a community. What is evolution in one case, granted an appropriate time scale, is catastrophe in another. Although there is a geochemistry, a geobiology, and a global ecological system, there is an immediate significance related to site—the conditions at a particular place and time.

Man is no exception. He, too, is both creature and creator of his environment. In a strictly biological sense, contemporary man is little different from early hominoids of tens of thousands of years ago; but in a technological sense, as a manager of his environment, man has no congener. He is one of a kind. The biological, physical, and social scientists will continue to specify how and why man became what he is, and humanists, philosophers, and poets will offer other explanations. For present purposes, however, it is sufficient to point to man's social organization, to his proclivity to institutionalize his actions for cooperative effort, to his tool-making, and, perhaps especially, to his harnessing of external energy to supplement the physiological energy of food expended on work by muscle and brain.

Beavers build dams, migratory birds and fish make their amazing thousand-mile voyages, physiological sensory receptors allow subtle communication and muscle power applied to primitive tools built the pyramids and Amerind temples, but these accomplishments permit only the faintest comparisons with modern feats of man that derive from machines driven by the energy of fossil fuels, hydroelectricity, and nuclear power.

*Reprinted from *Public Administration Review*, XXVIII (July–Aug., 1968), 320–326. (By permission of the American Society for Public Administration.)

Social and industrial development have been slow, halting, and un-
even through the millenia. Only in recent centuries, starting perhaps with
steam engines, and especially in recent decades with electrical power, has
physical change become explosive. It is not surprising, then, that the high
dam, the bulldozer, and the nuclear bomb have become the *bête noire* of
some, while to others the scientist and engineer have become the high
priests of progress. The forces for environmental change have outpaced
our institutional inventions for environmental management.

Enough of the conditions that we live with have become unsatisfactory to many of us that it is timely for the PUBLIC ADMINISTRATION
REVIEW to take a look at public administration and the shaping of the
human environment.

Secretary Stewart L. Udall has referred to the Department of the
Interior as a department of natural resources. He has also stressed its
conservation orientation in resources management and the ecological
basis for its vast and intertwined responsibilities. Furthermore, he is the
architect of its national image and the instigator of its growing concern
for the urban and densely populated regions of the nation. The goal of
maintaining a quality environment where it exists and restoring where
possible an environment of quality for all the people is a fundamental
administrative reorientation from the days when Interior was mainly a
"Department of the West" and patron of those who were concerned with
the extraction of economic goods from the environment.

For an evaluation of what this means to the administration of such a
department, it is necessary to look at some of the words that are used.
My definitions follow:

Environment is the aggregate of surrounding things, conditions, and
influences to which an organism is sensitive and capable of reacting, man
included.

Natural resources for man are the things, conditions, and processes in
the environment that he has the personal, technical, economic, social,
political, or other capability to use; that is, to turn into a good or a
service.

Human resources are man's personal and social capabilities to meet his
needs, especially through his institutionalized means for cooperative
action for social or community benefit.

Ecology is the fledgling science, growing in sophistication, that is
concerned with interactions between life and environment. As a consequence, to think ecologically is to try to cope with systems as they exist
in nature and society; to synthesize rather than just analyze; to try to see
problems whole, not only their parts; and to be concerned for the consequences of separate actions.

Conservation is a philosophy and a program of action based upon
ecological understanding of the world about us and of ourselves. It is

directed to the management of the environment and its riches of resources for achieving greatest net benefits over time. It is a theory and practice of use, rather than nonuse as many mistakenly believe, or as some perversely argue for self-serving ends. Even an inviolate sanctuary of nature serves some human ends, although these ends are not necessarily commodities and a market economy.

The problems of conservation management—of environmental management and of natural resource management—are those of allocation of resources to uses, some of which are incompatible at places and times, according to national goals or, more broadly, to those of humanity.

The Department of the Interior is so sprawling, its statutory missions so diverse, its capability for environmental management (or mismanagement, for that matter) so great that it is impossible to do more than suggest its scope in the present context. . . .

AGENCY MISSIONS AND FUNCTIONING

Of Interior's two dozen bureaus, services, and offices, all have some role in environmental management, and some have very important roles. I cannot report on all of them, nor in detail about any of them. A few of them can be grouped because they are responsible for public lands and resources that are largely in a natural condition, have a strong biological base, and receive minor management only.

The National Park System includes more than 26 million acres. The work of the National Park Service is less involved in actively shaping the environment than in keeping a bit of it from being bent completely out of shape. This applies clearly to the great national parks and similar national monuments and to some small but precious natural areas in the new category of recreation units, such as the national seashores. Ranging from large landscapes to local ecological complexes, they preserve vignettes of the pristine continent, reminding us of the vast changes we have wrought in a few centuries, sometimes in decades.

The Bureau of Sport Fisheries and Wildlife, with its nationwide system of wildlife refuges and game ranges, manages a public land estate of over 28 million acres, comparable to the National Park System in that much of the system is essentially wild and the management constructions minimal. In cooperation with other federal agencies and the states, the bureau is concerned with the quality of most continental waters.

In my opinion, these two agencies have had tremendous influence on public concern for conservation and the recent developing awareness of the accumulative deteriorative and destructive processes affecting our environment. The public sense of the profound importance of the quality of the environment is demonstrated only in part by the more than 150 million visits to the park and refuge system last year. Many millions of sportsmen and nature lovers are aware of the contrast between the beauty, naturalness, and integrity of these well-managed properties and often the unplanned, mismanaged, and ugly look of contiguous private properties, as well as our widely abused landscape. The policies of these agencies are ecologically based and help foster in Americans a perception of the unity of the world about us.

An earlier public awareness was an indispensable requirement for the creation of the Bureau of Outdoor Recreation. Although it administers no lands, it administers the Land and Water Conservation Fund which other agencies—federal, state, and local—need in their land programs. The bureau's programs are directed toward planning for preserving and enhancing the outdoor environment, not only in the countryside but also in the cities.

The Bureau of Commercial Fisheries, concerned largely with coastal waters and the open ocean, like the National Park Service, works with nature as yet little-affected by human management except for those species, such as salmon, which use the estuaries and migrate into fresh waters to spawn.

The Bureau of Land Management's responsibility for the residual public domain of nearly one-half billion acres makes it the nation's largest land manager. Although much of this land has been used, even abused, vast acreages, especially in Alaska and the mountainous West, are still wildlands, and present policies incorporate the best management principles.

Although the programs of the agencies already mentioned have a strong base in natural landscapes and their protection, they are clearly and properly oriented to human needs. The Bureau of Indian Affairs and the Office of Territories are similar in that they assist in the management of land and water resources; they differ in that the human interests are principally those of residents on the properties or with ties relating to the special federal trusteeship. These beneficiaries include nearly 400,000 American Indians, Aleuts, and Eskimos, and some 200,000 persons in the United States territories and the Trust Territory of the Pacific Islands. They seek to make the best use of both the human and natural resources. These assignments are as difficult and challenging as the terrain and climate (often raw, rugged, and not very rich), as obscure as the path to the human mind, and as rewarding as the material benefits of the resources that can be taken from the environment. Indian reservations and the territories include some of the *cul-de-sacs* of the modern world, in the past promising little for human greed and the technical capacity to fulfill it. Management emphasis today is on human resources and their better utilization, some of it through the extraction of natural resources, but much of it in recognition of the beauty of landscape that attracts tourists, and thereby brings indirect benefit to cultural and economic development.

I turn now to a different constellation of Interior's agencies. The Geological Survey has been describing and interpreting the environment for nearly a century, a prerequisite for intelligent efforts to shape, control, or preserve it. It maps the physical and cultural features of the land and by aerial photographs provides a record of changes over time, thus forming a basis for land use planning and interpretation. The structural and historical geology of the nation provides a guide to useful minerals and fuels, and is basic to an understanding of soils. Reliable knowledge about water is necessary for inland navigation, flood control, power development, irrigation, municipal and industrial water supplies, pollution abatement, fish and wildlife, and recreation. Geological research plays a supporting role for many federal agencies, state programs, and private enterprises on land, at sea, and in space.

The Bureau of Mines is oriented to research and information services, with some regulatory functions relating to health and mine safety. Minerals, metals, and fuels touch every aspect of daily life through agriculture, manufacturing, transporation, communication, and security, and these activities affect the environment in myriad ways.

The programs of both these bureaus are aimed at minimizing ecological disturbances while providing maximum goods and services to the nation. While industry cannot be made subject to injurious regulation that would seriously disrupt our way of life, primary and concurrent attention must be given to the protection of living and other resources of air, land, and water. This produces an obvious need for reconciliation of diverse objectives and establishment of priorities among natural resource uses, especially when there are incompatibles at a given place.

Other interests in the field of energy are well illustrated by the Bonneville Power Administration. Its mission is to market power from federal hydroelectric projects in the Pacific Northwest. In order to accomplish this, BPA constructs, operates, and maintains a regional electric transmission system with regional interconnections. Control of the Columbia River system for optimum multipurpose use includes flood control, navigation, irrigation, municipal and industrial water supplies, recreation, fish and wildlife interests, as well as power development. As hydroelectric sites diminish, the region will turn to thermal generation, especially nuclear-fueled plants.

High dams, large impounds, thermal plants and transmission lines have numerous impacts on the environment. The Bonneville Power Administration is concerned at all times with the physical and social effects of its program. Its power sales contracts have long incorporated a natural resources conservation clause for the Columbia Gorge. Now this feature is extended to the service region.

With the advent of high multiple-purpose dams, the Bureau of Reclamation came into the hydroelectric business. The bureau program includes numerous environmental benefits, such as: 43 million acre-feet of active storage capacity allocated to flood control, 546 billion gallons of water provided for municipal and industrial needs, and irrigation water for over 8 million acres of land (paid for, in most part, by power revenues). It does research to aid development and conservation of water resources, to enhance water supply by weather modification, and to reduce losses by evaporation. Silt retention in reservoirs and temperature-controlled water releases improve fish habitat. Reservoirs themselves and land acquired for mitigation and enhancement of fish and wildlife habitat provide for increased recreational opportunities.

The Office of Water Resources Research seeks to stimulate, sponsor, and supplement present programs of research and training in the field of water and of resources that affect water. This is done through grants and contracts with academic and private institutions, private firms, individuals, and public agencies through operations in 50 states and Puerto Rico. Most of the studies are on water supply augmentation and conservation, while others are concerned with water quality management and protection, water quantity management and control, and water resources planning.

The Federal Water Pollution Control Administration faces a fantastically complex problem that touches the lives of all of us. In addition to its direct operations and special studies, it carries out a diverse program of grants.

The Federal Water Pollution Control Administration grants provide support for activities that contribute directly or indirectly to the prevention and control of water pollution, including grants for waste treatment works construction, state and interstate agency programs, research and development, training, and comprehensive basin plans for water quality control. FWPCA special studies are on estuarine pollution, watercraft pollution, manpower evaluation, cost estimates, and industrial incentives. Its direct operations include review of water quality standards proposed by the states, an enforcement program, control of oil pollution and reduction of pollution from federal installations. In addition it carries on pollution surveillance, technical assistance, training, information, and other services. It operates a series of field and research laboratories and does research and development in the field of water quality.

ADMINISTRATIVE ARRANGEMENTS

The preceding paragraphs are sketchy. They treat the missions and functioning of the agencies in a most perfunctory manner, and they do not account for their accomplishments. Each is worthy of treatment in depth. However, some frame of reference has been presented for certain aspects of the administrative arrangements for environmental management.

Experience is a great teacher and man has had a long period of trial-and-error in resources utilization and management. Nevertheless, Interior's agencies seek a more adequate basis for operations through resource appraisal, inventory, and research, including technology based on scientific facts and understandings. Some agencies are heavily committed to research, such as the Bureau of Commercial Fisheries, the Geological Survey, and the Office of Water Resources Research. Every other agency carries on some in-house studies, and many have extramural programs.

I think it is not unfair to say that old-line agencies had a rather narrow orientation to the nature of resources and their use, together with a receptivity to the views of the resource exploiters. For some time now, and at an accelerating rate, such sharply focused missions are being supplemented and complemented by a broader outlook, including acceptance of responsibility for the environmental consequences of single-purpose actions.

Definitions of environment and resources through survey and research must precede intelligent action. Traditional knowledge, sometimes verging on folklore, and the bias of special or vested interests often seem to characterize many of Interior's clients, but if the public is to be well served they cannot prevail in Interior's administration and environmental management. Dr. Richard A. Cooley, in his *Politics of Conservation*, 1963, stresses that resource use alternatives and their social and economic costs vary greatly, and that it is impossible to make a rational choice of means unless the ultimate goals to be accomplished are stated in human terms.

The implicit difficulty at this point, of course, is the determination of goals. Whose goals? Individuals, firms, public agencies of all levels of government, and the people of geographic areas may have different goals according to the impact of a proposed allocation of natural resources to a given use, each according to economic, political, social or ideological interests.

Natural resources do not occur in isolation in the environment, but in intimate associations. Any given natural resource is subject to more than one use. The ability to command a certain use and to benefit from it is not a universal phenomenon. All these variables make determination of "wise use," as conservationists like to say, a difficult matter. Which administrative decisions and consequent actions best serve the "general welfare" may be a moot question. Despite such difficulties, public agencies must act. And they do so according to congressional mandate and administrative decision.

For a department as heterogenous as Interior, there are many mandates and administrative policies, and they are by no means always compatible. This is not surprising. Conflicts of purpose exist for historical reasons. For example, acts of Congress often are for a single purpose. Previous acts with different purposes may be overlapping. Any such acts concerning a given resource or construction may authorize procedures that have unknown, inadvertent, or ignored consequences for other resources and conditions of the environment. As a result, conflicts between missions are not uncommon. For example, carried to completion, the dam-building programs of the Bureau of Reclamation and the Corps of Engineers would preclude any wild or scenic rivers in natural state, at least on major streams. Also, the pressures for outdoor recreational developments can be incompatible with strict wilderness and natural-area preservation.

Turning to relations between Interior and other departments and major federal agencies, there are many points at which the missions of the Department of Defense, the Atomic Energy Commission, the Department of Transportation, and others are at variance with certain of Interior's objectives.

Interior has numerous relationships with the states through grant-in-aid programs, training programs, regulations, and enforcement, while there are some programs that relate directly to cities. Its contacts with citizen interests are multitudinous. Some are direct and personal, as with many millions of hunters and fishermen, park visitors, and other recreationists. Others are indirect and with the entire population, as in Interior's water pollution control program.

As S. J. Makielski, Jr., has pointed out in his "Preconditions to Effective Public Administration," appearing in the June, 1967, PUBLIC ADMINISTRATION REVIEW, public administration requires an array of basic skills appropriate to its particular projects and programs. For example, the Fish and Wildlife Service of Interior requires some 30 different scientific skills ranging from biochemistry and genetics to taxonomy, physiology, and biometry. And within such familiar skill-groups as these very special requirements need to be met—not just a taxonomist, for example, but a fish taxonomist. There needs to be organizational experience and the willingness and capability of reorganizing to profit from experience in order to meet changing conditions. Frozen bureaucratic mechanisms are capable only of glacial movement. Yet when there is flexibility, administrative norms and appropriate organizational language are needed if confusion is to be avoided.

I will close these observations with some examples of new arrangements in Interior and its agencies that help to shape the environment more effectively according to present goals for America. Interior has grown up over a century and a quarter. It was never designed as a department. To a considerable degree, it accumulated, but elements of design have been infused from time to time especially in recent years.

There was truth in the description of Interior as "a loose confederation of sovereign agencies often at war with each other."

The department has been experimenting with the programming, planning, and budgeting system. The results have not destroyed any bureau structure nor affected the budgeting process materially, but it has caused the agencies to look closely at one another's areas of responsibility and has fostered more understanding and cooperation than existed previously.

Interior even experimented with an "environment" program category for two years but discarded it. This decision was based on several considerations, but on the fact that so much of what we do in Interior through traditional program missions is related to understanding and using the resources of our environment.

The Federal Water Pollution Control Administration is responsible for water quality standards. It works closely with the states, but because water quality affects so many of Interior's interests a task force has been formed with members from several Interior bureaus to comment on proposed standards and criteria. The Bureau of Outdoor Recreation and the National Park Service work together on new area planning, often with participation by the Bureau of Sport Fisheries and Wildlife. The Bureau of Commercial Fisheries and the Bureau of Sport Fisheries and Wildlife have, after more than a decade as a service, recently formed several inter-bureau committees on such matters of common interest as anadromous fish, estuaries, and conflicts between commercial and sport fishermen. Task forces on an ad hoc basis are constantly being formed for special interbureau purposes. The examples are many; these few will have to do for now.

Interior certainly does not exist in a vacuum. It has cross-connections with most of the departments and major agencies of government. One illustration will suffice. The Marine Resources and Engineering Development Act of 1966 established a Commission and a Council. The Council has formed five intergovernmental committees. One of these, the Committee on Multiple Uses of the Coastal Zone is chaired in Interior. Its membership is made up of representatives of 15 major departments and agencies. While this committee seeks to clarify the problems of the coastal zone, its effectiveness will lie in administrative changes, statutory or by memoranda of agreement, that will help resolve conflicts, divide the labor rationally, and serve the nation better by the way the environment is shaped by governmental programs.

Administrative wheels within wheels are being meshed better than ever before to match the interconnectedness that characterizes the real world. While the specialities and bits and pieces of human affairs cannot be dispensed with, administrative systems must have congruence with the systems of nature, because single impacts can reverberate throughout an entire system.

George R. Hall

The Myth and Reality of
Multiple Use Forestry*

"Multiple use" is the current magic phrase in forestry. The Forest Service has even converted this principle into a slogan and designed a five-part multiple-use emblem to symbolize the multiple contributions of the forests to national well-being. But is multiple use really a principle which insures that the national forests will make the best possible contribution to our welfare? Supporters claim that it is the closest we can come in the forest sector to having our cake and eating it too.[1] Others claim that it is merely a psychological weapon in the perennial cold war among federal land managing agencies and is more useful to public relations officials than to forest managers. This paper will consider, therefore, the extent to which current multiple use doctrine and practice promote the socially best administrative decisions for the national forests. The reasons for developing a theory of multiple use management and current doctrine will first be examined. Then, how this doctrine is reflected in forest management procedures will be considered. Finally, some suggestions for reorienting multiple use forestry will be presented.

In 1960 multiple use forestry was officially declared to be a part of our national forest public policy. The Multiple Use Act,[2] sponsored by the Forest Service, authorizes and directs the forests to be managed "under principles of multiple use." These are defined as follows:

'Multiple use' means: The management of all the various renewable surface resources of the national forests so that they are utilized in the combination that will best meet the needs of the American people making the most judicious use of the land for some or all of these resources or related services over areas large enough to provide sufficient latitude for periodic adjustments in use to conform to changing needs and conditions; that some land will be used for less than all of the resources; and harmonious and coordinated management of the various resources, each with the other, without impairment of the pro-

*Reprinted by permission from *Natural Resources Journal* (School of Law, University of New Mexico), III (1963), 276–290.
(Notes to this selection will be found on pp. 433–434)

ductivity of the land, with consideration being given to the relative values of the various resources, and not necessarily the combination of uses that will give the greatest dollar return or the greatest unit output.[3]

What does this mean for forest administration? The answer is that there are two doctrines purporting to interpret what the legal commitment to multiple use implies.[4]

I

CURRENT DOCTRINE

A fundamental attribute of forests is that they can produce a variety of products. At present the major products are timber, grazing, water, wildlife, and recreation. The common input for all these outputs is forest land and this means that a decision about one product will affect the other outputs. Thus multiple use forestry is a necessity.

Interest in both the technical and public aspects of multiple use forestry has increased substantially in the last 15 years. The growth in population, leisure time, national income and highways has meant rapidly growing demands for all forest products. Consumers of each product would like to see their demands receive the primary attention of forest managers. As conflicting demands on the forests have increased, an ancillary dispute has arisen among the land management agencies. Some of these agencies—particularly the National Park Service—advocate that nontimber use of land be placed under the jurisdiction of "specialists" rather than the Forest Service.

To deal with both the substantive and bureaucratic aspects of this problem, the Forest Service developed a multiple use doctrine and promoted the passage of the Multiple Use Act. The service has emphatically maintained that passage of the act in no way changed traditional forest management practices. The statutory authorization for multiple use is traced back by the service to such early forestry laws as the Act of June 4, 1897.[5] The Multiple Use Act, according to the Forest Service, protects the forests from the encroachments of single use advocates.[6] It also protects the Forest Service from the encroachments of other agencies on its area of authority.

The interpretation which the Forest Service and its supporters place on the language in the Multiple Use Act can be called the "equal priorities" doctrine. It has two tenets. The first is that multiple use involves "harmony and coordination" of uses but does not necessarily require a combination which produces the maximum yield per acre of land of any one output. Nor does it require a combination which produces the maximum economic benefits. Thus maximization of per acre production as well as a benefit–cost analysis such as is used for water resource management is rejected. The second tenet is that no one use has priority over another. In the hearings on the Multiple Use Bill the Acting Secretary of Agriculture made much of this point. Secretary Peterson said:

The order in which the resources and uses are enumerated in the bill is merely alphabetical and has no significance insofar as the relative priority of one resource to another. One of the basic concepts of multiple use is that all of the named resources in general are of equal priority, but the relative values of the various resources on particular or localized areas, and viewed in the broadest public sense, will be considered in the administrative application of management plans.[7]

While these two tenets are the foundation of the equal priorities position there are other aspects to be considered. The former Chief of the Forest Service, Richard E. McArdle, has listed six points which he feels are important. First, multiple use "does not require maximum production for all resources or for any one resource."[8] Intangible and nonmonetary values are just as important as economic factors. Second, not all resources should necessarily be produced on each acre. Third, haphazard occurrence of more than one use is not multiple use; positive direction is required. Fourth, multiple use does not require that all uses be practiced concurrently and so the time period must be at least a year and often longer. Fifth, central decision-making is necessary to obtain coordination of outputs. Sixth, the administrative unit of land to which multiple use is applied ordinarily must be large.[9] The first four points are concerned with the definition of a multiple use while the last two assert the competence of the Forest Service to handle any job which might arise on forest land.

This interpretation is far from unanimously accepted. The opposing doctrine may be called the "dominant use" view. Holders of this position reject both basic tenets of the equal priority school. They assert that land should be used to the fullest extent possible and that priorities must be established. To adherents of this position priorities usually involve some social ranking of consumption needs plus some ranking of land on the basis of technological capabilities. Thus, Warren A. Starr holds that:

Our land resource now has to accommodate a host of *primary* and *secondary* uses.

Primary needs for land are those involving production of essential commodities for food, shelter and raiment needed by an increasing population. Secondary needs are those involving sports, recreation, wildlife habitat, and embrace the specific sites needed for research and education in the natural sciences. The differentiation of these two needs are [sic] . . . considered as priority needs.[10]

Later he concludes that:

[We should] allow single, alternate, or multiple use choice of single tracts to be decided upon the competitive comparison of the single tract potentials. In this manner, land quality will determine use potential, and use potential will determine ultimate planned use.[11]

Dominant use supporters seldom specify the relationship of the "social" priority of needs and the ranking by physical characteristics of land. They are firmly convinced, however, that multiple use is not a social goal but merely a planning technique to enable one to decide for what uses a tract of land might be best adapted. Dominant use supporters would decide on a major use for each piece of land. Subsidiary uses then would be allowed *to the extent they did not interfere with the output of the major use.*

The cornerstone of the dominant use position is the belief that benefits from different land uses are not necessarily additive. As Howard Stagner illustrated this view:

[On] a critical watershed, sheep grazing is a negative value and actually reduces the greatest benefit. Likewise, mining and lumbering are minus values when one is talking about national parks or recreation areas.[12]

Equal priority supporters would not deny that some areas should be devoted to the production of a single good or service. Where then is the disagreement? The fundamental difference is that the equal priorities school sees diversity and a multiplicity of products as good itself; the dominant use school argues that some combinations of goods and services affect either the quantities or the qualities of the products and this should be avoided. The argument that combining many uses is *per se* desirable has been summed up by one observer as follows:

My conception of the phrase, 'the greatest good to the greatest number' is that the objective of management must be to satisfy the needs and desires of as great a cross section of the public as the physical limitations of the land and the abilities of the [forest] managers will permit. Thus the goals [of the national forests] are quantity, quality and variety, so that to the extent possible there is something for everyone.[13]

Thus a management plan which provided a substantial range of land uses would then be preferable to one with only a few uses even if the latter had more net economic benefits or had a higher output per acre of land for the goods actually produced. This reflects the belief that the forests belong to everyone and no user group has a right to exclude another.[14]

The dominant use school rejects this philosophy and asserts that what is important is to preserve "inherent values." There is an important insight here; for many forest products, the other uses combined with its production will affect the nature or characteristics of the product. Thus, while recreation can almost always be combined with timber production, the *kind* of recreational activities possible will depend upon how much timber is produced and the way in which the timber is managed and harvested.

The two doctrines are not, as is sometimes asserted,[15] merely different statements of the same idea. They represent opposing viewpoints about the goals of forest policy and when applied at the managerial level lead to radically different decisions about output and land use.

The effect of combinations of use on product characteristics has been too often overlooked in the discussion of forestry. In economic textbooks multiple use is usually discussed under a heading such as "allocation of factors among products." In the examples given, such as a farmer deciding on combinations of oats and wheat to grow on a specified acreage, the implicit assumption is made that his decisions will only affect the quantities of the two commodities produced and that the oats will remain the same oats regardless of how much wheat is produced. In forestry, the interdependence among outputs makes such an assumption inadmissible. A forest under intensive management for timber will have, for example, different forms of wildlife from an old-growth virgin stand. The amount of grazing allowed will also affect not only the amount of game but their species. Many other examples could be given, for this is the heart of the multiple use problem: Different decisions will affect not only how much different consumers get but also the characteristics of the outputs they receive.

Dominant use advocates go further and point out that some uses are exclusionary. Stagner cited grazing and watershed management; the most common example is wilderness recreation and timber production. This school feels that noncompatible or exclusionary use conflicts can be resolved only through land use planning on the basis of "inherent values."

While the existence of exclusionary uses and the effects of different combinations on quality are points well taken, the supposed solution can be rejected out of hand. To devote all land to its "major" use and then allow only those "minor" uses which are completely compatible ignores three points. The first is that, as the equal priorities school argues, it often may be socially beneficial to permit either a decline in the quantity or quality of one product if the quantity or quality of another product is increased sufficiently. The second is that it may be possible through more complicated or costly managerial techniques to permit "minor" uses without damaging the quantity or quality of the "major" use. Thus in a campground it is often possible to harvest almost as much timber as would be possible under single use management. The timber will have to be cut in off-seasons and more costly roads, stump clearance, and slash removal techniques will be required. If, however, one is willing to expend the money and effort this is possible. Finally, the dominant use position is based on a fallacy: Social priorities cannot be set on the supposed "basicness" of some products, nor can one assert as a social goal the maximization of per unit output land or the maximization of the quality of some product.[16] The national forests are to be managed for the good of the public. There is little point to producing goods that people do not want—even if they are somehow more "basic." Nor is the goal to see how high we can push up per acre productivity; to accept this would be to reverse the causation and argue that the purpose of the public is to work for the good of the forest land.[17]

Therefore, neither of the two interpretations of multiple use is satisfactory. The equal priorities doctrine glosses over the effect of land use combinations on product characteristics. It also fails to provide a criterion for resolving the conflicts among demands except for the general and unspecified standard of "the best interest of the public." The dominant use doctrine falls down because it fails to state how priorities can be established and also because it implies that maximization of per unit output or product quality should be the goal.

One might accept this conclusion and yet argue the issue is academic because Congress has chosen, in passing the Multiple Use Bill, the equal priority approach. The language in the act, however, permits either interpretation. Nor can one say that the intent of Congress was to enact one view or the other. The hearings on the bill indicate that this conflict among interpretations was not brought out.[18] Many of the witnesses supporting the bill clearly held a dominant use position and believed that the act supported their interpretation.[19] It appears that in voting for multiple use Congress believed it was voting for virtue and against sin without having a definite idea about just what actions constituted virtue or sin. The conclusion seems warranted that the meaning of multiple use has not been established—either by a consensus among natural resource experts or by legislative decree.

II

MULTIPLE USE IN PRACTICE

It has been argued previously that multiple use problems arise from the technical nature of forest production. Therefore, some public policy rule must be established to settle the inherent conflicts among user groups. Before turning to this problem, however, it is important to consider multiple use as seen on the operating level by forest managers. The following account is generalized from procedures of one forest, the Jefferson

National Forest in southwest Virginia. However, the attitudes described are broadly representative of those throughout the Forest Service and the practices are typical of those found on most national forests.[20]

Long-range planning of land use takes place on three levels. The first is with the forest supervisor who prepares multiple use guides for the district rangers. Planning on this level establishes general methods for handling conflicts arising from competing demands among activities. Planning on the second level is done by the staff specialists in the forest supervisor's office. The supervisor's assistants are experts in the various aspects of forest management, timber, water, etc.; each specialist prepares management plans for the activity directly under his cognizance. Typically, the only plan in full operation on most forests is the timber management plan but the others are usually in some stage of preparation and implementation. This situation reflects the preoccupation until recent years with timber management on the national forests. A management plan lists the overall targets to be achieved and the criteria to guide the operating personnel in decisions specifically relating to the resource use in question.

The ranger district or working block is the third and vital planning level. Working blocks are the operating units of the forest under the direct supervision of a district ranger. Each block has a plan which translates the plans prepared at higher levels into specific programs. There is interaction between the various levels in the preparation of all plans. The forest supervisor and his staff work closely with the district rangers in order to insure that plans made at higher levels will reflect local conditions and problems and that working block plans are consistent with the more general guides.

Forest planning has two dimensions: volume control and area control. Volume control operates through specification of the allowable timber cut and outputs of other forest products for each working block. Area control operates through specification of the use to be made of each compartment. Compartments are homogenous land areas of perhaps 500 to 1,000 acres or larger areas; for example, a small valley or hillside slope. Working blocks are subdivided into compartments and records are kept for each compartment. To illustrate, on the Jefferson the foresters try to make a detailed examination of each compartment at least once every ten years. Upon the basis of the examination, decisions are made about the needed investment or change in the compartment's management.

The key decisions are those which go into making the working block plans; therefore, the district ranger is the key man in multiple use management. His importance is recognized in the higher echelons of the service. It is common knowledge that one ranger may be "recreation conscious" and view each plot of land as a possible camp site. Another may be fascinated by opportunities to improve wildlife habitat. Still another may be a "timber beast" and view all other activities as distractions from his main job of growing wood.

Attitudes are important because most of the decisions involved in the day-to-day administration have such complex multiple use effects that a considerable degree of managerial discretion is unavoidable. To take an example from a Virginia situation, assume a forester must decide how to harvest the timber on a small compartment of mixed hardwoods. If the compartment is clear cut (all the trees removed), the deer population will likely increase because they need open areas. On the other hand, the turkey population will likely decline because they need old-growth timber. If the timber is cut one way the area might be developed for a picnic area, but this will probably require special roads, slash removal, etc. Development of the area for recreation may lead to land compaction and erosion problems which may present watershed difficulties. Thus, any one of a variety of different land management programs could be selected each capable of being justified on the basis of multiple use management.

The wide range of choice leads forest managers to stress the subjective factors in multiple use management. One hears again and again that the vital element in land use decisions is "savvy," "good judgment" or "professional competence." This leads foresters to conclude that primary reliance must be placed on the judgment of the district rangers and only very general rules can be established by higher authorities.

The forest supervisor's role is also important. Particularly he must insure that his operating personnel are conscious of the various possibilities for multiple use of the forest. His chief weapon is inspections by himself and the specialists on his staff. The wildlife specialist, for example, in his periodic visits to the working blocks, can consult with the foresters, point out possibilities for habitat improvement and emphasize the need for the rangers to remain conscious of the need for attention to wildlife management.

The conclusion is warranted that, in practice, multiple use at the operating level is not a rule such that two foresters faced with the same objective situation will necessarily make the same land use decision. It is a subjective commitment to a "philosophy" that forest managers should take a "broad" view of the potentialities of the forest. Let us examine this view in somewhat more detail.

The flood of publicity about multiple use has made all foresters extremely conscious of the term. On the operating level, however, multiple use is seen as a problem of coordinating separate resource programs rather than being a matrix into which an individual activity can be fitted. That is, multiple use starts with individual resource plans and tries to fit them together rather than beginning with an overall multiple use program.

This is explained by history. Forest managers have had long experience in planning for particular resources, especially timber. Multiple use objectives are currently being superimposed on the older procedures. This poses some difficulties. For example, working blocks and compartments are geographical units which have long proved useful for timber management. They may or may not be useful for multiple use planning.[21] On the other hand, foresters are accustomed to working with the traditional tools and concepts of timber management and probably the easiest way to obtain multiple use objectives is by building on this base.

A vital aspect of multiple use in practice is what one forester described as the "hub" concept. In this explanation multiple use is thought of as similar to a wheel. A wheel is an integral unit in which all parts are dependent upon the other parts but do not have the same function, and all points revolve around the hub. Likewise, the forester explained, for each plot of ground there should be a hub use or one product around which the other outputs could be joined. While this theory was expounded as a personal view and does not represent Forest Service doctrine, it is an accurate description of how decisions about product mixes are usually made in practice.

A third aspect of multiple use stressed by foresters is that the time period involved is very important. Because some uses of an area are chosen as best now, for many areas this does not preclude other uses in the future. For example, a plot presently used as a campground might be shifted in twenty years to wildlife use by moving the camp facilities and seeding the area to grain. When trees have reseeded themselves and grown to marketable size, the area might again be used for camping or devoted to timber production. This shifting over time, it is argued, greatly reduces the conflict among competing uses for the service of the land.

Foresters also regard the multiple use problem as resolvable through variation of the production process. They tend to argue that under multiple use management one can obtain the same outputs of the various commodities and services that would be obtained were the land area devoted to single use management; however, more inputs would be required. For instance, timber can be cut in a scenic zone along a highway or the shore of a lake. But in such a zone the amount of timber harvested at any one time will ordinarily be much smaller than if the land were managed solely for timber. Also, logging roads may have to be disadvantageously located in order to keep them from view, and more attention will have to be given to land rehabilitation and trash removal. All of these requirements would make the logging operation more difficult and costly. Regardless, foresters claim that over time one can harvest almost the same physical amount of timber without affecting the scenic values. While in any specific period, say ten years, nearly the same number of board feet of timber might be obtained, note that the cost per board foot would be higher due to harvesting the timber in small lots, building high standard roads and engaging in more careful lumbering practices. Also, to be precise, the total amount of timber cut, though nearly the same as under single use management, would never be quite identical. There would be some difference in growth due to the change in management. Rotation ages of trees might be changed in recreation areas, or certain overripe trees might be left for wildlife management purposes. Foresters argue, nevertheless, that such effects are sufficiently small as to be *de minimis*.

Of course, to argue that with sufficient inputs multiple use management may produce the same quantities of outputs as would single use management does not mean that in fact this should be the goal. It is likely that the inclusion of some item in a multiple use plan will change other output quantities. Hopefully, there will be a social advantage to the shift. The important point to note is that in the thinking of forest managers outputs quantities and characteristics can be substantially maintained by increasing the inputs, if this is desired.

For example, commercial logging often can be made compatible with watershed protection. The methods used will raise the cost per board foot of the extraction process and decrease the stumpage price received by the forest. Of course, under some topographical conditions watershed protection may completely preclude logging. But to a large extent, the combination of timber production and watershed protection is a question of the expense one is willing to incur.[22]

In sum, foresters regard multiple use not as a decision-making rule but as a commitment to the principle that a variety of different demands will be considered when making professional judgments. Multiple use is seen as requiring the selection of a hub use and then a process of mutual adjustment of the hub use to the production of other goods and services, and vice versa. Foresters argue that the conflict between competing demands can be lessened considerably through various adjustments in management plans. Temporal adjustments are particularly important; foresters argue that because different parts of the land area of the forest can be used serially for different products, a variety of competing demands can be provided for on the same area. Another adjustment is through variation of the inputs in the production process. Such adjustments may make it possible to add more products to the output mix without affecting the other outputs. This adjustment will likely be more expensive than single use production.

National forest managers strongly support what they believe to be the Forest Service's commitment to multiple use and feel that in practice it yields the best possible product-mix decisions. However, do the current interpretations of multiple use and current administrative practices carry out the mandate of the Multiple Use Act—to manage the forests to "best meet the needs of the American people"?[23]

III

AN EVALUATION OF MULTIPLE USE FORESTRY

The most important conclusion about multiple use is that it works best where conflicts can be resolved by intensive management and temporal variation. It will not resolve the conflicts which arise over forest product-mixes where decisions about combination change the characteristics of one product or substantially lower its "quality." This situation occurs where the essence of a product is a nonintensive, "leave nature alone" form of management. Obvious examples of such products are wilderness recreation and scientific nature study. To the extent that conflicts can be resolved through modification of nature, present multiple use practices hold the promise of living up to the claims made for them.[24] Nevertheless, the hard-core problem of modification of output characteristics and "quality" remains.

From an economic standpoint the major issue of multiple use forestry is determination of the optimum product combination where product characteristics are a variable. This problem becomes acute when one product is exclusionary. People who like both ice cream and garlic don't necessarily want them mixed. Exclusionary products must be taken into consideration when making product-mix decisions. Thus the conclusion is warranted that multiple use is no easy solution to the conflicts now raging about the appropriate uses of the national forests.

From a political standpoint the major issue of multiple use forestry is whether it satisfactorily reflects the wishes of the citizenry about the kinds of goods and services to be produced by the forests. As pointed out above, neither the theory nor the practice of multiple use provides a clear rule for selecting one land use plan over another; the main reliance is on "savvy" or professional judgment. This has led Charles A. Reich of the Yale Law School to argue that present legal and administrative procedures provide few, if any, safeguards to insure that public wishes will determine operating decisions.[25] He points out that the power of the Forest Service is awesome, for

the Service recognizes, in the matter-of-fact pages of its manual, that its ultimate job is nothing less than the definition of 'the public good,' a task once reserved for philosopher-kings. This is the tremendous responsibility that Congress has delegated to all the forest agencies and with it the power to determine the very character of the American land.[26]

This poses a dilemma. The multiple use ramifications of any management decision are so great that nonprofessionals cannot be expected to evaluate all the possibilities and alternative advantages. Further, the Forest Service has an *esprit de corps* and professional dedication unmatched in the federal service which should not be damaged. The present fine condition of the national forests is a monument to the devotion and ability of the Forest Service and this is an important factor in any decision about the appropriate scope of professional responsibility. On the other hand, land use should reflect public wishes and desires. Forest management, like war, is too important a task to be left strictly to professionals however competent and dedicated.

Reich's suggestion for increasing the protection of the public interest in forest management is to establish more formal procedures for public hearings on land management decisions. This is not persuasive. Does any one familiar with natural resource administration really believe we need additional talk? More basic measures are required. The fundamental difficulty is that there are no methods whereby the advantages of alternative plans can be compared. Considerable adjustments in forest use to increase outputs or maintain or improve the quality of the products are possible. Such adjustments are not free of cost, and we need to know whether the multiple use adjustments will produce sufficient benefits to make them worthwhile. When confronted by exclusionary use situations, some type of analysis is required to allow one to compare the advantages and disadvantages of limiting the product-mix to the exclusionary product. This requires procedures similar to those used to analyze water resource investment.[27]

Development of such analytical tools will not be easy—as we are aware from the history of water resource administration. However, such procedures have the outstanding advantage of forcing administrators to specify the expected results of their action and they provide the lay public with a basis for deciding whether the professional judgment accords with popular wishes.[28]

SUMMARY

The current multiple use forestry situation involves both myth and reality. The myth is that such practices are capable of resolving all conflicting demands and allowing us to have our cake and eat it too. Resolution, of course, occurs in the sense that *some* land use plan is selected. Yet, present theoretical interpretations of multiple use are based on weak foundations, and professional administrative judgments are heavily dependent on intangible factors. Thus there is little assurance that the main objective of the Multiple Use Bill, to insure that the national forests will make the best possible contribution to our economic and social well-being, will be realized.

The reality behind the discussion of multiple use is that forestry decisions are primarily judgments about the characteristics of the goods and services produced. Decisions about product-mixes and output quantities affect the nature or "quality" of the outputs. Some outputs are even "exclusionary" in that their essential characteristics will be destroyed if combined with certain other land uses. A further part of the reality is that resolution of considerable conflicts is possible through temporal adjustments and changes in production techniques. This means that multiple use becomes a problem of evaluating the costs and benefits from alternative decisions. Present procedures do not exist which would allow such evaluation. Future attention to both the theory and practice of multiple use should concentrate on developing operational procedures to allow such analysis.

Our forests are a vital heritage. It is both a practical and moral concern to see that they are managed in the best possible manner. The past and present contributions of the forest to our welfare point up the tremendous future potential of these social assets. This means that it is of prime importance to clarify the meaning of multiple use and develop managerial techniques for applying the principle.

Vincent Ostrom

The Water Economy
and Its Organization*

Questions about organization have been the source of more extensive debate and controversy in the field of water resources development than in most other phases of American economic and political experience. Controversies over "public ownership" have reflected substantial ambiguity over whether the provision of water supplies and electric services should be organized in the public or the private sector of the economy. In the public sector, the problem of organization has been plagued by questions of functional and territorial allocation of jurisdiction among public agencies. The question has been often posed as one involving the organization of agencies devoted to single-purpose development as against agencies devoted to comprehensive, multiple-purpose development. Similar questions have often been posed about the need of special regional agencies for water development as opposed to reliance upon the states and national governments as the traditional units of political organization. Sometimes, demands have also been articulated for the creation of regional authorities with responsibility for comprehensive multi-purpose development of river basins.

In undertaking a new examination of this problem of organization for water resource development I shall, first, turn to an analysis of the different types of goods and services which can be derived from a water supply system and of the amenability of these goods to allocation in the private market economy as against their provision in the public economy. The second section of the paper will examine the types of organization that have been developed in American experience to provide these different types of goods and services. The final section of the paper will explore some aspects of the problem of organization in relation to the task of planning for comprehensive multiple-purpose development of water resources.

*Reprinted by permission from *Natural Resources Journal* (School of Law, University of New Mexico), II (April, 1962), 55–73.
(Notes to this selection will be found on p. 435.)

TYPES OF GOODS IN THE WATER ECONOMY

Water is the source of a complex multiplicity of "goods" which have value to us as human beings. In a fundamental way, water is essential to the continuity of life itself. All living organisms require a regular supply of water in order to sustain their survival, growth and development. In addition to supplying water to meet the consumptive requirement of living organisms, flowing water may also be used to provide a major source of power. The same water course may provide a habitat for valuable supplies of fish and wildlife and a place for human recreation. It may be used to transport a variety of goods and commodities along its course. A stream may also be used to dilute and purify waste products, or it may be used for washing or processing purposes or as a cooling agent in industrial production. Finally, water may be the source of a substantial "negative good" when floods wreak injury and havoc upon human endeavors. To control or prevent floods then becomes a positive good.

The bundle of goods which can be derived from a water course include both the uses of water as water and the uses that can be made of the flow of a stream. The various uses of water are highly interrelated. One pattern of use frequently precludes some other possibility of development. As demands for water increase, the elements of competition and conflict among the various users of a stream are apt to become accentuated. The wastes of an industrial civilization, for example, place an increasing load upon waterways at the same time that new opportunities for leisure reflect a bounding demand for water sports. When demands exceed certain minimal levels, the use of a stream for sewerage is not easily reconciled with its use for recreational purposes. The maintenance of anadromous fisheries may pose a substantial conflict for large-scale water storage facilities essential to flood control and hydroelectric power production.

Theoretically, the competition for the different "goods" to be derived from the uses of a water resource system might be resolved by economic allocation in the market. Under market conditions, priorities would be determined by the preferences of users spending their earnings upon one or another water resource products. However, market mechanisms are only partially available in allocating water resource products or uses because a number of the goods derived from a water resource system do not meet the criteria for allocation in the market economy.

A private good must be "packageable" in the sense that it can be differentiated as a commodity or service before it can readily be purchased or sold in the market economy. It must also be appropriable in the sense that the commodity or service is subject to the legal claim of a property right which vests control in the owner as against other possible claimants and users. A loaf of bread, for example, is both packageable and appropriable. Those who are not willing to pay for the loaf of bread can be excluded from enjoying its benefits. These are the conditions for meeting the exclusion principle and the exclusion principle is the criterion which must be met as a necessary condition for the operation of a market economy.

In considering the economic character of the different uses of water, a rather basic distinction can be made between consumptive and non-consumptive uses. A consumptive use implies that water is taken from its natural course and is used upon the land. Irrigation, domestic consumption, municipal and industrial uses are among the consumptive or "on-the-land" uses of water supply. Nonconsumptive uses on the other hand are "in-the-channel" uses. These include navigation, dissipation of wastes, recreation, propagation of fish and wildlife and flood control.

The Consumptive Uses as Goods—The consumptive or on-the-land uses are generally appropriative uses since they involve a taking of the water and placing it under control in an out-of-the-channel storage and distribution system. Both water used for consumptive purposes and electricity can be metered and sold in measurable units whether in gallons, cubic feet or in kilowatt hours. The conditions of the exclusion principle can be satisfied. Water can be sold as a commodity in relation to the demands of the various users who are willing to pay the market price to meet their various consumptive demands. As a result, the water supplies and water products which can be appropriated for on-the-land uses are generally more amenable to private organization and distribution in a market-type economy than are the nonconsumptive or in-the-channel uses.

The competitive dynamics of the water economy, however, is seriously constrained by the relatively large proportion of investments required in fixed diversion and distribution facilities. These relatively large capital costs in fixed distribution facilities lead to two separate consequences. One result is the tendency to require organizations of a larger scale than the individual proprietor to undertake the provision of water supplies. The other result is that each water supply system tends to function as a natural monopoly in its service area. Both of these factors limit the operation of market forces in the water economy.

In the arid West, the individual proprietor could thrive only on land in close proximity to a stream or where there was an abundant ground-water supply. Beyond the limit of these opportunities, the provision of consumptive water supplies has generally been organized through non-profit cooperatives or mutual water companies, limited-profit public utility companies, municipal utility systems or public distribution systems organized by a variety of special public districts of quasimunicipal corporations established to provide special water supplies for various groups and communities of people. Today the special public water districts which have evolved from the irrigation districts and the municipal water systems are the organizations which assume the dominant role in the distribution of water supplies for consumptive use.

None of these agencies operate their water supply systems in a way that would conform to the rule for maximization short-run of profits. Even the privately owned water company, which is organized for profit, is considered to be a public utility whose service arrangements and rate structure are subject to detailed control by state public utility commissions. Water is generally priced so that it functions as an intermediate product in the economy. The payoff is derived not by the water producer but by those who make use of water in the land-related economy. Instead, water simply becomes one of the factors contributing to the land promoter's development scheme in which he derives his return from land values; or, in the case of a local community, water may be used as an instrument to attempt to control patterns of economic and political development in the community. The history of the growth and development of Los Angeles, for example, reveals its conscious use of water as a tool to build the "great metropolis of the Pacific".

The Nonconsumptive Uses as Goods. Most in-the-channel or nonconsumptive uses do not meet the criterion of the exclusion principle. The benefits of flood control, for example, cannot be distributed only to those individuals who are willing to pay for the benefits. When flood control programs are undertaken all individuals in comparable situations on the flood plain are benefited alike. If the flood control measure is a local levee or dike, the group benefited may be relatively small and the enterprise might be organized as a public diking or flood control district. Where the flood control program involves the general regulation and control of a whole river system through large storage reservoirs, it becomes more difficult to allocate food control benefits among the various beneficiaries even if they could be encompassed within a common political jurisdiction.

The fish resources of a river system pose a somewhat ambiguous problem for economic organization. The fish which are taken from a stream are as readily subject to the market allocation as are loaves of bread. The taking, processing and distribution of fish products are, thus, largely conducted in the private sector of the economy. However, the operation of a fishery is not subject to the same type of organization and control. An entrepreneuer who decided to "farm" salmon, for example, would not be in a position to assure the exclusion of others from the benefits of his crop. As a result, the management of fish resources has generally been conducted as a public function.

The use of streams for the dilution and discharge of waste deals with a negative good or by-product which communities, firms and households attempt to dispose of at minimal costs to themselves. Unregulated use of a stream for pollution abatement is apt to poison the stream and destroy its usefulness for many other purposes. As a result the use of a stream for pollution abatement has never been recognized as a "good" for which a private property right vests. Rather it has been the subject of extensive regulation by state governments under police powers which emphasize the public character of the use of streams for pollution abatement.

The use of water in a water course for recreation poses another ambiguous problem for economic organization. Where access can be controlled, the conditions for the operation of the exclusion principle can be met and recreational uses can be organized by private enterprises. In this case, control of the land may afford control over the use of the adjoining stream. However, the use of the water course, *per se*, for recreational purposes is usually subject to the public use of all of those who can gain access.

The same principle applies to the use of a stream for navigation. All of those who can gain access to the stream are generally free to use it as a public highway subject to public regulations and control. However, particular works that may be constructed to circumvent natural obstructions to navigation could be amenable to private organization and use through the charge of a toll.

Other types of in-the-channel uses of a stream are usually intermediate aspects of transactions that are more clearly directed to the use of the water product for some on-the-land function. Hydroelectric power production, for example, requires the regulation of the flow of the stream to produce electrical energy, but the product is controlled and marketed on the land. Private development of hydroelectric power, thus, is usually associated with rather detailed public regulations which take cognizance of the public interest in the control of river flow.

Each of the various in-the-channel uses of a stream, thus, is not easily packageable or appropriable. They are not generally amenable to control by an individual proprietor who may want to produce the good or service for sale in the market economy. As a result, we must generally turn to public agencies to take appropriate courses of action in assuring adequate provision of in-the-channel uses of water resources.

The problem is further complicated by the high degree of interdependency among the various in-the-channel uses. It is the interdependency of one use pattern upon the other that requires those who plan any in-the-channel development to take account of the effect that each development will have upon the various possible patterns of use. This requirement for multi-purpose planning of interdependent uses poses one of the fundamental problems in the organization for the planning and administration of water resource programs.

Any effort to optimize output of in-the-channel uses of a river system depends upon the general regulation and control of flow characteristics. Reducing flood flows increases the benefits to be derived from flood control. Increasing minimum flows in turn increases the benefits that can be derived from most of the in-the-channel uses as well as increase the supply for on-the-land consumptive uses. Under these circumstances any water works project which modifies the flow of a stream must be evaluated in relation to the consequences which it produces. Each project which effects the flow pattern, then, has consequences for each other project and it becomes necessary to take account of each project as it affects the total pattern of development in a river system. This condition imposes another basic requirement that a water resource management system be organized so as to account for water production in a river system as a whole.

TYPES OF ORGANIZATION IN THE WATER ECONOMY

The types of organization associated with the uses of water in the water economy have derived from quite different vantage points in the American political system and in response to different patterns of demands at different points in time. These organizations constitute quite different commitments to the relative importance of different patterns of water resource development in relation to many different communities of interest. Since the different forms of organization tend to determine the capabilities for undertaking programs of water resource development, and, at the same time, to articulate demands in relation to planning for those interests, this analysis of the water economy and its organization will turn to a review of the different types of agencies and their function in water resource development.

Organizations for the Development of Consumptive and Land-Related Uses of Water Resources—The earliest use of water resources in the United States simply involved the use of the flow of a stream in its natural state. Under these circumstances no special form of organization was required for the individual entrepreneur to use the stream for navigation, for water power, for fishing or for the number of other uses that might be made of a stream in its natural state. The early water works which were constructed to make greater use of a stream's potential tended to be local single-purpose developments. These developments tended to emphasize consumptive or nonconsumptive uses depending upon the region of the country.

In the humid regions of the eastern portion of the United States local projects involving nonconsumptive uses took a higher order of importance. These uses might involve the diversion of water into a mill race where the flow could be directed over a water wheel to provide water power for the individual proprietor before the water was returned to continue its course in the natural channel of the stream. In other cases, local navigation canals and locks might be provided by private entrepreneurs or by public agencies to circumvent local obstructions to navigation. In a similar way, people in a local community might construct and maintain dikes and develop drainage works in order to reduce flood damage to their property. Diking and drainage districts were among the first local improvement districts used to undertake public water resource projects in the United States.

In the arid West, the use of water for consumptive demands took priority. The first appropriators were largely individual proprietors who diverted water from a local stream to their adjoining land. The centrifugal pump later gave many individual proprietors direct access to ground water supplies. As a result, the individual proprietor who directly appropriates at least a portion of his own water supply comprises a relatively large portion of the agricultural and industrial users in California, for example.

Apart from the individual proprietor who directly appropriated water from a stream or from ground water supplies to meet his own requirements, the early settlers of the arid West tended to rely upon mutual water companies as cooperative organizations to supply water for individual irrigators on a nonprofit basis. These mutual water companies were either organized by a group of individual farmers who would pool their resources in developing a common water supply or by a land developer who organized a water company as an adjunct of his land development and conveyed shares of stock in the water company proportionate to the amount of land sold in each farmstead. When the developer had completed the sale of land to local settlers, he had at the same time conveyed control of the water company to these same settlers who were then responsible for their own operation and management of the water company. In the course of time, the organization of mutual water companies developed a rather complex structure with new companies being organized by established companies to develop large-scale supplementary water supplies which would then be distributed on a pro-rata basis among the cooperating mutual water companies.

Where private companies have been organized to provide water supplies for a profit, they have uniformly come under state laws governing public utilities. These laws require a company to secure a license of "public convenience and necessity" in order to engage in a public service enterprise and the rates which they may charge for their services are subject to detailed approval by a public utility commission. Private companies providing water supplies as a public service are in effect limited profit enterprises.

The Wright Act, adopted in California in 1887, is generally used to date the rise of the special public district as an agency for the development of public water supplies. Earlier use had been made of special assessment and improvement districts to develop water supply or drainage systems in which local beneficiaries were assessed to pay for the local improvements made under the jurisdiction of local county authorities. The Wright Act, instead, made the general principles of organization in municipal corporations applicable to neighborhoods or communities which sought to develop common water supplies.

A municipal corporation is a legal device whereby a local community of people are permitted substantial authority to organize themselves and to govern their own local affairs. The government of a municipal corporation is usually vested in a governing board or council elected by the local people. The municipal corporation is usually vested with authority to enact ordinances, resolutions and by-laws in relation to its purposes and functions which are binding upon the people comprising the corporation, unless contrary to the general laws of some higher political jurisdiction. Similarly, a municipal corporation is usually vested with control over its internal administrative organization and the management of its own affairs. It may purchase, hold and dispose of property. If necessary, it may exercise the power of eminent domain to acquire property for public purposes. A municipal corporation is usually vested with the power of incurring bonded indebtedness to finance capital improvements, of taxation and of the management of its own fiscal affairs. A municipal corporation stands as an individual before the law; it can sue and be sued; and it has perpetual succession in its corporate name. In general, a municipal corporation has competent powers to develop, operate and maintain a public service program subject primarily to local responsibility and control. It is primarily an instrument of local self-government where the people of a local community are able to take public action in furtherance of their common interests.

From a beginning with irrigation districts, the special public districts, organized along the model of the municipal corporation or the quasimunicipal corporation, have come to include a vast range of activities related to water resource administration. These institutions have enabled a local community of people to use public authority to raise the necessary capital as a charge against the local community and upon the local water users subject to local political control. In California alone the state law authorizes the organization of some 30 different types of local government districts for various aspects of local water resource administration. The function of the local public district has been primarily directed to storage and distribution of water for consumptive, on-the-land use for both rural and urban populations. These have included the irrigation districts, reclamation districts, municipal water districts, utility districts, county water districts, as well as the cities themselves which maintain municipal water supply systems.

In more recent years other types of districts such as water conservancy districts, water replenishment districts, water storage districts, metropolitan water districts, county water authorities and county water agencies have been created to develop supplemental water supplies or to realize more efficient forms of water management by reducing the increasing costs of pumping or of salt water intrusion. This latter type of district often encompasses an area that may serve a variety of local water distribution systems. However, their function in the water economy is completely dominated by the consumptive demand of the various types of water distribution systems which are served by the supplemental supplies and the regulatory measures. They serve as water producers and wholesalers for the local distribution systems. The new form of organization simply allows the various units distributing water for consumptive purposes to develop a scale of organization adequate to undertake joint activities in larger-scale water production and transportation programs.

In Southern California, where these various local government agencies have seen their fullest development, a complex structure of private and public agencies function as an interrelated system. Some are engaged in water production including surface storage and ground water spreading. Others regulate pumping, and control ground water extractions. The Metropolitan Water District maintains its Colorado River aqueduct to provide a supplemental supply for most of the region. Beyond this is a vast complex of private and public distribution systems. Each of these distributors may produce a portion of its own water supplies. Finally, there are thousands of industrial and agricultural users who maintain their own individual water supply systems largely by pumping from the ground water supplies.

Since an adequate supply of water tends to be the critical element in controlling patterns of development in the arid West, the policy pursued by many of the private and most of the local public agencies is one of securing an adequate supply of water to assure a favorable competitive position for economic and social development of their local communities. As a result, a major investment is made in political efforts to influence decisions which will assure control over ample reserves of water and thus maintain a favorable competitive position in relation to other communities. The payoff is not measured in terms of the immediate dollar return upon the operation of the water distribution system but upon the adequacy of the reserve supply to meet future contingencies of growth. In many communities, the basic capital costs for developing new sources of supply are financed as a general demand upon taxpayers with the water utility, whether public or private, paying only a portion of the capital charges for its operation and maintenance costs. As a result, pricing policies rarely reflect the cost of water production and distribution, and values associated with the nonconsumptive uses of water are apt to be completely subordinated to demands for consumptive supplies.

This vast substructure of local private and public agencies concerned with consumptive uses and land-related development of water resources function largely within the framework of state law. Since agencies will articulate the demands which they are organized to represent, the overwhelming political tendency of the western states has been to reinforce the commitments of these local agencies. Western water law, for example, is built around the concept of appropriating water for beneficial consumptive use. Water flowing to the ocean is frequently looked upon as wasted water.

The role that the states have defined for themselves in relation to nonconsumptive uses of water has largely been that of a policeman seeking to regulate the behavior of persons making nonconsumptive use of water systems for fishing, recreation, boating, pollution abatement and other such purposes. The emphasis is upon the regulation of the conduct of persons rather than regulating the behavior of the water course so as to realize a greater resource potential. The states have done surprisingly little in water resource management *per se*.

Rarely have the states developed a coherent water policy that takes cognizance of both consumptive and nonconsumptive uses in a comprehensive state water plan. An exception to this general state of affairs exists in Oregon where a state water resources board has, since 1955, been charged with the responsibility of formulating a comprehensive state water program which recognizes both consumptive and nonconsumptive uses including, but not limited to, domestic use, municipal water supply, fire protection, irrigation, power development, mining, industrial purposes, navigation, sanitation, flood control, protection of commercial and game fishing, public recreation and scenic attraction as beneficial uses of the state's water resources. However, even in Oregon with a clear statutory mandate recognizing the beneficial character of nonconsumptive public uses, it has been difficult to change the perspectives of some state administrative officials who are inclined to recognize only consumptive use as having a valid claim for a commitment of the state's water resources.

Organizations for In-the-Channel Development of Water Resources—The organization for the management of in-the-channel control of large-scale river systems has posed a complementary set of problems which are fully as complex as the creation of institutions for the distribution of water supplies for consumptive uses. In fact, the two types of organization for consumptive and nonconsumptive use may not always stand in contradistinction to one another. In-the-channel management of a river system affects the total production of the water economy in both the consumptive and nonconsumptive uses. The stored waters captured during flood flows substantially increase the yield of a stream for both types of uses when these waters are released during the low water season. Many of the early reservoirs built to store flood flows for subsequent use during the irrigation season also contributed to the general function of river regulation. As an agency responsible for some of the first large-scale, multipurpose water resource projects, the Bureau of Reclamation was definitely committed to the priority of the consumptive use of water for an irrigated agriculture. Nevertheless, its operating responsibilities also involved major commitments to in-the-channel management of water resources for nonconsumptive purposes.

Few questions of organization as such have been the subject of as persistent inquiry and controversy as the organization of programs of large-scale water resource management of America's major river systems. On the one hand there is the task of constituting a pattern of organization which recognizes the functional interdependencies among the various uses that can be made of a river system. On the other hand, in-the-channel management of water resources needs to recognize the integrity of the river system so that projects are operated in a way that will complement one another in a comprehensive system of control for the river basin as a whole.

Thus far the states have not demonstrated a capacity to negotiate a satisfactory interstate arrangement that would provide an adequate vehicle for the regional management of an interstate watershed system. The hope that the interstate compact might become the appropriate vehicle for realizing "the principle of a regional problem, regionally administered" has been marked with disillusionment since the first negotiation of the Colorado River Compact. The states with their orientation to the dominance of consumptive uses have been primarily concerned with getting their "piece of pie" rather than with the development of regional programs related to regional and national communities of interest as well as to state, local, and private interests.

As a consequence, the federal government has become the most appropriate level of organization to undertake the development of water resources of the large interstate river systems. Furthermore, the U.S. Supreme Court has recognized that the authority over the development of waterways for purposes of navigation vests exclusively in the federal government by virtue of constitutional powers pertaining to interstate and foreign commerce. This constitutional authority coincidentally constitutes an important commitment to recognize the values of nonconsumptive, in-the-channel uses of a river in planning the development of its water resources. However, the proprietary interest of the federal government in large tracts of western lands has also been the source of important commitments to the development of the consumptive uses of water in that region.

With federal responsibility for in-the-channel water resource management in the large river systems has come the problem of formulating institutional arrangements which recognize the diversity of interests and potentialities for development among the different river basins while at the same time recognizing the extensive interdependence of interests within particular river basins. The Columbia River with its anadromous fisheries and arid lands, for example, poses quite a different problem of development than the Tennessee River. But within the Columbia basin the anadromous fisheries must be taken into account in the development of nearly every water works project. This task of recognizing a diversity of interests and potentialities as between different river basins and an interdependence of interests within individual river basins has been approached with some variations in patterns of organization in each major river basin in the United States. However, for purposes of analysis specific reference will be made only to experience in the Tennessee valley and in the Columbia basin.

The most heralded American experiment in the regional development of water resources is the Tennessee Valley Authority. The Tennessee Valley Authority Act stood for an integrated multiple-purpose river development program by a federal public corporation with jurisdiction over the whole Tennessee valley, a region impinging upon seven different states. The act included sweeping powers to provide flood control for the Tennessee basin, the improvement of navigation upon the river, and the development of hydroelectric power. In addition, the TVA was authorized to encourage the conservation and development of natural resources generally in the Tennessee basin and specific reference was made to reforestation, the production and sale of cheap fertilizers and the proper use of marginal lands. The TVA, thus, was charged with the task of undertaking the comprehensive development of the Tennessee valley, which had been a seriously depressed economic area. Since this responsibility was primarily vested with one agency functioning at the regional level, the program was characterized as an integrated regional approach to comprehensive resource planning.

As a water resource management agency, The TVA is primarily concerned with in-the-channel management and control of the river system for purposes of flood control, navigation and power production. It excluded power distribution from its operating responsibilities while encouraging the organization of local electric distribution systems by municipal and cooperative organizations in local community areas. The TVA has also divested itself of responsibility for providing shipping terminal facilities and is inclined to look upon the construction of levees and dikes not directly related to the management of the river control system as a local matter which should be provided by the local community.

In regard to other values or uses to be derived from the management of a water resource system the TVA has indicated sensitivity to the problems while avoiding any primary operating responsibility. The TVA, for example, operates no recreational areas or facilities of its own, but has encouraged state and local government agencies to take advantage of the recreational opportunities created by the TVA river control project. It has maintained a small recreational staff in its division of reservoir properties to advise and consult with state and local officials and with representatives of private groups regarding the development of facilities and the management of programs in the field of recreation.

The TVA operations in the areas of resource management which relate to the general social and economic development of the Tennessee valley have also been conducted with primary reliance upon previously existing agencies and institutional arrangements. The TVA has defined its role as an agency to provide technical assistance, financial support and demonstration projects rather than to assume operating responsibility in those fields. Its operating methods have emphasized cooperative arrangements, advice and consultation. In these areas the TVA is obviously dependent upon the decisions of others regarding the course of action taken in these cooperative programs concerned with resource management and economic development.

Thus, the TVA has tended to impose functional boundaries upon itself which limit its commitments in relation to interests that diverge from what it has defined as its primary operating responsibility over the mainstream river control system. It is much less than a fully integrated water resource management agency for the Tennessee River basin. It has avoided or divested itself of responsibility for values that relate primarily to local communities of interest. It has greatly limited its operating responsibility for resource management problems that are directly involved in flood control, navigation and power production. What has been integrated are the dominant values relating to flood control, navigation and power production. Other values are realized only as other cooperating agencies are willing to coordinate their programs with the TVA.

These commitments are also reflected in choices made regarding fiscal policy. TVA's commitment to low-cost public power has led to rigid restrictions limiting the use of power funds to finance power developments only. This fiscal inflexibility has led a sympathetic commentator to observe that, over time, the nonpower programs have suffered "both a relative and an absolute decline." These nonpower resource activities, "almost wholly dependent upon congressional grants, have seen their appropriations dwindle year after year until they are in some instances little more than shadow operations."[1]

There is evidence that TVA's initial period of enthusiastic growth and development has been replaced by a more routine administration of an in-the-channel river control program operated as an adjunct of an electric power production and wholesale business. Since the early 1950's, the TVA has expanded its electric steam plant generating facilities until its hydroelectric facilities are being dwarfed by comparison. When hard decisions require choice about the employment of limited funds for resource management activities, those decisions are apt to reflect values which conform to the central commitment of an agency while sacrificing other values with a lower order of priority. In the long-term process, the TVA's experience seems to indicate that an integrated comprehensive approach to the regional development of water resources is apt to become something less than fully "integrated" and wholly "comprehensive."

In contrast to the valley authority approach to water management problems, the Columbia basin has often been referred to as a "piecemeal" approach involving competing agencies with overlapping jurisdictions. The traditional water resource management agencies of the federal government with their special-purpose orientation are all involved in the administration of water resource programs in the Columbia basin. The Corps of Engineers with its commitment to functions of navigation and flood control is probably the most significant single operating agency on the Columbia River. The U.S. Bureau of Reclamation has developed some of its largest reclamation projects and river control structures in the Columbia basin. The U.S. Fish and Wildlife Service has substantial program obligations in the Columbia with its vital runs of salmon and steelhead as well as other sport and commercial fisheries. The Federal Power Commission has jurisdiction in the Columbia basin over some of the best hydroelectric power sites to be found anywhere in the United States. Only the Bonneville Power Administration among the federal agencies has a regional jurisdiction exclusive to the Pacific Northwest. The Bonneville Power Administration is responsible for operating an integrated power transmission grid which distributes hydroelectric power from the various power plants at dam sites to the principal load centers in the Pacific Northwest.

In addition to these functions performed by federal agencies, the states have had important responsibilities for controlling stream pollution, in regulating both commercial and sport fishing and in operating fish hatcheries in cooperation with federal fisheries programs, in developing and operating recreational facilities, in determining water rights among different types of consumptive water users, and more recently, in comprehensive planning for the multi-purpose development of local water resources. The states of Washington and Oregon, in particular, conduct major programs in their fields of responsibility for water resource administration. Local government agencies or districts also perform essential responsibilities in the operation of local distribution systems for electrical power supplies, irrigation, municipal water supplies and for the maintenance of local levees and channel improvements for flood control. Several private electric utilities maintain extensive service areas in the Columbia basin. Both privately owned public utilities and the publicly owned utility districts and municipal power systems operate large water control projects which produce a portion of the power load distributed to their local customers.

The growth of regional interests in the Pacific Northwest has been associated with the development of institutional arrangements for the preparation of research studies and planning reports and for fuller communication, consultation, deliberation and negotiation on a regional, interagency basis. The first effort to give a general regional focus to considerations of regional resource planning was the organization of the Pacific Northwest Regional Planning Commission as a part of the effort of the National Resources Committee (later the National Resources Planning Board) to deal broadly with questions of social and economic development. Its report on *Regional Planning, Part I: Pacific Northwest* was an important milestone in formulating basic perspectives regarding problems of regional development.[2] The development of the water resources of the Columbia River formed the central part of that report.

The regional planning commission's concern for the development of a public power policy which would encourage the general economic growth and development of the Pacific Northwest region led to the creation of the Bonneville Power Administration and its low-cost public power policies. The regional planning commission was also instrumental in organizing the Northwest Regional Council of Education, Planning and Public Administration to provide a common agency for the organization of research activities and a common forum for the exchange of ideas among professional personnel of the region's academic institutions, planning agencies and public administrative agencies concerned with resource problems and economic development.

Changing conditions of war and peace and of national politics and public policy lead to the demise of the regional planning commission, of the Northwest Regional Council and of other particular institutional arrangements, but these have been replaced by rich and varied institutional arrangements for planning, consultation and negotiation on an interagency, regional basis. Many of the primary resource agencies have regional advisory committees which have become a part of their planning and decision-making processes. Interagency intradepartmental and interagency interdepartmental field committees have seen extensive use. The departments of Interior, Agriculture and Commerce have maintained regional representatives to facilitate coordination among and between departmental agencies. Finally, many of these arrangements have been coordinated since 1946 with the organization of the Columbia Basin Inter-Agency Committee. The CBIAC serves in part as a forum for the exchange of ideas and a conference for the negotiation of interagency interests. It also provides an important means for professional administrative personnel to coordinate operations through the work of the vital water and power committees.

As these arrangements have led to decisions and to programs of action, basic operating commitments have been formed which require the various operating agencies to take each other into account in the conduct of a coordinated resource development program. Today, the Corps of Engineers is dependent upon the Bureau of Reclamation, which operates the larger upstream reservoirs, to provide its principal regulation for flood control. The Bonneville Power Administration depends upon the coordinated operations of the Bureau of Reclamation, the Corps of Engineers and a variety of publicly and privately owned electric power systems to produce the electric power transmitted over its regional grid. All of these electric power facilities are coordinated in a regional power pool. The financial feasibility of most of the region's reclamation projects are in turn dependent upon the pricing policies of Bonneville Power Administration. Some of the most imaginative work in engineering of fish facilities is being done by a private electric utility and by a municipal power system. These interagency operations have made regional, inter-agency institutional arrangements an imperative necessity in the Pacific Northwest. Independence of action without regard to other coordinated values can no longer be tolerated in the development of the Columbia River.

The differences between the patterns of water·resource management in the Tennessee valley and in the Columbia basin is largely one of degree rather than one of kind. The TVA has a relatively more dominant position in the control of the Tennessee River than any one of the water management agencies in the Pacific Northwest. Even the TVA, however, has divested itself of primary operating responsibility for such nonconsumptive, in-the-channel uses as recreation, and fish and wildlife. In both basins, the primary federal agencies can be viewed as the basic water producing agencies.

Water production is more nearly monopolized by the TVA in the Tennessee valley while a number of local government agencies and private companies maintain water producing facilities to supplement the basic federal control system in the Columbia basin. However, the licenses for these projects usually specify conditions that the utilities conform to requirements for maintaining public values regarding recreation, fish life and flood control in the design and operation of their projects. The problem of coordinating these systems in a water production program has been the source of some of the most intense controversies over water resource developments in the Pacific Northwest.

Organization for Comprehensive, Multi-Purpose Development—As the evolution of American institutions concerned with the development of water resources has unfolded, the earlier period of development saw a reliance upon private and local public agencies which placed emphasis upon the consumptive use of water supplies or upon water works related to on-the-land developments. These institutions were primarily related to local communities of interest in land and land-related developments. It was only much later that the concern for large-scale river control and management programs on a multi-purpose, regional basis came to the forefront in water resource developments. These tasks have been predominantly organized through agencies of the federal government. Both sets of agencies have performed vital roles which are essentially complementary to each other. The one set emphasizes the retail, distribution function. The other set emphasizes the production function.

This specialization in function has resulted in selective commitments and biases in the development of water policies at the different levels of government. The private and local public agencies have been overwhelmingly committed to the priority of values related to the consumptive use of water supplies. The predominant interest of these agencies in state politics has tended to reinforce a comparable commitment in state water law and water policies. The federal water production agencies, on the other hand, have tended to emphasize the interests associated with non-consumptive uses of water supply to the extent that these interests have been reflected at all.

If all of the goods in the water economy were amenable to production and distribution in the market, the solution to the problem would be relatively simple; or, contrariwise, if all of the goods realized in the use of water resources were subject to provision as public goods for a single community of interest, the problem of comprehensive multi-purpose development could be solved in a relatively simple way. Instead, the water economy includes a variety of goods some of which are more or less amenable to allocation in the private market, others which might be organized through private agencies but are involved in substantial questions of public interest and finally there are those goods which seem to be amenable only to public provision if they are to be provided at all.

Furthermore, these goods affect many different communities of interest. The variety of local communities of interest alone is immense. In addition, regional interest in water resource development has been one of the chief factors directing attention to the problems of regional organization within the American political economy. Finally, inter-basin transfers of water and hydroelectric power indicates that the watershed basin is not an isolable unit for definining interests in water resource development, but these transfers tend to point up interbasin regional and national interests of substantial proportions.

Theoretically, the allocation of water among competing demands for consumptive uses would be relatively simple to solve by market-type arrangements except for the essentially monopolistic character of water distribution systems and the necessity for making choices concerning the relative balance between consumptive and nonconsumptive uses in the water economy. Any effort to recognize the place of both consumptive and nonconsumptive uses of water will require a fundamental re-evaluation of state water law and of public bodies regulating the consumptive use of water supplies.

State water law requires re-evaluation since it determines the nature of the property to which various proprietors can make enforceable claims to water supplies or in reallocating surplus or waste waters.

The character of the use that can be made and the degree of transferability of a water right are defined within the framework of water law. Unfortunately, the bramble bush which some of the states have permitted to grow under the name of water law defies comprehension by even those who are the most learned in the mysteries of law. Many proprietors, unwilling to risk the security of their rights, insist upon an exclusiveness of control which denies many obvious economies of scale in interrelating distribution systems, in the interchange of water supplies or in reallocating surplus or waste waters.

If greater reliance is to be placed upon market allocation of water for consumptive use, the law must define the property in a water right with a view to the exclusiveness of proprietary interests, in relation to some readily specifiable and measurable unit of water which can be simply transferred in whole or in part. A definition of rights by reference to various correlative doctrines simply creates unavoidable confusion for market economies.

The interest of others, and especially the public interest in nonconsumptive uses can best be recognized by an enunciation of public policies which specify the conditions for the allocation of water for consumptive uses as against the reservation of water for nonconsumptive uses together with an indication of the public responsibilities of the various appropriators making consumptive demands upon water supplies. Here the state of Oregon has pointed the way with its emphasis upon comprehensive multi-purpose planning for water resource development. The amount of water available for appropriation for consumptive use is related to the development of plans which, when adopted by the State Water Resources Board, become a part of the state's water policy indicating the order of preferences among various consumptive and nonconsumptive uses and the stream flows to be maintained for nonconsumptive uses in particular watershed areas.

Any resolution of the conflicting interests of the federal and state governments over the validity of state water rights should take cognizance of the necessity of defining the public interests especially in relation to various public, nonconsumptive uses of water resources. A comprehensive water policy can be developed only when these interests are articulated. The special federal interests regarding in-the-channel water management programs suggests that federal agencies should be concerned that these interests be formulated as a part of the federal water policies that bear upon state water law.

The task of making plans regarding the relative allocation of water resources to nonconsumptive uses or in making allocations among the nonconsumptive uses is the most difficult area for decision-making in water resource development. Reliance upon methods of economic analysis where a dollar value is assigned to public uses is only a partial solution. Since the nonconsumptive uses do not have a directly salable market value an approximate dollar value must be assigned and this assignment of value must necessarily be somewhat arbitrary.

It is entirely possible that the commercial potentialities of the salmon fisheries, for example, have been seriously underestimated. Anadromous fish have a built-in guidance system which takes them to the ocean to pasture and to mature unattended, and then leads them back to spawn in the stream of their birth. It is even unnecessary for people to engage in such inefficient games as salmon fishing when fish ladders could direct a run of salmon to a fish market as easily as they can pass brood stock upstream. If a reasonable portion of the effort that our state universities and agricultural experiment stations have devoted to animal husbandry had been devoted to salmon husbandry, we might find salmon to be an extraordinarily valuable water product which should be given a much more important place in the water economy.

Since economic analysis at best provides a tool for making a gross approximation to questions of evaluation in planning for resource developments, attention should also be given to the way that organizations are constituted and related to one another as a political framework for making decisions and exercising control over events. The structure of organizational arrangements implicitly determines the basis for distinguishing the sets of events to be controlled, the order of preferences for ranking the values to be achieved by organized activities and the standards for determining the relevancy of information to be communicated in the decision-making process. Since the patterns of organization have a fundamental influence upon the development of perspectives, values and ideas regarding resource policies and patterns of resource development, any question of comprehensive planning must necessarily involve comparable questions about the design of organizational arrangements.

All aspects of administration and of economic development are based upon the assumption that efforts to control events will produce some greater benefits than if the events were not controlled. The initial problem in organization is to determine which sets of events is to be controlled in relation to some value reflected in the consequences to be realized. What these interests are and how they are ordered in relation to one another comprises the basic task in constituting any general system of organization.

In dealing with the development of water resources, the interests that are related to the various uses of water and of the flowing stream can theoretically be tied together in an integrated water agency. But such a decision necessarily means that land and water interests in recreation, energy, transportation, fish and wildlife and rural and urban community developments cannot be organized in similarly integrated agencies. The fact that the universe is not organized in mutually exclusive sets means that any form of organization must take account of the patterns of interrelationships among the different sets of events that are being controlled.

The experience in both the Tennessee valley and the Columbia basin would seem to indicate that the comprehensive development of water resources cannot be organized within the framework of a single integrated agency. Too many values are at stake in relation to too many different communities of interest. Changing requirements and conditions of life do not permit a simple ordering of values in which one set of values can be arbitrarily rejected and subordinated to another set of values. The organization of planning for comprehensive development must be able to tolerate conflict so that the various interests about controversial issues can be clarified, adequate intelligence can be organized and decisions can be negotiated. If the diverse interests can be negotiated and decisions reached, program can then be coordinated, each with the other, through a variety of operational agreements and contractual arrangements.

Water resource administration, because of the rich interrelationships among the various values or goods which can be derived from water, will require a very rich and complex system of organization in realizing the diverse values of multipurpose development. As patterns of demand change, we can anticipate that the patterns of organization will also change. Increasing competition for the available water supplies will certainly require a much greater clarification of the place of nonconsumptive uses in relation to the various consumptive uses of water. The choices among these uses will reflect the preferences which we as individuals make when we function as consumers and as citizens. If we are organized so that we can inform and articulate our interests both as consumers and as citizens, we should be able to arrive at those settlements in the use of water resources that represent the requirements for comprehensive development at any given period of time. A rich variety of both private and public agencies would be required in order to realize any such objective.

Joseph L. Fisher †

Resource Policies and
Administration for the Future*

The adequacy of raw materials and natural resources for the future has been a matter of major concern to people throughout history. It is of concern to people everywhere at the present time, although the contrast between the optimistic outlook in the United States and a few other advanced countries and the difficult outlook in the less developed countries is sharp. The need exists in both types of places, however, for well-conceived resource policies and their efficient administration. A continuation of present affluence, let alone its increase, depends upon maintaining the flow of low-cost raw materials and resource services of many kinds. Escape from the circle (where it exists) of low income, poverty, inefficient production, and low income again, requires major augmentation of the supply of cheap food, hydroelectric power, fuels, metals, and fresh water. National security is impossible without large capacity to produce or otherwise obtain those raw materials necessary to support major military strength, and this now includes virtually all raw materials.

Therefore, natural resources, both in the sense of products and in the sense of aspects of the environment such as amenities and economic location, remain important objects for national attention. This is true despite the declining role they play when their value is viewed as a per cent of the national product or when employment in their production is viewed as a per cent of total employment. In a real and inescapable sense the resource base supports the increasingly high and complicated structure of manufactures and services which characterizes the modern American technological economy.

*Reprinted by permission from *Public Administration Review*, XXI (Spring, 1961), 74–80. [Copyright by the American Society for Public Administration.] (Notes to this selection will be found on p. 435.)

†NOTE: For statistical and other material this article draws from the comprehensive appraisal of the trends and outlook for natural resources in the United States prepared in Resources for the Future, Inc. under the title *Resources for America's Future*.

CONTRADICTORY RESOURCE POLICIES

In the past and down to the present time resource policies in this country have been contradictory and have been devised in response to numerous problems and objectives arising mainly in nonresource fields. For example, during most of our history public land policy has responded successively to the need for frontier defenses and public revenues, to the desire for continental aggrandizement and land ownership, and to the urgency of providing roads and railroads. Water policy has evolved in response to successive single-purpose uses of water for navigation, irrigation farming, electric power, and flood control. Much of what passes for national minerals policy has come about as a means of encouraging and accommodating private enterprise in this field through such measures as tariff protection, rather easy terms for leasing mineral rights on public lands, tax advantages, and government regulation in the interests of conservation and more orderly private business. Only here and there in an unsustained way have resource policies been conceived and administered with primary concern for resource development as a whole or for the broad role that resources play in national development. This is true despite outstanding studies that have been commissioned at various times to address broad resource problems and recommend policies.[1] The difficulty has been not so much the absence of good studies and sets of recommendations as it has the failure for these to be translated into adequate legislative and executive action so that administration can proceed with the application of policies.

A basic reason for poor performance in this area of public concern is the failure to provide a framework within which resource problems can be visualized and policies shaped. There has not been an organized way of looking at the situation which permits a policy structure to be built. Without such a framework the nation is doomed to piecemeal attempts at national resource policy, characterized by inconsistencies which frustrate sensible and broad-gauged administration. For example, in the face of enormous surpluses of basic agricultural crops, how much and what kind of emphasis should be placed on soil conservation which ultimately will permit us to raise even more crops? How much quota protection and tax preference should be granted the domestic oil industry in view of the present glut of oil in the world? How much money and precious scientific talent should be spent in an effort to desalinize brackish and ocean water at lower and lower cost when most of the existing fresh water supply in the arid west is now used for low-return purposes? How much should be spent for the development of outdoor recreation facilities through land acquisition, investment in camping and other facilities, protection of nature and wildlife, in view of competing demands for both funds and the land and water resources?

DEMAND-SUPPLY POLICY FRAMEWORK

A serviceable framework within which resource trends can be seen and policies developed is the demand-supply framework. Such a framework consists of a display of the historical trends in demand for and supply of the variety of raw materials and natural resources which people want, along with a projection of these trends in an interrelated way for some years into the future—at least 20 years and perhaps even 40. Demand projections for the various intermediate products and basic resources can be made by extrapolating into the future past trends as they relate to the larger movements in the economy, such as production, income, investment, and the like. Allowances are made also for foreseeable demographic and technologic factors. The following table illustrates such a demand–

Table 29-1—Selected Economic and Resource Estimates for 1980 and 2000[a]

	1960	1980	2000
Economic Aggregates			
Population (millions)	180	245	330
Labor force (millions)	73	102	140
Households (millions)	53	73	100
GNP (billions)	503	1,060	2,200
GNP. per worker	7,000	10,000	15,000
Government expenditures ($ billion)	100	230	500
Private investment ($ billion)	73	160	340
Personal consumption expenditures ($ billion)	228	660	1,320
Intermediate Products			
Meat consumed (billion lbs.)	29	46	65
Cotton produced (billion lbs.)	7.5	10.4	16
Autos produced (millions)	7	13	27
New dwelling units (millions)	1.5	2.7	4.2
Steel produced (million tons)	99	175	340
Construction lumber produced (billion bd. ft.)	31	48	79
Fertilizer consumed (million tons)	25	41	67
Basic Resource Requirements[b]			
Cropland, including cropland pasture (million acres)	440	440	450
Forest land, commercial (million acres)	484	484	484
Grazing land (million acres)	700	700	700
Outdoor recreation land (million acres)	44	75	136
Urban land (million acres)	21	32	45
Timber (billion cu. ft.)	11	21	36
Water (billion gal./day)	250	340	480
Fuel (quadrillion BTU's)	45	83	136
Oil (billion bbls.)	3.2	5.4	9.6
Coal (million tons)	398	610	702
Iron ore (million long tons)	102	200	375
Aluminum (million tons)	2.1	9.6	20.0
Copper (million tons)	1.7	3.5	7.1

[a] Source: Taken from work in progress at Resources for the Future under the provisional title of "Resources in America's Future,"
[b] From domestic and foreign sources.

supply framework by showing a few of the items. Medium estimates are shown, although there is actually a range of possibilities.

From this presentation of current and projected future demand one may turn to the consideration of supply potentialities and difficulties, item by item. One can look first at the domestic capacity for producing an item, and then in turn, examine possibilities for new discoveries, new technology, increased productivity, substitutions, larger imports, and so on. In the first instance, it may be assumed that costs and prices remain in their present relative position. If on this basis a supply problem is brought into view, either on the shortage or on the surplus side, one may then consider the various reaction paths which may ensure as costs and prices move upward or downward. For example, if there appears to be an impending shortage of a particular item, say lumber or fresh water, one may consider the chain of effects that might follow an increase in cost and price in terms of price elasticities of demand and supply, possibilities for substitution, incentive to exploration and adoption of new technology, possibilities for increasing imports, and so on. What are some of the general lines of policy and administrative action in the resource fields that seem to be indicated?

Croplands

Our medium projection of the amount of cropland which will be needed by 2000 shows only a slight increase over the 440 million acres needed now. (Actually an estimated 460 million acres were in use in 1960, resulting in some overproduction.) That is to say, continued increases in yields per acre will more or less counterbalance increases in demand arising chiefly from increased population but also to some degree from improved diet, higher consumption of meat, and other factors. Over the next ten or so years some reduction in acreage would be helpful, perhaps 5 or so per cent, until such time as the tendency toward overproduction can be brought in hand. Some good agricultural land favorably located with respect to markets undoubtedly will have to be shifted into urban and suburban uses as metropolitan areas extend outward into rural land. Perhaps some 160,000 acres a year on the average will be added to urban and suburban uses. Other farm land will go to highways and airfields. But still for at least the next few years overproduction of many crops will point to the need for farm land retirement.

Recreation Lands

Present trends indicate that much additional land will be required for outdoor recreation as the next few decades pass. With nearly 85 per cent larger population in 2000, with per capita income about twice as high, with a shorter work week and longer vacations, and with perhaps four times as many automobiles and very great increases in air travel, it seems perfectly clear that the demand for outdoor recreation 40 years hence may increase by as much as five or ten times over what it is now. This will mean the acquisition and development of much more land for public recreation, as well as for private recreation, the intensification of use in present recreation areas, the need for much more careful location of recreation areas to encourage greater use, the development of water resources and wilderness for appropriate recreation purposes, and so on.

Lumber

Of all the truly basic raw materials, lumber seems to present the sharpest problem. This has been true for some years in the past as may be seen from the relatively large increases in price of lumber compared to other raw materials and in the fact that we produce domestically and consume no more now than we did 40 or 50 years ago. This has stimulated some new technology in the use of low grade and scrap wood and has led to the substitution of plastics, paper, and metals for lumber in certain uses. For the future, however, it is clear that vigorous policies should be pursued to increase the yield of sawtimber from our forest land. The greatest potential seems to lie on the smaller private holdings, predominantly in the south and northeast. This problem reduces itself largely to finding ways of encouraging better forest management on these holdings through extension services, tax alterations, better credit, appropriate insurance, and a host of other measures. A frontal attack on this problem might yield good returns, rather than looking upon it in a fractured way as a small part of several other types of policy having to do with agriculture, land tenure, soil conservation, credit generally, and forest policy oriented to national forests.

Water

In water the visible problems include insuring a more adequate supply in the more arid west and cleaner water in the more populated industrial areas where rainfall is relatively plentiful. In the arid portion of the country, in addition to the development of new supply through dam and reservoir construction and conserving water generally, there is an obvious need for redirecting the use of water, at least new supplies of water, from lower-value to higher-value uses; that is, toward domestic, industrial, and recreational use as this may prove possible through changes of public and private policy. In the more plentiful water supply regions, especially in the Northeast, the Midwest, and the Southeast, the problem can be pinpointed as one of preventing and abating pollution so that supplies may be used and reused for a variety of purposes. Beyond this there is a critical need for maintaining at all times minimum flow in the streams as a means of diluting and carrying off wastes. A good beginning has been made in estimating demand for and supply of water by some

22 river basins in the country, having in mind costs of developing additional supply and minimum flow requirements.[2] Water problems have to be dealt with by major river basins. Thus, if the prospect in a region is for shortage or increasing cost of fresh water, and the magnitude of the shortage can be portrayed, it becomes possible for a set of policies to be established which is designed to provide direction and consistency to the variety of actions for overcoming the shortage or moderating its harmful effects. Actions in this case can be varied and may include more intensive research on desalinization, reservoir films to reduce losses from evaporation, means for long-distance transport of water, as well as construction of storage facilities. Some of these actions may be taken at the national level while others are more appropriate for states, localities, or even the individual users. They can be held together in a pattern more readily if all of them flow from a comprehensive view of the trends and probabilities and are thus directed more consistently toward solutions.[3]

Energy

In energy several objectives will continue to be important: low cost, convenience, certainty of supply. The prospect is that the American economy could obtain from domestic sources the energy supplies it will require for the next 15 or so years at no general increase in cost.[4] Cheaper supplies of oil might be imported. For the last 20 or 25 years of the century one cannot now say that domestic supplies will be available in sufficient volume to prevent cost and price increases without resort to nuclear energy on a fairly large scale, at least for production of electric power and in high-cost regions. But this, in turn, will depend upon further scientific and technological developments for reducing the cost of nuclear power. The energy economy is characterized by flexibilities and substitutions. This has been true in the past as we have shifted first from wood to coal and then to oil and natural gas. Maintaining flexibility should continue to be a principal object of policy. This implies an emphasis on research and pilot plant operations into new ways of handling conventional fuels, as well as the new sources such as nuclear fission, oil shale, tar sands, and others. The demand–supply way of portraying the situation and outlook can provide a framework within which problems of shortage or surplus, cost, substitutions, exports and imports, and the like can be seen to good advantage, and in terms of which alternative policies can be tested.

Metallic Minerals

For the metallic minerals many of the policy objectives cited for the energy commodities also hold. There may be greater advantages in importing many of the metallic minerals, and frequently there is somewhat less opportunity for substitution. Already we depend heavily on imports of copper, lead, zinc, nickel, manganese, bauxite, tungsten, and numerous others. The degree of dependence on foreign supplies has now become so great that military security requires stockpiles. This country now has some $8.5 billion invested in various nonagricultural stockpiles, principally metals, but it is a debatable question whether this is too much, just about right, or not enough. Much hinges on the kind of war that is hypothecated—its intensity, duration, the degree and kind of damage, and the recovery time. The outlook for as far into the future as one can see will be for large imports of metallic minerals, implying a need for lines of policy which can accommodate this.

Resource policies for minerals or for anything else are not sufficient unto themselves, but are part of yet broader national policies. For example, policies having to do with the disposal of surplus food crops in less developed countries, or with oil and metallic minerals imports, are strongly interrelated with foreign economic policy and foreign policy generally. Water development policy, insofar as it involves public works, has to be viewed as a part of public works and development policies generally, and as a part of employment policy since certain kinds of water projects may be speeded up to aid in counteracting economic recession. Energy policies are very closely related to national security policy in the broad sense; indeed, the major justification for tax-depletion allowances in the oil and gas industries has to do with the need of special treatment to insure an adequate rate of exploration and discovery to meet conceivable defense situations.

Natural resource policies, like other policies, aim to provide a general guide to the flow of decisions on how to deal with foreseeable problems, in this case resource problems. If the problems cannot be seen with some clarity and quantitative perspective, the policies which aim to solve them have little chance of success. But the demand–supply framework, important and useful though it is, is not the only way of looking at resource problems policies. Many questions have to do with equities, returns, and special benefits among segments of the population and for various industries and regions. These are not seen in any full sense through a demand–supply window, even though the demand–supply framework can be exceedingly useful for such problems, and no resources policy should be established without some reference to the demand–supply outlook.

LESSONS FOR PUBLIC ADMINISTRATION

In the final part of this paper I shall direct attention to more closely defined matters of public administration. What lessons for public administration may be drawn from this long-range. comprehensive, demand–supply way of looking at resource problems and policies?

Policy and Action

Administrative decisions and actions, in resource as well as other fields, are best when they flow from clearly enunciated general policies. The long-range comprehensive demand–supply way of looking at resource problems can aid greatly in furnishing broad and consistent policies. Administrators should be concerned not only with policies themselves but also with the factual and analytical basis for them. This is obviously a necessity for administrators at the upper levels; it is of almost as much importance for administrators at lower levels in understanding their own jobs and as training for advancement to higher positions. That is, an administrative decision down the line relating to a land or mineral lease or to a contract for purchase of timber stumpage should reflect a high fidelity to broad policies relating not only to leases and government contracts, but also to land or forest policy in the broadest sense. Furthermore, an administrator down the line should understand the close connections between administrative policies strictly speaking and substantive policies, and the need for flexibility in applying the former to serve the purposes of the latter. Frequently this kind of flexible administration is to be sought in the timing of an action, for example the letting of a government contract, the placing of a purchase order, or even the scheduling of a crucial meeting.

Administrative Flexibility

Diversity of local conditions, both bureaucratic and geographic, points to the desirability of wide latitude and discretion in administration at the several administrative levels. For example, any program to improve management of small private forest holdings should be adapted to local forest conditions, local management practices, alternative land uses in the area, various educational and skill levels, local credit institutions, and to the ways in which government administration has been successfully carried out locally. That is to say, policy built for the long range should be flexible, and policy flexibility will be thwarted unless administration can also be flexible to an appropriate degree all down the line.[5]

Administering Long-Range Programs

Administrators will have to be prepared to cope with administering longer-range programs than they have had to administer heretofore. They will also have to deal increasingly with interrelated and multiple-purpose resource programs. Neither of these features is new; for example, administrators of the Tennessee Valley Authority have long regarded resources as both long-range and multiple-purpose in character. In the future nearly all resource administration will take on these characteristics. Furthermore, the span of interrelated purposes is being widened even beyond the resource fields proper into foreign policy, research and educational matters, full employment and production, and so on. All of this implies the need for broader training for resource administrators, both in the schools and through job experiences.

Administration and Research

Administrators in coming years will have to handle much larger research programs since the long view ahead of resource problems points clearly to the necessity for new discoveries, new techniques of extraction and handling, development of cheaper and more plentiful substitutes, and so on. A rich flow of innovations can only be sustained by generous support of basic research and education for such research. It may be anticipated that in the future all resource agencies throughout federal, state, and local government will be more concerned with research than they have been in the past; indeed this item in resource budgets may well prove to be the most rapidly growing item. Research personnel in some respects are a special breed requiring special attention. Their job is to come up with new ideas, think them through, and perhaps test them out; administration in all its aspects must be adapted to this primary objective. Beyond this, administrators will have to know more about the world of universities and private research institutes since much research in the public interest will continue to be done in them, either on their own or with the aid of government funds.

Education and Training

In order to bring along the trained professional specialists that will be necessary if we are to have the flow of raw materials our future needs indicate will be required, government agencies will find themselves increasingly involved in the education and re-education of their employees. Expansion of the federal executive's training program, by means of which government employees go back to school as it were, can be expected. If there is no school to which they can go and receive the kind of training they need, it will be imperative that government agencies aid in the establishing of such programs. The federal government has long been involved in agricultural education, not only in its practical aspects but in basic research and theory. In the future the federal government may also have to provide help in the establishment or expansion of education and research programs in other resource fields such as hydrology, plant and forest genetics, mineral economics, multiple-purpose resource administration, among others. Special attention should be given in the universities to natural resources as a field of study to be approached through various science and social science disciplines. Any re-evaluation of the land grant colleges might consider these possibilities.

Policy Conflicts

Administrators will have to foresee policy conflicts before they become acute and be prepared to point out the administrative pros and cons of the alternative solutions, to undertake the administration of whichever solution is decided upon, and to audit the ensuing administrative experience. Policy conflicts may be foreseen in many resource fields: the shift from rural to urban land use on the outskirts of metropolitan areas, increasing production on small forest holdings, acquisition of recreation land, water allocation especially in the west, water and air pollution control in metropolitan areas, import regulations for oil and certain metallic minerals, stimulation of domestic mineral exploration through special tax and other incentives. One of the best ways to get a glimpse of possible future conflicts is through a careful examination of the trends of demand and supply as outlined earlier. This kind of format of the future also gives clues as to which present conflicts may dissolve more or less without any effort from policy and program and which ones will have to be dealt with forthrightly.

Structure for Policy-Making

As a final point it may be noted that responsibility for providing the framework of demand–supply estimates will have to be pinned down. It could be done in the Department of the Interior or the Department of Agriculture where much long-range projection work is already done for agricultural crops, although the job is essentially broader than the scope of any one department. Or it could be assigned to an interdepartmental committee established for the purpose, although this might prove clumsy and involve endless hassles. Or it could be done in the Executive Office of the President, possibly in the Council of Economic Advisers or under the leadership of that agency. Objectivity and close tie-in with general economic projections might best be achieved in this case, but at the sacrifice of more detailed knowledge of natural resources. The task would fall naturally to a Council of *Resource* Advisers, should the bill calling for this be passed by the Congress. A workable arrangement, short of new legislation, would be to create by presidential action a resources council made up of top representatives from the Council of Economic Advisers and the Bureau of the Budget, from the Executive Office of the President, and from the departments of the Interior, Agriculture, Army, and Health, Education, and Welfare, the so-called resource departments, preferably with an independent chairman appointed by the President to the White House staff for this purpose. A council of this sort would have to have some professional staff and be able to call on departments and agencies for assistance. Presumably, it would do other things besides furnishing a long-range demand–supply framework; it might make policy studies and provide guidance, and it might evaluate and perhaps coordinate development programs.[6]

To get the job done of creating the long-range perspective and framework within which alternative policies and administrative actions can be conceived and tested is the important thing. Precisely where it is done—in connection with the Council of Economic Advisers, by a new council of resource advisers of some sort, or through some combination—is also important, but is open to choice.

Notes

Lynton K. Caldwell: Environment—A New Focus for Public Policy?

1. For an historical account of environmental theories, including a criticism of environmental determinism, see Franklin Thomas, *The Environmental Basis of Society* (New York and London, 1925). For an example of a far-reaching theory of political development based upon indirect effects of man–environment relationships, see Karl A. Wittfogel, *Oriental Despotism: A Comparative Study of Total Power* (New Haven, 1957).

2. Some of these have been analyzed by Gilbert F. White in "The Choice of Use in Resource Management," *Natural Resources Journal*, I (March, 1961), 23–40.

3. A major political reason for segmental decision-making on environmental matters has been developed by Clyde S. Wingfield in "Power Structure and Decision-Making in City Planning," *Public Administration Review*, XXIII (June, 1963), 74–80. An illustration of the political consequences of our traditional approach to resources policy is developed by Roy Hamilton in "The Senate Select Committee on National Water Resources: An Ethical and Rational Criticism," *Natural Resources Journal*, II (April, 1962), 45–54.

4. For example, the influence of the new regional science. See Walter Isard, *Methods of Regional Analysis—An Introduction to Regional Science* (New York, 1960).

5. Cf. Henry C. Hart, *Administrative Aspects of River Valley Development* (New York, 1961).

6. Cf. Daniel R. Mandelker, *Green Belts and Urban Growth—English Town and Country Planning in Action* (Madison, 1962).

7. Cf. William L. Slayton, "The Administrator's Role in Bringing Better Design into City Rebuilding," *Journal of Housing* XIX (Sept. 14, 1942), 365–368.

8. C. A. Doxiadis, *Ekistics—The Science of Human Settlements* (Southampton, England: Town and Country Planning Summer School, 1959).

9. As a sample, see:

U.S. Public Health Service, *Environmental Planning Guide*, Publication No. 823 (Washington, D.C.: Government Printing Office, 1961) [note Preface and Introduction].

Kevin Lynch, *The Image of the City* (Cambridge, 1960).

Philip L. Wagner, *The Human Use of the Earth* (Glencoe, Ill., 1960).

Journal of the American Institute of Architects, XXXV (March, 1961) [special issue on urban design].

Jane Jacobs, *The Death and Life of Great American Cities* (New York, 1961).

Jean Gottmann, *Megalopolis: The Urbanized Northeastern Seaboard of the United States* (New York, 1961).

August Heckscher, *The Public Happiness* (New York, 1962), Chaps. 13–14.

10. This viewpoint is rapidly gaining acceptance among urban renewal administrators; cf. remarks by William L. Slayton relative to "the need for a comprehensive approach to the development and renewal of urban areas" in a talk, "Towards a

Comprehensive Urban Policy: National Interest" at the Annual Conference, American Institute of Planners, Detroit, Michigan, Nov. 29, 1961.

11. Cf. Norman Wengert, "Resource Development and the Public Interest: A Challenge for Research," *Natural Resources Journal*, I (Nov., 1961), 207–223.

12. This opinion seems consistent with a conclusion reached by some students of natural resources administration that better policy guidance is a concomitant, if not a necessary antecedent, of more effective administrative coordination; cf. Irving K. Fox and Lyle E. Craine, "Organizational Arrangements for Water Development," *Natural Resources Journal*, II (April, 1962), 31 ff. [especially 34 and 39]. But the development of policy and organization are inseparable because, as Vincent Ostrom puts it: "Since the patterns of organization have a fundamental influence on the development of perspectives, values and ideas regarding resource policies and patterns of resource development, any question of comprehensive planning must necessarily involve comparable questions about the design of organizational arrangements." "The Water Economy and Its Organization," *Natural Resources Journal*, II (April, 1962), 72.

Hans H. Landsberg: The U.S. Resource Outlook—Quantity and Quality

1. See Harold J. Barnett and Chandler Morse, *Scarcity and Growth: The Economics of Natural Resource Availability* (Baltimore, 1963).

2. Ibid., p. 86.

3. Ibid., p. 235 ff.

4. John R. Platt, *The Step to Man* (New York, 1966), pp. 185–203.

5. Hans H. Landsberg, Leonard L. Fischman, and Joseph L. Fisher, *Resources in America's Future* (Baltimore, 1963); and Hans. H. Landsberg, *Natural Resources for U.S. Growth* (Baltimore, 1964).

6. A cautionary view of prospects for rising yields in developed countries was advanced by Lester R. Brown at the December, 1966, meeting of the American Association for the Advancement of Science. (See *Journal of Commerce*, January 3, 1967; no published version as yet available.)

7. For a recent attempt, see, for instance, Joseph L. Fisher and Neal Potter, *World Prospects for Natural Resources* (Baltimore, 1964).

8. Mason Gaffney, "Applying Economic Controls," *Bulletin of the Atomic Scientists* (May, 1965), pp. 20–25.

9. J. W. Milliman, "Can People Be Trusted with Natural Resources?", *Land Economics* (August, 1962), pp. 199–218.

10. Ibid.

11. Appreciation is expressed to the Cooper Foundation Committee, Swarthmore College, for permission to utilize material first developed in connection with a talk on conservation presented to a symposium in February, 1966.

Raymond A. Bauer: The Policy Process

1. For a fuller discussion of how these assumptions are not appropriate to what happens in policy formation, see Martin Patchen, "Decision Theory in the Study of National Action: Problems and a Proposal," *Journal of Conflict Resolution* (June, 1965).

2. The pioneering work in this field is Robert Schlaifer, *Probability and Statistics for Business Decisions* (New York: McGraw-Hill, 1959).

3. Raymond A. Bauer, Ithiel de Sola Pool, and Lewis A. Dexter, *American Business and Public Policy* (New York: Atherton Press, 1963).

4. For an articulate and detailed discussion of this distinction, see the contrast between the views of human behavior held by psychologists and that held by policy-makers in Sir Geoffrey Vickers, *The Art of Judgment* (New York: Basic Books, 1965), pp. 31–34.

Robert H. Salisbury: The Analysis of Public Policy

1. David Easton, *The Political System* (New York: Alfred A. Knopf, Inc., 1953), pp. 129 ff.

2. In a more recent statement Easton defines policy as "decision rules adopted by authorities as a guide to behavior. . . . In this sense, policies would be just a term for a kind of authoritative verbal output" (*A Systems Analysis of Political Life* [New York: John Wiley & Sons, 1965], p. 358). See also pp. 6–9 and 27–29, above.

3. Thus Easton: "But the term [policy] is used in a second and broader sense to describe the more general intentions of the authorities of which any specific binding output might be a partial expression" (Ibid.). From the days of Frank Goodnow on, the distinction is a familiar one.

4. Harold D. Lasswell and Abraham Kaplan, *Power and Society* (New Haven: Yale University Press, 1950), p. 71.

5. Carl J. Friedrich, *Man and His Government* (New York: McGraw-Hill Book Co., 1963), p. 79.

6. Reitzel, Kaplan, and Coblentz suggest rather the reverse, however: that policy refers to specific actions designed to achieve objectives or realize interests (*United States Foreign Policy, 1945–1955* [Washington: Brookings Institution, 1956], p. 473).

7. Lewis A. Froman, Jr., "An Analysis of Public Policies in Cities," *Journal of Politics*, XXIX (Feb., 1967), 95.

8. Thus, though these studies differ on many other dimensions too, one may contrast the findings of Maurice Pinard, to the effect that communities with certain demographic characteristics that presumably indicated high alienation are likely to refuse fluoridation of water, with those of Robert Crain and Donald Rosenthal, who argue that the *process* by which the fluoridation issue is diffused in the community makes a critical difference to the question of adoption. Pinard uses a simple dichotomy of yes–no on the issue ("Structural Attachments and Political Support in Urban Politics: The Case of Fluoridation Referendums," *American Journal of Sociology*, LXVIII [March, 1963], 513–26). Crain and Rosenthal use more continuous variables and get a richer result ("The Fluoridation Decision: Community Structure and Innovations," unpublished manuscript, 1965).

9. See the imaginative efforts along this line of James A. Robinson in *Congress and Foreign Policy Making*, rev. ed. (Homewood, Ill.: Dorsey Press, 1967).

10. Froman, "Analysis of Public Policies," summarizes much of the list.

11. Thus comparative state policy analysis has proceeded faster than its counterpart at the urban level in part because of the much readier comparability of state expenditure categories. On the difficulties of comparative urban studies, see the essay by James Q. Wilson, "Problems in the Study of Urban Politics," in *Essays in Political Science*, ed. Edward Beuhrig (Bloomington: Indiana University Press, 1966).

12. Froman, "Analysis of Public Policies," p. 104.

13. Theodore J. Lowi, "American Business, Public Policy, Case-Studies, and Political Theory," *World Politics*, XVI (July, 1964), 677–715. Lowi actually seems to go both ways; he conceptualizes policies in "terms of their impact or expected impact on the society" (p. 689), but in discussing redistributive policy he says, "Expectations about what it *can* be . . . are determinative" (p. 691).

14. It would seem to me appropriate to subject, for example, agricultural policy decisions and bills of the past 30 years to content analysis. My hypothesis would be that over time the structure of policy has grown increasingly complex, especially in its treatment of commodities. This change would, I think, be more or less systematically related to the "commoditization" of agricultural production. See John P. Heinz, "The Political Impasse in Farm Support Legislation," *Yale Law Journal*, LXXI, (April, 1962), 952–78.

15. I propose to beg the question, important though it be, of how to get at the appropriate perceptual data. I suspect much of it can be taken and ordered from the public record, but much would depend too on sophisticated interviewing instruments whose shape is beyond the scope of this paper.

16. This is why the conversion of a dispute over substance to one over procedure may be expected to reduce the intensity of the conflict. I should also note that what Lowi means by regulation may be somewhat different. He stresses the "sector" level at which regulatory policy operates, an indicator that would be compatible with my argument. Beyond that, however, either he or I remain unclear as to the precise meaning of his usage.

17. Good examples of self-regulation policy include not only professional licensing (see V. O. Key, *Politics, Parties and Pressure Groups*, 5th ed. [New York: Thomas Y. Crowell Co., 1964], pp. 122–23), but the successful quest of the National Association of Retail Druggists for fair-trade legislation (see Joseph Palamountain, *The Politics of Distribution* [Cambridge: Harvard University Press, 1955], chap. 8).

18. Another typology I think especially suggestive is one that differentiates between incremental and innovative outcomes. There is thus far little reported research that explores this distinction, and I shall not attempt to explore it here. Nevertheless, it seems reasonably clear that there are innovative policy breakthroughs from time to time which do not, as incremental choices may, reflect comparable shifts in system resources or, in any easily observable way, major changes in the structure of political demands. Once made, in the area of state spending policy, for example, they often establish new and lasting levels from which incremental adjustments may depart. But how and why they are made, especially if they are made in the absence of system crisis of some kind, remains mysterious, to me at least. William Buchanan has called my attention to the major increase in Virginia's state spending which has occurred since the death of Harry Byrd, Sr., despite the continued presence in authoritative positions of former Byrd protégés. A comparable jump shift took place in Kentucky some years ago without any obvious political explanation. For an effort to explore the incremental character of the federal budgetary process, see Otto A. Davis, M. A. H. Dempster, and Aaron Wildavsky, "A Theory of the Budgetary Process," *American Political Science Review*, LX (Sept., 1966), 529–48.

19. For a recent attempt, see Froman, "Some Effects of Interest Group Strength in State Politics," *American Political Science Review*, LX (Dec., 1966), 952–63. At different levels of complexity and contextual richness are Forrest McDonald, *We the People* (Chicago: University of Chicago Press, 1958); Robert S. Friedman, *The Michigan Constitutional Convention and Administrative Organization: A Case Study in the Politics of Constitution-Making* (Ann Arbor: Institute of Public Administration, University of Michigan, 1963); and Robert H. Salisbury, "The Dynamics of Reform: Charter Politics in St. Louis," *Midwest Journal of Political Science*, V (Aug., 1961), 260–75.

20. See especially Robert A. Dahl, *A Preface to Democratic Theory* (Chicago: University of Chicago Press, 1956) and *Pluralist Democracy in the United States* (Chicago: Rand McNally & Co., 1966).

21. See, for example, John H. Kessel, "Governmental Structure and Political Environment," *American Political Science Review*, LVI (Sept., 1962), 615–20; Raymond E. Wolfigger and John Osgood Field, "Political Ethos and the Structure of City Government," *American Political Science Review*, LX (June, 1966), 306–26; Edward C. Banfield and James Q. Wilson, *City Politics* (Cambridge: Harvard University Press, 1963); and a large number of others.

22. See the summary of this literature in Froman, "Analysis of Public Policies."

23. The proportional-representation debate may still be sufficiently alive to call this conclusion into question.

24. I take this to be the thrust of James McGregor Burns' argument in his

Deadlock of Democracy: *Four-Party Government in America* (Englewood Cliffs, N.J.: Prentice-Hall, Inc., 1963).

25. See, generally, David Truman, *The Governmental Process* (New York: Alfred A. Knopf, Inc., 1951), and Grant McConnell, *Private Power and American Democracy* (New York: Alfred A. Knopf, Inc., 1966).

26. A recent discussion of the relationship between pluralism and consensus is Dan Nimmo and Thomas Ungs, *American Political Patterns* (Boston: Little, Brown & Co., 1967).

27. See Stephen K. Bailey, *The Condition of Our National Political Parties* (Santa Barbara, Calif.: The Fund for the Republic, 1959), or E. E. Schattschneider, *Party Government* (New York: Farrar & Rinehart, 1942).

28. Ivo K. Feierabend and Rosalind L. Feierabend, "Aggressive Behavior within Polities, 1948–1962: A Cross-National Study," *Journal of Conflict Resolution* (Sept., 1966).

29. See Truman's discussion to the effect that pluralism, at least when combined with overlapping memberships, leads to consensus on the rules of the game (*Governmental Process, passim*, and especially pp. 503 ff.).

30. See, for example, C. E. Lindblom, *The Intelligence of Democracy* (New York: Free Press, 1965).

31. Aaron Wildavsky's *Dixon-Yates* (New Haven: Yale University Press, 1962) is an impressive study of this kind of case.

32. William Riker's *Democracy in the United States* (New York: Macmillan Co., 1953) is one of the clearest among the many statements of this general position.

33. Thomas R. Dye, *Politics, Economics, and the Public*: *Policy Outcomes in the American States* (Chicago: Rand McNally & Co., 1966), p. 300.

34. Richard E. Dawson and James A. Robinson, "Inter-Party Competition, Economic Variables, and Welfare Policies in the American States," *Journal of Politics*, XXV (May, 1963): 265–89.

35. Richard I. Hofferbert, "Ecological Development and Policy Change in the American States," *Midwest Journal of Political Science*, X (Nov., 1966), 464–85, and "The Relation between Public Policy and Some Structural and Environmental Variables in the American States," *American Political Science Review*, LX (March, 1966), 73–82; Dye, *Politics*; and Phillips Cutright, "Political Structure, Economic Development and National Social Security Programs," *American Journal of Sociology*, LXX (March, 1965), 537–50.

36. For an application of this argument in explaining differences in state political systems taken as wholes, see John Fenton, *Midwest Politics* (New York: Holt, Rinehart & Winston, 1966), and Daniel Elazar, *American Federalism*: *A View from the States* (New York: Thomas Y. Crowell Co., 1966). Fenton has elsewhere attempted to rehabilitate party competition as a significant variable by distinguishing between issue-centered and job-centered or traditional party competition. The argument has appeal, but his evidence is not persuasive. See *People and Parties in Politics* (Chicago: Scott, Foresman & Co., 1965).

37. I am indebted to Ira Sharkansky for an advance look at his *Spending in the American States* (Chicago: Rand McNally & Co., 1968), which demonstrates this relationship. Also cf. Lindblom, *Intelligence of Democracy*, and Davis, Dempster, and Wildavsky, "Theory of the Budgetary Process."

38. Cf. Dahl, *Who Governs?* (New Haven: Yale University Press, 1961).

39. V. O. Key's classic contribution in *Southern Politics* (New York: Alfred A. Knopf, Inc., 1949) and his contention that *political*, as distinguished from party, competition has an important bearing on policy outputs have not yet been shown to be invalid, since the more recent studies employ interparty competition as the measure.

In any event, as Key shows, demand patterns can be observed, and they vary profoundly from state to state.

40. Stephen K. Bailey, *Congress Makes a Law* (New York: Columbia University Press, 1950).

41. See Heinz, "Political Impasse."

42. Illustrative references for the points that follow can be cited at length but, I think, without improving the persuasiveness of the argument. Hence I have omitted them.

43. The literature on teacher certification, much of it polemical, makes this point: See, for example, James Koerner, *The Miseducation of American Teachers* (Boston: Houghton-Mifflin Co., 1960).

44. See Palamountain, *Politics of Distribution.*

45. This seems to me the essence of Samuel Gompers' classic position regarding the feasibility of labor's entry into politics.

46. See the discussion of Agriculture Department agency proliferation in Charles Hardin, *The Politics of Agriculture* (Glencoe, Ill.: Free Press, 1952), and in Grant McConnell, *The Decline of Agrarian Democracy* (Berkeley: University of California Press, 1953).

47. See Marver Bernstein, *Regulating Business by Independent Commission* (Princeton, N.J.: Princeton University Press, 1955), and Samuel Huntington, "The Marasmus of the ICC," *Yale Law Journal*, LX (April, 1952), 467–509.

48. See Harry Eckstein, *Pressure Group Politics* (London: Allen & Unwin, 1960). Eckstein concludes his analysis by arguing that to understand pressure groups in a system one must incorporate the system's policies, governmental structures, and political culture. Thus he says very nearly what I argue here, though I think without fully developing the theory that links these components together.

49. It should perhaps be added that a decisional system that, as in Congress, employs as a primary unit the geographically defined district or state must think of demands and encourage others to think of themselves in largely distributive terms. Rather than thinking of labor, farmers, businessmen, or the poor in general, such a system disaggregates them into particular geographically specialized unions, commodity groups, firms and industries, and neighborhoods.

50. See, for example, James Burnham's outspokenly conservative defense of congressional fragmentation, *Congress and the American Tradition* (Chicago: Henry Regnery Co., 1959), and James McGregor Burns' outspokenly liberal defense of Presidential integration, *Deadlock of Democracy.*

51. Lowi, "American Business."

52. See Richard Neustadt, "Presidency and Legislation: The Growth of Central Clearance," *American Political Science Review*, XLVIII (Sept., 1954), 641–71, and "Presidency and Legislation: Planning the President's Program," *American Political Science Review*, XLIX (Dec., 1955), 980–1021.

53. American farm policy and politics during the past several decades presents, I believe, a persuasive case study illustrating this general argument, and with Professor John Heinz of the Northwestern University School of Law I hope to complete this study in the near future.

54. See Harmon Zeigler, "Interest Groups in the States," in *Politics in the American States*, ed. Herbert Jacob and Kenneth N. Vines (Boston: Little, Brown & Co., 1965), chap. 4.

55. Joseph A. Schlesinger, "The Politics of the Executive," in ibid., chap. 6.

56. Richard Fenno's brilliant analysis of the appropriations process in Congress shows, however, that as the House Appropriations Committee has achieved a high degree of integration for itself, it is able to convert appropriations policy into an effective means of regulation (*The Power of the Purse* [Boston: Little, Brown & Co., 1966]).

57. See my discussion of the local unity norm of the Missouri legislature, whereby demand integration is required as a condition of granting local self-regulation authority: "Schools and Politics in the Big City," *Harvard Educational Review*, XXXVII (Summer, 1967), 408–24.

58. Gilbert Steiner, *Social Insecurity: The Politics of Welfare* (Chicago: Rand McNally & Co., 1966), especially p. 239 ff.

Arthur Maass: Benefit–Cost Analysis—Its Relevance to Public Investment Decisions

1. Robert Dorfman (ed.), *Measuring Benefits of Government Investments* (Washington: Brookings, 1965).

2. For conditions under which regional redistribution in the United States can be achieved without any significant loss in economic efficiency, see Koichi Mera, "Efficiency and Equalization in Interregional Economic Development," unpublished Ph.D. thesis, Harvard University, 1965. For a more general statement of the relations between economic efficiency and income distribution, see Stephen A. Marglin, "Objectives of Water-Resource Development: A General Statement," in Arthur Maass, Maynard M. Hufschmidt, Robert Dorfman, Harold A. Thomas, Jr., Stephen A. Marglin, and Gordon Maskew Fair, *Design of Water-Resource Systems* (Cambridge: Harvard University Press, 1962), pp. 63–67.

3. This example is adapted from Marglin, "Objectives of Water-Resource Development."

4. For a discussion of these problems as of 1961, see Chaps. 2 (Marglin), 3 (Dorfman), and 4 (Marglin) in Maass, Hufschmidt, *et al.*, *Design of Water-Resource Systems*; and Maynard M. Hufschmidt, John Krutilla, and Julius Margolis, with assistance of Stephen A. Marglin, "Report of Panel of Consultants to the Bureau of the Budget on Standards and Criteria for Formulating and Evaluating Federal Water Resources Developments" (Washington, June 30, 1961), mimeo. For examples of more recent developments see Peter O. Steiner, "The Role of Alternative Cost in Project Design and Selection," *The Quarterly Journal of Economics*, LXXIX (Aug., 1965), 417–30, and Kenneth J. Arrow, "Discounting and Public Investment Criteria," paper presented at Water Resources Conference, Fort Collins, Colorado, July 6, 1965.

5. The term has been used also to describe a small class of *efficiency* benefits that are *induced* rather than *produced* directly, by the public investment, but this distinction is of questionable utility.

6. Hubert Marshall, "Politics and Efficiency in Water Development," Fort Collins, Colorado, July 7, 1965.

7. There are causes, in addition to what I consider to be the principal cause, for so-called benefit overestimation, and these, but not the principal cause, are given in Marshall's Fort Collins paper.

8. Arthur Maass, "System Design and the Political Process: A General Statement," in Maass, Hufschmidt, et al., *Design of Water-Resource Systems*, p. 588.

9. The origin of this provision of the Flood Control Act of 1936 (49 Stat. 1570) did not, incidentally, come from a Presidential initiative.

10. U.S. Federal Inter-Agency River Basin Committee. Subcommittee on Benefits and Costs, *Proposed Practices for Economic Analysis of River Basin Projects* (May, 1950).

11. U.S. Bureau of the Budget, *Circular A-47*, Dec. 31, 1952.

12. See for an example Richard A. Musgrave, *The Theory of Public Finance* (New York: McGraw Hill, 1959). The first of these labels is perhaps correct technically, but even this cannot be said of the others, for efficiency is not necessarily either less or more value laden, or altruistic, or meritorious than other objectives.

13. In essence this is what Dorfman proposes for West Pakistan. Robert Dorfman, "An Economic Strategy for West Pakistan," *Asian Survey*, III (May, 1963), 217–23.

14. Stephen A. Marglin, "Objectives of Water-Resource Development," pp. 17–18, 62–67. Jan Tinbergen, *On the Theory of Economic Policy* (Amsterdam: North Holland, 1952), observes that in the normal case *n* programs (or instruments) are required to maximize a welfare function that includes *n* objectives (or targets). But for his normal case Tinbergen assumes that only the results of the programs, not their qualitative characteristics, affect welfare and that planners are free to select that level of achievement of each objective that maximizes the overall welfare function. This freedom is theirs only if *n* programs are available to the planners. Our discussion, on the other hand, proceeds from the assumptions that the qualitative characteristics of the programs affect welfare, and that the number of acceptable programs may be fewer than the number of objectives, which necessitates the trade-off among objectives. This would be an abnormal case in Tinbergen's formulation.

15. W. W. Charters, Jr. and Theodore M. Newcomb, "Some Attitudinal Effects of Experimentally Increased Salience of a Membership Group," in Eleanor E. Maccoby, Theodore M. Newcomb, and Eugene L. Hartley, *Readings in Social Psychology* (New York: Henry Holt, 1958), pp. 276–81.

16. Arthur Maass, "System Design and the Political Process: A General Statement."

17. Anthony Downs, "The Public Interest: Its Meaning in a Democracy," *Social Research*, XXIX (Spring, 1962), pp. 18–20, 27–32; Gerhard Colm, "The Public Interest: Essential Key to Public Policy," in C. J. Friedrich (ed.), *The Public Interest* (New York: Atherton, 1962), p. 121; Jerome Rothenberg, *The Measurement of Social Welfare* (Englewood Cliffs, N.J.: Prentice-Hall, 1961), pp. 296–97.

18. Marglin's 1962 analysis is one demonstration of this.

19. For an excellent summary of this research see Rothenberg.

20. See Stephen A. Marglin, *Public Investment Criteria* (London: Allen and Unwin, 1966).

21. My data are taken from David C. Major, "Decision Making for Public Investment in Water Resource Development in the United States," unpublished Ph.D. thesis, Harvard University, 1965, chap. 5. See this thesis for citations of statutes and reports referred to here.

22. This design standard was amended in 1963 to provide for predicted traffic volumes twenty years from date of approval of project plans.

23. The Act of 1956 contemplated completion by fiscal year 1969, but both estimated costs and year of completion were later amended.

24. The Clay report's proposals on tax policy and accounting procedures for financing the road system, which we do not discuss here, were altered significantly in the legislative process.

25. Except where otherwise noted, the facts of this case are derived from legislative documents relating to the Housing and Urban Development Act of 1965: President's Message (H. Doc. 89–99); Hearings before Subcommittees on Housing of the House and Senate Committees on Banking and Currency (Mar.–April, 1965); Reports of House and Senate Committees on Banking and Currency (H. Report 89–365, S. Report 89–378); Debate in House and Senate (*Cong. Rec.* for June 28–30 and July 14–15); Conference Report (H. Report 89–679; Debate in House and Senate on adoption of Conference Report (*Cong. Rec.* for July 26–27). Dr. David C. Major has assisted in developing the facts and interpretation of this case.

26. Under the Administration bill the rent supplement would be the difference between rent for standard housing and 20 per cent of a moderate-income family's income. Under the act as approved, the rent supplement is the difference between the same rent and *25* per cent of a *low*-income family's income. The two changes made by Congress work in opposite directions, but they do not offset each other.

Charles E. Lindblom: The Science of "Muddling Through"

1. James G. March and Herbert A. Simon similarly characterize the literature. They also take some important steps, as have Simon's recent articles, to describe a less heroic model of policy-making. See *Organizations* (John Wiley and Sons, 1958), p. 137.

2. "Operations Research and National Planning—A Dissent," *Operations Research*, V (Oct., 1957), 718. Hitch's dissent is from particular points made in the article to which this paper is a reply; his claim that operations research is for low-level problems is widely accepted. For examples of the kind of problems to which operations research is applied, see C. W. Churchman, R. L. Ackoff and E. L. Arnoff, *Introduction to Operations Research* (John Wiley and Sons, 1957); and J. F. McCloskey and J. M. Coppinger (eds.), *Operations Research for Management*, II, (The John Hopkins Press, 1956).

3. I am assuming that administrators often make policy and advise in the meking of policy and am treating decision-making and policy-making as synonymous for purposes of this paper.

4. Martin Meyerson and Edward C. Banfield, *Politics, Planning and the Public Interest* (The Free Press, 1955).

5. The line of argument is, of course, an extension of the theory of market choice, especially the theory of consumer choice, to public policy choices.

6. A more precise definition of incremental policies and a discussion of whether a change that appears "small" to one observer might be seen differently by another is to be found in my "Policy Analysis," *American Economic Review*, XLVIII (June, 1958), 298.

7. The link between the practice of the method of successive limited comparisons and mutual adjustment of interests in a highly fragmented decision-making process adds a new facet to pluralist theories of government and administration.

8. Herbert Simon, Donald W. Smithburg, and Victor A. Thompson, *Public Administration* (Alfred A. Knopf, 1950), p. 434.

9. Elsewhere I have explored this same method of policy formulation as practiced by academic analysts of policy ("Policy Analysis," *American Economic Review*, XLVIII [June, 1958], 298). Although it has been here presented as a method for public administrators, it is no less necessary to analysts more removed from immediate policy questions, despite their tendencies to describe their own analytical efforts as though they were the rational–comprehensive method with an especially heavy use of theory. Similarly, this same method is inevitably resorted to in personal problem-solving, where means and ends are sometimes impossible to separate, where aspirations or objectives undergo constant development, and where drastic simplification of the complexity of the real world is urgent if problems are to be solved in the time that can be given to them. To an economist accustomed to dealing with the marginal or incremental concept in market processes, the central idea in the method is that both evaluation and empirical analysis are incremental. Accordingly I have referred to the method elsewhere as "the incremental method."

Morton Grodzins: The Many American Governments and Outdoor Recreation

1. J. Frederick Dewhurst and Associates, "America's Needs and Resources, A New Survey," (New York: The Twentieth Century Fund, 1955), chap. 2. See also Marion Clawson, "The Crisis in Outdoor Recreation," *American Forests*, March, 1959, p. 5, [Resources for the Future, reprint No. 13].

2. Laurence I. Hewes, Jr., "The Demand for Outdoor Recreation—Implications for Natural Resource Allocation," speech presented Aug. 24, 1960, before the Western Resources Conference, Boulder, Colo.

3. Personal communication from Colorado Game and Fish Department.

4. "Public Recreation in Private Forests," *American Forests*, April 1958, p. 72.

5. Since the paragraph was written, the Corps of Engineers has evolved new policies placing "major emphasis on comprehensive planning. . . . Recreation is . . . dealt with in the same manner as any other use of water resources." In addition, "steps have been taken . . . to assure that adequate lands are acquired to meet the needs for future recreation use and development in accordance with the policy of the administration . . ." Personal communication from office of Assistant Secretary of the Army, "Financial Management," Aug. 25, 1961.

6. The text of Secretary Udall's moratorium notice is given in the *Federal Register*, Feb. 16, 1961, p. 1382.

7. For discussion of actual and potential conflicts in multiple-use administration of national forests, see Evan W. Kelley, "Problems of Land Management and Administration Arising from Associated Uses of Land for the Various Services which the Public Seeks from the National Forests," *Proceedings of the Western Farm Economics Association*, 1938; Marion Clawson and Burnell Held, *The Federal Lands: Their Use and Management* (Baltimore: The Johns Hopkins Press, 1957), chaps. 2 and 3. I have also profited from reading an unpublished paper by Prof. Michael McCloskey of the University of Oregon.

8. Federal Inter-Agency Committee on Recreation, "The Role of the Federal Government in the Field of Public Recreation," Washington, D.C., mimeographed, rev. ed., 1956, p. 21. (This report is hereafter cited as "The Role of the Federal Government.") The Fish and Wildlife Service also has important responsibilities in recreation planning for reservoirs of the Bureau of Reclamation and the Corps of Engineers.

9. "Directory of State Outdoor Recreation Administration," a commission staff project based on an American Political Science Association study, ORRRC Study Report 14.

10. Ibid., chapter on Arizona.

11. Clayton E. Anderson, "Cooperation Helps to Build Parks in Oregon Counties," *The County Officer*, May 1961, p. 146.

12. "A Progress Report to the President and to the Congress by the Outdoor Recreation Resources Review Commission," Government Printing Office, Washington, 1961, p. 62.

Mister Z: The Case for a Department of Natural Resources

1. Hoover Commission—Report on Organization of the Executive Branch of the Government, 1949, p. 267.

2. H.R. Doc. No. 255, 86th Cong., 2d Sess. (1960).

3. Address on Natural Resources, *N.Y. Times*, Feb. 24, 1961, p. 12, col. 1.

4. S. 2549, 86th Cong., 1st Sess. (1959); S. 239, 87th Cong., 1st Sess. (1960); S. 1415, 87th Cong., 1st Sess. (1961).

5. Reorganization Act of 1949, 1 U.S.C. § 133z (1949).

6. Ibid., § 133z–4.

7. Note 5 above.

Orris C. Herfindahl: What is Conservation?

1. Gifford Pinchot, *Breaking New Ground* (New York: Harcourt, Brace and Co., 1947), p. 326.

2. *Proceedings of the Joint Conservation Conference*, Sen. Doc., 60th Cong., 2nd Session, Vol. 10, p. 123.

3. Quoted in Samuel P. Hays, *Conservation and the Gospel of Efficiency* (Cambridge: Harvard, 1959), p. 41.

4. Ibid., passim.

Norman Wengert: Resource Development and the Public Interest—
A Challenge for Research

1. *N.Y. Times*, Mar. 26, 1961, p. 22, col. 1.

2. It might be noted, interestingly, that although Massachusetts, when still a colony, reserved title in the so-called "Great Ponds" in the state, this foresight (obviously not in contemplation of the automobile and the population pressure of 180 million people) did not include provision for public access. As a result in this and many another state, questions of public access to recreation resources are among the most difficult pressing for solution.

3. 72 Stat. 238, 16 U.S.C. 17 (k) note.

4. The most significant recent work on the political process remains Truman, *The Governmental Process* (1951). See also Gross, *The Legislative Struggle* (1953); and *Political Behavior* (Eulau ed.) (1956).

5. The pragmatic aspect of administration is trenchantly described by Long, "Power and Administration," *Public Administration Review* (1949), 257–64. This is also a dominant impression of the description of the Roosevelt administration by Burns, *Roosevelt: The Lion and the Fox* (1956).

6. Schubert, *The Public Interest* (1960), p. 220.

7. The implicit logical dilemma posed by legislative action in which both majority and minority declare that they voted "in the public interest" illustrates well the analytical problem.

8. The account of how this principle was developed is recorded in Pinchot, *Breaking New Ground* (1947), p. 326.

9. See McConnell, "The Conservation Movement—Past and Present," *Western Political Quarterly* (1957), p. 463.

10. Soil scientists, speaking professionally, do not make such statements. But much of the pamphlet literature and popular articles suggest this point of view.

11. For a discussion of this topic see Department of Agriculture, Handbook No. 18, Soil Survey Manual 25 (1951).

12. This point of view is frequently stated. For example, Kenneth D. Morrison, Vice President, National Audubon Society, wrote: "It seems clear that we cannot long maintain our present standard of living if we continue to destroy land as rapidly as we have since 1800. . . . Some 500 thousand acres of crop-land are lost by erosion each year. An average cultivated acre yields from $15 to $50 in newly created wealth each year. Over a century, the return from an acre would be $1500 to $5000—and that acre could still be on the job producing wealth. . . . It has often been said that our civilization rests upon six to nine inches of topsoil. Destroy that layer and we destroy the 'land bank' on which our farm economy depends." From *The Voice*, XXI (March 1956), p. 1, published by Carlton College. Contrast this view with that expressed in the Soil Survey Manual mentioned in note 11, pp. 268–69: "Erosion by itself . . . means little or nothing. Tons or inches of soil lost through erosion have little general meaning in terms of soil productivity. . . . Many eroded soils were very poor for crops or pasture to begin with. The erosion of such soils does not greatly reduce their capability for use. . . . It cannot be accepted that even dramatic-appearing erosion has destroyed the soil for crop production unless it has been established that the soil was suitable for crops before it was eroded. It may originally have been suited only to forest and may still be well suited to forest with proper management, even after it is eroded. . . ." See also Simonson, "The Soil Under Natural and Cultural Environments," *J. Soil and Water Conservation*, VI (April 1951), p. 7, who concludes: "Looking broadly at the changes in soils following their shift to a cultural environment, we should be hard pressed to prove that the net result had been either good or bad. . . . We can say that we could have used many of them better, both for our immediate purposes and for the future, had we known more about them. . . . Someone looking back upon our

handling of our soils from a vantage point in the distant future may well find that our stewardship on the whole was good." And see Simonson, "Changing Place of Soils in Agricultural Production," *Scientific Monthly,* LXXXI (Oct., 1955), pp. 173–82; and Kellogg, "Conflicting Doctrines About Soils," *Scientific Monthly,* LXVI (June, 1948), pp. 475–87.

13. Dr. Charles E. Kellogg, U.S. Department Agriculture, Chief of the Soil Survey, has stressed that an impoverished, troubled people pass their sufferings on to the land. By this he means that the root causes of most bad land management are social and economic. See Kellogg, "Soil and the People," *Annals Ass'n Am. Geog.,* XXVII (Sept., 1937), pp. 142–48.

14. For these views see Roos and Maass, "The Lobby that Can't be Licked", *Harpers Magazine,* August, 1949, p. 21; Miller, "The Battle That Squanders Billions," *The Saturday Evening Post,* May 14, 1949, p. 30; Maass, *Muddy Waters* (1951) and the U.S. Committee on Organization of the Executive Branch of the Government, Task Force Reports 1–2 (1949), and the Hoover Commission—Report on Organization of the Executive Branch of the Government (1949).

15. The most authoritative works on the flood problem are: Leopold and Maddock, *The Flood Control Controversy* (1954) and Hoyt and Langbein, *Floods* (1955). Leopold and Maddock state, p. 30: "There will always be a flood bigger than the one experienced," and ". . . unless construction costs exactly keep pace with increases in development within the flood-plain, which is not likely, it is but a matter of time till benefits will exceed costs. Then when the flood exceeding the one planned for comes, the damage will be tremendous."

16. Some progress has been made toward eliminating doubtful projects by use of cost-benefit analyses. But the scope of these analyses is in practice severely limited with the result that there is considerable controversy as to who shall do the cost-benefit studies. Leopold and Maddock, on p. 134, discuss some of the limitations of the cost-benefit approach. See also Wengert, "The Politics of River Basin Development," *Law and Contemporary Problems,* XXII (1957), pp. 258–75.

17. 4 U.S.C. §§ 1001–18 (1959).

18. For an analysis of the objectives of water policy see Fox, "National Water Resources Policy Issues," *Law and Contemporary Problems,* XXII (1957), pp. 472–509.

19. The literature on economic decision-making in monopoly situations is suggestive in this connection. For a summary see Wilcox, *Public Policies Toward Business* (1955), especially chaps. 1, 30 and 31.

20. A somewhat similar point is made in Dahl and Lindblom, *Politics, Economics and Welfare* (1953), especially in chaps. I and II.

21. For example, dramatic appeals are made for expansion of public power facilities in the Northwest. Forgetting the issues of private vs. public power, these appeals miss the fundamental question of national economic policy, i.e., whether and to what extent the Pacific Northwest should be the location for public investment in general, and in power facilities in particular.

22. Some of these terms are analyzed in Wengert, "Politics of River Basin Development."

23. Although sometimes cited as supporting the urgency argument, a close reading of The President's Materials Policy Commission, *Resources for Freedom* (1952), indicates quite clearly that the problem of shortages is a long-range problem. See also the interim report on resources and national growth research in Resources for the Future, Inc., *Annual Report* (1956), pp. 62–70.

24. See Wengert, *Natural Resources and the Political Struggle* (1955), especially chap. 3, where the exceptionally difficult problem of projection into the future is discussed.

25. For a discussion of this approach, see ibid., chap. 5, "The Search for the Public Interest."

25. As quoted in Van Dyke, *Political Science: A Philosophical Analysis,* (1960), p. 4.

27. As quoted on the fly leaf of Frank, *Law and the Modern Mind* (1936).

28. Simon, *Administrative Behavior* (1949), p. 62.

29. Ibid., p. 68.

30. Ibid., p. 70.

Gerald F. Vaughn: In Search of Standards for Preserving Open Space

1. New York Open Space Act (1960), Section 875, Part 2.

2. Jeanne M. Davis, "Getting and Keeping Open Space," 1963 Yearbook of Agriculture—*A Place to Live* (U.S. Government Printing Office: Washington, D.C., 1963), p. 337.

3. See Davis, pp. 337–338 for the best effort at such definition.

4. Outdoor Recreation Resources Review Commission, *The Future of Outdoor Recreation in Metropolitan Regions of the United States*; Study Report 21, Volume I (U.S. Government Printing Office: Washington 25, D.C., 1962), p. 40.

5. Ibid.

6. American Public Health Association, *Planning the Neighborhood: Standards for Healthful Housing* (Public Administration Service: Chicago, Ill., 1960), pp. 47–49.

7. George D. Butler, *Introduction to Community Recreation* (McGraw-Hill Book Co., Inc.: New York, N.Y., 1949), p. 157.

8. Institute of Public Administration, *The Future of Outdoor Recreation in Metropolitan Regions of the United States*, ORRRC Study Report 21, Volume II (U.S. Government Printing Office: Washington 25, D.C., 1962), p. 50.

9. Outdoor Recreation Resources Review Commission, *Outdoor Recreation for America* (U.S. Government Printing Office: Washington 25, D.C., 1962), pp. 30–32.

10. Summarized from Baltimore Regional Planning Council, *Standards for Parks, Recreation Areas, and Open Spaces* (Maryland State Planning Commission: Baltimore, Maryland, 1958), p. 15.

11. Ibid.

12. Ibid., p. 17.

13. Baltimore Regional Planning Council, *Open Spaces*, Technical Report No. 5, 1960, p. 24.

14. F. Stuart Chapin, Jr., *Urban Land Use Planning* (Harper and Brothers: New York, 1957), p. 309.

15. University of California (Los Angeles), Graduate School of Business Administration, *The Future of Outdoor Recreation in Metropolitan Regions of the United States,* ORRRC Study Report 21, Vol. III (U.S. Government Printing Office: Washington 25, D.C., 1962), p. 74.

16 Ann Louise Strong, *Preserving Urban Open Space,* (Washington: U.S. Housing and Home Finance Agency, Feb., 1963), p. 5.

17. Outdoor Recreation Resources Review Commission, *Outdoor Recreation for America* (Washington: U.S. Government Printing Office, 1962), p. 183.

John Kenneth Galbraith: How Much Should a Country Consume?

1. References here are to *Resources for Freedom* (Washington: U.S. Government Printing Office, June, 1952). Summary of Volume I, hereinafter cited as PMPC, Summary.

2. New York: The Ronald Press, 1954.

3. J. Frederic Dewhurst and Associates, *America's Needs and Resources: A New Survey* (New York: The Twentieth Century Fund, 1955).

4. PMPC, Summary, p. 5.

5. Ibid., p. 10.

6. Ibid., p. 16.

7. *The Affluent Society* (Boston: Houghton Mifflin, May, 1958).

Ashley L. Schiff: Outdoor Recreation Values in the Public Decision Process

1. Frederick Burk Foundation for Education, *Federal Agencies and Outdoor Recreation* I (U.S. Outdoor Recreation Resources Review Commission Rep't No. 13, 1962). The agency responsible for this report will hereinafter be referred to as ORRRC.

2. Official Proceedings of the White House Conference on Conservation 29 (U.S. Government Printing Office, 1962).

3. *Hearings on Department of the Interior and Related Agencies Appropriations for 1965 Before the House Committee on Appropriations*, 88th Cong., 2d Sess. 3 (1965).

4. U.S. Bureau of Outdoor Recreation, *Manual: Nationwide Plan, Planning and Survey Series* (1964).

5. I. K. Fox, *Trends in River Basin Development*, Proceedings of the Ninth National Watershed Congress (1962).

6. P. Diesing, *Reason in Society* (Univ. of Ill. Press, 1962), pp. 179–80.

7. *N.Y. Times*, Oct. 17, 1963, p. 25, col. 4.

8. *Hearing on S. 859 Before the Senate Committee on Interior and Insular Affairs*, 88th Cong., 1st Session 14 (1963).

9. Staff of Subcommittee on Intergovernmental Relations, Senate Committee on Government Operations, 88th Cong., 1st Session, *Impact of Federal Urban Development Programs on Local Government Organization and Planning* (Committee Print 1964), p. 34–35.

10. 77 Stat. 49 (1963), 16 U.S.C. § 460 (*l*) (1964). See also 109 *Congress Record* 8779 (1963).

11. E. Cliff, "Multiple-Use Planning in National Forest Management," in *Land, and Water: Planning for Economic Growth* (Western Resources Conference, Univ. of Colo. 1961), p. 73. See also statement of Conrad Wirth in *Hearings on H.R. 6289 Before the House Committee on Agriculture*, 87th Cong., 1st Session 126 (1961).

12. ORRRC, Proceedings of the Fourth Joint Meeting With Its Advisory Council (1961), p. 44.

13. U.S. Bureau of Outdoor Recreation, "Federal Executive Branch Policy Governing the Selection, Establishment, and Administration of National Recreation Areas" (Policy Circular No. 1, Recreation Advisory Council, 1963).

14. 109 *Congress Record* 25167 (1963).

15. *Hearings on Watershed Projects Before Senate Committee on Agriculture and Forestry*, 87th Cong., 1st Session (1961), p. 20.

16. *Hearings on California Wildlife Land Withdrawals Before House Committee on Interior and Insular Affairs*, 87th Cong., 1st Session, ser. 5 (1961), p. 37.

17. E. Crafts, *Federal Focal Point in Outdoor Recreation* (U.S. Bureau of Outdoor Recreation 1964), p. 13.

18. R. Nash, "The American Wilderness in Historical Perspective," *Forest History* (Winter, 1963), p. 5.

19. Ibid., p. 11.

20. Ibid.

21. S. Olson, "A Philosophical Concept," *First World Conference on National Parks* (U.S. National Park Service, 1964), pp. 47–48.

22. E. Swift, "Planning for Resource Availability," *Conservation News*, Jan. 15, 1965, p. 3.

23. Statement of Secretary of the Interior Stewart W. Udall in *Proceedings of the*

Fourth Joint Meeting of the Outdoor Recreation Resources Review Commission With Its Advisory Council (ORRRC, 1961), p. 13.

24. A. Green, *Recreation, Leisure, and Politics* (McGraw-Hill, 1964), p. 39.

25. A. Etzioni, *Modern Organizations* (Prentice-Hall, 1964), p. 9.

26. R. Lucas, "Wilderness Perception and Use: The Example of the Boundary Waters Canoe Area," *Natural Resources Journal* (1964), p. 102. [Also p. 308 this volume]

27. W. H. Whyte, *Open Space Action* (ORRRC Report No. 15, 1962), p. 2.

28. 72 Stat. 238 (1958).

29. 75 Stat. 183 (1961), 42 U.S.C. § 1500(e) (1964); Whyte, p. 34.

30. U.S. National Park Service News Release of May 30, 1961.

31. ORRRC, Outdoor Recreation for America (1962), p. 83.

32. Ibid., p. 49.

33. *Hearings on H.R. 6423 Before the House Committee on Banking and Currency*, 87th Cong., 1st Session (1961), p. 740.

34. ORRRC, *Proceedings of the Fourth Joint Meeting With Its Advisory Council* (1961), p. 135.

35. Green, p. 34.

36. H. S. Perloff and L. Wingo Jr., "Urban Growth and the Planning of Recreation," in *Trends in American Living and Outdoor Recreation* (ORRRC Report No. 22, 1962), p. 96.

37. 369 U.S. 186 (1962). This is the landmark reapportionment case.

38. *Hearings on S. 1381 Before the Senate Committee on Interior and Insular Affairs*, 87th Cong., 1st Session (1961), p. 120; *Hearings Before the House Committee on Agriculture*, 87th Cong., 1st Session, ser. W, (1961), p. 268.

39. 78 Stat. 903 (1964), 42 U.S.C. § 460(*l*) (1964).

40. 75 Stat. 183 (1961), 42 U.S.C. § 1500(e) (1964).

41. Advisory Commission on Intergovernmental Relations, *1965 Legislative Program* (U.S. Government Printing Office, 1964).

42. In the White House Message on Natural Beauty, H.R. Doc. No. 78, 89th Cong., 1st Session (1965), p. 3, note the recommendation that broadens the program by "permitting grants to be made to help city governments acquire and clear areas to create small parks, squares, pedestrian malls and playgrounds."

43. Consider the Saarinen Arch in St. Louis.

44. One example is the Mt. Auburn Cemetery operated by the Massachusetts Horticultural Society.

45. M. Grodzins, "The Many American Governments and Outdoor Recreation," in *Trends in American Living and Outdoor Recreation* (ORRRC Report No. 22, 1962), p. 73. [Also p. 131 this volume.]

46. 72 Stat. 563 (1958), 16 U.S.C. § 661 (1964).

47. U.S. Department of the Interior News Release of Feb. 5, 1963.

48. National Wildlife Federation, "New Regulations May Cut Highway Stream Damage," *Conservation News*, July 15, 1963, p. 5.

49. *Congress Record* 21469 (1963), p. 109.

50. Interview With Marion Clawson, Director, Land Use and Management Program, Resources for the Future, Inc., in Los Angeles, Fall, 1963.

51. J. Shanklin, *A Study of Multiple Use of Land and Water Areas* (ORRRC Report No. 17, 1962), p. 9.

52. 75 Stat. 183 (1961), 42 U.S.C. § 1500(c) (1964).

53. A. Wildavsky, *Politics of the Budgetary Process* (Little, Brown, 1964), p. 167.

Gilbert F. White: Formation and Role of Public Attitudes

1. *Quest for Quality*: U.S. Department of the Interior Conservation Yearbook (Washington: U.S. Government Printing Office, 1965), p. 13.

2. Lynton K. Caldwell, "Environment: A New Focus for Public Policy?", *Public Administration Review* (1965), p. 138. [Also p. 18 this volume.]

3. Herbert Simon and J. March, *Organizations* (New York: John Wiley and Sons, 1958).

4. William J. Gore, *Administrative Decision-Making: A Heuristic Model* (New York: John Wiley and Sons, 1964).

5. *Outdoor Recreation for America*, U.S. Outdoor Recreation Resources Review Commission (Washington: U.S. Government Printing Office, 1962), p. 27.

6. *Quest for Quality*, p. 6.

7. The report currently is in preparation under the title of *Attitudes Toward Water: An Interdisciplinary Exploration*. Principal participants have been Fred L. Strodtbeck, Meda White, William Bezdek, and Don Goldhammer from the Laboratory of Social Psychology, and W. R. Derrick Sewell, David Czamanske and Richard Schmoyer, from the Department of Geography. Several of the cautions as to definition were suggested by Fred Strodtbeck.

8. David Lowenthal, "Geography, Experience, and Imagination: Towards a Geographical Epistemology," *Annals of the Association of American Geographers*, LI (1961), pp. 241–60.

9. Jerome S. Bruner and Cecile C. Goodman, "Value and Need as Organizing Factors in Perception," *Journal of Abnormal and Social Psychology*, XLII (1947), pp. 33–44.

10. Leon Festinger, *A Theory of Cognitive Dissonance* (New York: Harper and Row, 1957).

11. Robert Beck, "Spatial Meaning, and the Properties of the Environment," in *Environmental Perception and Behavior*, ed. David Lowenthal (Chicago: University of Chicago Geography Research Papers, in press).

12. Lowenthal, "Geography, Experience, etc."

13. Clarence J. Glacken, "Changing Ideas of the Habitable World," in *Man's Role in Changing the Face of the Earth* (Chicago: University of Chicago Press, 1956), pp. 70–92; and "Man's Attitude Toward Land: Reflections on the Man-Nature Theme as a Subject for Study," in *Future Environments of North America*, the papers of the Conservation Foundation Conference of 1965 (New York: The Natural History Press, 1966). See also Alexander Spoehr, "Cultural Differences in the Interpretation of Natural Resources," in *Man's Role in Changing the Face of the Earth*, pp. 93–102.

14. Yi-Fu Tuan, "Attitudes Toward Environment: Themes and Approaches," *Environmental Perception and Behavior,* ed. David Lowenthal (Chicago: University of Chicago Geography Research Papers, in Press).

15. Bernard Berelson, *Content Analysis in Communication Research* (Glencoe: Free Press, 1952). David Czamanske applied this type of analysis to the Boulder data, using material printed in the *Boulder Camera* during one month and compiled by Mary B. White.

16. Ruth Miller Elson, *Guardians of Tradition: American Textbooks of the Nineteenth Century* (Lincoln: University of Nebraska Press, 1964), pp. 39–40.

17. Douglas R. McManis, *The Initial Valuation and Utilization of the Illinois Prairies, 1815–1840* (Chicago: University of Chicago Geography Research Series. No. 94, 1964), pp. 49–58, 89–85.

18. The Program Surveys were initiated by farseeing officials and social psychologists who sought to understand more precisely why farmers accepted certain government measures and rejected others, why some were concerned about eroding soil or sustained woodland management and others were not. Political exigencies of the period soon drove the effort into assessment of responses to international policies and wartime controls, and other data collected then has received little notice. It would merit re-examination for its revelations of attitudes prevailing in the 1940's and for

its suggestions of factors which then seemed relevant. Comments on the work are to be found in Rensis Likert, "Opinion Studies and Government Policy," *Proceedings of the American Philosophical Society* (1948), pp. 341–50.

19. Studies published by the National Opinion Research Center involving assessment of environment: Paul N. Borsky, *Community Reactions to Sonic Booms,* Oklahoma City Area, Pt. 1, University of Chicago, National Opinion Research Center, Report No. 101, 1965; Community Conservation Board, City of Chicago, *The Hyde Park–Kenwood Urban Renewal Survey,* University of Chicago, National Opinion Research Center Report No. 58, 1956; and Community Conservation Board, City of Chicago, *The Near West Side Conservation Survey,* University of Chicago, National Opinion Research Center Report No. 63-B, 1957.

20. Studies of the Survey Research Center, Institute for Social Research, University of Michigan, Ann Arbor, published by the Institute unless otherwise noted: Angus Campbell and Charles A. Metzner, *Public Use of the Library and Other Sources of Information* (1950); Eva L. Mueller and Gerald Gurin, with Margaret Wood, *Participation in Outdoor Recreation: Factors Affecting Demand Among American Adults,* (Washington: U.S. Government Printing Office, 1962); Eva L. Mueller, Arnold A. Wilken, and Margaret Wood, *Location Decisions and Industrial Mobility in Michigan, 1961* (1962); John B. Lansing, Eva. L. Mueller, William M. Ladd, and Nancy Barth, *The Geographic Mobility of Labor: A First Report* (1963); John B. Lansing and Eva L. Mueller, with Nancy (Morse) Samuelson, *Residential Location and Urban Mobility* (1964); John B. Lansing and Nancy (Morse) Samuelson, *Residential Location and Urban Mobility: A Multivariate Analysis* (1964); John B. Lansing, *Residential Location and Urban Mobility: The Second Wave of Interviews* (1966).

21. *The Future of Outdoor Recreation in Metropolitan Regions of the United States,* Vol. I, The National View—Present Conditions and Future Prospects of Outdoor Recreation for Residents of the Metropolitan Centers of Atlanta, St. Louis, and Chicago, A Report to the Outdoor Recreation Resources Review Commission, Study Report 21 (Washington: U.S. Government Printing Office, 1962). *The Quality of Outdoor Recreation: As Evidenced by User Satisfaction,* Report to the Outdoor Recreation Resources Review Commission, Study Report 5 (Washington: U.S. Government Printing Office, 1962).

22. Nahrum A. Medalia, *Community Perception of Air Quality: An Opinion Survey on Clarkston, Washington,* Environmental Health Series (Cincinnati: U.S. Department of Health, Education, and Welfare, 1965).

23. *Public Awareness and Concern with Air Pollution in the St. Louis Metropolitan Area,* Public Administration and Metropolitan Affairs Program, Southern Illinois University (Washington: U.S. Department of Health, Education, and Welfare, 1965).

24. Paul N. Borsky, *Community Reactions to Air Force Noise,* WADD Technical Report 60–689, parts I and II (Dayton: Distributed by U.S. Department of Commerce, Office of Technical Services, 1961).

25. E. J. Baur, "Opinion Change in a Public Controversy," *Public Opinion Quarterly,* XXVI (1962), pp. 212–26.

26. Nathaniel Wollman et al., *The Value of Water in Alternative Uses* (Albuquerque: University of New Mexico Press, 1962), pp. 6–19.

27. Orris C. Herfindahl and Allen V. Kneese, *Quality of the Environment: An Economic Approach to Some Problems in Using Land, Water and Air* (Washington: Resources for the Future, Inc., 1965), p. 29.

28. Gore, *Administrative Decision-Making* . . . An interesting description of opinion in relation to land and water use organization is given in Charles K. Warriner, "Public Opinion and Collective Action: Formation of a Watershed District," *Administrative Science Quarterly,* VI (1961), pp. 333–59. He concludes, "the 'need' arises as the organization comes into being and thus is as much a creator of the need as the needs is the creator of the institution" (p. 358).

29. Robert C. Lucas, "Wilderness Perception and Use: The Example of the Boundary Water Canoe Area," *Natural Resources Journal*, III (1964), pp. 394–411. [Also in this volume, p. 308.]

30. Ian Burton and Robert W. Kates, "The Perception of Natural Hazards in Resource Management," *Natural Resources Journal*, III (1964), pp. 412–41.

31. Robert W. Kates, *Hazard and Choice Perception in Flood Plain Management* (Chicago: University of Chicago Geography Research Papers, No. 78, 1962).

32. Thomas Frederick Saarinen, *Perception of the Drought Hazard on the Great Plains* (Chicago: University of Chicago Department of Geography Research Paper No. 106, 1966).

33. Meda M. White, "Role Conflict in Disasters: A Reconsideration," paper presented at American Sociological Association, 1962. See also Harry Estill Moore, F. L. Bates, J. P. Alston, M. M. Fuller, M. V. Layman, D. L. Mischer, and M. M. White, *And the Winds Blew* (Austin: Hogg Foundation for Mental Health, 1964).

34. Studies published by the National Academy of Sciences—National Research Council, Disaster Research Group (formerly Committee on Disaster Studies), Washington, D.C.: Lewis M. Killian, *A Study of Response to the Houston, Texas, Fireworks Explosion*, Disaster Study No. 2, Publication No. 391 (1956); Anthony F. Wallace, *Tornado in Worcester: An Exploratory Study of Individual and Community Behavior in an Extreme Situation*, Disaster Study No. 3, Publication No. 392 (1956); Fred C. Ikle and Harry V. Kincaid, *Social Aspects of Wartime Evacuation of American Cities, with Particular Emphasis on Long-Term Housing and Re-Employment*, Disaster Study No. 4, Publication No. 393 (1956); George W. Baker and John H. Rohrer (ed.), *Symposium on Human Problems in the Utilization of Fallout Shelters*, Disaster Study No. 12, Publication No. 800 (1960); *Field Studies of Disaster Behavior: An Inventory*, Disaster Study No. 14, Publication No. 886 (1961); Raymond W. Mack and George W. Baker, *The Occasion Instant: The Structure of Social Responses to Unanticipated Air Raid Warnings*, Disaster Study No. 15, Publication No. 945 (1961); George W. Baker (ed.), *Behavioral Science and Civil Defense*, Disaster Study No. 16, Publication No. 997 (1962); F. Bates, *The Social and Psychological Consequences of a Natural Disaster: A Longitudinal Study of Hurricane Audrey*, Disaster Study No. 18, Publication No. 1081 (1963); Harry E. Moore, *Before the Wind: A Study of the Reponse to Hurricane Carla*, Disaster Study No. 19, Publication No. 1095 (1963).

35. Robert S. Ingolds, "Taste Test Taxes Theories," Engineering Experiment Station, Georgia Institute of Technology, Atlanta, Georgia. Reprint No. 176 from *Water Works and Wastes Engineering* (1964).

36. Joseph Sonnenfeld, "Variable Values in Space and Landscape: An Inquiry into the Nature of Environmental Necessity," *Journal of Social Issues*, p. 22 (in press).

37. Florence Rockwood Kluckhohn and Fred L. Strodtbeck, *Variations in Value Orientations* (Evanston: Row, Peterson and Company, 1961), pp. 1–48, 363–65.

38. Kluckhohn and Strodtbeck, pp. 341–42.

39. Benjamin D. Paul, William A. Gamson, and S. Stephen Kegeles (editors), "Trigger for Community Conflict: The case of Fluoridation" (eight articles), *Journal of Social Issues*, XVII (1961), No. 4, pp. 1–81, quotation on page 7. See also: "Fluoridation" (special issues of 22 articles), *Journal of the American Dental Association*, LXV (1962), pp. 578–717; Robert M. O'Shea and S. Stephen Kegeles, "An Analysis of Anti-Fluoridation Letters," *Journal of Health and Human Behavior*, IV (1963), pp. 135–40; Arnold Simmel and David B. Ast, "Some Correlates of Opinion on Fluoridation," *American Journal of Public Health*, LII (1962), pp. 1269–73.

40. R. Burnell Held and Marion Clawson *Soil Conservation in Perspective* (Baltimore: The Johns Hopkins Press, for Resources for the Future, 1965), pp. 254–62.

41. Robert W. Kates and J. F. Wohlwill (eds.), "Man's Response to the Physical Environment," *Journal of Social Issues*, p. 22 (in press).

42. Everett C. Hughes, *Student's Culture and Perspectives* (Lawrence: University of Kansas School of Law, 1961).

43. William E. Henry and John M. Schlien, "Affective Complexity and Psychotherapy: Some Comparisons of Time-Limited and Unlimited Treatment," *Journal of Projective Techniques*, XXII (1958), pp. 153–62.

44. For a review of changes in attitudes toward culture groups, see E. E. Davis, *Attitude Change: A Review and Bibliography of Selected Research*, Social Science Clearing House Documents, No. 19 (Paris: UNESCO, 1965).

45. "Alternatives in Water Management," National Academy of Sciences Research Report No. 1408, August, 1966 (Washington, National Academy of Sciences–National Research Council).

T. F. Saarinen: Attitudes Toward Weather Modification— A Study of Great Plains Farmers

1. The derivation of the Thornthwaite moisture index is described in C. W. Thornthwaite and J. R. Mather, "Instructions and Tables for Computing Potential Evapotranspiration and the Water Balance," Drexel Institute of Technology, Laboratory of Climatology, *Publications in Climatology*, X, No. 3 (Centerton, N.J., 1957).

H. George Frederickson and Howard Magnas: Comparing Attitudes Toward Water Pollution in Syracuse

1. See Roberta A. Sigel and H. Paul Friesema, "Urban Community Leader's Knowledge of Public Opinion," *Western Political Quarterly*, XVIII (1965), pp. 881–895; and Warren E. Miller and Donald E. Stokes, "Constituency Influence on Congress," *American Political Science Review*, LVII (1963), pp. 45–56.

2. See Robert A. Dahl, *Who Governs?* (New Haven: Yale University Press, 1961); and V. O. Key, *Public Opinion and American Democracy* (New York: Alfred A. Knopf, 1961).

3. See Gordon Tullock, "Excess Benefits," *Water Resources*, III (1967), pp. 643–644.

4. Key.

5. Alex Inkeles, *Public Opinion in Soviet Russia* (Cambridge: Harvard University Press, 1950).

6. State of New York, Executive Department, *New York State Population Changes Since 1960* (Albany: State of New York, Dec., 1966).

7. Onondaga Lake Scientific Council, *An Environmental Assessment of Onondaga Lake and Its Major Contributory Systems*, mimeograph (Syracuse: Onondaga Lake Scientific Council, 1966).

8. Key.

9. *Acknowledgments.* The authors are especially indebted to Dr. Glenn Nesty, Vice President for Research, and A. J. von Frank, Director, Air and Water Pollution Control, Allied Chemical Corporation. Jane Weiss and Susan Spencer, to whom we are greatly indebted, provided research and typing support. The Allied Chemical Corporation supported this research.

M. M. Kelso: Resolving Land Use Conflicts

1. In a fundamental aggregative sense, even the elemental content of land is absolutely inflexible for what is an *increase* in one site necessitates an equal and off-setting *decrease* somewhere else. Only "capital" and the elemental content of land viewed as partial units are increasable or depreciable. In the strict fundamental aggregative sense, land is absolutely inflexible in all its attributes.

2. *Increasing* the elemental supply content of a site by the decision maker is an act of *investing*; the increase is *capital ex ante*. Thus, *ex ante*, all *increases* in land content

are capital. However, when, *ex post*, such "capital" turns out to be "sunk" and irremovable, it transforms conceptually into "land" and the then enhanced elemental content of the site may be depreciated through use. Consequently, from this point of view, the elemental content of land can never be *appreciable* but only *depreciable*. Technology has a similar character *vis-a-vis* land. The discovery of "new" elemental content in a site, such as an increase in productivity, is a "knowledge" input or a form of capital when first applied but, once "known," the knowledge remains and subsequent decisions are made in the context of such existing and unchanging knowledge.

3. "There are therefore special attitudes toward land, sometimes mystic, recognizing its permanence and man's dependence on it. The result seems to be a more frequent, conscious, often economically purposeful elaboration of rights and regulations of land use and disposal. 'Land . . . has hardly ever or anywhere ceased to invest even its most private users with at least a touch of public character.' " Frank E. Horack, Jr., and Val Nolan, Jr., *Land Use Controls*: *Supplementary Materials on Real Property* (St. Paul, Minn.: Webb Publishing Co., 1955). Their quotation is from Brinkmann, "Land Tenure," *Encyclopedia of the Social Sciences*, IX and X (1933), pp. 73 ff.

4. I am not defining "land use development" as progression "ever onward and upward." The resolution of conflict over land use simply permits "change" to occur. The ultimate determinate of whether the conflict resolution that permits change has been development or retrogression in some value sense must be left to the judgment of history and of moral philosophers. All that can be said here is that the resolution of land use conflicts will facilitate land use changes. We can only hope that history proves them to be developments in the ever upward and onward sense.

5. "If we endeavor to find a universal principle, common to all behavior known as institutional, we may define an institution as Collective Action in Control of Individual Action. . . .

"Collective Action is more than *control* of individual action—it is, by the very act of control, as indicated by the auxiliary verbs, a *liberation* of individual action from coercion, duress, discrimination, or unfair competition, by means of restraints placed on other individuals. . . .

"And Collective Action is more than restraint and liberation of individual action— it is *expansion* of the will of the individual far beyond what he can do by his own puny acts. The head of a great corporation gives orders which execute his will at the ends of the earth. . . .

"Since liberation and expansion for some persons consist in restraint, for their benefit, of other persons, and while the short definition of an institution is collective action in control of individual action, the derived definition is: collective action in restraint, liberation, and expansion of individual action."

John R. Commons, *Institutional Economics* (New York: Macmillan Co., 1934), pp. 69 and 73.

6. John R. Commons, *The Economics of Collective Action* (New York: Macmillan Co., 1950), p. 74.

7. Commons, *Institutional Economics*, pp. 67 ff.

8. I am not unmindful that in not infrequent situations in the United States, it appears and, in fact may be true, that parties in conflict over land use appear before the court not as equals but as unequals due to economic, social, or racial differences. In such cases it is not that the individuals appear before the court as unequals but that the working-rules laid down by the legislative process of the sovereign, and as interpreted and enforced by the executive and judicial arms of the sovereign, have classified persons into groups to which different rights, duties, liberties, and exposures pertain.

Robert Rienow: Manifesto for the Sea

1. *Christian Science Monitor*, Jan. 13, 1958, p. B-7. [Italics added to quote.]

2. John Clark, *Fish and Man, Conflict in the Atlantic Estuaries* (Highlands, N.J.: American Littoral Society, 1967), p. 1.

3. H. H. Carter, J. H. Carpenter, and R. C. Whaley, "The Bacterial Effect of Seawater Under Natural Conditions," *Journal of Water Pollution Control Federation*, XXXIX, No. 7 (July, 1967), 1184.

4. See Y. Hata, H. Miyoshi, H. Kadota, and M. Kimata, "Microbial Production of Sulfides in Coastal and Estuarine Regions," Second International Conference on Water Pollution Research, Section III. Marine Disposal; Tokyo, Japan, Aug. 24–28, 1964, abstracted in *Journal of Water Pollution Control Federation*, XXXVI, No. 3 (March, 1964), 327.

5. "Estuarine and Marine Pollution, Biological and Chemical Features of Tidal Estuaries," a review of the literature by Werner N. Grune, *Journal of Water Pollution Control Federation*, XXXVII, No. 7 (July, 1965), 973 ff.

6. Lloyd Berkner, "Man Versus Technology," *Social Education*, XXXI (April, 1967), 281.

7. Robert and Leona Train Rienow, *Moment in the Sun* (N.Y.: Dial, 1967), p. 156 [citing Fish and Wildlife Service news release, Sept. 7, 1965].

8. L. R. Pomeroy, E. P. Odum, R. D. Johannes, and B. Roffman, "Flux of ^{32}P and ^{65}Zn Through a Salt-Marsh Ecosystem," *Proceedings of Symposium, International Atomic Energy Agency*, (Vienna, May 16–20, 1966), p. 186.

9. Rienow and Rienow, p. 195.

10. C. S. Taigvoglon and R. L. O'Connell, *Waste Guide for the Uranium Milling Industry*, HEW Technical Report, W62-12, 1962, pp. 45–56.

11. R. J. Lowton, J. H. Martin, and J. W. Talbot, "Dilution, Dispersion, and Sedimentation in some British Estuaries," International Atomic Energy Agency, *Disposal of Radioactive Wastes into Seas, Oceans, and Surface Waters* (Vienna, 1966), pp. 189 ff.

12. W. Feldt, "Radioactive Contamination of North Sea Fish," ibid., p. 739.

13. F. G. Lowman, D. K. Phelps, R. McClin, V. Roman de Vega, I. Oliver De Padovani, and R. J. Garcia, "Interactions of the Environmental and Biological Factors on the Distribution of Trace Elements in the Marine Environment," ibid., p. 251.

14. "Disposal of Radioactive Waste," *IAEA Bulletin*, II, No. 1 (Jan., 1960), 4.

15. Ibid.

16. "Is the Ocean in Danger?", UNESCO *Courier* (English ed.), July–Aug., 1959, p. 30.

17. Ibid.

18. Feldt, p. 752.

19. See Robert and Leona Train Rienow, "The Oil Around Us," *New York Times Magazine*, June 4, 1967.

20. See Henry Reiff, *The United States and the Treaty Law of the Sea* (Minneapolis: Univ. of Minnesota Press, 1959), p. 322.

21. Edward W. Allen, "Freedom of the Sea," *American Journal of International Law*, XL (1966), 814.

22. William L. Griffin, "The Use of Waters of International Drainage Basins Under Customary International Law," *American Journal of International Law*, LII (1959), 50.

23. Ibid., p. 59.

24. P. Eleson, "Underwater Ordnance," *Ordnance*, May–June, 1967, p. 548. See also Jan.–Feb., 1967, issue, p. 418, for the program of the National Council on Marine Resources; and the March–April, 1967, issue, pp. 454–455, for a budgetary analysis of oceanography programs.

25. A. P. Lester, "River Pollution in International Law," *American Journal of International Law*, LVII (Oct., 1963), 833ff.

Robert C. Lucas: Wilderness Perception and Use—The Example
of the Boundary Waters Canoe Area

1. Huth, *Nature and the American* (1957), pp. 2–9.

2. Nash, "The American Wilderness in Historical Perspective," *Forest History*, VI (1963), 3.

3. Huth, pp. 10–53.

4. Leopold, *A Sand County Almanac* (1949), pp. 188–94.

5. Nash, pp. 10–11. For an interesting criticism of this view see Lowenthal, "Not Every Prospect Pleases—What is Our Criterion for Scenic Beauty?," *Landscape*, XII (Winter, 1962–1963), 19.

6. Wildland Research Center, Univ. of Calif., *Wilderness and Recreation* (Outdoor Recreation Resources Review Commission Study Report No. 3, 1962), pp. 16–26.

7. There have been a series of wilderness bills. S. 174, 87th Cong., 1st Session (1961), is quoted here.

8. USDA, Forest Service, Wilderness (1961), p. 5.

9. USDA, Forest Service, The National Forest System and Outdoor Recreation (Prepared for the Outdoor Recreation Resources Review Commission, 1960), p. 52.

10. Wildland Research Center, Univ of Calif., p. 4.

11. USDI, National Park Service, The National Park Wilderness (no date), p. 17.

12. Wildland Research Center, Univ. of Calif., pp. 40, 50–51.

13. Thompson, "Politics in the Wilderness: New York's Adirondack Forest Preserve," *Forest History*, VI (1963), 14.

14. Wildland Research Center, Univ. of Calif., p. 50.

15. For a full discussion of the problem of defining and attaining "primitive America" see the Leopold Committee Report to the Secretary of the Interior, "Wildlife Management in the National Parks," *American Forests*, LXIX (1963), 32, 61.

16. Marshall, *The Forest for Recreation*, A National Plan for American Forestry, S. Doc. No. 12, 73d Cong., 1st Session (1933), pp. 473–76.

17. Outdoor Recreation Resources Review Commission, *Outdoor Recreation for America* (1962), p. 71.

18. Wildland Research Center, Univ. of Calif., pp. 11, 303.

19. Carhart, *Planning for America's Wildlands* (1961).

20. USDA, Forest Service, *Report of the Chief of the Forest Service, 1961* (1962), p. 40.

21. Wildland Research Center, Univ. of Calif., pp. 119–21.

22. USDI, National Park Service, *Public Use: National Parks and Related Areas*, (1960), table 2a.

23. USDA, Forest Service, *Report of the Chief of the Forest Service, 1961*, p. 10.

24. The Forest Service's definition of a "visit" requires counting a person every time he enters the reporting area. Thus, a person camping or staying at a resort just outside a wilderness area and entering it every day for a week would technically produce seven visits.

25. Wildland Research Center, Univ. of Calif., p. 124.

26. Ibid., p. 236.

27. Outdoor Recreation Resources Review Commission, p. 46.

28. The probability of a party of a given type, e.g., resort guests, falling in the sample was equal everywhere. The probabilities were not equal between types—e.g. between campers and canoeists—because of necessary differences in the way of contacting the different types. For example, each access point was sampled on six randomly chosen days, two weekend days for one hour each day, and four weekdays for $1\frac{1}{4}$ hours each day, and every returning party was interviewed during these times. Each campground was visited on one randomly selected weekend day and two weekdays, and one-half of the occupied campsites were randomly chosen for interviews.

29. For a more complete history of the management policies see Lucas, *The*

Quetico-Superior Area: *Recreational Use in Relation to Capacity* (Unpublished thesis, Univ. of Minn., 1962), pp. 70–111.

30. Carhart, *Preliminary Prospectus*: *An Outline Plan for the Recreational Development of the Superior National Forest* (no date, 1921 ?).

31. International Joint Commission on the Rainy Lake Reference, Final Report (1934), p. 48.

32. 46 Stat. 1021 (1930), 16 U.S.C. § 577b (1958).

33. 46 Stat. 1021 (1930), 16 U.S.C. § 577a (1958).

34. 46 Stat. 1020–21 (1930), 16 U.S.C. § 577a (1958).

35. Superior National Forest, *Plan of Management*: *Superior Roadless Areas* 11–12, 14 (1948), pp. 11–12.

36. Exec. Order No. 10092, 14 Fed. Reg. 7637, 7681 (1949).

37. For a full discussion of the President's decision to issue this order and the subsequent cases see Andrews, *Wilderness Sanctuary* (Inter-Univ. Case Program No. 13 rev. ed. 1954).

38. From the files of the Superior National Forest, Duluth, Minn.

39. Jardine, *The Policy of the Department of Agriculture in Relation to Road Building and Recreational Use of the Superior National Forest, Minnesota* (1926), pp. 1–2. Actually, the most popular section of the present Boundary Waters Canoe Area—northeast of Ely—was not a part of the National Forest until later.

40. 62 Stat. 568 (1948), as amended, 16 U.S.C. §§ 577c-h (1958).

41. Wildland Research Center, Univ. of Cal., p. 319.

42. Superior National Forest, p. 15.

43. For a general discussion of the internal, subjective definition of "wilderness" see Carhart, *Planning for America's Wildlands* (1961), p. 34–42.

44. Taves, Hathaway and Bultena, *Canoe Country Vacationers* (Univ. of Minn. Agri. Expt. Sta. Misc. Rep. No. 39, 1960); Bultena and Taves, "Changing Wilderness Images and Forestry Policy," *Journal of Forestry*, LIX (1961), pp. 167–71.

45. See Lucas, *Visitor Reaction to Timber Harvesting in the Boundary Waters Canoe Area* (USDA, Forest Service Res. Note LS-2, Lake States Forest Expt. Sta., 1963).

46. Wildland Research Center, Univ. of Calif., *Wilderness and Recreation* (Outdoor Recreation Resources Review Commission Study Report No. 3, 1962), p. 153.

47. Ibid., p. 159.

48. See Burch and Taves, *Changing Functions of Recreation in Human Society*, Outdoor Recreation in the Upper Great Lakes Area (USDA, Forest Service, Lake States Forest Expt. Sta. Paper No. 89, 1961), pp. 8–16.

49. This conclusion agrees with the suggested system of concentric zones of progressively less primitive character surrounding strict wilderness cores in Carhart, *Planning for America's Wildlands.*

George Hagevik: Legislating for Air Quality Management—
Reducing Theory to Practice

1. § 101(a)(3), 81 Stat. 485.

2. §§ 101(b), 016, 107, 81 Stat. 485.

3. E.g., A. Pigou, *The Economics of Welfare* (1932), 160–61.

4. A detailed statement of this approach is found in Crocker, "The Structuring of Atmospheric Pollution Control Systems," in *The Economics of Air Pollution*, ed. H. Wolozin (1966) [hereinafter cited as Wolozin]. For a refinement of the problem of determining which abatement expenditures are justifiable, see notes 69–70 and accompanying text.

5. Wolozin, "Discussion," in *Proceedings*: *The Third National Conference on Air*

Pollution (public Health Service Pub. No. 1649, 1967) p. 580 [hereinafter cited as *Third Nat'l Conf. Proceedings*].

6. Ibid.

7. But cf. comments by Linsky, Mills, and Wolozin, ibid., p. 589.

8. W. Vickrey, "Theoretical and Practical Possibilities and Limitations of a Market Mechanism Approach to Air Pollution," a paper presented at the Air Pollution Control Association Conference, Cleveland, O., June, 1967.

9. See generally A. Kneese, *The Economics of Regional Water Quality Management* (1964), pp. 193–95; Mills, "Economic Incentives to Air Pollution Control," in Wolozin, p. 40.

10. Mills, "Federal Incentives to Air Pollution Control, "in *Third Nat'l. Conf. Proceedings*, pp. 575–76.

11. See Mills in Wolozin, pp. 45–46.

12. Working Committee on Economic Incentives, Federal Coordinating Committee on the Economic Impact of Pollution Abatement, Cost Sharing with Industry? XXVII (Summary Report 1967) [hereinafter cited as Federal Coordinating Committee.]

13. Ibid.

14. For a full discussion of federal powers under the statute, see Martin and Symington, "A Guide to the Air Quality Act of 1967," in this symposium, p. 239.

15. Staff of the Senate Committee on Public Works, 88th Cong., 1st Session, *A Study of Pollution—Air* (Comm. Print 1963), p. 20.

16. Crocker, in Wolozin, p. 79.

17. P. Gerhardt, "Some Economic Aspects of Air Pollution," a paper presented at the Mid-Atlantic States Section, Air Pollution Control Association Conference, Oct. 4, 1967.

18. Federal Coordinating Committee, p. 14.

19. Ibid.

20. See *Air Quality Act of 1967*, § 211(a), 81 Stat. 485.

21. The main technological problem that remains to be solved is the development of a method of monitoring levels of emission accurately and at low cost.

22. Turvey, "Side Effects of Resource Use," in *Environmental Quality in a Growing Economy*, H. Jarrett ed. (1966), p. 52.

23. This is essentially a benefit–cost view of air quality management since one may alternatively refer to (1) damages (costs) avoided as benefits and (2) costs incurred for abatement as costs, and say that waste reduction up to but not beyond a certain point will maximize benefits minus costs. Cost minimization (including damages as a cost) and net benefit maximization are in this case identical.

24. It is significant, as Gerhardt points out, that there has been far more interest in assessing the value of the damage by air pollution than in the costs of control. The costs of recent attempts at control have generally been accepted as a fraction of total damages. The interest in incremental costs of control will increase as the point of equality between incremental control costs and incremental damages is approached. See Gerhardt. For an argument suggesting that abatement costs should be a matter of immediate concern, see notes 69–70 and accompanying text.

25. Ridker, "Strategies for Measuring the Cost of Air Pollution," in Wolozin, pp. 87, 100.

26. For a useful review of the major contributions in the area of decision theory, see Robinson and Majak, "The Theory of Decision-Making," in *Contemporary Political Analysis*, J. Charlesworth, ed. (1967), p. 175.

27. See, e.g., J. Anderson, *Politics and the Economy* (1966).

28. See T. Schelling, *The Strategy of Conflict* (1966), p. 3–20.

29. K. Boulding, *Conflict and Defense: A General Theory* (1962), pp. 310–13.

30. Schelling, "What is Game Theory?," in *Contemporary Political Analysis*, p. 213.

31. See Banfield, "Notes on a Conceptual Scheme," in *Politics, Planning and the Public Interest*, eds. M. Meyerson and E. Banfield, (1953), p. 307.

32. In the terminology of game theory, bargaining is a positive-sum (as opposed to zero-sum), frequently nonsymmetrical game between participants with a mixture of conflict and cooperation. Zero-sum games are those in which one player's loss is the other's gain. The sum of gain plus loss is zero—hence "zero-sum." A positive-sum game is one in which the gain of one party is not equal to the loss of the other. For example, a gain for A of one unit of value may only cause a loss to B of one-half unit. A nonsymmetrical game results when B's loss varies from move to move even though A's gain with each move is constant. These variations from the zero-sum prototype make the mathematics of a game extremely complex.

33. This dichotomy gives the bargaining game its unusual character and raises issues quite different from pure conflict or pure cooperation games.

34. McKean, "The Unseen Hand in Government," *American Economic Review*, LV (1965), 494.

35. See R. Cyert and J. March, *A Behavioral Theory of the Firm* (1967), p. 31.

36. See, e.g., Schelling, p. 219, and Shubik, "The Uses of Game Theory," in *Contemporary Political Analysis*, p. 260, both.

37. See T. Schelling, *Strategy of Conflict*, p. 170.

38. See K. Boulding, *The Impact of the Social Sciences* (1966), p. 43.

39. See T. Schelling, *Strategy of Conflict*, p. 45.

40. This learning process is detailed in A. Rappaport and A. Ghammah, *Prisoner's Dilemma* (1965).

41. See § 108, 81 Stat. 485 (1967). See Martin and Symington, pp. 244–47.

42. See Douglas, "The Peaceful Settlement of Industrial and Intergroup Disputes," *Journal of Conflict Resolution*, I (1957), 69.

43. See K. Boulding, *Conflict and Defense . . .* , p. 311.

44. T. Schelling, *Strategy of Conflict*, p. 114.

45. Ibid., p. 111.

46. See ibid., p. 114.

47. See R. Cyert and J. March, *Behavioral Theory . . .* , p. 33.

48. Local Law 14, May 20, 1966, *N.Y. City Admin. Code* §§ 892–2.0 to 897–2.0 (Supp. 1967–1968).

49. *N.Y. City Admin. Code* §§ 892–4.3 (Supp. 1967–1968).

50. Task Force 2 of the Committee for Implementing Local Law 14, "Economics of Upgrading or Discontinuing Incineration" (mimeo.) Oct. 3, 1967.

51. Holden notes the inadequacies of state water pollution control legislation for this purpose. M. Holden, *Pollution Control as a Bargaining Process: An Essay on Regulatory Decision-Making* (1966).

52. *Illinois Revised Statute*, chap. 111½, § 240.11 (1967).

53. The reference to the constitutional problem simply refers to the general principle that the state cannot curtail one's use of his property without paying "just compensation." The concept of "taking," which appears in the statute, is a constitutional concept which defines whether or not compensation must be paid, and it is applied rather inconsistently. Still, it is possible that curtailment of the property owner's rights to pollute may be classified as a "taking" unless a strong case can be made based on regulation for public health and use of the police power. When aesthetic and generalized environmental quality goals are emphasized, constitutional doubts are increased. See Pollack, "Legal Boundaries of Air Pollution Control—State and Local Legislative Purpose and Techniques," in this symposium, p. 331; see also Michelman, "Property, Utility, and Fairness: Comments on the Ethical Foundations of 'Just Compensation' Law," *Harvard Law Review*, LXXX (1967), 1165.

54. §§ 107(c), 108(c), 81 Stat. 485. See Martin and Symington, p. 259.

55. The Air Quality Act of 1967, § 107(c), 81 Stat. 485, provides, "Such recommendations shall include such data as are available on the latest available technology and economic feasibility of alternative methods of prevention and control of air contamination including cost-effectiveness analyses."

56. The state control plan will be approved if the Secretary finds, among other things, "that such State *standards* are consistent with the air quality criteria and recommended control techniques issued pursuant to section 107." § 108(c) (1), 81 Stat. 485. (Emphasis added.) Section 107(c) provides that control techniques should be based on technological and economic feasibility. See note 55. But the state enforcement *plan* need only be "consistent with the purposes of the Act insofar as it assures achieving such standards of air quality within a reasonable time," and must provide "a means of enforcement by State action, including authority comparable to" certain emergency powers provided in the act. § 108(c) (1), 81 Stat. 485. Thus the emphasis arguably is on achieving prompt compliance and not on cost effectiveness.

57. One possible, perhaps even a likely, evolution from the present system would require polluters to *pay* for the variances they seek, the fee to be set in accordance with damage estimates. If variances were purchased rather than granted, the system would change profoundly, with variances becoming more palatable to the public and the control agency. Bargaining over the fees would yield some of the benefits sought in the program hypothesized below.

58. The inadequacies of a litigation-oriented approach are detailed in National Research Council, National Academy of Sciences, *Waste Management and Control* (Pub. No. 1400, 1966), pp. 203–221

59. See generally Welch "Constant Surveillance: A Modern Regulatory Tool," *Villanova Law Review*, VIII (1963), 340. See also note 65.

60. Californian Health and Safety Code §§ 24260 (West, 1967).

61. N.Y. City Administration Code §§ 894–2.0, 892–3.0, 892–5.0 (1966); Californian Health and Safety Code §§ 24261–63 (West, 1967).

62. Hagevik, "Decision Processes in Air Quality Management" (unpublished dissertation, forthcoming in 1969).

63. The Air Quality Act of 1967, § 108(c) (5), 81 Stat. 485, states that in connection with hearings conducted under the act, "no witness or any other person shall be required to divulge trade secrets or secret processes." Some confidentiality must be provided by any regulatory scheme.

64. Evaluation of agency performance by the legislature is one of the more important aspects of a rational decision process. See A. Maass and M. Hufschmidt, *Design of Water Resource Systems* (1962), chap. 15.

65. Testimony to the importance of establishing such a framework appears in an opinion of the FCC defending the decision to commence the first full-scale rate case against AT&T. In response to Bell's stated preference for bargaining as a rate-making method, the commission stated, "Indeed, we believe that the standards and criteria developed on the record here will enable us to employ continuing surveillance [i.e., bargaining] even more effectively in the future." *Re* American Tel. & Tel. Co., 61 P.U.R.3d 554, 559–60 (1965). The words "even more" are self-serving.

65a. See note 70 on the derivation of such objectives.

66. § 107, 81 Stat. 485 (1967). *But see* note 70 on the theoretical deficiencies of the HEW criteria.

67. One of the reasons given for the success of the Los Angeles Air Pollution Control District is that there has been a great deal of cooperation between the technical staff of the district and the technical staffs of the regulated industries.

68. Although making the use of low-sulfur fuel mandatory is in conflict with the economists' rational model, it can still be viewed as a sound decision in keeping with

our strategy, which would allow mixing of necessary approaches. At a later stage another approach should probably be substituted.

69. Since the aggregate cost curve for damage abatement within an airshed is almost certainly non-linear—costs increase as the more obvious sources of pollution are controlled and as the more serious damage is eliminated—an estimate of the amount of damage reduction obtainable from a unit of abatement by the first polluter proceeded against might be high if this polluter was considered as an isolated source. This would apparently justify imposition of equally high abatement costs. Such a view of marginal control expenditures and benefits is deceptive, however, in that if other firms or groups of firms were forced to abate sequentially, their positions on the curve would be lower and their expenditures would yield a lower return, thereby decreasing the amount of required investment. Thus, a simplistic comparison of marginal costs and benefits is not enough, since this would result in applying a different standard to each polluter depending on the sequence in which they are attacked.

70. See Thomas, "The Animal Farm, A Mathematical Model for the Discussion of Social Standards for Control of the Environment," *Quarterly Journal of Economics*, LXXVII (1963), 143. Thomas points out that to set a quality criterion is to impute a cost–benefit ratio. (P. 147.) Thus the starting point for pollution abatement programs should be cost–benefit analysis and not arbitrarily determined quality criteria or emission standards. *But see* H.R. Rep. No. 728, 90th Cong., 1st Session 16 (1967), which states that economic considerations are to have no place in the development of HEW's criteria.

71. For a more optimistic view, see National Research Council, pp. 204, 207–09, 214–17.

George R. Hall: The Myth and Reality of Multiple Use Forestry

1. See, e.g., Neff, "Multiple Use Is A Reality," *American Forests*, LXVII (1961), 18.
2. 74 Stat. 215 (1960), 16 U.S.C. §§ 528–29 (Supp. IV, 1963).
3. 74 Stat. 215 (1960), 16 U.S.C. § 531 (Supp. IV, 1963).
4. No attempt will be made to present a complete bibliography of the many articles on multiple use. In recent years almost every issue of *American Forests* and the *Journal of Forestry* has dealt with the theory or practice of multiple use forestry. In addition to the articles cited elsewhere in this article, notable contributions include: Clawson and Held, *The Federal Lands* (1957), pp. 51–57, McConnell, "The Multiple Use Concept in Forest Service Policy," Sierra Club Reprint Series No. 3 (1960); Shanklin, *Multiple Use of Land and Water Areas* (1961); Gulick, *American Forest Policy* (1951); Greeley, "Today's Opportunities for Conservation in Forests, Parks and Wilderness," Transactions at the 23rd Wildlife Conference (1958), p. 18.
5. 30 Stat. 35 (1897). Other statutes specifying the authority of the Forest Service are 64 Stat. 82 (1950); and 58 Stat. 132 (1944) (Sustained Yield Unit Act).
6. Statement of E. C. Peterson at *Hearings Before the Subcommittee on Forests of the House Committee on Agriculture*, 86th Cong., 2d Session, ser. RR, at 4 (1960).
7. Ibid., p. 3.
8. "The Concept of Multiple Use of Forest and Associated Lands—Its Values and Limitations," Address by Richard E. McArdle, 5th World Forestry Cong., Aug. 29, 1960, p. 5.
9. Ibid., pp. 5–6.
10. Starr, "Multiple Land Use Management," *Natural Resources Journal*, I (1961), 288. (All italicized in original.)
11. Ibid., p. 300.
12. Stagner, "A Second Look at Multiple Use," *American Forests*, LXVI (1960), 24.
13. Letter from Norman R. Tripp to George R. Hall, April 10, 1962.

14. See McArdle, "Multiple Use—Multiple Benefits," *Journal of Forestry*, LI (1953), 323.

15. See Gregory, "An Economic Approach to Multiple Use," *Forest Science*, I (1955), 11.

16. These are old fallacies but they continue to pop up in forestry literature. The exchange value of a good is not determined by the total "worth" of the commodity if the good had to be obtained in one lump amount. What is relevant is the demand for, and cost of, obtaining an extra or marginal unit. Thus, while food is in some sense more "basic" than wilderness recreation, the importance of obtaining an extra unit of wilderness may outweigh the importance of an extra unit of food in a country with a great deal of food and little wilderness. Nor is maximizing the quality of a product always a desirable objective. A Cadillac has more "quality.' than a Ford, but we would be a poorer instead of a richer country if car manufacturers produced only "high quality" automobiles. Finally, it can be shown that maximization of per-unit output is also a false goal. If the value of the extra inputs exceeds the value of the resulting additional output, there is little point to the additional effort regardless of the technological efficiency.

17. Scott, *Natural Resources: The Economics of Conservation* (1955), pp. 20–21.

18. *Hearings Before the Subcommittee on Forests of the House Committee on Agriculture*, 8th Cong., 2d Session, ser. RR, (1960), p. 3.

19. See, e.g., statement of C. R. Gutermuth of the Wildlife Management Institute, ibid., p. 112.

20. I am greatly indebted to the staff of the Jefferson National Forest for the effort they extended in instructing me in the fundamentals of multiple use forest practice. The following discussion is based on my observations and judgment and is not a statement of the official position of the Forest Service or of the Jefferson's administration. In fact, many conclusions presented here are opposed to the current view of the Forest Service. That the Jefferson's procedures are reasonably typical can be seen in Neff, note 1; Kaufman, *The Forest Ranger* (1960); and Pike, "Recreation Plans for the Superior National Forest," *Journal of Forestry*, LI (1953), 508.

21. I am indebted to Norman R. Tripp for this point. See also Starr, note 10.

22. The illustrations used are drawn from competitive situations where the inclusion of an item in the product-mix affects adversely the quantity or characteristics of some other product. Foresters insist that many complementary and supplementary situations exist where no conflict difficulties present themselves. Clearly, one should capitalize on such situations. Stress on the competitive cases is not intended to indicate that such cases are the only ones that arise. They are, however, the ones which pose hard problems of choice and, therefore, pose public policy problems.

23. 74 Stat. 215 (1960) 16 U.S.C. § 531 (Supp. IV 1953).

24. The division between intensive and non-intensive forest management is a subcase of the more general split among conservationists over "development" and "preservation." My views on this subject are presented in Hall, "Conservation as a Policy Goal," *Yale Review*, LI (1962), 400.

25. Reich, *Bureaucracy and the Forests* (1962).

26. Ibid., p. 13.

27. For descriptions of the analytical techniques applied to water resource development, see Eckstein, *Water Resource Development* (1958); Hirshleifer, DeHaven and Milliman, *Water Supply: Economics, Technology and Policy* (1960); Krutilla and Eckstein, *Multiple Purpose River Development* (1958); Maass, Hufschmidt, Dorfman, Thomas, Marglin and Fair, *Design of Water-Resource Systems* (1962).

28. For an example of a dispute in which the data produced by the evaluative procedures required of the water resources agencies played an important role in the popular discussion, see Stratton and Sirotkin, *The Echo Park Controversy* (1959).

Vincent Ostrom: The Water Economy and Its Organization

1. Martin, "The Tennessee Valley Authority: A study of Federal Control," *Law and Contemporary Problems*, XXII (1957), 351, 374.

2. National Resources Committee, *Regional Planning, Part I: Pacific Northwest* (1936).

Joseph L. Fisher: Resource Policies and Administration for the Future

1. See, for example, *Resources for Freedom*, the report of the President's Materials Policy Commission, 1952; the report of the President's Water Resources Policy Commission in three volumes, 1950; the reports of the two Hoover commissions that bear on natural resources; the report of the Mid-Century Conference on Resources for the Future, *The Nation Looks at Its Resources* (1953). Prior to these studies of the most recent decade were the numerous reports of the National Resources Planning Board in the late 1930's and early 1940's as well as occasional earlier studies going back 50 and 75 years.

2. See Nathaniel Woolman, *Water Resources Activities in the United States: Water Supply and Demand*, U.S. Senate Select Committee on National Water Resources, Committee Print No. 32 (U.S. Government Printing Office, 1960).

3. A principal recommendation of the Senate Select Committee on National Water Resources calls for "biennially an assessment of the water supply–demand outlook for each of the water resource regions of the United States . . . ," Senate Report No. 29, 87 Cong., 1st Session (1961), p. 19.

4. Schurr, Netschert et al., *Energy in the American Economy, 1850–1975* (Johns Hopkins Press, for Resources for the Future, Inc., 1960).

5. Insights into forest administration may be found throughout Herbert Kaufman's *The Forest Ranger: A Study in Administrative Behavior* (The Johns Hopkins Press, for Resources for the Future, Inc., 1960).

6. Shortly after the draft of this paper was completed, President Kennedy recommended a strengthening of the Council of Economic Advisers "to report to the President, the Congress, and the public on the status of resource programs in relation to national needs." He also recommended that a Presidential advisory committee be established under the council, representing the resource agencies of the government. Message to the Congress, dated February 23, 1961.

Subject Index

Name Index